CULTURAL EXPRESSION AND GRASSROOTS DEVELOPMENT

CULTURAL EXPRESSION AND GRASSROOTS DEVELOPMENT

Cases from Latin America and the Caribbean

edited by

Charles David Kleymeyer

Lynne Rienner Publishers • Boulder & London

Front cover photo (Mitchell Denburg/IAF): Capacitación Integral de la Mujer Campesina (CIMCA), a renowned Bolivian women's training organization, uses puppets and oral tradition to train indigenous women in themes such as agricultural production, nutrition, and health.

Back cover photo (Julia Weise-Vargas/IAF): Residents of the indigenous community of Bazán in Chimborazo, Ecuador, watch a sociodrama about local problems. The drama is being presented by the Feria Educativa, or Educational Fair, a group of young Indian artists that has visited more than 800 such communities with its consciousness-raising message. (See EC-053 and EC-165 in the Appendix.)

Published in the United States of America in 1994 by
Lynne Rienner Publishers, Inc.
1800 30th Street, Boulder, Colorado 80301

and in the United Kingdom by
Lynne Rienner Publishers, Inc.
3 Henrietta Street, Covent Garden, London WC2E 8LU

Library of Congress Cataloging-in-Publication Data
Cultural expression and grassroots development : cases from Latin
  America and the Caribbean / edited by Charles David Kleymeyer.
    p.   cm.
Includes bibliographical references and index.
ISBN 1-55587-461-4 (alk. paper)
ISBN 1-55587-499-1 (pbk. : alk. paper)
  1. Community development—Latin America—Case studies.
2. Culture—Case studies. I. Kleymeyer, Charles D.
HN110.5.Z9C62632   1993
307.1'4'098—dc20
                                                        93-30868
                                                        CIP

British Cataloguing in Publication Data
A Cataloguing in Publication record for this book
is available from the British Library.

Printed and bound in the United States of America

Contents

PART 3
CONCLUSIONS

About the Contributors

Patrick Breslin is the representative for Honduras at the Inter-American Foundation (Arlington, Virginia).

Mac Chapin is the director of the Central America Program for Cultural Survival (Arlington, Virginia).

María Chumpí Kayap is an alumnus of the Instituto Normal Bilingüe Intercultural Shuar and now is a schoolteacher (Macas, Ecuador).

Juan García Salazar is the director and founder of Etno-publicaciones (Quito, Ecuador).

Brent Goff is a writer and radio producer (San Francisco, California).

Kevin Healy is the representative for Bolivia at the Inter-American Foundation (Arlington, Virginia).

Xochitl Herrera and Miguel Lobo-Guerrero are codirectors of ETNOLLANO—the Fundación para· el Etnodesarrollo de los Llanos (Bogotá, Colombia).

Miguel Jempékat was the director of the Instituto Normal Bilingüe Intercultural Shuar (Bomboisa, Ecuador) and now is the provincial director of the Educación Intercultural Bilingüe of Morona Santiago (Macas, Ecuador).

Charles David Kleymeyer is the representative for Ecuador at the Inter-American Foundation (Arlington, Virginia).

David Maybury-Lewis is president and founder of Cultural Survival and professor of anthropology at Harvard University.

Carlos Moreno is the president and cofounder of Comunidec—Sistemas de Investigación y Desarrollo Comunitario (Quito, Ecuador).

Paula R. Palmer is a consultant and writer who collaborates with ANAI—The Asociación de los Nuevos Alquimistas (San José, Costa Rica).

Caryl Ricca is an anthropologist who was the research assistant for this book (Boulder, Colorado).

The *Sistren Theatre Collective* is a women's theater group (Kingston, Jamaica).

Alaka Wali is an anthropology professor at the University of Maryland (College Park, Maryland).

Elayne Zorn is a doctoral candidate in anthropology at Cornell University (Ithaca, New York).

Foreword:
Culture and Development
•

DAVID MAYBURY-LEWIS

People have speculated since ancient times about how to improve the moral and physical lots of humankind. In the years immediately following World War II, there was an optimistic feeling among economists and in international agencies that at last we knew how to do this and that we had the means at our disposal. What now seems curious, as we look back on that age of innocence, is that specialists in the relatively new field of international development thought that abolishing want and raising the standard of living worldwide were technical problems for which there were universally applicable technical solutions. The Protestant ethic may originally have had something to do with the spirit of capitalism, but now the techniques of capitalism, stripped of any ethical or cultural concomitants, would improve the lives of all who would employ them correctly, be they Muslims or Marxists. It was assumed, of course, that Marxists would be neither willing nor able to use the techniques. They had, after all, their own prescriptions for development, which they thought to be even more scientific and impervious to cultural considerations than the capitalist ones. As a result, theorists and practitioners from the First and Second Worlds alike instructed the peoples of the so-called Third World in how to improve their standard of living.

A generation later, when their prescriptions had had only modest success (and in many cases no success at all), development theorists remembered culture. This agreeably flexible concept was conveniently introduced to "explain" why things had gone wrong, or at least why they had not gone according to plan. Culture therefore usually had negative connotations. Indian culture was blamed for India's problems in Gunnar Myrdal's *Asian Drama,* and theorists lamented that cultural factors succeeded in applying the brakes to development in other parts of the world. It was still assumed that the process of development was unilinear and that, as Daniel Bell put it in *The Coming of the Post-Industrial Society,* those countries that sought development would become progressively industrialized, modernized, and Westernized. In the theories of leading sociologists and economists, culture had thus become a sort of residual category. It was treated as an externality, like sand that gummed up the works of proper theory. There were, of course, cultural specialists—anthropologists—but, to the extent that they were brought in at all, their job was to try to eliminate the cultural residues, to clean out the engines of development, so to speak, so that they could function properly.

This way of thinking about development derived not only from the simplistic economic axiom that countries would "take off" as soon as they had gotten up sufficient speed but also from the theories of modernization current at the time. The latter assumed that modernization, which looked very much like Westernization, was regularly accompanied by individualization and secularization. Therefore, if developing countries wanted to increase their standards of living, they would have to put up with the social ailments that afflict the West—overall loss of faith, a weakening of the ties that bind people together in communities, individual rootlessness, and so on. A reluctance to pay this price was interpreted as a sign of backwardness and underdevelopment. It was as if development was thought to bring with it not only the abandonment of outdated beliefs but of outdated cultures as well.

Nor was it only technocrats who thought this way. Frantz Fanon, who passionately opposed colonialism and the developmental pretensions that were used to justify it, argued in *The Wretched of the Earth* that the only salvation for the colonized was to get rid of their cultures. These had been deformed by colonialism and should therefore be replaced. Development was for him the process by which new cultures and new individuals, with an integrity and dignity of their own, would emerge phoenix-like from the ashes of colonialism. The idea is reminiscent of the emphasis that used to be placed until recently on the "new Soviet man," whose emergence would facilitate and ensure the success of communism in the Soviet Union.

Nowadays, as we contemplate with a kind of awe the spectacular collapse of Soviet revolutionary pretensions, it is easy enough to see how they were unsuccessful in remolding the various cultures of the Russian empire. Yet Western thinking about development still tends all too often to assume that cultures not only can but should be made over, and furthermore to assume it casually, as if this will happen incidentally to the important "developmental" changes being planned. I believe such thinking is misguided. I do not mean to say that cultures do not and should not change. On the contrary, culture, in its broad anthropological sense (meaning the way of life of a people and particularly the shared understandings that underlie it), is constantly changing. Development, too, is a process of change, often of induced change. The questions, then, are what sort of change is contemplated, how rapid it will be, and whether the advantages it brings will make it worth putting up with the dislocations it effects.

Development, as Charles Kleymeyer points out in this volume, is a profoundly cultural matter, in the sense that it is intertwined with and affects a people's whole way of life. Yet it is not always carried out in a way that is respectful of a people's culture. The most dramatic recent example of this type of development is Iran under the Shah. The Shah was praised in the West for modernizing his country, though some people wondered if he was doing it too fast. The fact that he was doing it in a way that profoundly affronted the values of many of his subjects was discounted. Their explosion of outrage therefore caught the West by surprise and plunged Iran into its revolution; as a result, the world has had to live ever since with an Iranian nation that is embittered, anti-Western, and anti-modernistic.

The point is that the Shah and those who applauded his policies thought that the Iranian traditions he was affronting were archaic and should be changed. This view, apart from the fact that it led to disastrously unsuccessful policies, raises very difficult questions. Who decides whether a people's traditions, or perhaps their whole way of life, should be condemned, and on what grounds? Such decisions are normally made by the powerful and for reasons that are prejudiced and specious.

In the Americas, for example, the invading Europeans have been arguing since the conquest that Indian cultures are backward and should disappear. The Indians were considered savages because customs such as cannibalism or human sacrifice put them beyond the pale. Those Indian societies that did not engage in such practices were considered savage because they were naked. If they went clothed, then they were held to be savage for being too egalitarian or un-Christian. These judgments were passed, with no sense of irony, by Europeans who practiced, for example, slavery and judicial torture. It is clear to us now that the justifications used by the conquerors were rationalizations for their determination to seize the new lands and rule over their inhabitants.

The invaders felt justified at first because they claimed they were Christianizing the Indians. Later they argued only that they had an obligation to civilize them. Others simply insisted that the Indians, as savages, had to get out of the way of the forces of civilization. That was Teddy Roosevelt's view, as he summed it up in *The Winning of the West:* "This great continent of ours could not have been left as a playground for squalid savages."

In the nineteenth century, even many who sympathized with the Indians felt that the Indian cultures of the Americas should cease to exist. They felt that the only way Indians could escape discrimination was to abandon their Indianness and take their places as individuals in the mainstream of the civilization that had engulfed them.

Similar arguments are being made nowadays, but the modern rationalization is development. According to this view, Indian cultures should cease to exist, either because they stand in the way of economic development or because the presence of unassimilated Indian populations is thought to undermine political development. These contentions are often considered self-evident, yet I would challenge them both.

In Brazil, for example, the recent assaults on Indian peoples have been excused in the name of development. Yet it is clear that the Brazilian model of development favors business and agribusiness interests but marginalizes not only Indians but all of the rural poor. Neither of these categories of people stands in the way of development. On the contrary, both are victims of a particularly skewed and indefensible set of "development" policies that have benefited a few, impoverished many, and driven the country into economic crisis. Nor does the current Indian demand for the right to maintain their own cultures threaten the political development of the state. Indians, after all, make up less than 1 percent of the total population of Brazil, and they are scattered in small societies in the more inaccessible parts of the country. This demand only threatens Brazil's self-image as a melting-pot society, forcing Brazilians to confront the question of whether or not they are willing to permit ethnic pluralism in their nation.

Nor can it be argued that in places where the Indian populations are much larger—in the Andean countries, for example, or Guatemala—the Indians impede economic or political development by maintaining their Indian cultures. On the contrary, the Indians have been used as scapegoats as well as workhorses in these societies. National development has certainly been deformed, but the causes are the policies of the elites, who have historically excluded the bulk of the population of their respective countries from full participation in the national life. Thus, the reluctance of these countries to consider the possibility of Indian cultural autonomy or even, on occasion, to admit the existence of their Indian populations at all derives from a reluctance to rethink and revise the traditional inequalities of neocolonial states.

Such rationalizations are by no means confined to the Americas. African pastoralists have been targets of development programs aimed at putting an end to their nomadic way of life, which is claimed to be contributing to desertification. Yet studies have shown that it is not pastoralism that creates deserts but the pressures exerted by settled populations on pastoralists. Similarly, governments the world over try to stop people from practicing swidden, or slash-and-burn, agriculture on the grounds that it impoverishes the soil. Again, study after study has shown that there is nothing inherently harmful to the soil in swidden agriculture. Indeed, it is often the most effective form of agriculture available to people who have few tools or other agricultural aids. Problems are created only when the pressure on such populations reduces their land base and they are forced to shorten the time the ground is allowed to remain fallow before replanting. The real reason pastoralists and swidden agriculturalists receive so much negative attention is that they are normally marginal populations, looked down on for their "backward" ways of life and considered therefore to be appropriate targets for modernization.

Let me be clear that I am not defending traditional practices as *invariably* possessing more wisdom than is supposed. I am merely arguing that they *often* do. It is therefore more sensible to start with the assumption that the locals know what they are doing and to try to understand their practices in their own terms. Yet in development work, this simple precept is often ignored. Developers tend to assume that there is a single, demonstrably better way to development, a way that is most clearly understood by experts. I disagree with this view, for which I can find no convincing evidence. Instead, I argue that development professionals have an important contribution to make, but of a different kind: They have the general knowledge and experience to be able to put local findings in context and thus understand them better. But they cannot succeed without this local knowledge. Their best results come when they take it seriously and base their thinking on the dialectic of the general and the particular.

This perspective implies a different way of going about development—abandoning the monolithic thinking of the past in favor of a pluralist outlook. Such pluralism should not be confused with an eclectic "let us take each case as it comes" approach that does not allow us to learn from experiences in other times or other places. It is rather a more open approach, whose general propositions can be modified in the light of particular knowledge and in which planning and practices can be adapted to local circumstances.

Such an approach has another great advantage. By its very nature it depends on the cooperation of the people who are the beneficiaries (or, as it is sometimes more aptly phrased, the targets) of development policy. In effect, it includes them in the process of development planning. Such inclusion is an excellent precept to follow. The worst disasters and injustices committed in the name of development come about when people are excluded from the decisions that affect them or even excluded from consideration when such decisions are being made.

The pluralism I am advocating thus entertains a wide variety of development strategies and deals openly with the populations to be affected by those strategies. It also accepts their right to be different, if they so wish. This is particularly important when the populations are culturally or ethnically different from the mainstream.

Here again it is necessary to deal with some misconceptions. Ethnicity has often been considered an atavistic and explosive force that has to be abolished or at least kept in check in the interests of progress and nation building. I have elsewhere criticized the modern world's fascination with the nation-state and argued that the divisive effects of ethnic attachments have been systematically overemphasized and contrasted with the hypothetical benefits of the idealized nation-state.[1] If we reexamine the role of ethnic subcultures, particularly in "Third World" countries, we find that allegations of ethnic divisiveness, backwardness, and separatism are often used by governments as cloaks for exploitation, authoritarianism, and hegemonic privilege. This ploy is particularly ironic given that our modern preoccupation with the nation-state and its needs derives from the French revolutionary idea of the state, based on equality and fraternity for all. Yet nowadays people are resorting to their ethnicity in many parts of the world as a sort of civil rights movement to achieve the equality of treatment that has been denied them in the name of modernization or development. We need, then, to rethink the supposed "needs" of the state, particularly the relationship between the state and its constituent populations.

But people do not cling to their cultures simply to use them as interethnic strategies. They do so because it is through them that they make sense of the world and have a sense of themselves. We know that when people are forced to give up their culture, or when they give it up too rapidly, the consequences are normally social breakdown accompanied by personal disorientation and despair. The attachment of people to their culture corresponds, then, to a fundamental human need.

That is why development programs that build on cultural traditions are likely to be the most successful. This volume describes such programs. The essays gathered here are practical demonstrations of the theoretical position I have been outlining. I have argued, essentially, that there is no monolithic science of development that can serve as an unerring guide for action. Development strategies are therefore political and technical programs, which depend for their success on a mixture of cultural, social, and economic factors. It follows that no development policy should be deemed to be beyond question, and none should be put into effect until the alternatives to it have been carefully considered—and considered furthermore in terms of whose is the gain and whose is the pain. That is why I have stressed pluralism and inclusion. These are the best means at our disposal to avoid arrogance and injustice.

I am particularly pleased to be able to introduce the essays gathered in this volume, for they demonstrate that what I am advocating is not impractical. It is not easy either, as Mac Chapin shows in his article on traditional knowledge among the Kuna of Panama. Yet even Chapin's essay is more optimistic than it might seem at first reading. It may be that younger Kuna no longer find it worth their while to go through the arduous apprenticeship necessary to learn traditional Kuna lore. Nevertheless, the Kuna have maintained a strong sense of themselves and have jealously preserved their way of life and their local autonomy. That way of life will change and some aspects of Kuna tradition may be lost in the process, yet one comes away with a sense of a people who are capable of making their own decisions and in a position to do so. This ability is the essence of cultural survival.

This volume, then, is a series of examples of how to go about grassroots development, an area in which the Inter-American Foundation has done pioneering work. Most of the essays deal with the expressive culture of the peoples being assisted—their art, music, dance, theater, puppets, and so on. They describe in moving terms how relatively small amounts of money invested in a people's expressive culture served to promote their social cohesion and enhance their self-respect. I was reminded when I read these essays of the many Indian societies throughout the Americas who now want to write their own histories. They feel ignored or maligned in the histories written by non-Indians and want now to compose their own and have them taught to their children so that the next generation may get a sense of the dignity of their ancestors.

This is a point that is sometimes overlooked. Development is as much about dignity as it is about consumption.[2] The cultural productions described in this volume belong to that realm of human life that is often referred to as folklore, especially when we are speaking of ethnic minorities, or even of ethnic majorities who are otherwise underprivileged. Folklore in its turn is not usually taken seriously in development circles. It tends to be regarded either as a quaint production of backward cultures or as a sentimental backward glance to a vanished way of life, when it is indulged in by properly "modern" ethnic minorities. These essays show just how wrong that perception is. A people's expressive culture, which is at the heart of its folklore, has a profound significance. It is a powerful statement of what is most deeply felt and of what gives meaning to people's lives. If it flourishes, so too does their way of life. Being poor does not mean being impoverished culturally. The essays in this volume understand this and go on to show that this understanding is not only the stuff of poetry. It is also the basis of sensible and sensitive development, which is, after all, about improving the quality of people's lives.

NOTES

1. See David Maybury-Lewis, "Living in Leviathan: Ethnic Groups and the State," in David Maybury-Lewis, ed., *The Prospects for Plural Societies* (1982 Proceedings of the American Ethnological Society, Washington, DC, 1984).

2. See Patrick Breslin, *Development and Dignity* (Rosslyn, VA: Inter-American Foundation/Westview Press, 1987).

Acknowledgments

There are no pieces of work in life that are accomplished entirely by individuals; all work and all creativity is collective. Such has been the case with this book, and not only because to a large degree it is a collection of articles written by past and present employees, grantees, and other colleagues of the Inter-American Foundation (IAF). The collective effort in this case reaches much further.

First, it includes those who aided in the conceptualization of the book: Marion Ritchey Vance and the IAF Cultural Committee that she headed during the 1970s and 1980s; Sheldon Annis, who saw the need for a book that would focus on the connection between cultural expression and grassroots development; the editors of the IAF's journal, *Grassroots Development,* especially Sheldon Annis, Kathryn Shaw, and Ron Weber, who developed and polished the more than twenty articles on culture and grassroots development that have been published in that journal over the past two decades; Caryl Ricca, the research assistant contracted for the study that formed the basis for this book; the members of the book's advisory committee—David Bray, Patrick Breslin, Kevin Healy, Caryl Ricca, Marion Ritchey Vance, and Julie Sutphen Wechsler; and countless cultural activists and analysts in Latin America and the Caribbean, who are the true artisans of the book's conceptual framework, especially Juan García Salazar and Carlos Moreno.

I acknowledge the vision and work of the other authors who contributed to this book. Their varied points of view, experience, and backgrounds have made the book far richer than any single author could have done. Also participating in this collective effort, with general comments and detailed editing suggestions, were Diane Bendahmane, Patrick Breslin, Charles Reilly, Kathryn Shaw, and Ron Weber.

I thank the Inter-American Foundation and its Office of Learning and Dissemination for providing me with the time and institutional backup necessary for carrying out this collective effort it has been my honor to direct—especially Sheldon Annis, Leyda Appel, Maria Barry, Linda Borst, Patrick Breslin, Comunidec (the in-country service organization that works with the IAF in Ecuador), Chris Krueger, Pam Palma, Bill K. Perrin, Ann

Prestidge, Walter Price, Charles Reilly, Marion Ritchey Vance, Kathryn Shaw, Deborah Szekely, Anne Ternes, David Valenzuela, Steve Vetter, and Ron Weber.

But above all, I wish to recognize the dedication and creativity of every storyteller, singer, musician, dancer, actor, puppeteer, folk poet, painter, and traditional artisan who carries the torch that illuminates the path leading from the past into the future. They provide people with inspiration, pride, and cultural energy in their constant efforts to construct a more humane and just society for our children. To these cultural activists, and to those who join hands and hearts with them, I dedicate this book.

CDK

Introduction

●

CHARLES DAVID KLEYMEYER

After many years of waiting, a remote village in Africa finally received electricity. One of the first things the villagers did was to pool their money and buy a television set from a salesman who was traveling through the region. Lots of people from outside the community had been telling them what a good thing television was.

Little else went on for the next couple of months while everyone in the village stayed glued to the TV. Then, one by one, people got tired of it, until almost no one watched anymore.

The man who sold the television set showed up again one day, expecting to sell dozens more. Puzzled, he asked the people, "Tell me, why aren't you all watching your new TV?"

"Oh, we don't need it," was the answer. "We have our storyteller."

"Don't you think," said the traveling salesman, "that the television set knows a lot more stories than your storyteller?"

The villagers were quiet for awhile. Finally an old man spoke up: "You're right. The television set knows many stories. Probably more than our storyteller." He paused. "But our storyteller . . . knows us."

> —Told by Native American Ron Evans,
> at the National Storytelling Festival,
> Jonesboro, Tennessee, October 1982

Culture is at the center of the human experience. It is a major force that shapes behavior and social structure; in turn, it is formed and re-formed by the cumulative impact of those behaviors and structures. Culture helps to define who we are and how we think of ourselves and act toward others—both inside and outside the groups to which we belong. Just as people have material needs, we have social and cultural needs as well:

to relate to others, to achieve survival and fulfillment through collective efforts, and to express what we perceive, feel, and yearn for. Our material and sociocultural needs are inextricably linked; we must not only attend to our physical wants but carry on and elaborate our cultural traditions and social orders as well, continually reforming them to adapt to changing conditions. This is where the storyteller, as illustrated in the vignette above, and cultural expression in general can play a key role.

This book describes development activities in Latin America and the Caribbean that have encouraged social and economic change by both drawing upon and reinforcing the cultural traditions of low-income and ethnic peoples. This promising but as yet largely neglected approach to grassroots development has evolved from experience in the developing world, as well as in poverty-stricken areas and ethnic enclaves of the industrialized world. Rooted in respect for the wisdom and ways of ethnic peoples and the poor in general, this approach seeks to retain their special cultural strengths and contributions while enabling them to achieve necessary changes in their social and economic condition. The purpose is not to romanticize these people nor to maintain them in some static, pristine state (were that even possible). Rather, it is to improve their chances for survival and well-being through change that they control and carry out. Their own cultural heritage becomes the foundation upon which equitable and sustainable development is built.

The cases described in this book are drawn from social and economic development efforts supported by the Inter-American Foundation (IAF) in more than thirty countries of Latin America and the Caribbean over a seventeen-year period. From September 1973 through September 1990, the IAF directed $20.9 million (nearly 7 percent of its total funding) to more than 200 groups, institutions, and individuals, supporting 215 projects in which cultural expression was an integral part. The recipients of this funding included federations of ethnic minorities, agricultural cooperatives, youth groups, communities, artisan groups, nonformal education institutions and radio stations, church-related organizations, and social science institutes, as well as individual folklorists, social scientists, writers, artists, actors, musicians, and other performers, researchers, and activists. Their projects ranged from handicraft production, adult literacy centers, and community bread ovens to collection of black folktales and Indian harvest chants to reforestation of Andean highlands and conservation of a rain forest. For a complete listing and description of these projects and the groups that carried them out, see the Appendix at the end of this volume.

CULTURAL EXPRESSION

The projects mentioned above included activities that can be considered "cultural expression"—such as music, dance, popular theater, puppetry, artisan work, poster and mural art, and oral tradition. Cultural expression is the representation in language, symbols, and actions of a particular group's collective heritage—its history, aesthetic values, beliefs, observations, desires, knowledge, wisdom, and opinions. It includes things material, such as a weaving or a woodcarving, and immaterial, such as a dance, a song, or a legend. At times the material is combined with the immaterial, as in an illustrated book of animal tales, or a street theater pageant with enormous colorful banners and human figures, or a patchwork *arpillera* that depicts an historical event. These forms of cultural expression are presented through media as varied as festivals, street and stage theater, art and historical exhibits, radio and television programs, classrooms, and photography, film, and video. They are also manifested informally in the course of everyday life—in homes, in the streets, and in other places where people meet. Some of these activities are not usually thought of as artistic. Examples are traditional technologies, products, and work forms. But from the point of view of, say, Amazonian Indians, the physical beauty of cooking and eating utensils cannot be separated from their utilitarian aspects—and thus the creation of a ceramic bowl or a reed basket is a form of cultural expression. For the Andean Quechuas, the *minga,* or traditional work party, is often imbued with cultural expression in the form of songs, food, and clothing. Local festivals are not merely expressive in a cultural manner: they also have political and economic functions—i.e., they are also "productive" or "utilitarian" in the Western sense. This characteristic is mentioned to warn readers of occasional uses of the term "cultural expression" that may be nonconventional for industrialized societies but closer to how many native peoples view the world.

An underlying theme of this book is how a cultural expression approach to development can contribute ideas on how to address abject poverty among the lowest strata of society, particularly among so-called "traditional" or "minority" peoples. These peoples, although neither immune nor averse to the process of modernization, are at the same time attempting to maintain their cultural heritage, not in a static state but with continual adaptation to new realities and surrounding cultures. Throughout human history, people have expended time, energy, and resources to both produce and adjust to change while preserving their culture from being assimilated wholesale into another one. For the most part they prefer to integrate themselves into the larger society on their own terms, without having to deny who they are. They accept and affirm their ethnic identity but not the material and social conditions to which they are subjected. In fact, their ethnic identity may grow in importance if they feel discriminated against.

The term "minority," or "minority group," will be used here in the sociopolitical rather than the demographic sense; in some parts of Latin America and the Caribbean, groups such as Indians or blacks may represent the majority of the population statistically but function socially and politically as minorities. They suffer the consequences of low social and political power, discrimination, and exploitation based on their physical characteristics, beliefs, lifestyle, language, dress, or other traits. Other groups living in Latin America and the Caribbean—North Americans, Europeans, Middle Easterners, or Asians—may form minorities in numerical terms but dominate politically and economically.

As this book will demonstrate, experience indicates that participatory, broad-based development at the grassroots level is best built upon a foundation of strong cultural identity and pride and the resulting increases in group solidarity and energy. Cultural expression, in all its richness and variety, is a major means of generating and focusing a vital social force that can be called *cultural energy*. This force is a prime source of motivation that inspires people to confront problems, identify solutions, and participate in carrying them out.

Weakened identities and negative group image, on the other hand, are obstacles to development. They reduce motivation and energy. They also reduce clarity of purpose and direction—people cannot discover where they want to go if they do not first know where they have come from. For many minority groups, oral histories, songs, and other forms of traditional expression are the best if not the only sources of their own history. As Ecuadorian educator and development practitioner Carlos Moreno puts it: "Only when we recuperate our history, and when we are capable of critically analyzing and knowing the reality in which we live, will we be ready to change that reality, to transform it in order to return to being the authors of the new history and to begin the construction of the just and unified society to which we all aspire."[1]

GRASSROOTS DEVELOPMENT

The central focus of this book is the relationship between cultural expression and grassroots development—as opposed to other areas of human endeavor in which cultural expression can play a significant role, such as entertainment, advertising, political campaigning, religious proselytizing, and even group conflict. Grassroots development is a process in which disadvantaged people *organize themselves* to overcome the obstacles to their social and economic well-being. The strategies they employ include conducting self-help development projects, pressuring public and private institutions for resources, and representing the group's common interests before governmental agencies and the body politic.

Ideally, members of grassroots groups *participate* fully in identifying problems, setting priorities, designing strategies and programs, and carrying them out. These activities normally involve small-scale, practical efforts to achieve change, and are carried out by organizations such as village or neighborhood associations, production or service cooperatives, cultural groups, workers' associations, ethnic coalitions, or federations of such organizations. The breadth and intensity of participation typically generated by this approach is one of its major strengths relative to other styles of development.

This participatory development approach is often called "bottom-up," in contrast to the more common "top-down" approach. In bottom-up development, the potential beneficiaries themselves take the initiative to identify problems and possible solutions; then, with their own human and material resources, or sometimes with outside assistance, they address those problems. The bottom-up approach is typically characterized by a unique perspective on problems and solutions, one grounded in the cultural traditions of people in the lower strata of society. Their responses to social and economic dilemmas frequently are imaginative, unconventional, and highly innovative.

In the more common top-down approach, outsiders from higher up the socioeconomic and political scale choose the problems to be addressed, then design and carry out the solutions, at times consulting to varying degrees with the prospective beneficiaries. Outsiders are also frequently involved in bottom-up, grassroots development, though in a more collaborative role. They commonly provide services, technical assistance, and resources such as materials or funding, and they either share decisionmaking with project organizers and beneficiaries or leave it to them entirely. The key point is that these outsiders usually respond to the initiatives of local organizations and collaborate with them in a supportive role.

Grassroots development efforts are often based on a broader concept of deprivation and well-being than are programs initiated from the top. Rather than limiting themselves to economic and material goals, grassroots organizations and the professionals that support them often try to achieve social and cultural objectives as well. Because they typically believe that economic change must be built upon a solid social and cultural foundation, they include among their goals, for example, building collective confidence and self-respect or fostering a positive group identity, particularly if the group's members form part of a cultural minority.

Results of grassroots development efforts can be intangible—improved skills in communication, leadership, management, or production; increased group pride and a strong sense of self; the establishment of rights to civil liberties and to land and water usage; or the increased ability to leverage services from the state. Results can also be tangible—increases in production of agricultural or manufactured goods; a building to be used for organizational or project activities; or a road or water system used by several communities.

A grassroots development strategy is necessarily people-oriented, stressing the development of human resources over physical infrastructure. The belief is that broad-based, sustainable development at the lower levels of society results primarily from the promotion and strengthening of local organizations. Within this strategy, empowerment and democratization replace charity and the treatment of the symptoms of poverty. Improved organizational and problem-solving capacities are crucial for each group, as is the formation—among like-minded organizations—of mutually supportive coalitions and networks.

In sum, the long-term objective of grassroots development is to produce more viable, productive, and effective local organizations that can carry out further development efforts on their own, long after a specific project has ended.

Many of these grassroots development efforts, whether consciously or not, employ cultural expression as a key method, in collaboration with other approaches, for achieving their goals. Music, dance, stories, myths and legends, popular theater and puppets, and crafts and artwork sometimes are used as an end in themselves—e.g., to maintain aspects of a culture for purposes of group identity and esteem, or as a source to be tapped for cultural energy. Alternatively, they are used as means to broader programmatic ends—e.g., harnessing cultural energy to promote increased participation, teaching new practices or knowledge, or raising group consciousness about a problem or potential solution. These uses will be a major focus of this book.

THE SOCIAL AND HISTORICAL BACKDROP

Historically, most development efforts imposed from above or imported from the outside, ostensibly on behalf of traditional or minority populations, have failed—sometimes dramatically. The reasons for these failures are numerous and complicated. Such programs often have a tendency to ignore or downplay the beneficiaries' culture, at times going so far as to make it the scapegoat, if not the target, of the efforts at change. Rather than building upon existing cultural strengths and strategies, these imposed development projects have imported solutions and structures from alien cultures, sometimes cultures that have competed against the traditional group for generations.

These projects generally define poverty and development in relatively narrow terms, emphasizing material ends and imported technology and downplaying basic human needs such as self-esteem, a strong identity, group cohesiveness, creativity, and free expression. Programs that attend only to material factors by, for instance, increasing the production of cash crops for export often miss the point as to what brings about lasting improvements in a group's capacity to develop. These programs also frequently miss the point as to what people in poverty feel they need. When people lack dignity, self-esteem, and group solidarity, they can feel culturally and socially impoverished, which can perpetuate their being disadvantaged in a material sense.

In the aftermath of decades of failed development efforts among ethnic minorities, and in the context of rapid modernization and changing political realities, the gap is generally widening between minority peoples and those in the higher strata of their societies. Modernization, war, and economic deterioration have hit traditional peoples harder than most and left them more vulnerable than ever. Massive geographical dislocation, national integration policies that emphasize cultural homogenization and assimilation into the dominant sector of society, and the penetration via mass media of the values and needs of urban, Western-style consumer society often overwhelm marginalized, politically weak, traditional peoples.

These factors lead to reduced life chances and increased suffering of all kinds—but that is not all. In many cases—for example, in the Amazon Basin—not only the cultural but also the physical survival of traditional ethnic groups is in question.

All of society is made poorer by the demise of any one of its groups. Not only the moral stock of the society but also its cultural diversity is drastically reduced by such tragedies. Traditional ethnic groups offer vital practical knowledge in the areas of health, sustainable agriculture and forest management, and even social and political organization. If the ethnic group dies out, its knowledge goes with it.

The problem of overwhelming poverty among minority ethnic populations and the challenge of cultural survival are important issues in the developing world and the industrialized world alike. In the United States, for example, many African-Americans and Native Americans are locked in an underclass, with little hope of improving their prospects. In Australia, aborigines struggle for land, civil rights, and cultural integrity. In Japan, the Ainu minority group and many ethnic Koreans face persistent poverty and discrimination.

Beyond the complicated problem of poverty, another important theme prompts us to focus on cultural approaches to development. Throughout the twentieth century, the enterprise of nation building and the achievement of peace have continually foundered on the rocks of racial and ethnic conflict and discrimination. The question of how to achieve ethnic coexistence—if not mutually beneficial cultural pluralism—is still largely unanswered, not just in the developing world but also in Eastern and Western Europe and the United States, as daily headlines remind us.

The cases are numerous and the numbers of people are large, underlining the significance of ethnic conflict at this time in world history. Jason Clay of Cultural Survival, the human rights group that supports the efforts of indigenous ethnic groups to preserve their physical and cultural integrity, states the problem in very stark terms:

The outlook for indigenous peoples, who number 600 million worldwide and live in more than 5,000 groups, is deteriorating. In excess of 5.5 million tribal people have been killed as the result of warfare waged by their own governments since World War II, and 150 million have been displaced. This century has witnessed more extinctions of native peoples than any other.[2]

It is significant that culturally diverse grassroots groups in this hemisphere and throughout the world are addressing the threats of ethnic discrimination, disaggregation, and misunderstanding. They frequently employ cultural expression to change how people think about and treat one another. Their first step often is to challenge harmful stereotypes about ethnic minorities, educating members of other groups to change their perceptions and expectations.

Proponents of a culture-based approach to development believe that free choice is a crucial ingredient in just development for any group of people but especially for ethnic minorities. Making choices is the crux of self-determination, and self-determination is not only a human right but also the most effective way, in the long run, to bring about broad-based, equitable change. In the words of Rex Nettleford, artistic director of the National Dance Theatre Company of Jamaica, "I don't want to *enter* anyone's mainstream; I want to help *determine* it."[3]

Cultural expression activities can provide a rich forum for considering and making choices. Observes Ecuadorian folklorist Juan García Salazar: "Choice means there are alternatives with which to compare, and cultural activities present those alternatives. They offer people options from which to choose and to take control over their lives. Without these choices, people are not free; their values and lifestyles are imposed upon them."[4]

CURRENT CULTURAL EXPRESSION APPROACHES

The culture-based approach to development is not a panacea for human suffering and inequality. It is one facet of a diverse strategy with many mutually reinforcing methodologies. A culture-based approach goes hand in hand with other approaches that encourage people to achieve empowerment by strengthening organizations and coalitions; increase productivity by forming cooperative enterprises; heighten individual and group capacity through consciousness-raising and nonformal education; or sustainable agricultural production through increased environmental sensibility.

People from *all* levels of society, not just ethnic minorities and the poor, employ the link between cultural expression and socioeconomic development, although they may not recognize it as such. When a country celebrates its independence day with pageants, parades, and fireworks; when a chain of hamburger outlets produces a snappy song-and-dance routine promoting its product; when an antidrug campaign utilizes poster art and rap music; when a military band marches down the street; or when a church choir goes on tour—in all cases, cultural forms are being used to preserve and promote ideas or identities or to change behaviors.

Clearly, cultural expression does not cause social or economic change to take place, but it can facilitate those changes by tapping into cultural energy, motivating people to analyze and to act. It would be misguided to view all forms of cultural expression as universally positive and acceptable activities. They can be used for social control or manipulation as well. Militaristic and totalitarian societies are most apt to misuse cultural forms in this way, although all societies are susceptible.

THE INTER-AMERICAN FOUNDATION'S PERSPECTIVE

The Inter-American Foundation was established in 1969 by the U.S. Congress as an experimental foreign aid program to support the self-managed development efforts of disadvantaged peoples throughout Latin America and the Caribbean. As stated in its founding legislation, the purpose of the IAF is to:

- Strengthen the bonds of friendship and understanding among the peoples of this hemisphere;
- Support self-help efforts designed to enlarge the opportunities for individual development;
- Stimulate and assist effective and ever wider participation of the people in the development process; and
- Encourage the establishment and growth of democratic institutions, private and governmental, appropriate to the requirements of the individual sovereign nations of this hemisphere.

Rather than export solutions to the southern part of the hemisphere from the northern part, the IAF responds to initiatives from local Latin or Caribbean organizations, based on strategies they design and carry out to address their own priorities. IAF grants go directly to beneficiary groups or support organizations without passing through governmental channels and with no political or religious conditions attached.

The IAF has always striven to be apolitical, secular, and nonpartisan. Its first president, William Dyal, described the institution's responsive stance in this way:

The Inter-American Foundation has never attempted to establish a precise formula for development or social change. We recognize there are many paths and many approaches contingent on the local political context, the level of development, and the desires of the people most concerned.

The Inter-American Foundation has learned, for example, from listening to groups in Latin America and the Caribbean, that people do not necessarily aspire to modernization and forms of economic growth as do people in the U.S. They often consider economic growth subordinate to other human aspirations. The funder must understand the qualitative concerns of people. Herein there is harmony between our basic values and theirs. We are attempting to perceive what the potential for change and accomplishment will be even more than what the actual change and accomplishments have been.

Responsiveness then involves listening to, understanding, and supporting with grant funds the activities people themselves are carrying out. It means to facilitate what others want to do without intervening in, creating, or shaping their activity. As funders we are concerned about the vested interests of the mind and the spirit. We are learning that knowledge, history, experience, and privilege can be tyrannies when imposed or used against others.[5]

Because of this responsive approach, the IAF has not funded culture-based development projects as part of a preconceived strategy, nor has it solicited proposals that focus on culture. Rather, groups and individuals in Latin America and the Caribbean independently identified the approach as promising and subsequently designed and carried out projects using it, often with support from the IAF.

People of the developing world recognize that culture and development are linked and choose to connect them in striving to improve their lives. One close observer of the IAF's support for this approach put it as follows:

The Foundation has come to appreciate the importance of cultural aspects of development, because it has learned *from* people that these aspects are important to them. It has not introduced a new variable or capriciously aggregated two unrelated elements—culture and economic development. Rather it has merely acknowledged that cultural and economic aspects are inextricably interwoven when observed in their natural state. In fact, culture is an holistic concept: economic aspects are one element of that whole. Instead of having to justify the *inclusion* of cultural considerations in the development process, it would seem more likely that the more conservative "developmentalists" should be forced to justify their isolation of economic factors and their disproportionate concentration on these to the *exclusion* of other relevant factors.[6]

Other bilateral and international institutions have also supported cultural expression. Among them are the African Development Foundation (the IAF's sister organization), CEBEMO (a Dutch funding agency), Coordination in Development, Inc. (CODEL), Cultural Survival, the Ford Foundation, the International Development Exchange (IDEX), the Organization of American States, Oxfam-America and Oxfam-UK, the Rockefeller Brothers' Fund, Traditions for Tomorrow, and the United Nations

Educational, Scientific, and Cultural Organization (UNESCO)—especially the International Fund for the Promotion of Culture. UNESCO has declared 1988–1997 the "World Decade for Cultural Development." It is important to underline, however, that the efforts of all international organizations represent only a small fraction of the activity in the area of cultural expression and grassroots development. The *vast* majority of such activity is supported locally by the participants themselves, through donated time, materials, equipment, funds, and facilities.

CULTURAL EXPRESSION AND GRASSROOTS DEVELOPMENT

In 1978, a group of IAF employees, the Learning Committee on Cultural Awareness, produced "Cultural Expression and Social Change," a report on twenty-five projects supported between 1973 and 1977 that involved the performing arts (theater, music, and dance). The report generated such interest that the foundation's journal devoted a special edition to "The Arts and Social Change,"[7] followed by a series of articles over the next decade that focused on culture-based development projects (for examples, see the bibliography under the following names: Breslin, Breslin and Chapin, Chapin, Cotter, Dorfman, Palmer, García Salazar, Goff, Healy and Zorn, Herrera and Lobo-Guerrero, Kleymeyer, Kleymeyer and Moreno, Sistren Theatre Collective, and Wali). Nine of these articles, several of them revised and updated, are included in this volume.

All of these studies made important steps in describing the issues, techniques, and problems surrounding the use of cultural expression in grassroots development efforts. It is now time to take a look at the breadth and depth of this rich set of experiences. During a sabbatical in 1988, I began a formal study of the 215 projects that the IAF has supported in the area of cultural expression and grassroots development. I visited Bolivia, Chile, Colombia, Ecuador, Jamaica, Mexico, Panama, and Peru to observe firsthand more than seventy development efforts having a significant cultural expression component. In addition, I interviewed more than two dozen people in the United States (many of them individuals from Latin America and the Caribbean who were passing through Washington, D.C.). This work was aided by Caryl Ricca, an anthropologist who collaborated on the extensive bibliography and the project inventory. She also gathered qualitative data on approximately 100 of the projects most likely to produce insights on the relationship between cultural expression and social change.

The book begins with a conceptual overview of the uses and functions of cultural expression (Kleymeyer) and a treatment of the critical importance of identity and self-respect (Breslin). This section is followed by case materials illustrating how cultural action is used in practice as a strategy for grassroots development. Two chapters demonstrate the role of cultural expression in generating the energy needed to drive grassroots development efforts and enable people to reflect on their situation (Kleymeyer and Moreno, and the Sistren Theatre Collective). The next three chapters describe efforts to preserve and revive cultural traditions—especially oral traditions—as a source both of cultural energy and of present-day answers to long-standing questions about survival and human betterment (Chapin, García Salazar, and Palmer). Following are a series of chapters that focus on practical applications of the culture-based development methodology to crucial areas of endeavor such as handicrafts and education (Goff), textile production and tourism (Healy and Zorn), agricultural production (Chumpí Kayap, Jempékat, Moreno, and Kleymeyer), general peasant productiveness (Wali), and health (Herrera and Lobo-Guerrero).

This book has three primary goals. The first is to offer readers *descriptions* of the ways in which groups of disadvantaged people, and the organizations that support them, use cultural expression in development. Exactly how and why do they employ cultural expression in their work? What is the process by which they do so, and what are the results? Several cases will be described more than once—by different authors, and at different points in time—to provide readers with a longitudinal view of these efforts from varying perspectives. When possible, the description is done by cultural activists themselves, thereby giving voice to practitioners, with their insider's perspective.

The second goal is to provide readers with a few useful tools—the bibliography, the inventory of projects studied, and certain analytical concepts presented in the various chapters. These tools are intended to increase readers' understanding of a culture-based approach to social change. The bibliography, for example, should help people find the best written materials available in more than a dozen thematic categories on cultural expression and grassroots development. The inventory of projects is designed to provide brief summaries of the content of cultural expression projects and illustrate the breadth and depth of such endeavors. The concepts include the two major topics of discussion—cultural expression and grassroots development—as well as related topics, such as cultural rescue, maintenance, revitalization, and cultural activism.

The third goal of the book is to identify the key issues and questions regarding a culture-based approach to grassroots development that need to be addressed by those who apply it. In general, how viable is this culture-based approach? Is it worth spending scarce resources—time, money, and materials—on cultural expression? What are some of the positive effects, and what are the risks and pitfalls? It is premature to make definitive statements about the impact—but hopefully this volume will demonstrate that there is a connection and above all make clear that the beneficiaries of development assistance, when allowed to choose, see that connection.

NOTES

1. This quotation, by Carlos Moreno M., introduces a book edited by Segundo Moreno Y., *Alzamientos indígenas de la audiencia de Quito: 1534–1803* (Quito: Ediciones Abya Yala, 1987), p. 3.

2. Jason Clay, "Radios in the Rain Forest," *Technology Review,* Vol. 92, No. 7 (October 1989): 52–57. The quoted figures were updated in a phone call with Clay on April 5, 1992.

3. In a seminar presentation at the Inter-American Foundation, Rosslyn, Virginia, September 18, 1988.

4. In a discussion at the Encuentro Nacional de Programas de Educación Bilingüe, Latacunga, Ecuador, July 1989.

5. William Dyal, "Report from the President," *Annual Report 1979* (Inter-American Foundation, 1980), pp. 5–6.

6. Felisa M. Kazen, "Culture and Development: An Inquiry into Policy and Practices in Selected International Agencies and Private Foundations," unpublished report (1982): 4–5.

7. Patricia Haggerty, et al., "The Arts and Social Change," *Journal of the Inter-American Foundation,* Third Quarter (1979): 1–15.

Part 1
●
Overview

1

The Uses and Functions of Cultural Expression in Grassroots Development

•

CHARLES DAVID KLEYMEYER

In recent decades, throughout the developing world and in poverty-stricken areas of industrialized countries, many promising but largely overlooked development efforts have drawn upon and reinforced cultural traditions. Sometimes cultural expression is an end in itself—for example, when blacks collect their own folktales in pamphlet form so that children will learn about the escapades of Br'er Rabbit[1] as well as those of Donald Duck. Sometimes it is a means of reaching an objective—for example, when groups use songs or puppets to stir up interest in a development program.[2] In either case, cultural expression is central to the development enterprise.

Grassroots development workers and community organizations have shown how the unique cultural strengths and contributions of ethnic peoples, and the poor in general, can be retained while significant social and economic changes are achieved. The experiences of these workers strongly suggest that a cohesive and adaptive cultural identity is necessary to achieve just and lasting development among ethnic peoples and other groups that have suffered discrimination—the physically handicapped, members of a minority religion, or individuals in a deprecated occupation. For adherents of this approach, any acceptable definition of development at the grassroots level must take into account the *sociocultural* as well as the economic dimensions of deprivation and well-being. The poor in Latin America and the Caribbean frequently turn to their own popular culture to express and affirm themselves because they are commonly marginalized in a world where others have far more access to the media and the levers of government and commerce.

Sociocultural deprivation—be it manifested in spoiled identity, racial discrimination, lack of ethnic autonomy, or alienation from cultural roots —can be as damaging and limiting as material deprivation. Unfortunately, current development strategies and programs focus heavily, if not exclusively, on material deprivation. The potential impact of cultural impoverishment

17

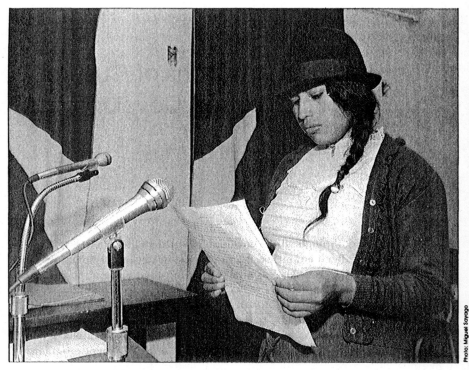

An indigenous announcer reads the news in Quichua for Radio Latacunga, a nonprofit station broadcasting bilingual educational and cultural programs to more than 1,000 Indian communities in highland Ecuador. Using portable transmitters and community-based recording booths, the indigenous audience prepares their own programs of music, stories, or news. (See EC-136 in the Appendix.)

is described eloquently by Léopoldo Sédar Senghor, ex-president of Senegal:

> White men, go into the distant villages of my land with your tape recorders, your cameras, and collect what the shamans, the street performers, and the old people tell you; the final keepers of a long human history, entrusted only to their voices. When they die, it will be as if for you, for your civilization, all the libraries were to be burned.[3]

As this book demonstrates, the conscious uses and the unconscious functions of cultural expression in grassroots development efforts are numerous and diverse. This chapter discusses eight ways cultural expression can have an impact on development. All eight can be employed by development workers who wish to make their programs more culturally appropriate and to channel a high level of participation and creativity. Nothing motivates people quite like cultural expression; it unlocks creative forces that otherwise remain dormant or go unrecognized.

The categories presented here are not a comprehensive typology. Several of the categories overlap, and many are related in mutually reinforcing ways. The chapter ends with a discussion of who controls the evolution of cultural expression.

STRENGTHENING GROUP IDENTITY, SOCIAL ORGANIZATION, AND COMMUNITY

Our organizations offer us life. Without them, we will disappear.
—A lowland Indian leader from the Ecuadorian Amazon

A strong sense of shared identity can energize people and inspire them to take collective action to improve their lives. When individuals see themselves as proud members of a culture, they are more likely to organize and work for change. Organizations built on the bedrock of cultural identity seem better able to single out common problems and collectively seek appropriate solutions.

Without a sense of community, individuals retreat into their families or themselves, to the detriment of collaborative efforts at survival and betterment. They might work in isolation to increase productivity and improve themselves, but collaborative social action withers or never even starts.

Many groups—particularly indigenous communities—depend upon the shared perception of their own uniqueness vis-à-vis other groups for their very survival as an identifiable and viable entity. This uniqueness may be based upon physical characteristics, dress, rituals and traditions, geography, or worldview. Such expressions of culture as feast days, work parties, celebrations, special songs, dances, and costumes establish and shore up a group's sense of identity and pride. Recognizing this, many groups actively promote such activities as an integral part of everyday life. When people's shared notion of uniqueness is lost or weakened, so is their sense of belonging to any community at all, and social organization is the first victim.

Los Yumbos Chahuamangos, a music and dance group of lowland Quichua Indians from the Amazonian region of Ecuador, exemplifies this use of cultural expression. Los Yumbos's members are drawn from a large agricultural cooperative made up of eleven communities and 500 families.[4] The group regularly performs at local festivals and important cooperative meetings, attracting broader attendance by injecting vitality into the proceedings and promoting organizational participation through song lyrics and by example. One of its songs explains in Quichua how a cooperative functions. Group members are also involved in mobilizing participation in a local Indian federation.

Another example of community recognition of the importance of cultural traditions is given in the following passage from a proposal to the Inter-American Foundation by the Taquile islanders of Lake Titicaca in southern Peru:[5]

> We want to make a request that we think is very important for our future and that of our children. We ask for a fund to construct and equip a small, "on site" museum on our island. Economic reasons and pressures from tourists have forced us to sell inherited weavings left by our ancestors, the value of which we had ignored. We are a community of artisans, and weaving is our heart. Our visitors know this, and it is the reason for their visits. We want an exhibition room to show off our culture; and more important than that to perhaps preserve our patrimony and tradition. In this manner we would avoid the selling of our patrimony; we would have the means for teaching our children the art of weaving; and we would not lose something that is difficult to recuperate.

Cultural expression also contributes to the sense of shared identity, group solidarity, and strength necessary for protection against outside incursions. For example, the Kuna in Panama,[6] the Kayapó in Brazil, and the Shuar in Ecuador use a variety of cultural forms in self-defense, ranging from legends to songs to physical symbols of ferocity. The Kuna warn intruders away from their land with prominently placed wooden guardian spirits, and the Shuar promote their image as a people unconquerable by Incas and Spaniards alike. Other groups, such as the Mapuches in Chile and the Zapotecs and Mixtecs in Mexico, realizing that they risk losing their cultural integrity and even their homelands, attempt to preserve their forms of cultural expression through music, dance, community museums, open-air drama, and the like.

The risks inherent in building up group solidarity in a chauvinistic or aggressive way are reverse discrimination and increased friction among ethnic groups. A prime example is the high level of ethnic conflict in cities such as New York. Racial tension exists throughout the world, sometimes reaching such extremes as Ku Klux Klan or Nazi ideology. Ethnic pride can encourage separatist tendencies that lead groups to reject assistance, provoke enemies, and break up alliances. The trick is to emphasize the positive aspects of solidarity and community, not the negative impulses of fear and hatred.

AN ANTIDOTE TO SPOILED IDENTITY AND ALIENATION

Maintaining our culture gives us a sense of pride, of vigor.
—Kuna Indian leader, San Blas Islands,
Panama, June, 1987.

In contrast to the energizing capability of cultural expression, there is little that disheartens people more than a negative ethnic identity or sense of self, a shared perception of inferiority and low value within a larger social structure. People who feel inferior or despised participate less actively and perform poorly.

Negative stereotypes can limit the access of ethnic peoples to opportunities offered by the larger society—e.g., education, social services, and other resources. Viewed through the prism of these stereotypes (e.g., that blacks in the Andean countries have no culture or that Indians lack intelligence and creative initiative), the conditions of denigration and poverty appear to be inalterable. Blacks in Ecuador, for example, observe that although Indian peoples may be deprecated, they are at least present in the history books. As folklorist and community organizer Juan García Salazar points out in a later chapter, blacks in Ecuador are absent from history, an invisible population of uncertain origins. Even in the tourist industry, stores feel compelled to sell black handicrafts as Indian products. As García Salazar has put it, "We must prove we are here. We must say who we are. And if *we* don't know who we are, who does?"

Central to the development process, therefore, is the projection of an alternative, more positive image of ethnic peoples and the poor. A revitalized and revalued culture assists ethnic peoples in counteracting negative stereotypes they may have internalized and that others in society may have of them. Cultural expression can shore up people's self-perceptions and demonstrate the richness and complexity of their creative capacities to outsiders. The resulting reassessment by the surrounding society can have a positive impact on how a stigmatized group sees itself.

Most important, a shared sense of self-worth provides the foundation for self-help—a "we can do" attitude—encouraging a group to maximize the use of its own internal resources rather than turning too often, too much, or too soon to outsiders. Jamaica's most renowned reggae singer, the late Bob Marley, recognized this point in "Redemption Song," where he advised people in postcolonial societies to "emancipate yourself from mental slavery."

Cultural expression can be an especially effective way of weakening negative stereotypes minority groups may have about one another because traditional cultural forms communicate particularly well to ethnic peoples. For example, in the Occupied Territories in the Middle East, ethnic groups in conflict have formed theater groups to address social tensions before local audiences. Real-life incidents are dramatized. Israeli and Palestinian actors play the parts of members of the *other* group—a rock-throwing youth and a patrolling soldier, perhaps. Discussion among actors and audience follows.

Cultural revitalization can also serve as a preventive measure or an antidote to the alienation inherent in abject poverty, particularly among ethnic peoples. For the most part, development thinking and practice continue to be guided by strategies of social change that see modernization as a uniform, categorically desirable process and economic change as virtually the sole basis for a better life. Ethnic peoples of the developing world are encouraged to join the modern world, largely by assimilating into urban-centered nations. This process asks them to abandon what many development professionals see as picturesque but counterproductive folkways, and it often pushes them into towns and cities. Yet the infrastructures of developing world cities are already overwhelmed. Many inhabitants of urban barrios demonstrate remarkable creativity and energy in confronting the odds against them. However, others form part of an apathetic underclass of culturally dispossessed people who lack the group solidarity and sense of identity necessary to solve their problems. These people can be embittered, confused as to who they are, disconnected from social groups and institutions, deeply distrusting, and pessimistic about the prospects for positive change.

An approach to development (as distinct from modernization) that respects and builds upon existing cultural systems is preferred by ethnic groups that wish neither to deny who they are nor to cling to the past and pass up the opportunity for better lives and reduced suffering. Hence, cultural revitalization efforts can develop or reinforce a people's outlook about what they can accomplish as individuals and as a group. Music, dance, and oral tradition can counteract pessimism and the effects of cultural rootlessness and alienation, reinforcing a sense of belonging and a positive self-image, both prerequisites for successful social change.

TEACHING AND CONSCIOUSNESS-RAISING

Ethnic history is like a bow and arrow. The farther back you pull the bowstring, the farther the arrow flies. The same is true with historical vision: The farther back you look, the farther you can see into the future. If you pull the bowstring back only a little, the arrow only goes forward a short way. The same with history: If you only look back a short distance, your vision into the future is equally short.

—A Navajo teacher speaking to a public forum
on intercultural education on the Navajo Reservation,
October 1985.

Forms of cultural expression effectively store and transmit information. They can preserve local history and lore, describe and delimit a cultural group and its roots, define and interpret dilemmas, and pass on lessons—especially to youth. They play a central role in the discovery of new possibilities and the encouragement of group reflection about poverty and development. Members of grassroots groups frequently say they need to know where they have come from, where they are, and why they are there in order to plan for the future.

Forms of cultural expression can also be very effective ways of teaching because they capture people's attention and imagination in ways that other means of communication do not. In their very essence they are culturally appropriate, using understandable language and symbols to transmit messages in nonformal training programs, in formal education, or in the course of everyday life. According to Juan García Salazar,[7] the oral traditions of black Ecuador tell people "when to plant and what to plant, how to live, and love, and raise a family." If the oral tradition dies, these lessons die with it. García Salazar says the power of the storyteller lies in his or her ability to simplify and interpret traditional messages that are relevant to a group's current experiences. Valdemar Neto, a Brazilian nonformal educator,[8] notes that engaging people in a context of leisure and fun is a highly effective manner of reaching them with a message. Consequently, his organization, Centro Luiz Freire, uses humor, theater, and storytelling in its "T.V. Viva" community-oriented television programs. Similarly, Teatro Nuestro, a bilingual theater and music group from Eugene, Oregon, tours the West Coast of the United States presenting educational dramas to farm workers about the dangers of pesticides. One of its plays, *La Quinceañera,* was created with the collaboration of migrant laborers and legal services workers. In Washington, D.C., one of the more popular antidrug programs is carried out by a rap group of black teenagers who write and perform all their own material. In the same city, another antidrug and alcohol message is given by Blue Sky Puppet Theatre, a troupe of brilliant, irreverent puppeteers who get kids (and adults) to roar with laughter and shout encouragement and answers to the characters. The use of drama and participation seems far more effective than a speech by an official in the school auditorium at communicating messages and encouraging reflection.

Many other social change programs throughout the world use forms of cultural expression for teaching and consciousness-raising. Often the message is direct and well defined, ranging from the specific and practical in mother-child health programs—"boil water to avoid infant diarrhea"—to the broad and abstract message of a Yumbos Chahuamangos performance at an Amazonian festival—"dedicated participation in our local federation is the first step toward progress." Other educational and consciousness-raising uses of cultural expression are less direct—as, for example, when the Rastafarians of Jamaica or the musical group Los Masis[9] in Bolivia convey messages about the intrinsic worth of their respective ethnic groups.

If cultural expression is used in a heavy-handed or patronizing manner, it can put off its intended audience. An example is the practice of adding an obvious moral to radio broadcasts of folktales sent in by peasants. In Lima,

I visited one such radio program that received a tape from a peasant with a short note attached to it, exhorting the programmers, *"No me cambias mi voz!"*—"Don't change my voice!" He wanted his story to be disseminated by the media, unadulterated by cultural intermediaries.

Cultural expression can be used to manipulate people to consume under the guise of "educating" them to act "correctly" or be good "modern mothers." Using traditional culture to aggressively sell baby formula in the developing world is an example of such manipulation. To counteract the ensuing decline in breast-feeding, grassroots programs use similar methods, employing song and dramatization to convince mothers to nurse their babies. In the end, we see advertising locked in a struggle with consciousness-raising efforts to win the minds of low-income mothers. Political propaganda battles do the same on an even broader scale. It is usually not the strategy per se that is distorted and objectionable, it is the *content* of that strategy and the *intent* behind it.

At least one writer[10] openly advocates using folk traditions for commercial as well as development objectives: "I hope this will not only be useful as a guide book to extension workers, rural communicators, field publicity personnel, as well as radio and TV programmers, but will also provide material for new avenues of thought to ad men, sales promoters and PR men." This attitude illustrates the fine line between promotion/education on the one hand and social marketing and even political manipulation on the other.

An eloquent discussion of the negative side of a utilitarian approach to cultural expression is offered by Juan Díaz Bordenave, a communications specialist with the Organization of American States:

> I see in this discovery (using folk media to achieve development goals) a lot of good and a lot of evil. The good is that the folk media are legitimate possessions of the people, an intrinsic part of their culture, and so they have the right to be respected, supported, and used. However, and this is the evil part, the development thinkers' obsession with goal achievement and not with human growth may take up these folk media as another set of instruments for changing a people's way of thinking, feeling, and behaving. And this is not the purpose and the function of the traditional communications media. Their purpose is expression, relationship, communion, escape, fantasy, beauty, poetry, worship; never persuasion of people to vaccinate, to implant I.U.D.s, to fight parasites, or to eat vegetables. I am afraid that as soon as the people realize that their folk songs, poems, and art are being used for subtle propaganda, they will let them die. Of course, the contemporary forms of folk media must reflect the new preoccupations of a people in movement towards development. New dreams and anxieties will appear naturally in the songs and poems of the masses.[11]

CREATIVITY AND INNOVATION

*Without tradition, there is no creation. Without creation, you
cannot maintain a tradition.*
                                        —Carlos Fuentes, in his lecture "Crucible of
                                            Fiction," at George Mason University,
                                                                April 14, 1988.

Creative thinking often happens in the form of metaphors. An image flickering through the mind casts light on a seemingly unrelated subject— as many scientists and inventors have reported. When thinking about a difficult problem, another thought intrudes and mysteriously moves one closer to a solution or an understanding. Where a direct line of thought might have foreclosed possibilities, open-mindedness can be facilitated by viewing a situation that is parallel to, but not the same as, one's own. All of a sudden the answer for the problem at hand is revealed in the form of a metaphor. One is in the relatively free realm of "as if."

What does this realm have to do with cultural expression and grass-roots development? What is Br'er Rabbit if not a metaphor for the weak, who have to use their wits to escape danger or to prevail against the strong? Rabbit is ever present among the blacks in Esmeraldas Province of Ecuador. According to Juan García Salazar, Rabbit is mentioned at meetings when a person or a group seems to be in a fix similar to one of the familiar folk characters. Most Quechua riddles in the Andes are nothing but metaphors.[12] What is a loudmouth in the forest but silent on the pampa? A hatchet. What is pregnant every night and gives birth every morning? A bed. A bread roll flung on a plain strewn with dried corn kernels represents the moon and stars. Such riddles may have less direct relevance to human dilemmas than do the Rabbit stories, but they give people (especially youth) practice in thinking metaphorically and in associating seemingly unrelated images or ideas. Many folk dances are also metaphorical in nature, quite a few of them dealing with issues of domination and defense. For example, police, military, landowners, and priests are depicted satirically in Central American and Andean folk dances, giving vent to people's collective distaste for past abuses. The Brazilian *capoeira* transformed an outlawed form of traditional martial arts practiced by blacks into a folk dance. And, of course, many annual carnival dances and costumes throughout the hemisphere are highly symbolic in nature.

Forms of cultural expression are primary sources of collective and individual creativity. They provide people with rare opportunities for looking at the world in a new way. They teach and inspire people of all ages, particularly the young, to express and innovate—two essential processes in broad-based development. By providing the opportunity to assess new possibilities and ponder how things might be, this exercise of imaginative reflection can be the first step in the development process, an arena where problems and potential solutions can be identified, defined, and redefined. As community awareness increases, more effective strategies can be formulated. For example, sociodramas presented by Ecuador's Feria Educativa stimulated villagers to rethink a persistent problem: adult illiteracy.[13]

Participating in cultural expression can help prepare people for an unknown future where problems will be both new and old, exciting and frightening, life-enhancing and life-threatening—just as they are in folktales and songs. Such participation is especially important for people without access to stimulating written materials or to the creative or performing arts that historically have shaped a group's shared consciousness and soul. By encouraging the human imagination, the creative and performing arts promote the idea that change is possible and that the future can be made more livable. This perspective, characterized by optimism and initiative, is a prerequisite for successful bottom-up social change.

Successful development strategies are best built on a sociocultural foundation that is well established but capable of sustaining new growth. Some assume that traditional cultural forms are by their very nature immutable, but the evidence is that they have evolved over generations in a never-ending process of invention, elimination, and active borrowing from other cultures. Such change is significant not only for the development of culture but also for the culture of development. Because cultural forms are creative and dynamic, they are especially compatible with what should be the most basic elements of the development process—creativity and dynamism. Thus, traditional culture and socioeconomic development need not be opposing processes but rather can be two facets of the integral process by which human beings confront, interpret, and ultimately transform their reality. In short, cultural expression and humane socioeconomic development are, in practice though not always in theory, parallel and often mutually reinforcing manifestations of human creativity.

THE LINK TO PRODUCTION

Value systems and ethics, far from being peripheral, are the dominant, driving variables in all economic and technological systems.

—Economist Hazel Henderson, in a speech to the
World Future Society, Toronto, Canada, 1980;
as reported by Joanna Macy, *Dharma and Development,* p. 19.

Traditional forms of cultural expression are related to production, although the relationship is frequently more contextual than direct, particularly in rural settings. Here, music and dance are not set off from the rest of the human enterprise as mere entertainment but are integral to social structure and to forms of work. For example, the Andean *minga*—a pre-Columbian collective work system often used for harvests or for community projects—is commonly mobilized and energized by songs and special foods, and the work is followed by a festive celebration.[14] Cooperatives and worker-managed enterprises also use cultural expression to promote group solidarity and pride. Even though their resources may be extremely limited, these groups commission songs, organize festivals, design colorful banners (which are proudly presented to honored visitors), and so on—a clear sign that cultural expression is an integral part of the group's productive process.

A number of grassroots development projects draw upon this connection by promoting traditional handicrafts such as weavings, embroidery, leatherwork, and woodcarving and employing pre-Columbian agricultural processes, water systems, plants, grains, and small animals, as well as the *minga*.[15] Many projects try to revive or preserve traditional products as a strategy for maintaining ethnic identity and solidarity as well as for producing income and better diets. Such efforts may succeed socially but fail economically. Sometimes, though, traditional products and systems are clearly better than what replaced them (e.g., imported plant varieties, increasing dependency on mechanization, and dangerous pesticides).

PRESERVING AUTONOMY— THE CHALLENGE OF PLURALISM

Herein lie buried many things which if read with patience may show the strange meaning of being black here at the dawning of the Twentieth Century. This meaning is not without interest to you, Gentle Reader; for the problem of the Twentieth Century is the problem of the color line.

—W.E.B. Du Bois, in his 1903 preface to
The Souls of Black Folk: Essays and Sketches.
Greenwich, Connecticut: Fawcett Publications, 1961.

Minority ethnic groups are frequently locked into the lower strata of society and commonly blamed for causing its problems, retarding its development or obstructing its integration as a nation. This blame often involves a labeling process—the "Indian problem," the "black problem," and so on. The solutions frequently offered for these "problems" challenge the very essence of the group's ethnicity, usually by threatening to assimilate the group into the dominant culture.

Maintaining ethnic autonomy and cultural self-determination is a basic human right and is fundamental to broad-based development. Such a right is enunciated in various international statements, including two prominent ones by the United Nations: the Universal Declaration of Human Rights and the International Covenant of Civil and Political Rights. This concept is discussed at length in a UNESCO publication, *Cultural Rights as Human Rights*.[16]

Ethnic pluralism contributes to the richness and breadth of choices in a society's repertoire. It may be that each subculture in a society has dominion over one piece or several pieces of the development puzzle but not over all of them. In the quest for development, the questions may be the same, but the answers are different. Cultural expression helps keep diverse technologies and worldviews alive, transmitting and supporting them within a broader cultural webbing. Efforts to produce a monocultural society have often result in increased conflict and alienation, and such efforts ultimately impoverish us all.

The present situation in the Amazon Basin is a vivid example of the need to meld native and Western technologies. In this case, the objective is to promote sustainable resource use in the interest of human survival, local as well as international. In agriculture, nutrition, environmental protection, and health care, native techniques have been adapted frequently by the Western world. Pharmacies and grocery stores are filled with products first developed by Native Americans. Where native technologies have been lost, the chances for broad-based and lasting development have radically decreased. Although these cultures should not be romanticized, neither should they be written off as quaint, primitive, or useless. Nor should they be asked to jettison their pragmatic technological heritage in favor of questionable "modern" implants.

Forms of cultural expression play a key role in defining interethnic boundaries and in preserving the autonomy and basic character of subgroups—thereby maintaining the ethnic pluralism of a given society and the survival of minority cultures. Many grassroots organizations actively promote this process by means of public festivals, photography, recorded music, and publication of transcribed oral traditions.[17]

DEMOCRATIC DISCOURSE AND SOCIAL MEDIATION

We feel that Cultural Exchange will not just express secular or national cultures, but will bind all events to put us one step further in achieving global and cultural attitudes for world peace, as there is one race, the human race. The power of culture is one language, not just linguistically but the general

*rhythm of human vibration which is most needed in the world
peace endeavor.*

> —Samuel J. Clayton of the Mystic Revelation of
> Rastafari Co-operative Society and Cultural Centre
> (see the Appendix, JA-034), Kingston, Jamaica,
> March 1978.

Cultural expression can serve as a public forum in which to examine issues such as poverty and racial discrimination; it can be the ground upon which disparate groups come together and seek increased understanding, compromise, and tolerance. Alberto Minero, executive director of the Theatre of Latin American (TOLA; see the Appendix, LA-046 and LA-052),[18] in a proposal to the Inter-American Foundation in 1982, stated the case for the arts as follows:

> Because of the universality of their "language," the arts have long served to enhance communication. The modern, technologically oriented world tends to forget the arts—and theatre in particular—as being useful tools of analysis. One of the historical functions of theatre has been to offer social critique, to stimulate creative thought, and to suggest alternatives. The arts also play a vital role within any community of nations or ethnic groups in correcting misunderstandings and prevailing stereotypes. The thread linking participants in the network reinforced by TOLA is each group's dedication to theatre as a mirror of contemporary social phenomena. Those affiliated with TOLA believe that theatre is a revitalizing force within the socially and culturally marginated populations of Latin America and the Caribbean.

Many cultural activists and artists throughout the hemisphere share Minero's views on the role of the arts in society. Cultural expression is seen as a means for two prominent ends: democratic discourse and social mediation.

Democratic discourse is lacking in many societies. Frequently, the disadvantaged are kept at the margins of political participation and public debate. In repressive societies, the vast majority of the population may be similarly marginalized. Intimidation keeps individuals from expressing their opinions and pressuring officials openly. In these situations, threatened people turn to various forms of cultural expression—frequently popular songs and humor—to make their opinions known, to protest injustices, and in some cases merely to reaffirm a social consensus. Poster and mural art play a similar role.

In Chile, the culture of protest developed to a high form over the past two decades. Chilean protest songs and groups are some of the most popular in all of Latin America, and Chile's poetry and theater is unsurpassed as social commentary. The successful "Campaign of the No" led by the opposition during the 1989 referendum on the Pinochet government was based on brilliantly executed songs, videos, posters, and other manifestations of cultural expression that touched and moved the Chilean people at their core. For some time, two other forms of expression had sent powerful, if less widely disseminated, messages to Chileans and foreigners—namely, the *"cueca sola"* and the innovative *arpilleras,* both of which depict scenes of disappearances and other injustices and convey collective hope.[19]

In the *cueca sola*, a line of women wait silently, each wearing a white blouse to which is pinned a photograph of a disappeared relative. One at a time, the women come forward and raise a handkerchief to eye level. To the rhythm of the folk music, each woman in turn dances the *cueca,* Chile's national dance. The cueca is always danced by a man and a woman together, but these women dance alone. The cueca sola presents a powerful visual image to other Chileans of the pain and injustice of disappearances. The image was spread around the world by the popular singer Sting with his song, "They Dance Alone."

The arpilleras emerged spontaneously in the early years of the Pinochet dictatorship. Poor women, many of whom had lost family members to government repression, began to craft powerful scenes on small wall hangings made out of pieces of cloth. The arpilleras allowed them to voice their pain and to earn a few pesos to support their families. The idea was adopted by Peruvian women, who have now become as proficient as their Chilean neighbors. In both countries, these crafts produced by poor women represent some of the best documentation of how common people have survived desperate periods in their history. The crafts communicate with the present generation and will endure as an invaluable record to inform future generations.

Cultural expression has been used from time immemorial, in democratic as well as totalitarian societies, to voice protest and to pressure authorities. Caribbean calypsos and Colombian *vallenatos* are songs that frequently carry a critique—a well-known example is the music of the calypso singer Sparrow. As the chapter by Juan García Salazar illustrates, many of the oral poems (*décimas*) of black Ecuador have social commentary as their theme. They serve as history book and newspaper, recording and disseminating events and opinions about them. A telling example is the *décima* "Complaint Against the Railroad," which describes an incident in which local boys were killed by a train.[20]

Cultural expression also can play a role in social mediation. In the right circumstances it can help reduce conflict by bridging sociocultural gaps between people who would otherwise have little or no contact. A form of expression as basic as a handicraft can overcome barriers of language, race, and social class to bring people together, at least momentarily, on a common ground of mutual appreciation. Crafts can raise the estimation of a disadvantaged group in the eyes of others far more than verbal appeals or formal educational programs can. As goods of obvious aesthetic and practical value pass from hand to hand, they transform perceptions and meanings in a very personal but effective manner.

Other forms of cultural expression are used more consciously for social mediation. In Oaxaca, Mexico, in an area where intraregional conflict has been persistent and cooperation among communities low, village musical bands travel to neighboring communities to perform, keeping the lines of communication open. In Ecuador, the two existing major concentrations of blacks—in Esmeraldas Province and in the Chota Valley—are separated by geographic as well as cultural barriers. Historically, they have maintained some economic ties but very little cultural exchange. The Grupo de Danza, Teatro, y Música "Angara Chimeo"[21] is taking steps to change this pattern, promoting the first cultural encounters between the two populations. These contacts have met with enthusiastic responses in both regions as people recognize their common heritage and the variations within it.

When politics enters the picture, however, cultural promotion and exchange activities can take a negative turn. Political parties sometimes manipulate ethnic groups. Governments can co-opt cultural activists, as has happened in Mexico, or set up a hollow superstructure, as in El Salvador. In Mexico, the leaders of cultural groups are often also in the employ of a government agency, greatly limiting their ability to act independently and breeding a passive, supplicatory style. In El Salvador, the Ministry of Culture's Casas Culturales serve mainly as patronage plums for party loyalists and as structures for political mobilization when necessary.

Cultural expression, democratic discourse, and social mediation are perhaps less directly connected to grassroots development efforts than some of the other uses and functions discussed in this chapter. Still, for grassroots development to be truly participatory, broad-based, and responsive to locally identified needs, complicated problems having to do with equitable public debate, social tension, and group conflict must be addressed. Forms of cultural expression represent a flexible and often uniquely effective way to address these kinds of conflict.

GENERATION OF CULTURAL ENERGY

In the term from our oral tradition—"nosotros gente," we the people—lies much power to generate the energy needed to move people. There was a day when we owned our world, when we were capable. And we can still recuperate that capacity.
—Juan García Salazar, Ecuadorian folklorist,
at the Highlander Center, New Market,
Tennessee, July 1989.

Albert O. Hirschman, after visiting forty-five grassroots development programs in 1983, inductively developed the useful concept of the "conservation and mutation of social energy." "Social energy" was defined as a renewable source of motivation to join in a collective movement or cooperative action in spite of—at times because of—hardship, adversity, and even failure.[22] Based on my own inductive fieldwork for this book, I have found a supplementary concept, called "cultural energy," that can help us understand the broad forces that motivate and mobilize human beings.

Cultural energy not only provides the collective force necessary to begin and sustain group action, it is also the force that enables a culture to renew itself. One could even say that a culture is alive to the extent that cultural energy is generated and maintained.

Cultural energy entails individual and social or collective behavior, as well as behavior and sentiment that is unwittingly shared by people who do not consciously belong to a mutual group. These two aspects make it different from social energy.

Cultural energy is a primary basis for human motivation, cohesion, and persistence. As Hirschman illustrates, there are numerous other sources of collective energy. These include unsuccessful prior attempts at mobilization, the shared instinct for physical survival, natural and social disasters, and external threats. In contrast, cultural expression is an economical source of social energy that is more within the reach and control of the people themselves.

Cultural energy both is called forth by cultural expression and acts back upon that expression to reshape it and perpetuate it. The numerous forms of cultural expression treated in this volume—from the songs of the Feria Educativa, the dramas of the Sistren Theatre Collective, and the Shuar chants to the oral tradition of the Talamanca coast and the Kuna, the Taquile textiles, and the Quichua collective work parties—are all major sources of cultural energy within the life of the group. All of these forms, in turn, are carried forward and transformed through practical application.

Cultural energy is undeniably a primary requisite for broad-based grassroots development. Although hard to measure, it can be felt—sometimes immediately, sometimes much later—and its impact can be readily observed. Cultural expression can energize participants and instill in them strong feelings of group pride, reaffirmation, optimism, collective strength, and vitality. It is especially effective in calling forth and directing group energies toward shared goals.

Examples can be found in development projects as well as in social movements. In Jamaica, members of the Mystic Revelation of Rastafari (see the Appendix, JA-034) told me how they use music, accentuated by traditional drumming, to create a sense of identity and pride and to energize their youth training programs.[23] In highland Ecuador, I was present when a new campesino federation of twenty-six communities launched a major development project by inviting each community to send a dance or music group to the federation's inauguration.

In one dance presentation, a team of oxen, led by the festive music of a local village band, plowed a single furrow around the entire village plaza. Behind the plow, a line of Indian women did a serpentine dance, reaching down at each beat of the music to plant a seed in the furrow. Around the borders of the plaza were 3,000 local campesino men and women wearing bright red ponchos or shawls; they had gathered to plant the seeds of the first federation of organizations in that region. Each community organization had brought its own music and dance group—no two of which were alike—and all waited their turn to contribute to this historic event and reaffirm their Indianness. This was the largest such gathering by a local Indian organization in living memory, and it stirred up an enthusiasm for organizational efforts that had a lasting effect on the surrounding population.

Sometimes cultural expression is used to tap into cultural energy as a means for promoting participation in a specific program. I witnessed this function in a rural health effort in Tarabuco, Bolivia, when a medical doctor from the Centro Cultural Masis (see the Appendix, BO-087) raised the panpipes to his lips and began playing an Andean song as hundreds of indigenous campesinos crowded around a large new medical kit sent from Germany. After finishing the song, the physician filled a small glass with local *aguardiente* and slowly poured it over the aluminum lid of the kit—a traditional inaugural rite. The crowd broke into an enthusiastic cheer. This Western import—the medical kit and the health program it represented—had become *theirs*, in fact and in symbol, and it would amplify their future commitment to making the health program work.

Social movements such as the civil rights movement in the United States in the 1950s and 1960s made conscious use of cultural expression. One cannot forget the scenes of blacks in churches in Alabama or Mississippi singing songs from their folk tradition before marching out to meet the police dogs, fire hoses, and threatening crowds.[24] Songs also played an important role in the popular uprising against the Marcos dictatorship in the Philippines. Some were borrowed from other cultures. For example, the Philippine liberation movement used protest songs from the repertoire of the folksingers Peter, Paul, and Mary, who were later invited to the first anniversary celebration of the fall of the Marcos regime.

The case material that follows in this book illustrates the concept of cultural energy and demonstrates how cultural activists call that energy forth and direct it toward the ends described in this chapter. It is an approach that can be abused as well as used for constructive purposes, and it only works well if the participants in grassroots development efforts have primary control over it.

CONTROL OVER CULTURAL EXPRESSION

Culture is a way of getting things done, of setting priorities about needs. In the Iroquois Nation this knowledge exists largely in the family oral traditions and lore, in stories. These are important matters I am talking about—the Iroquois, after all, developed representative democracy and the federating of tribal nations into a workable system long before American democracy was born. And the men who wrote the U.S. Constitution knew about that. What's important is that this culture be recognized as ours, and that it stay ours.

—John Mohawk, Seneca/Iroquois editor and
writer, at a Smithsonian conference,
Washington, D.C., 1988

We have seen that a cultural approach can be misused in pursuit of social control, exploitation, political or religious gain, or marketing ends. There is a fine line between encouragement and manipulation, between promotion and agitprop. Juan Díaz Bordenave's caveat in this chapter should lead us to be cautious, not to give up trying.

Is there anything to be lost by taking a utilitarian approach to cultural expression? Does such an approach drain the life from cultural forms? Or does it have a regenerative or broadening effect in pushing them toward new ends? Will people begin to feel that their culture is being taken from them and turned into a mere tool or, worse yet, used against them? What can cultural activists do at that point to enable the people to regain control?

The key issue is not *whether* traditional culture should change but *how* minority groups can maintain proprietorship over the forms and content of their own cultural expression and control over how they evolve. Who will manage the process of change? Will it be directed from above or by autonomous subgroups in a society? There is a parallel here with certain tenets of bottom-up development: Ethnic minorities should have a primary role in overseeing the evolution of their own cultures, just as they should have a primary role in deciding on development priorities and strategies and the programs that affect their communities. Were that to happen, they could begin to achieve what Shuar Indian leader Ampam Karakras cites as a goal of the indigenous peoples of Ecuador: "What we seek is integration *without* assimilation."[25]

Many of the cases discussed and cited in this book show how a cultural action methodology can maximize success in grassroots development efforts, especially when that methodology is controlled by the beneficiary groups. Beneficiary control is a safeguard against misuse of the method. It should be encouraged and explored further in evaluation and practice.

None of the issues arising from the use of cultural expression in development is simple or clear-cut. For instance, who should be in charge of changing cultural forms? An insider is not automatically more sensitive than an outsider to issues of value and preservation. Often the external and internal forces impinging on a group are stronger than the group's ability to define its destiny, and rarely is it possible to maintain control over how a group's forms of cultural expression are expropriated and utilized by others.

One of the obvious strengths of a cultural strategy as part of a broader grassroots development approach is its democratic nature—culture is made by the people, for the people. But what are the implications of outsiders, or of individuals within the group, reshaping cultural expression into a handy tool kit? Who is to judge when a use has slipped over into the arena of abuse? These are issues that cry out for open debate.

We need to increase our knowledge of what works, when, and how in this intersection between cultural expression and grassroots development. But assessment of utility and impact is no simple matter. As Lourdes Arizpe writes: "Culture has already been acknowledged as a basic concern in policies of national advancement but it still has not been taken up as an issue underlying the central problems of international development. Partly because it is an evasive concept for it is, at the same time a code, a tool, an industry and a dream."[26]

NOTES

1. See the Appendix, EC-074.

2. See the Kleymeyer and Moreno chapter in this volume, and the Appendix, EC-053 and EC-165.

3. As quoted in *Gente*, October 1978, No. 84, p. 21.

4. See the Appendix, EC-083.

5. See the Appendix, PU-093, and the chapter in this volume by Kevin Healy and Elayne Zorn.

6. See Chapter 5 in this book.

7. See the Appendix, EC-074, and García's chapter in this book.

8. See the Appendix, BR-644.

9. See Chapter 2 in this book.

10. Shyam Parmar in his preface to *Traditional Folk Media in India* (New Delhi: Gekha Books, 1975).

11. In Patricia Haggerty, et al., "The Arts and Social Change," *Journal of the Inter-American Foundation*, Third Quarter, 1979, p. 11.

12. See Kleymeyer, 1990.

13. This process is described and documented in the Kleymeyer and Moreno chapter on the Feria Educativa.

14. See Moreno in the chapter in this book entitled, "Work and Tradition."

15. For examples of such projects, see the Appendix: BO-026, BO-213, BO-222, BR-509, CH-402, CO-072, CO-121, CO-306, EC-053, EC-165, ME-217, ME-282, PU-093, PU-117, PU-256, SK-007.

16. UNESCO, *Cultural Rights as Human Rights* (Paris: UNESCO, 1970).

17. See the Appendix: BO-087, BO-213, BR-275, BR-314, CH-398, CO-046, CR-042, CR-103, EC-053, EC-074, EC-082, EC-116, EC-165, HO-046, LA-070, ME-106, ME-262, PY-025, SU-004, US-115.

18. See the Appendix, LA-046 and LA-052.

19. See the Appendix, CH-324.

20. See Juan García Salazar's chapter in this volume.

21. See the Appendix, EC-198.

22. For discussion and illustrations of the concept of social energy, see Albert O. Hirschman, "The Principle of Conservation and Mutation of Social Energy," *Grassroots Development,* Vol. 7, No. 2, 1983. A similar treatment can be found in Chapter 4 of *Getting Ahead Collectively: Grassroots Experiences in Latin America* (New York: Pergamon Press, 1984), pp. 42–57, as well as in Annis and Hakim (see Bibliography).

23. See the Appendix, JA-034.

24. There is an excellent documentary film on this subject directed by Jim Brown: *We Shall Overcome: The Song that Moved a Nation* (New York: Ginger Group Productions, 1989).

25. Conversation with the author, 1985.

26. Lourdes Arizpe, in "Culture and International Development," paper delivered at the 19th World Conference of the Society for International Development, New Delhi, India, March 1988; published in *Development* (Journal of the Society for International Development) 1 (1988), p. 17.

Part 2

•

Cultural Action
as a Strategy in
Grassroots Development

2

Identity and Self-Respect

•

PATRICK BRESLIN

"Who am I? Where do I come from? Where do I fit in?" In the gloom of the late afternoon in Quito, while storm clouds rumbled overhead, Juan García Salazar (see Chapter 6) recited the questions that drove him to become a one-man folklore commission for his people, the descendants of black slaves first brought to Ecuador in colonial times. Shelved on the office wall behind him were hundreds of cassette tapes filled with interviews from five years of work searching the riverbanks of Esmeraldas in Ecuador's coastal lowlands or the dry hillsides of the Chota Valley for the old men and women who carry in their heads the history, legends, stories, and poetry of their race.

Juan García Salazar's questions are asked frequently in Latin America and the Caribbean. They are voiced in Spanish, English, Portuguese, French, Creole, or in any one of dozens of Indian languages, sometimes in tones of intellectual curiosity, sometimes in pain and anger, often in desperation. The questions touch on some of the most serious and sensitive problems in the region: the tension between ethnic identity and national integration; the destructive effects of racial prejudice; the struggles for cultural independence and personal identity and dignity. Efforts to find answers to those questions have led toward a more complex understanding of development.

Development is usually thought to mean change for the better in material standards of living, or at least to be aimed at that goal. If material standards of living are to be improved, many other kinds of changes in society are usually required: changes in the patterns of use, ownership, and distribution of land; in the forms of ownership, management, and employment in the workplace; in access to and control of credit, capital, and commodity flows; in the observance of human and civil rights; in the treatment of minorities.

But there is another element to development besides change. Sometimes people must first fortify their base before they sally out to change the world. No matter how poor their material conditions, people always

A Bolivian puppeteer participates in a program run by Capacitación Integral de la Mujer Campesina (CIMCA), a women's training center specializing in issues important to indigenous women, such as human rights, agriculture, family health and nutrition, and cultural preservation.

have resources available: intelligence, imagination, language, the skill of their hands, history, a sense of identity, a cultural heritage, pride, a certain piece of land. Sometimes the development process is not so much about change as about the preservation and strengthening of those resources. Without them, Juan García Salazar's questions go unanswered.

García Salazar's questions go back to his school days. His father was a Spaniard who arrived at the Esmeraldas coast of Ecuador around 1940,

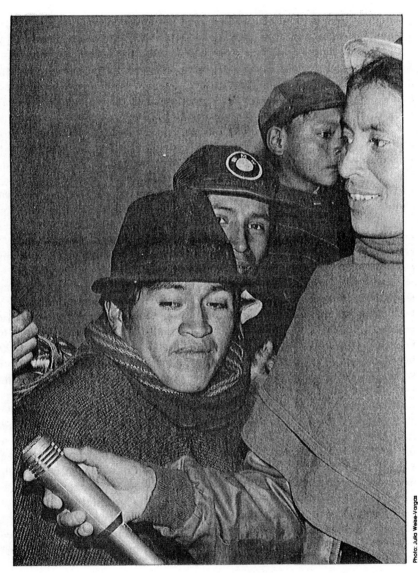

Paulina Paca, a member of the Feria Educativa, or Educational Fair, asks an audience member to react to a sociodrama that was just presented in the community of Bazán in Chimborazo, Ecuador. The Feria only presents a problem, allowing the community to draw its own conclusions. (See EC-053 and EC-165 in the Appendix.)

dedicated himself to mining, and married a local black woman. "Down on the coast, we have a saying, that one takes his culture with his mother's milk. If your mother is white, you're white. If she's black, you're black." But in school, he began to wonder where he fit in. "The identity of

Ecuador is Spanish and also Indian. The Indians have managed to insert elements of their traditions into the schools. There are monuments to Indian leaders. But as a black boy in school, I had the problem of not finding anything in Ecuador to identify with. Schoolchildren learn of Indian and Spanish heroes. But nothing of the blacks. No one identifies with the blacks, and blacks find no ancestor mentioned in the history books they read in school. There are no monuments to blacks."

García Salazar was born near the sea, and his earliest memories are of swift trips to market in southern Colombia, riding the Pacific currents in outrigger canoes, and then the long return, poling the canoes through the dim light of the mangrove swamps and spending the nights in isolated houses on stilts above the riverbank while old men spun stories. As a young man, he continued to travel, and eventually wound up in Bogotá, the Colombian capital, where he ran a small factory. He frequented the university, took some classes, and talked with students. "There I learned that one ought to have a cultural tradition. I began to think about Ecuador. I decided to return to my own country to do something. I didn't know what."

Back home, he found himself caring for his dying grandfather and teaching in the local school. His grandfather's illness was prolonged. "It's because he knows so many secrets," the people said. "He can't die until he passes them on." The grandfather began to tell his stories and legends to García Salazar. "That's what began my interest in the old people, and the hoard of stories they have. And then I began to look in the books. Who are we, the blacks of Ecuador? Where did we come from? And there was nothing. No one knew anything. No one had written anything.

"I began to travel the rivers in my own canoe to talk with the people. Whenever I'd see an old person, I'd stop to talk. And I began to see that there was a marvelous treasure in all the traditions but that it was going to die, to disappear. I started to think: 'Why not try to gather this material?' But I didn't have the means to do it right. I talked to a woman who could make *guarapillo*, a medicinal drink, and she told me she picked 100 herbs to make it. How was I to remember the names of a hundred herbs?

"I went to a foundation here in Quito, and they suggested I write a proposal and they would send it to someone." (García did not know anything about the Inter-American Foundation, but one day someone introduced him to Charles Kleymeyer, the foundation's representative for Ecuador.) "I said that what pained me most was the loss of this tradition, because every time I went back on the river, another old person had died.

"When the Inter-American Foundation came through," García Salazar said, "I could get the equipment I needed to record. And I just went out and started taping. *Décimas* at first, our poetry. And then other things started coming out, legends that I hadn't even heard before. There were stories of white and black magic, of a man who could turn into a hen or a bunch of bananas when the police came looking for him. The police would kick the hen out of the way or take two bananas, and afterwards, the man would limp or be missing two fingers."

Some of the stories told of the dark bargains people would strike with the devil so they could become wealthy. In one a man raises a family from a dozen eggs he hatches with incantations and his sons and daughters become, as he intended, expert thieves, rustlers, pirates, spies who amass great wealth for him. In another, a godfather violates the baptism ceremony by willing the priest's blessing to bypass the infant and enter a coin he holds in his clenched fist. The infant is left spiritually adrift, but the coin now has the magic power to attract all other coins it comes in contact with and bring them home to its master. Such stories of conjuring up dark powers bespoke the powerlessness of the slaves' lives.

Other stories recounted the history of Ecuador's blacks; how their ancestors were brought down from Colombia; how some gained their freedom by fighting in the war of independence; how emancipation finally came in 1860, but only after the slave owners were recompensed. There were religious stories, children's stories, tales of animals, very like the Br'er Rabbit stories from the American South.

As García Salazar probed deeper into his people's folklore, he began to see in the old storytellers the monuments he had sought in vain as a schoolboy. "I realized they are the only monuments we have. But no one is going to make a monument to them. So I said to myself, the next best thing to a monument is paper. Get it down on paper.

"Now, the question is what to do with the material. I want to give it to the young people. I want to be sure that other black children don't have the problem I did of lacking a sense of identity. See how alienating the educational system is? Nowhere, not in stone, not on paper, do you find our people remembered. And this is a serious problem for the integration of the nation. It tells you you're not here, you don't exist. That's what this work is aimed at."

Of some 1,500 hours of interviews already taped, García Salazar has transcribed over 300. He has published more than a dozen booklets containing samples of the collected material. He hopes that it can be gradually introduced into the educational system. But he knows that his real work is for posterity. "This collection probably won't be really used for years, until the country realizes what it has lost. Especially the black people. In 50 years maybe, someone will come looking for it, saying, 'There was a guy named García Salazar who collected stories.' That's why I'm working."

Meanwhile, he's rekindled interest in the old storytellers. "In some places, we were able to reactivate the tradition of storytelling by the old people. What happened was we would visit the house of a storyteller and arrange to go back the next day to record some stories. These houses have large open areas. We would bring a few packs of cigarettes. And gradually, other people would come by, old people, youths. Sometimes we'd be there until dawn. Afterwards, the youths would ask us where we were going the next day. And so, during a month we'd spend in a small town, we'd reactivate a whole tradition."

AN OUTPOST OF ENGLISH

Nearly 20 years ago, about the same time that Juan García Salazar returned to Esmeraldas, a young North American teacher on an extended trip wandered into Cahuita, a town south of Limón on Costa Rica's Caribbean coast. Paula Palmer (see Chapter 7) says she was just looking for a good beach when she came to Cahuita, but what she found was an opportunity to help preserve a unique culture that was starting to disappear, a task that has consumed her ever since. "I guess I was something of a hippie," Palmer said. "I'd worked in the civil rights movement at home, and then traveled through Mexico where I worked with some Indian groups, and then kept moving until I got to Costa Rica."

Discovering that Palmer was an experienced teacher, a woman in Cahuita urged her to prolong her stay and teach her seven grandchildren English. Palmer did not understand why the woman was so insistent but agreed. When she appeared for the first class, 35 children were waiting. Palmer called a parents' meeting and discovered the interest in English instruction for their children was intense. Soon she had eighty-five students and no reading materials.

Meanwhile, Palmer had been learning the Creole language common to the Limón region, as well as the local history. The English-speaking black population of the region originally came from the Caribbean islands. Some were fishermen and hunters who had followed the droves of turtles up along the Panamanian coast. Later, farmers from Jamaica came to settle. Still later, jobs on the banana plantations and the railroads drew many more.

Until midcentury, the Limón region maintained its distinctive cultural identity. People went to the English schools; links were maintained with Afro-Caribbean people from other parts of the Caribbean basin. A rich theatrical tradition flourished. "They were doing *Macbeth* in Puerto Viejo in 1915," Palmer said.

Changes came in the 1950s. President José Figueres was intent on integrating the nation and breaking down the barriers that separated Limón from the rest of the country. Under Figueres's policies, Spanish supplanted English in Limón's schools. "As it did," Palmer said, "the people began to lose all the things the English school had done, all the cultural activities that had formed a sense of being Afro-Caribbean."

As she listened to the older people recount the history of their community, it occurred to her that she could use their stories for her English classes. She began recording the oral history and then transcribed it. As the stories circulated in the community, the neighbors urged her to collect full-time. They were aware that many of the old people were dying, and with them, links to their own past. After teaching three years, Palmer followed their suggestion. Two more years of recording led to her book, *What Happen: A Folk History of Costa Rica's Talamanca Coast.* "But even though the people were very interested," Palmer said, "they were concerned that their children were not. That led me to think that I should be teaching high school kids to collect their history themselves, rather than having me do it. And that's what we did."

A local agricultural cooperative, many of whose members were parents of Palmer's students, secured a grant for research on the local culture and made Palmer coordinator. Soon many of the local youths were busy gathering material. "People have told me that it was important that I was a foreigner," she said. "They said the kids took it from me that this history and these traditions are rich and fascinating. They wouldn't have listened to their grandparents saying the same thing."

The gathering of oral history led to the renewal of cultural events and practices that had faded away. For the first time in 20 years, the people began to observe Slavery Day, a celebration commemorating their liberation. A cricket match was played for the first time in 35 years. Special ceremonies honored the old people of the community.

Eventually, the students gathered enough material for three publications on the history, culture, and economy of the black and Indian populations of the region. Impressed by their quality, the Costa Rican government reprinted them for distribution throughout the school system to increase public awareness of the country's heritage. But Palmer believes the project's main impact will be felt among the people of the coast. "More important than what we can teach the rest of the country about this region is what goes on in the souls of these thousand or so kids and what they'll do in Costa Rica because of the way they feel about themselves."

THE TECHNOLOGY OF SELF-RESPECT

Of Bolivia's estimated 6 million people, 60 percent are Indian and the rest are criollo. As is often the case in Latin America, the line that separates the two is drawn more by culture and history than race. An Indian is a person who comes from an Indian community, wears Indian dress, and speaks one of 30 Indian languages—most often, Quechua, Aymara, or Guaraní. A criollo is a white or mestizo—usually an urban person—who bears the language and traditions of the Spaniards.

Since the conquest, "Indian" has also meant the people who are exploited. Avid for the mineral wealth of the Andes, the Spaniards herded Indians into silver mines, and then out onto the haciendas that grew up around the mining centers. Institutionalized systems of mandatory labor preserved the serflike condition of the Indian for more than a century after independence. A common practice called *pongiaje*, from the Aymara word for door, required that every night an Indian protect the landowner's house by sleeping curled in the doorway. Even today, the word *indio* is so weighted with connotations of oppression and degradation that it is considered an insult. The more neutral term, *campesino*, has replaced it in polite language.

Despite the advances since the 1952 revolution, chasms of distrust separate Indians from criollos. Many Bolivians insist that the political instability and economic chaos for which their country is famous are only surface manifestations of these deeper rifts. They see scant possibility for genuine national development until there is both self and mutual respect among the groups that cohabit the country.

Development usually implies production. But for many multiethnic societies, even desperately poor ones such as Bolivia, the need for cultural integration is no less acute than the need for economic growth—or rather the two are linked. Each is a condition of the other.

Jorge Arduz, president of one of the groups described below, expressed the need in this way: "The important factor in any kind of development is the human factor. To be productive, man has to value himself, which means being able to understand where he stands in society and in history. That's why for us, cultural development goes hand in hand with economic development."

But how? What is the technology that restores self-respect after four hundred years of degradation? In recent years, many Bolivians—campesinos, community organizers, schoolteachers—have looked inward to their own traditions. These people approach their culture as developmentalists. They have found resources in their music, language, folktales, crafts, and dance. They see these cultural forms as the basis for educational programs that teach self-worth. By inverting the symbols associated with shame, they create a kind of cultural capital that is as important and valuable as land, water, or seed.

PROJECT AYNI: AESOPS OF THE ANDES

The Christmas tree light bulb in the control room window flashed red; and in the studio, three Aymara Indians leaned toward their microphones and began to dramatize the fable of the farmer and the fox. In the control room, an Aymara woman draped in an alpaca poncho expertly twirled the dials of the recording equipment, checking the oscillating needles and adjusting the sound levels. The bowler hat that normally crowns her black, braided hair rested beside her on a shelf.

This scene is repeated three times a week in the La Paz studio of Radio San Gabriel. Fifteen-minute tapes are recorded and then broadcast to the altiplano, where an estimated two million Aymara speakers live—three-quarters of them in Bolivia, and the rest across the border in southern Peru. Four centuries ago—before the European conquest—this was a prosperous area. But today the highland home of the Aymara is one of the bleakest, harshest, and poorest rural areas of the hemisphere.

The people in the recording studio are members of the Centro de Promoción Cultural Campesino Ayni. They are trying to reanimate the centuries-old fables of the Aymara people, and they are using the radio to do it. "The Aymara," said the Spanish Jesuit who directs Radio San Gabriel, "are like the Japanese. They are traditional and progressive at the same time."

Radio is the medium of mass communication in rural Bolivia. Newspapers circulate only in the cities, and then only to the minority who read Spanish. Television antennas are sprouting from the rooftops in the cities; but in the countryside, only radio reaches into every community and into practically every home. Many Aymara—such as army recruits stationed in distant corners of Bolivia—write to their families in care of Radio San Gabriel. The station broadcasts a mail call, and the letters—more than 50,000 a year—are promptly picked up at its office. It is the only station broadcasting exclusively in the Aymara language, and all but four of the radio staff of 48 are Aymara. Ayni's idea of broadcasting traditional fables blends well into San Gabriel's mixed format of cultural and educational programs.

The seven young Aymara who make up the Ayni group refer to themselves as "promoters of popular development." All seven come from peasant backgrounds. Although most completed primary school, only a few went for more than a year or two of secondary school. Each participated in leadership training programs for campesinos and then began working on rural development projects. As Aymara, they are conscious of their long history as an oppressed people. They bitterly recall the haciendas and the degradation of enforced labor.

One recent and typical Ayni activity was to help the Ministry of Education in a project to teach weaving, tailoring, electrical repair, and food preparation. Short courses were offered in several rural provinces. Groups of 20 to 30 men and women attended classes where they shared their subsistence skills and learned new ways to produce cash income.

Ayni's members, like a small but growing number of Aymara rural leaders, share a vision that culture is a foundation upon which to build. They speak of educational and cultural revitalization. Some of their projects are as straightforward as construction of "community cultural centers" that double as meeting halls and classrooms. Others are as sophisticated as the Radio San Gabriel education project.

Felix Tarqui, Ayni's director, explained the group's evolution this way: "We are all campesinos. We each began by participating in a course that sought to prepare us for educational work in the countryside. But as we went along, we saw that for education to be effective, it must build people's capabilities, not reinforce feelings of inferiority. It must be based on the culture of the people being educated."

The public educational system is a controversial subject in Bolivia, and the Aymara speak of its failings with vehemence. "Education here attempts to colonize us," one Aymara organizer said.

"The rural school in Bolivia is simply a jail for children," said another.

"It is all in Spanish," complained an Aymara linguist. "How can it *not* be an alienating education?"

Ayni cannot replace the national educational system, but its radio program does provide an educational experience with which the Aymara can identify. Not only is it effective because it is in the language of its listeners, but—as the example below illustrates—stories are perceived by the Aymara to be a method of teaching and learning. No Aymara is too "uneducated" to understand the implications of the laziness of sons who do not follow their mothers' instructions.

Another series of fables traces the adventures of a fox. No one misses the fox's symbolism as a deceitful middleman. In some fables, the allegorical fox represents the Aymara themselves, matching cleverness against the brute force of larger, fiercer beasts. The stories reinforce traditional Aymara values of shrewdness, hard work, and respect for elders.

To gather tales, the three Ayni members who work on the radio program first visited communities throughout the highlands. Once the program went on the air, however, they began to receive a stream of stories written and mailed in by listeners. Currently, two or three tales a day arrive by mail at the radio station—many painstakingly written out in a mixture of Aymara and Spanish. Other listeners, instead of writing down a story, come into La Paz to tell it.

The members of Ayni turn the narrative into a script. Lines are written for each character. Frequently, the same characters appear in several stories—for example, the wise grandfather and Susana and Paulino who come to him for advice:

Grandfather: Paulino, you're wandering around like a stray mutt. Don't you have anything to do? Haven't you heard the saying: "Loafers, like dust, are gone with the wind?"

Paulino: No, Grandfather, I never heard that.

Susana: Well, now that you have, you must never be lazy.

Paulino: Grandfather always has good advice. His experience makes him wise.

Susana:	That's right. We should always listen to his advice. Grandfather, what story will you tell us today?
Grandfather:	A story I heard in the province of Los Andes, about a widow who had three lazy sons. This was in ancient times. One day, she sent them to plant potatoes.
Mother:	My sons, it's time to plant potatoes. Take these seed potatoes to the field. Plant them and then come right back.
Roberto:	All right, Mother, we'll plant the potatoes.

(Musical transition)

Roberto:	Whew, these seed potatoes are heavy.
Manucho:	These hoes and picks are wearing me out, too.
Santico:	Oooh, I'm beat! Why did Mama have to make us walk so far? I need to rest. You plow the soil.
Roberto:	But, how can you want to rest, Santico? If we work together we can finish early.
Santico:	No, I can't. Didn't I tell you I'm exhausted?
Manucho:	Then let's forget about it. The rest of us are tired too.
Grandfather:	So the three lazy sons didn't plant the potatoes. Instead they cooked them and then, not being able to eat them all, amused themselves throwing them at one another. When it was late, they returned home where their old mother was waiting.

(Musical transition and sound of wind)

Grandfather:	When six months had passed, the mother told her sons to harvest the potatoes. No one wanted to. So the mother went herself. She had scarcely begun to turn up some plants when a man came along.
Man:	Hey, woman, why are you gathering my potatoes when you haven't planted your own?
Mother:	But, sir, I sent my sons here to plant. . . .
Man:	Your sons were loafers. The day we were all working, they didn't plant one potato. They spent the whole day eating and playing.
Grandfather:	The poor mother returned home, filled with bitterness at her sons. Not having any food in the house, she cut a piece of flesh from her leg and silently served it to them.

	Soon after, she died and her sons realized what she had done. In a flash, they were transformed: one into wind, another into frost, and the third into hail.
Paulino:	What punishment. No wonder our grandfathers are not loafers.
Grandfather:	That's right, my grandchildren. Otherwise, as the story teaches us, they would have been swept away with the wind.

How is Ayni's radio program received by its Aymara listeners? At an isolated farmhouse southwest of La Paz, one woman said: "Most people around here listen to it. It's more than entertainment. It's important, because each story makes you think. And often, after listening, the young people ask for more stories."

Others are less convinced. From a community near La Paz: "Some don't like to hear that this is the way we were. They think it confirms the picture the whites have of us: primitive, superstitious, that we have strange beliefs. Some even think that it could therefore do us harm."

In Bolivia, the Aymara have the reputation of being much more impermeable than other Indian societies. They have protected themselves from the outside by sealing themselves off. Asked whether there isn't need for more intercultural communication, an Aymara rural organizer said, "For now, it's important to preserve the culture for ourselves. When we go somewhere, people look at us and ask us, 'Well, what people are you? Are you Quechua or Aymara?' And when we say, 'We're Aymara,' then they want to know what kind of people we are, what are our customs. We need to know them ourselves in order to be able to show them to others. Later on we can think more about carrying our culture to other people."

HARMONIZING BOLIVIA'S CULTURE

When a group of youngsters play the haunting music of the Andes, Bolivia's discordant culture suddenly seems a bit closer to harmony. It is there in the instruments: the guitar brought from Spain; the *charango,* an Indian version of the guitar, its body fashioned from a humped armadillo shell; and the fur-trimmed drums, the *quenas* (flutes), and *zampoñas* (panpipes) that are as Andean as the snow on Illimani's peak. Together, they produce a rhythmic, piercing music tinged with the desolation of the altiplano.

Late one sunny afternoon in Sucre, Bolivia's nineteenth-century capital, four teenagers headed out Calle Pérez to the whitewashed, colonial-style building which then housed the Centro Cultural Masis. Warming up for their music classes, they capered along the street, blowing riffs at one another on their quenas and zampoñas. People passing them on the narrow sidewalk smiled.

There weren't always smiles for the quena and zampoña. Sucre is perhaps the best-preserved colonial city in all of South America, and it has always preened its Spanish heritage, which included a deprecatory attitude toward all things native. Until after the 1952 revolution, no Indian wearing traditional garments dared even enter the city's central plaza. Thus, when the young people who formed the original group, Los Masis, first began to play Indian instruments in Sucre, tomatoes sometimes came flying their way, and most people dismissed them as "hippies."

In those days, musical performance meant an occasional visiting artist from Europe. "Serious" music did *not* include sounds such as those produced by the flutes and drums of the villagers of nearby Tarabuco, whose feet, shod with rattling spurs and three-inch wooden clogs, shook the earth as they stomped through their monotonous dances. But when word filtered back from Paris and Rome in the 1960s that groups playing Andean music were the rage, many Bolivians began to listen with greater interest.

In 1969, several university students in Sucre formed a group to play Andean music. They called themselves "Los Masis." Roberto Sahonero, one of the original members, explained the name: "It's a Quechua word. It means someone of your class, your equal; someone who's neither more than you, nor less than you. An intimate friend, almost a brother."

During the next decade, Los Masis prospered. They released several records and traveled thousands of kilometers on concert tours.

Since it was composed of university students, Los Masis began losing members as they finished their studies and moved on to other careers. Tito Tapia, another original member, thinks it was this inherent instability of the group that motivated some members to begin teaching music and dance to children in Sucre. After 1975, they found themselves devoting more time to teaching, and in 1980, the original group known as Los Masis played its last concert together. But by then, the Centro Cultural Masis was well established. Subsequently, the group revived itself, toured Europe several times, made five records, and carried on its involvement in the center.

Since 1980 the center has offered nightly classes in guitar and Andean music instruments. In its workshop, students are taught to make as well as play the traditional instruments. More importantly, they learn to value the culture that they symbolize. There are also classes in theater, mime, and the Quechua language. Students who can afford it are asked to pay $4 for the two- to three-month courses. Those whose interest in the music continues are encouraged to form their own groups.

The Masis center's impact on life in the Sucre area is varied. For example, the center has placed its mark on Sucre's carnival—a four-day, pre-Lenten celebration—by reviving the traditional synchronized dances. In the weeks leading up to the pre-Lenten festival, the center offers classes in traditional dancing, and the number of people participating has doubled every year. The center directs an exhausting regimen of physical training and nightly practice. This year, 500 children, teenagers, and adults signed up for five weeks of strenuous conditioning every morning from six to eight o'clock plus an hour of dancing six evenings a week.

The efforts of the Masis center are felt especially in the poor barrios on Sucre's outskirts. There, many impoverished, Quechua-speaking migrants from the countryside face a daily struggle for survival in an alien world. Many of the barrio's residents are rural children sent by their parents to live with relatives during the school year. "A child will come in here crying because someone called him an Indian," said a foreign teacher in one barrio. "They have lovely legends, lovely traditions, but they're not valued, so they don't value themselves. The problem is how to learn to value those things again, in the face of a modern world that devours tradition."

El Tejar is one such poor neighborhood—dark, low-roofed houses that are crowded around the railroad tracks below the city. One Saturday night in February, 250 people jammed the parish hall while dozens more strained in the doorways and open windows for a program that included works in progress by the center's theater group, educational slide shows on local festivals, and traditional music by four newly trained groups.

That night, after each of the center's barrio performances, three scholarships for music classes were awarded. In fact, students from all the nearby neighborhoods now attend classes at the center. And instructors from the center are now beginning to work in more distant barrios.

The slide show at El Tejar was produced by the center's research unit, which documents the cultural legacy of the Sucre region. Similar narrated slide shows are presented in the schools. "Nanta Ruaspa," the center's twice-monthly radio program (in Quechua it means "to open a road"), draws upon those materials. The program reaches listeners in both rural and urban areas. Schoolchildren typically have been taught to esteem foreign cultures and to denigrate their own. This is the first systematic effort in the region to treat the culture, history, and geography of surrounding communities as educational tools.

A group called Raíces, seven young teenagers who have been playing together since they were ten years old, now teaches in San Juanillo, a poor neighborhood on the far side of Sucre. Raíces is clear evidence of the center's ability to train accomplished musicians and to imbue them with respect for traditional culture. They have already won top prizes in regional and national festivals. Their repertoire has grown from the days when, as one of them recalled, "If an audience asked for an encore, we'd play the same song again. We only knew two songs then." The group plays and dances in traditional Indian dress. It is the same clothing that, outside the center, still provokes middle-class disdain. The challenge, which Los Masis recognizes, is to generate the same respect for Indian dress on the street as it now generates on the stage.

The center's growth and diversification have more than met the hopes of the young musicians who gave up their performing careers to found it. Asked if he misses his days of touring with Los Masis, Tapia said, "Yes, a bit, but teaching at the center keeps me in touch with the music. More important, I have the sense that there's something permanent. Behind me there are 35 or 40 young people that I've helped to train. We've transmitted not only the music, but the tradition of teaching. Now Raíces, who are only kids of sixteen—they're already teaching the younger kids."

BREAD AND ROSES

In 1912, mill girls in Lawrence, Massachusetts, went on strike under the banner, "We want bread and roses too." Many Bolivians, surveying their country's poverty and disarray, have concluded that bread and roses—economic and cultural development—are inseparable, and that, in fact, the latter may well be a precondition to the former.

Ayni and Centro Cultural Masis are two responses to the cultural divisions that afflict Bolivia. Both projects emphasize Aymara and Quechua values of mutual assistance, solidarity, and equality. The members of Ayni and Centro Cultural Masis believe that until criollos better appreciate the values of the majority of the nation's inhabitants, Bolivia's future will remain bleak. Linguist Juan Yapita de Dios put it this way: "A great need here is to diminish the ignorance of the criollo, to educate him to the worth of the native values. It is the discrimination practiced by the criollo against the indigenous people and all the resulting distortions in education, in jobs, in possibilities for advancement which is the brake on Bolivia's development."

Centro Cultural Masis contributes to that educational process by legitimizing Indian culture. It distinguishes itself from music groups in Bolivia by its social commitment to the poor and its educational activities aimed at changing attitudes and values.

Since my 1981 visit, the Centro Masis has greatly expanded its scope. It has trained hundreds of young musicians to play traditional instruments, leading to the establishment in Sucre of more than 30 folk music groups, where before there were none. This has not only created a permanent opening for traditional Andean expression in the area, it has done so in a city that holds fast to the traditions of its shining colonial past. Some of the local citizens may be noticeably annoyed by Indians dancing carnival down Sucre's cobblestone streets, but the truth is that the Masis have captured the imagination of the urban youth and the rural Indians in a way that no one else has. Moreover, Sucre's only cultural center at this moment is the Masis's recently acquired locale. This makes the Centro Masis, with its indigenous focus, a major player in the re-formation of local identity during a time of broad challenges and change, as the people of Sucre, and Chuquisaca Department, ask the perennial question, "Who are we?"

In recent years the Centro Cultural Masis has also chosen to confront the issue of rural poverty and development. Masis members have worked with a Tarabuco Indian community several hours from Sucre, carrying out development efforts in accord with Indian priorities and ways of proceeding. Having worked first with rural migrants in the Sucre barrios, and then established links to the countryside through village-based Indian musicians from whom they collected songs, the Masis stepped unabashedly onto the uncertain ground of cross-cultural community development. While there have been initial successes and some disappointments in this new enterprise, it will be years before they know for certain whether their style of cultural activism is successful when carried beyond their own strong suits of music and dance.

CULTURE IS A PLACE

The projects described above are all based on the faith that if a fading cultural patrimony can be restored, it will strengthen the capacity of the people to deal with the challenges that surround them. But can it be demonstrated that such faith is justified? If people can answer Juan García Salazar's questions confidently, will they be more successful at solving other problems? Perhaps the best place to ponder that question is from an island in the Gulf of San Blas on Panama's Caribbean coast.

When a Kuna Indian awakens on one of the small coral islands where most of his people live, his gaze wanders past the thatched houses of his neighbors, out over the low-riding canoes of farmers headed for their mainland plots, and then across a mile or so of shimmering water to a mass of green forest rising, virgin and luxuriant, to the ridge of the San Blas mountains. At his back, the sun climbs above the calm Caribbean, and its first rays loosen the tufts of mist snagged like fleece in the clefts of the hills. For generations this dawn panorama, serene and unchanging, has greeted the Kuna people.

But if the Indian were standing atop the 2,400–foot-high San Blas range, the view down the other slope would be less reassuring. Large swaths of thick vegetation have fallen victim to the machete and the torch. Ash-gray tree trunks stand above the denuded landscape, skeletal remnants of the once-towering jungle.

For several years now, peasants from the increasingly arid interior of Panama have been slashing and burning—implacable as soldier ants

—toward Kuna land. Cattle ranches, producing beef for the international market, drove many of them from their previous farms, and cattle are close behind them again. In three or four years, when the newly cleared and shocked land will no longer support subsistence crops of bananas, rice, manioc, and corn, they will plant pasture and try to sell holdings to ranchers. In a few more years, the fragile soils will be so leached that even cattle ranching will fail. The tracks of the future can be read on the southern slopes and lower ridges of the San Blas, where the erosion that will inevitably claim all the cleared acres has begun.

Until recently, Kuna lands seemed safe from this specter. Although less than 100 miles from Panama City, they were practically inaccessible until the government announced plans to push a branch road from the Pan-American Highway over the ridge and down the northern slopes of the San Blas to the Caribbean coast. The Kuna were of two minds about the road. They welcomed the prospect of easier movement for themselves and their goods between San Blas and Panama. But they knew that the road had already brought settlers to the southern slopes, and they feared encroachment on their tribal land. With a fine sense of geopolitics, they realized that the point of maximum danger was a place called Udirbi, where the new road would enter their territory. It was there that they had to establish a presence.

First they attempted to carve out their own agricultural colony in the virgin forest. When they failed because of the poor soil, the Kuna began to explore the idea of creating a park for scientific research. As the plan developed, they saw major advantages in such a park. Twenty square kilometers around Udirbi would have clear, patrolled boundaries to bar intruders. Moreover, if the threat persisted, the international scientific community, handed an expanse of unstudied rain forest with richly unique flora and fauna, would be an influential ally in future struggles.

Eventually, the Kuna sought backing from development agencies as well as from several scientific and conservation agencies. They are now building housing and research facilities at Udirbi and are cutting nature trails to observation sites in the forest.

The completion of the park should forestall a serious threat to the land of the Kuna, but their determination to protect it springs from impulses much deeper than considerations of property rights. To the Kuna, this land is not just a physical resource, but a spiritual one as well. "We say that this land is our mother," Leonidas Valdez explained. Valdez is one of the three *caciques*, or chiefs, who are the principal spokesmen for the entire Kuna people. Kuna traditions say the green-clothed earth is the body of the Great Mother. In the beginning, they say, she was naked. Her union with the Great Father produced all of the vegetation—which became her garments—the animals, and finally humans. "The land is also the culture," Valdez continued. "Here are born all things necessary to our culture: the fronds we use for the puberty ceremonies, all the foods gathered for our communal feasts, the materials our artisans use, and what goes into the construction of our houses. All of this comes from the forest. If we were to lose this land, there would be no culture, no soul."

The Kuna have no trouble answering Juan García Salazar's questions. They are one of the very few Indian peoples to have survived into the twentieth century with their culture, their society, and their identity intact. Because of their self-confidence, they have been able to approach Western culture like careful department store shoppers rather than awestruck "primitives." They pick through the wares of Western culture, select those ideas and techniques that seem useful, and then tailor them to their own traditions. All this, the Kuna believe firmly, is because they have their own base in the land, to which they return for replenishment and reinforcement. Their historical experience suggests that self-confident people who know where they come from and who derive personal security and group pride from that knowledge, are best prepared to accept and implement the changes their societies need.

NOTE

This chapter is an updated version of two separate articles published in *Grassroots Development*: "The Technology of Self-Respect: Cultural Projects Among Aymara and Quechua Indians" (Vol. 6, No. 1, 1982) and "A Sense of Identity" (Vol. 10, No. 2, 1986).

3

La Feria Educativa:
A Wellspring of Ideas
and Cultural Pride

•

CHARLES DAVID KLEYMEYER & CARLOS MORENO

In the village plaza, high up in the Ecuadorian Andes, a dozen campesinos formed a tight knot around a single figure standing in the center. Each campesino in the group wore a red poncho woven from hand-spun wool, and a dark felt hat. Hundreds of other similarly dressed campesinos were milling about the plaza, reluctantly preparing for the trip home in the lengthening afternoon shadows. But the small knot of people in front of the white adobe chapel were clearly not about to leave. All had their eyes fixed on the figure in the middle, and each in turn spoke intently, gesturing with a hand that came out from under his poncho only long enough to emphasize a point before returning to its warm haven.

The man in the center spoke very little. As a truly captive audience, he could only listen, occasionally shrugging his shoulders or raising his palms shoulder-high in protest. His nylon aviator's jacket indicated a higher social status than that of the poncho-draped campesinos who pressed in around him, but his bronze face and felt hat showed that it was only slightly higher.

After a half-hour of intense discussion, the man in the center began slowly nodding his head up and down. In turn, each campesino pumped the man's hand and the group quickly broke up.

We hurried over to find out what had just happened. These dozen campesinos had come from a neighboring village to watch a performance by the Feria Educativa, or "Educational Fair." The Feria, a group of young indigenous musicians, had spent the entire Sunday afternoon in the village plaza, playing traditional Quichua[1] songs, staging sociodramas, putting on a puppet show, and encouraging members of the audience to comment on how the situations on stage reflected local problems, and how local people might find solutions.

57

The *Feria Educativa* has helped establish more than a dozen indigenous women's music groups, like this one, in highland Ecuador. This unprecedented cultural change has been accompanied by dramatic increases in Indian women's public participation in development project meetings and training programs. (See EC-053 and EC-165 in the Appendix.)

The sociodrama that received the most vigorous response depicted an illiterate campesino being taken advantage of by a sharp operator who was able to silently read an important letter, and then mislead the campesino regarding its contents. Many in the crowd murmured and nodded during that scene, remembering similar incidents.

After the final song and the tremor of the mandolin-like *charango* had died out, most of the audience set out for home, except for the men from the neighboring village who had spotted the local trainer from the government's new literacy program. They swiftly surrounded him to demand that he visit their village to help establish an adult literacy center. Identifying with the illiterate campesino in the sociodrama, the men felt the time had arrived to do something, and they would accept no excuses.

The trainer, whose nights were already filled teaching in his own village, finally agreed to visit the following Sunday. He added that he would bring along the area supervisor, who could actually assign a teacher to a new literacy center if the villagers prevailed—which, by the way, they did.

Seldom are the effects of the Feria Educativa's work so immediate. They seek to be the culturally appropriate groundbreakers for a broad development program for campesino organizations in highland Chimborazo Province. The Feria frequently is the first contact Chimborazo campesinos have had with this program, which is managed by the Servicio Ecuatoriano de Voluntarios–Chimborazo (SEV).[2] The SEV program itself emerged in 1986 from an earlier effort involving many of the same people and carried out by the Unidad de Educación para el Desarrollo,[3] whose main task was to implement a national literacy campaign begun by the newly democratic Ecuadorian government in 1979. These two successive programs used adult education as a platform for a variety of development activities in indigenous villages, including literacy training centers, communal bakeries, self-managed artisanal workshops, reforestation efforts, and other activities.

Over the fifteen-year period from 1975 through 1989, the grassroots development efforts of Unidad and SEV, in which the Feria Educativa has played a central role, received $1.2 million from the Inter-American Foundation. An additional $1.1 million was raised in counterpart donations—in cash, labor, materials, and land—from indigenous communities and public and private entities.

To appreciate the significance of the Feria's role, and the cultural action methodology which underpins it, requires a closer look at the history of grassroots development in Chimborazo. The province has one of the highest concentrations of poverty-stricken native peoples in Ecuador, even in South America. Living in more than 1,000 villages, at altitudes that sometimes exceed 4,000 meters (13,000 feet), the quarter of a million indigenous inhabitants of the province have only recently emerged from an exploitative hacienda system that greatly limited their possibilities for self-sufficiency, social advancement, and economic growth. Nature has been no kinder, as the land has been ravaged by drought, frosts, landslides, and erosion.

For more than two decades, national and international organizations have set up shop in Chimborazo, offering relief and change. Typically, the white collar representatives of these organizations have come from a social and cultural background far removed from that of the local campesinos. They would drive to villages accessible to the Pan-American Highway and meet with a small group of leaders, invariably men, explaining to them in Spanish how some institution intended to set up a development program for the benefit of the local residents. Lip service to "popular participation" often required a question-and-answer period, concluding with a request for campesino representatives to attend all future meetings. Then the visitors would pile into their jeeps for the three-hour drive back to Quito. Unfortunately, in spite of much goodwill and massive expenditures of national and foreign funds, the majority of these programs failed, and little positive evidence of them remains today.

Despite these experiences, the people of Chimborazo have not given up their often-expressed hopes for broad-based development and social justice. The most successful local grassroots programs have emerged from the province itself—from communities, federations, and urban-based, private support organizations. In the case of Unidad/SEV, a group of individuals, most of them born in indigenous villages, believed they could do better than the outsiders. Many had at one time or another been involved in the earlier efforts and thus knew firsthand their strengths and weaknesses.

In 1974, a small group of these people formed the first Feria Educativa, drawing primarily from local Indian youth. The objective was to promote cultural revitalization, ethnic pride, and self-help efforts among the Quichua-speaking masses, and to do so in the beneficiaries' own language and on their own terms. After much training, refining, and maturing, the Feria began to emerge as an important force in development throughout the province, facilitating a broad mix of strategies and methodologies that stand in stark contrast to the earlier incursions.

Above all, the Feria's task is to gain rapport with local indigenous communities. The campesinos of Chimborazo, with their long history of suffering from conquest, repression, and exploitation in their relations with hacienda and city, are understandably wary of imported schemes. From their point of view, these programs imposed upon them have been rife with hidden agendas, goals, and values that conflict with their own.

The Feria Educativa has a noticeably different approach. It enters a village only by invitation. Feria members—themselves indigenous men and women—arrive in traditional dress, play local music, sing songs in Quichua, and get people to dance and sing with them. For one night, the Feria is radio, television, stage, and newspaper to people hungry for information and new perspectives on a world that can seem hopelessly rigid and hostile to Indians. Often it is past midnight before the audience allows the Feria to finish. The songs are about historical events, the world of nature, love, festivals and ceremonies, death, planting and harvest, pride in being an Indian, the problems of alcoholism, domestic animals, favorite foods, religion, crime, and politics—in other words, the entire human drama.

Only after trust is established do Feria members begin to encourage people to identify their most important problems. The Feria Educativa does not offer answers or promises of support for projects. The sociodramas and puppet shows typically sketch out a common problem: illiteracy, unresponsive or abusive authorities, discrimination against indigenous people in the cities, poverty, deforestation and erosion, or the lack of schools and teachers. Then, almost in midperformance, they halt abruptly and the floor is given to the people, many of whom have been commenting openly or talking to each other or laughing in recognition, at times in discomfort, throughout the presentation.

Sometimes a woman will speak out in favor of establishing a local weekly market, or a man will ask how a neighboring village was able to start a community bakery or plant a mountainside with trees. But often people will simply talk about the performance and how it resembles, or differs from, their own experiences. According to the Feria's strategy, this collective recognition of how a problem is rooted within the local reality is a prerequisite for building the resolve and summoning the energy and creativity necessary for solutions. The trick is to promote a raised consciousness on the part of campesinos that prepares the ground for constructive future action, rather than to simply leave them more embittered and frustrated than before. Sometimes action results immediately; sometimes nothing happens. But usually the Feria's visit is the first step in a long process of reflection and planning, leading eventually to action.

This democratic, nondirective approach to helping people analyze their situation draws upon the people's own worldview, after first captivating them with their own songs and dances. This means being able to *listen* to new ideas that emerge from the people themselves. What makes the dialogue work is the Feria's ability to speak in the local idiom, using local symbols, with a constant back-and-forth flow of energy and humor. Accomplishing this is more than second nature, it is first nature—since every member of the Feria was born and raised in one of the thousand Indian villages of Chimborazo. They do not simply capture the essence of the local people, they embody that essence.

The Feria's sociodramas are generally scripted, at least in outline, and rehearsed, although in performance the actors at times will improvise a sociodrama based on the particular problems of a given group. Often comments from the audience provoke direct answers from the actors—and vice versa—or even a departure from the script. Puppet shows traditionally lend themselves to such give and take, and the Feria often takes advantage of the opportunity to tweak the noses of visiting dignitaries by having one of the puppets play them, with good-natured humor on all sides.

On a number of occasions, members of the audience go beyond verbal participation in the drama to literally step into it. Feria members often encourage such participation. If no one steps forward spontaneously, they will put a microphone before a potential speaker or take someone by the hand and lead him or her onstage. Usually there are roars of approval from the audience for the new actor, and the sociodrama takes a new direction, somewhat out of the hands of the Feria.

Roughly speaking, there are two types of sociodramas and puppet shows: those designed to culminate in some plan of action and those designed to encourage further reflection or to challenge old patterns of thought. The sociodrama of the illiterate campesino described earlier is an example of the first type. Another presents the problem of widespread ecological destruction in Chimborazo by portraying conditions that every campesino is struggling with on a daily basis—water and wind erosion, mudslides, flooding, and so on. This leads to a discussion of actual steps that campesinos can take, such as reforestation and control of overgrazing.

One of the Feria's "open-ended" sociodramas recently won second prize in a popular theater contest. It presents the history of the Ecuadorian peasant in six scenes, progressing from the conquest, through colonization, independence, and modern times. The goal is to provoke reflection and collective self-analysis and to avoid conclusions predetermined by outside perspectives and ideological filters.

In some sociodramas, the two types are mixed. For example, two sociodramas illustrate the challenges faced by campesinos meeting with government officials or simply taking a bus journey to Quito. These open the door to reflection on campesinos' civil rights and the ways for them to affirm those rights as they pursue and defend their interests in the bureaucratic mazes of the modern world. These sociodramas move back and forth from the concrete—actual strategies and techniques for getting the job done—to the abstract—the rights of campesinos to equal access to the goods and services of government and to human dignity as citizens of their country.

Other elements of the Feria's work, such as song, story, and dance, also demonstrate to campesinos the social value of their instinctive need to preserve their music, their festivals—each with its characteristic dances and costumes—their folktales and metaphoric riddles, and above all, the Quichua language. This message is both implicit and explicit and is transmitted through printed materials, cassette tapes, and practical workshops, as well as through public performances.

The most important result of a Feria visit can be a renewed affirmation of Indian culture and community. A song such as "Jacu Villa Mariaman" contributes to this by telling of everyday trade in a local village, of cattle, pigs, sheep, wool, leather, and small animals such as guinea pigs, and expressing affection towards these activities and the persons who carry them out. (This is a traditional quichua song, collected by the Feria Educativa, in the village of Amulá, Parroquia of Cacha, Riobamba Cantón, Chimborazo Province, Ecuador.) The meals that commonly accompany a visit by the Feria also create a sense of solidarity, for everyone shares the food, not just honored guests as can be the case when outside dignitaries visit.

"Jacu Villa Mariaman"	"Vamos A Villa María"	"Let's go to Villa María"
Jacu Villa Mariaman	Vamos a Villa María	Let's go to Villa María
jacu Santa Rosaman;	vamos a Santa Rosa;	Let's go to Santa Rosa;
jala Rosa María	hola Rosa María	Hi there Rosa Maria
jala Pachu Francisco.	hola Pacho Francisco.	Hi there Pacho Francisco.
Cambac cuchi catuna,	En tu negocio del chancho	In the sale of your pig
mana saquichishachu;	no te voy a hacer perder;	I won't let you lose money;
cambac huagra catuna	y cuando vendas tu vaca	and when you sell your cow
mana shitachishachu.	no voy a dejar de hacer.	I won't get in your way.
Alli cuyi catuni,	Yo vendo muy bien los cuyes	My guinea pigs are selling well
alli lulun catuni;	y vendo muy bien los huevos;	and my eggs are selling well;
mana canta shuyani,	yo no espero por ti,	I won't wait for you
mana canta chapani.	ni espero nada de ti.	Nor do I ask anything of you.
Jacu Villa Mariaman	Vamos a Villa María	Let's go to Villa María
jacu Santa Rosaman;	vamos a Santa Rosa;	Let's go to Santa Rosa;
jala Rosa María	hola Rosa María	Hi there Rosa Maria
jala Pachu Francisco.	hola Pacho Francisco.	Hi there Pacho Francisco.

Feria members know that pedantic or simplistic suggestions can insult people's intelligence. They know from their own experience that telling campesinos what they should want is not only demeaning but arouses suspicions of hidden agendas. Realizing that campesinos generally know what needs to be done, even though they may be unclear as to how, the Feria focuses more on strategies than on preconceived goals. And since local people set their own agendas, programs rarely need to be sold. Demand for support from Unidad/SEV has consistently overwhelmed available resources.

A key element in the Feria's work is follow-up. Music and sociodrama may be seed sown in fertile soil, but just as no seed will sprout without water and sunlight, the Feria's work does not generally bear fruit without subsequent support by Unidad/SEV or others. This support can be technical assistance, or pressure on government or private agencies to deliver services. It is offered in response to community interest, not imposed.

Although numbers alone cannot adequately describe the Feria's impact on the communities and organizations of Chimborazo, they are impressive:

- When the Feria was formed in 1974, there were only two campesino music groups in the province that promoted the playing of traditional music. In 1990 over 100 such groups were independently performing traditional music; many of them are also collecting and preserving it. At least 12 of these groups were formed by women.
- The Feria Educativa has conducted 16 training programs for young musicians, helped almost all the new musical groups to

form, sponsored four festivals of traditional music and dance, made three cassette tapes for sale locally, published a songbook and several pamphlets on local history and traditional arts, and collected and performed countless songs, stories, riddles, and dances.

- Since 1979, the Feria Educativa has visited over 800 communities throughout the province, a number of them more than once.
- These contacts helped pave the way for the local literacy campaign that established 1,050 training centers at the community level, achieving virtually blanket coverage of the province and becoming the most successful such program in Ecuador.
- Helped by the Feria's promotional work, the Unidad de Educación para el Desarrollo was able to establish 32 community bakeries and 45 artisan-managed workshops, and to enable villages to build 145 community centers and plant more than 200,000 trees in reforestation efforts.
- Partly as an offshoot of Unidad/SEV's community-level work, local federations of communities have been forming. In 1990, there were a dozen, representing more than 200 villages and organizations. Many of these federations sponsor their own cultural revitalization efforts, integrating them with training, production, and community development activities.

Not all of these accomplishments can be credited solely to the Feria's work. Yet it is difficult to argue that they would have been achieved without the Feria. Indeed, in other provinces accomplishments like this are not in evidence.

Other results of the Feria's work may be less quantifiable, but they are observable nonetheless: Ten years ago in Chimborazo Province, campesino women rarely if ever spoke in public gatherings, and as late as five years ago, they never played musical instruments in any setting. Now women are increasingly speaking out at meetings, and a number of women's musical groups have formed with help from the Feria. This increased participation of women spills over from the cultural realm into production. Many women's groups have organized to raise small animals, establish artisan workshops, and produce crops. This is due in part to a shift in the consciousness of Indian men in their roles as both organizational leaders and husbands. In the past, they were influenced by Western models of male-centered community development imported from outside the indigenous areas. They are now more open to the initiatives of indigenous women to establish their own projects—which was one focus of the Feria's work.

In contrast to the past, local campesinos now regularly express pride in their native language, and want literacy programs and schooling conducted in both Spanish and Quichua. Also songs in Quichua are sung more often. The renaissance of the Quichua language is due primarily to the bilingual literacy program that the Feria promoted in Chimborazo and the revival of traditional music to the Feria's tireless efforts at performing, collecting and disseminating it, and organizing music groups and festivals. Something similar has happened with other traditional forms such as stories, riddles, and dance.

The Feria's impact on organization building in Chimborazo is noticeable at the community level as well as among coalitions of communities. The Feria has been the major point of contact for various grassroots development projects and an important force in the emergence of a local federation movement in Chimborazo. Increasingly, the federations have become effective vehicles for development and for lobbying the government for services and for the respect of human rights. The Feria's role in all of these activities has been key—as consciousness raiser, promoter, model, and resource.

Undeniably, one of the Feria's most important achievements has been the encouragement and enabling of a collective sense of ethnic pride and "can do"—a sense that Indians in Chimborazo Province have a valuable culture and are capable of contributing to society as a whole. Indians are not as compliant and manipulable as they were in the past. They are more assertive, more questioning, and more skilled at dealing with Western-style bureaucracies. Local authorities were at first critical of the Feria's role in this process. Most now have come to accept the changed attitudes and to recognize that they were warranted.

The Feria has also had an effect on the schools, no surprise since education is its primary work. The Feria grew out of the literacy program of the Ministry of Education and Culture and was rooted in the theories and practice of nonformal education. It was natural that the Feria would be in close contact with rural schoolteachers. At first it met with indifference or resistance from the education establishment. At times, educators were the target of Feria performances. Over the years, many schoolteachers have changed their attitudes, perhaps as a result of their contacts with the Feria and with Indian colleagues. (Some Indians had become teachers themselves and many were literacy trainers and regional coordinators.) Now teachers frequently ask the Feria to give performances or teacher training courses or to provide educational materials for use in their classrooms.

Perhaps the most noticeable change wrought by the Feria is the frequency and intensity with which previously reluctant Indian communities now embrace and demand development aid. Indigenous leaders who once viewed development programs with suspicion now crowd into the offices of the Unidad and SEV, especially on market day, to present typed requests for a teacher, a training program, or funds for planting communal lands, building a community center, or reforesting an eroded mountainside.

After the community has made its request, the Feria plays only a supportive role, for example by performing at the inauguration of a new federation building. The Feria is just one piece in a broader sociocultural methodology employed by SEV. The Feria is commonly a local organization's initial contact and the catalyst that activates it, but the organization ultimately must carry out the activity. SEV provides follow-up services: securing funding, providing technical assistance, carrying out monitoring and evaluation, and pressuring government agencies to provide services and other resources.

In the course of its work the Feria itself has changed. It doubled from six to twelve members, including two women whose presence as group spokespersons has had a significant impact on Indian women throughout Chimborazo. Many of the Feria performers who joined as teenage students have taken on additional duties managing SEV's development work, or moved on to other positions related to campesino self-development. Several are schoolteachers. Another became a municipal official and federation leader and then entered law school in Quito. Another directed a major development program. Meanwhile, demand for the Feria Educativa's services has increased in the cities as well as in the countryside. New, local Ferias will need to be formed to fill the gaps left by these changes in the original Feria.

The history of the Feria Educativa, like the dance music it performs, has been generally upbeat. But the group has also had its share of dilemmas and disappointments. The Feria's style and message have not been universally accepted. Some city folk have objected to the content and delivery of the Feria's songs, as have fundamentalist church groups who charge that music and dance lead to a lascivious lifestyle. Once, a performance in the exclusive Quito municipal auditorium was abruptly halted by the event's organizers for being "inappropriate" for such a setting. On another occasion, a provincial agency head complained about "indios" being allowed to manage development activities. But opposition and intimidation have been sporadic and ultimately ineffectual.

More subtle societal pressures have had a greater impact. With the passing of the years, the men of the Feria wear their ponchos less and less, as they have become more integrated into the mestizo, urban world. The women, however, have maintained their traditional dress, as is customary in the general Indian population. The group has shifted somewhat away from traditional music toward playing more pieces in the mode of modern protest songs popular throughout Latin America. The Feria's members have been influenced by progressive, non-Indian performing groups that draw upon and interpret Andean music to make highly marketable records and go on international tours.

The Feria Educativa has had to resist commercial and political pressures. Many people would like to profit from a group and a method that has so successfully won the trust and the ear of campesinos. Repeatedly, Feria members turned aside offers to record their music for purely economic gain and to become paid performers. They chose instead to continue their grassroots development activities, at modest salaries, meanwhile depending on sales of tapes and booklets for partial self-financing. Finally, however, after returning home from participation in a folklife festival in Washington, D.C., the majority of the Feria members succumbed to temptations to return to the United States for an extended tour, abandoning their work in Chimborazo. Nevertheless, other local music groups stepped in to pick up the baton, thereby continuing the spread and the impact of the Feria methodology. In short, the Feria is no longer merely a group of specific performers, but a time-proven idea, a cherished local institution.

Over the years the Feria has also scrupulously avoided partisan politics. Members have refused numerous invitations to events sponsored by political parties. They know that many campesinos would become less trusting of the Feria were it seen to have its own political agenda, or loyalty to certain political parties or figures. In spite of the group's political neutrality, on at least one occasion Feria members were accused by authorities, falsely, of involvement in a national opposition political campaign. At the same time, government officials were pressuring the Feria to link its activities to the ruling party.

Another problem for the Feria has been recruiting more women members. The two women who have been part of the group since the beginning are self-assured and eloquent public speakers, and their visibility and hard work has been vital to the emergence of women's music groups throughout the province. Nevertheless, the Feria has not been able to incorporate other women, in part because campesino parents object to letting their single daughters travel about the countryside at night with a band of musicians. (The two women are the wife and sister of one of the original Feria leaders.)

Ironically, the Feria's greatest challenge may be in coping with its own success at promoting grassroots development. Since 1986, Feria members have taken on expanded roles as project managers in the broader SEV development program. As a result, the group has become more bureaucratic and inwardly focused. For a while, the everyday administrative duties which that shift entailed, and the challenge of retraining themselves as development specialists, brought the Feria to a point where it almost ceased to perform at all. In attempting to balance its two roles, the Feria ultimately risks not carrying out either one very effectively.

The solution is most likely the emergence of spin-off groups from among the many musicians the Feria has trained and encouraged. Such groups are already involved in the preservation and perpetuation of the living culture of the province. Whether they will obtain the necessary financial resources and permanently adopt the key philosophical and methodological approaches developed over the years by the Feria is still an open question. Without these resources and skills, the new groups will be unequipped to move from performance to cultural activism.

Meanwhile, the idea of using culture as a development tool in Ecuador is not confined to Chimborazo. Elsewhere, similar cultural groups have formed independently, most notably among the black population of the Chota Valley in northern Ecuador, among the lowland Indians of the country's Amazon region, and within the Society of Deaf Adults of Quito.[4] These groups are now beginning to collaborate, exchanging cassette tapes, publications, and other materials, and accepting invitations to perform in each other's communities. On occasion, they have performed together in other areas where such groups are not active. An example is a joint visit in 1989 by the Feria and the Chota group—Grupo de Danza, Teatro y Música "Angara Chimeo"—to the 26th annual congress of the Shuar Federation in the Ecuadorian Amazon.

Similar groups of cultural workers are active in Mexico, Colombia, Jamaica, and the United States.[5] A common thread running through all these experiences is their grassroots nature. Through these groups, minority peoples are able to preserve and disseminate their own cultural heritage and aspirations for their own purposes, and on their own terms.

As for Feria Educativa itself, although it is changing and may evolve into very different forms, it remains a rich source of new ideas and of burgeoning campesino support for local development programs and organization building within campesino communities and federations. By revitalizing local history and indigenous identity and pride, it has been a cultural means to promote development ends, as well as a cultural end in itself.

Perhaps most important, the Feria has encouraged tens of thousands of local indigenous people to reflect upon their lives and their organizations, and it has been an example for *all* the people of Chimborazo, and Ecuador, of what indigenous people can accomplish by drawing upon their own internal resources and cultural heritage.

All this was visible one cold, moonlit night in a remote shepherd's village in southern Chimborazo. We had stooped under the thatched roof of an adobe schoolhouse to pass through the small doorway. Once inside the single room—dimly lit by an ancient kerosene lantern, the dirt floor worn smooth by bare feet—we nodded our greetings to the class of adult literacy students sitting on wooden benches before us. We counted 17 women, many of them carrying infants on their backs, wrapped in woven blankets. Eight men were also present, most of them over 50 years old. All of the faces that stared at us showed the fatigue of the day's work in the fields and the household.

We had come to this scattering of huts high up on an Andean slope in part to find out why an adult bilingual literacy training center had been formed in a place so isolated and devoid of other services and infrastructure.

The literacy trainer, a woman from the same community, took the floor to explain:

"Some months ago, a group of indigenous musicians calling themselves 'Feria Educativa' passed through here. They performed in this very room. Their stories and music got us to reflect on our lives—our reality and our needs. After they left, the community asked me to teach reading and writing. And how to organize ourselves to improve conditions here, for ourselves and our children."

She paused and then asked us if we would like to hear some local music. We accepted without hesitation, and someone left the room to bring back seven young women, none of them older than 18. Shyly, they lined up in front of us, and each brought a simple instrument out from under her shawl. Drums and tamborines and maracas appeared. One young woman gave a signal, and with a burst they all began to play their instruments and sing in high, clear voices. They performed with a verve that kept our eyes riveted on their faces and made us forget our cold hands and feet and our empty stomachs. Glancing away to look at the crowd, we saw backs straightening and eyes brightening. Every face in the room glowed with pride.

When the group finished, everyone applauded enthusiastically. We urged them to sing again, and they did, treating us to the same song. More applause, sweetened with laughter this time. As a pot of steaming potatoes was brought in and passed around, we asked the inevitable visitor's question: "How did your group form?"

The group leader laughed nervously and said, "Some musicians came through our town, and they helped us."

"What were they called?" we asked. "The Feria Educativa?"

"They were called María," she answered. "And Paulina."

Then she added, "They're *Quichua women*. Just like us!"

NOTES

This chapter is an updated and expanded version of the article that appeared in *Grassroots Development* (Vol. 12, No. 2, 1988).

1. "Quichua" is the Ecuadorian form of "Quechua"—once the lingua franca of the Inca Empire, it is still spoken by millions of indigenous campesinos throughout the Andes.

2. The Ecuadorian Volunteer Service of Chimborazo Province; see the Appendix (EC-165) for a brief description.

3. The Education for Development Unit; see the Appendix (EC-053).

4. For brief descriptions of the latter two efforts, see the Appendix under Ecuador—(EC-198), (EC-082), and (EC-116).

5. Sna Jtz'Ibajom (ME-262); Teatro Identificador (CO-046); SISTREN Theatre Cooperative (JA-047); the Mystic Revelation of the Rastafari Community Cooperative (JA-034); Lati-Negro of Washington, D.C.; and Teatro Campesino of California.

There are also numerous cases of cultural activists who come from the outside to assist ethnic groups in attaining their development goals. Examples are: Grupo Proyecto Aty-Ne'e in Paraguay (PY-016); Fundación Cultural Teatro Taller de Colombia (CO-127); Garífuna Theater of Identity in Honduras (HO-046); Los Comediantes in Chile (CH-075); Centro de Indagación y Expresión Cultural y Artística also in Chile (CH-170); Joven Teatro in Bolivia (BO-138); Centro Cultural Masis also in Bolivia (BO-087); Casa de Teatro in the Dominican Republic (DR-040).

4

Women's Theater in Jamaica
•
SISTREN THEATRE COLLECTIVE

"Sistren," which means "sisters," is the only theater company in the Caribbean that has developed from the initiative of working-class women. Drawing on personal ghetto experiences, Sistren writes and performs plays that make audiences more aware of the problems that women face, particularly in this part of the world.

The women of Sistren came together in 1977 while being trained as teachers' aides in a special Jamaican government program. The trainees were picked from workers in the "Impact Programme," a government effort to make jobs, such as street cleaning, for thousands of unemployed women.

During the training, the 13 women were asked to do a theater piece for the annual Workers' Week celebrations. They approached the Jamaican School of Drama for a director to help prepare their performance and eventually met Honor Ford-Smith in the old, broken-down schoolhouse in Swallowfield. When she asked, "What do you want to do a play about?" they answered, "We want to do plays about how we suffer as women." Talking about their lives that day led to *Downpression Get a Blow,* their first theater piece, which dealt with women in a garment factory forming a union and achieving their demands.

From that performance, Sistren was born. The women decided to stay together, continue collaborating with the director, and make more theater pieces. Sistren's first major production was "Bellywoman Bangarang" in 1978. How that play emerged tells much about how the company works together and grows. The play developed using a method based almost completely on folk traditions. Actresses played ring games from childhood, told riddles, and sang songs that called up memories. One woman would tell a story or act it out, and as another member identified with it, she would link her experience through storytelling or action. From these improvisations, the theme of teenage pregnancy and the rites of passage from girlhood to adulthood emerged.

After creating a scene, an actress had to script it in Creole. This exercise revealed that some of the actresses were better able to read and write.

71

The more fluent helped those who were less able, and by Sistren's second production, everyone could read her own script. This informal learning process was reinforced later by various research workshops. Calisthenics were developed based on the alphabet; a dance was choreographed to spell out words. Writing exercises were linked to problem-solving skits involving conflict resolution, personal awareness, and group development. Some of the women would develop a skit on a particular problem, stop, then ask the rest of the group how the problem should be solved. After discussion, the solution was acted out. The desire to make theater increased the desire to master new skills.

Through four major productions, that growth has continued. Sistren's members have had to learn to be not only actresses, but also teachers, stage managers, secretaries, graphic artists, accountants, text designers, and printers. A textile project has been started, and members have been trained in stencil-cutting and silk-screening to make bags, aprons, and other objects to sell at crafts fairs and at acting performances. Sistren t-shirts and wall hangings are also printed, depicting themes from the company's major theater productions. This craftwork not only supplements individual incomes, it helps support the aims of the collective.

Since Sistren has a cooperative structure, each member helps evaluate everyone's work. The group is comprised of not just actresses and an artistic director. There are also "resource people," behind-the-scenes members who help with administration, fund-raising, and publicity. After six years of working together, Sistren's main goals are to

- Perform drama in working-class communities,
- Create theater and drama that comment on the position of women,
- Look at possible solutions to the problems of women in their day-to-day struggle, and
- Provide the members of our collective with the chance to participate in a self-reliant cooperative organization.

To accomplish these aims, Sistren mounts major commercial productions which develop themes that challenge and stimulate questions about the situation of women. The collective also conducts public workshops where drama is used as a problem-solving tool. Although these workshops are often free, they are as important as larger theatrical productions. Performed in prisons, community centers, and remote villages, these skits apply what has been learned in Sistren's research workshops. A sense of community is created so that an audience can be exposed to and deal with hidden or taboo subjects about women. The open-ended skits do not passively reflect life; they try to demystify it by fully exploring its realities. By facing what has been considered indecent or merely irrelevant, the actresses record women's rejections of the forces that thwart their lives.

Although grounded in the experience of our members, we at Sistren try to explore the experience of *all* women. The subjects of plays are thoroughly researched, but sometimes community workshops turn up new information and themes. In meetings with women from factories to schools, from sugar workers to the urban unemployed, many described themselves solely in terms of their work in and for the home. Meanwhile there was a void of information about this in official reports and research about our society. A continuing workshop series—"Domesticks"—explores this domestic labor, looks at how people migrate from rural to urban areas and even overseas looking for work, and tries to inform society through drama about our findings.

Sometimes that research recovers the past. The play *Nana Yah* is about Nanny, a real woman who led a guerrilla fight for independence against the British in the 17th century. Through understanding the past, and our African heritage, Jamaicans can come to grips with the present. As expressed in director Jean Small's program notes,

So mi min fall pon Nanny and mi aks misself ow Nanny did do wha she di do. Is whey she get de courage, eddication'n tins an strenk fe fight eeh? an mi see seh is causen Nanny ad she culcha an she belief an all dat appen is dat Nanny did believe dat she cudda dwit and she dwit. Strenk is a tin come outa de pas, an yuh av it deh all de time inna yuh ead an wen yuh noa seh is dat you believe yuh jes mek yuh spirit guide yuh and dwit.

(So my mind falls on Nanny and I ask myself how Nanny did what she did. Where did she get the courage, education in things and strength to fight, eh? And I see that because Nanny had her culture and her belief, and all that happened is Nanny believed that she could do it, and she did it. Strength is a thing out of the past, and you have it there all the time in your head, and when you know yourself, you believe, you just make your spirit guide you and do it.)

During the past six years, Sistren has been following its spirit, receiving critical recognition, and travelling widely. In 1979 the Inter-American Commission of Women awarded Sistren a certificate of merit for its work and a prize for the best mass media project encouraging women in development, specifically for *Bellywoman Bangarang.* After that, the Jamaica National Theater Critics Award was received for another play, *Q.P.H.* Recently, Sistren completed successful tours of Canada and the eastern Caribbean and will soon tour Europe. The company will perform plays at the London International Festival of Theatre and give workshops in West Indian communities all over England. Later performances will be given in such cities as Berlin and Amsterdam. In addition to the exposure these tours offer, they produce much-needed money to help support our educational workshops. Wherever we are, our work stays focused on the women of the Caribbean: as mothers, as workers, as sisters, and as partners of our men.

"You can't have pure seriousness going on."

—Lillian Foster

I am from Kingston. I went to Kingston Technical High School, and I went the domestic science way—nowadays they call it home economics—so that I could get into Kingston Public Hospital to train as a nurse. But I started having children from an early stage. I had to stop from school, and that is what blighted my prospects.

Although having the children early, I wasn't really such an out-and-out girl. My godmother held me inside—from school, to house, to church. Nowhere else. I couldn't even go to the gate and look out. So when I got pregnant with my first child, everybody around the neighborhood was wondering how that happened. You know, I was like a lamb that was led to the slaughter. I don't think it's the best way for parents to have their children—like on a chain in bondage. Maybe the least chance they get. . . .

So when I had the first child, the trouble started. Goddie didn't want to keep me, but you know, she looked it over and I stayed there. When I find myself pregnant with the second one, I was thrown out. Yes, she put me out. I had to go live with my sister, but she couldn't really keep me to have a baby: she occupied just one room. Well, it so happened that there was a man that says he used to see me going to school. But he didn't know that I had another child before. So when I was pregnant with the second child, he saw me and asked me what happened to me, and I said, "You don't see what happened to me? I'm in trouble. I'm pregnant."

And he said, "Where is the man that get you pregnant?" At that time, the father of my first and second child was getting ready to go to England. And this other man, seeing that I was pregnant, decided to take me with this pregnancy. He rented a room and put the both of us in there. He was the first man I was going to live with. And well, he treated me nicely. I got my clothes, my food, everything that I needed. But he was sort of on the rough side: he was very jealous. He didn't want me to talk to anyone, neither a man or a woman. And it go on and on, and I found myself pregnant with my boy, which was the third child. But then I couldn't take his jealousy, and I had to leave him when my son was six months old. And up to this day I don't live with another man. No, he let me become afraid, you know. My daughter's father, who I met after that, I don't live with him. I had two boys and two girls: four children, three different fathers. One girl died, so my oldest he's 24, one is 20, and my little girl is 13.

I worked for about eight years as a sales clerk. Then I left to go and do some nursing, but I went the wrong way. I went to a nursing home. There was one doctor who wanted to help me to get a job in the hospital, but a lady told me if I went to work at a nursing home, she would teach me the job. I was to watch her and the other nurses and to do whatever they were doing. I stay on there for around six months without pay and spent up all my money to buy uniforms and all those things. All that went down the drain: I thought that she would really teach me something, but she was just looking for somebody to do her job. If I had followed that doctor, I would have gone very far, because when you know one thing, you catch on quickly. Nursing was what I really wanted to do. So, you know, I got downhearted and stopped.

So there I was at home for a year, not working. And this Special Employment Programme came up. I said, "Well, let me go and do it, because I'm working for my honest bread." Soon after that, Sistren started—in 1977. And I'm in it until now, nearly five years. We do our plays by improvisation. We take our own experience—teenage pregnancy, mother and child experiences and so on—and we put bits and pieces together to form the play. And we make up our own songs. Yes, man, it's fantastic! We're far different from other groups. That is why whenever we put on a show, people always craving to come and see what we are doing. Most groups use scripts, while we just improvise, you know. Then we write a script, but whatever is written in the script is just what we say.

Our first major production was about teenage pregnancy. We saw teenagers going to school, getting pregnant, mother turning them out; man getting them pregnant and leaving them alone to bring up this child and look after it. It's a real mixed-up thing. So we call the play *Bellywoman Bangarang*, because we always like to give our plays a funny name. This play has two acts. In the first act, you have around six little scenes. The young people working, going to school, having games, and from there start growing up, 'til they start having boyfriends. Mother watching girls having their period and, after a while, lose their period, get pregnant, and the guy run off and leave, and the mother have to take over again. Maybe the mother can't bear it—your coming with more than one unwanted kid—so she put you out. Things like that. But within the seriousness of those scenes, you have a little humor coming between, because you can't have pure seriousness going on. That is in the first half of the play.

Then in the second half of the play, we show another type of problem that women face: rape. And—oh mercy—I would really like you to see that show! When that rape is going on, we don't do it with a man and a woman. We are only pure women; we do it in a different form. And I tell you, that thing come off. We have some people crying.

Our other major show is *Q.P.H.* Our acting director, Pencer Lindsay, said she would love to do a show based on the fire at the Eventide Home for the Aged. Year before last, on 22nd of May, Eventide Home was burned down. So we tell this story of three persons—Queenie, Pearlie, and Hopie (that is why we call it *Q.P.H.*)—and what happened to them. Pearlie, this woman come from a well-to-do family, but mother turned her out. From there, she started to drink and become a drunkard, and she also became a prostitute. She was one of the biggest prostitutes in Jamaica. And she went to Eventide, where she died from consumption. Hopie was handicapped from a young girl. She used to walk around and beg, and she end up in Eventide. She died in the fire. Queenie is still alive; she's still down at Eventide, in the part that didn't get burned out.

I want to tell you, we did research on that, too. At the time of the fire we went down there and talked to people. A lot of charred bodies: just bones, pure bones. Oh, my God!

In the play, we start with the lives of the three women, and then how they got to Eventide. When we come to the fire scene, everybody gets old at that time. You can just imagine that you are old, and the fire is in this building, and you can't move to get out. Somebody have to help you, and the only help is the same older people. The stronger ones tried to help the weaker ones. When we have that scene—mercy—a lot of people in the audience cry!

Now, our play *Bandoolu Version* is based upon three women living in a tenement yard in a ghetto and the problems that they face with their man. Two of the men are thieves, and one woman in that yard, she don't like those things. She don't put up with her man to be a thief. The other two women throw a word at her all the while and curse her and want to fight her. They come in and want to kick down her door and steal what she have in her house—just like what going on here now. So we did a play around that.

Another play, *Nana Yah,* is about this strong warrior woman Nanny from history. You've heard about Nanny and the guerrilla fighters who fought for their freedom. Well, that is what *Nana Yah* is based on. Just the same as the other plays, we put bits and pieces together. We use our own words to build up this play. But regardless of what we say and what we do, it's based on research. You can't just go about and do a thing and say, "This thing happened at such-and-such a time," and it's not true. You have to have true saying, and then you work around it to build your show. We did research work in St. Elizabeth to watch the type of dance they do, the ritual: how they set up the table to feed the spirits. We put different kinds of food on the table and rum and all those things. And the dance—we call it Etu—and for what reason they do the dance. And that is *Nana Yah.* It's fantastic to see women moving around as men, as soldiers, fighting for their freedom.

We also do workshops that mostly deal with women—you know, raising women's consciousness. It's not that men are left out, but we are a group that deals with women's issues. We go to the rural areas, to prisons, schools, community centers. We share our views with other groups and they share their views with us. And we have traveled abroad: we went to Barbados and to Canada. It was fantastic. People were clamoring that the time was too short; they wanted us to stay. It's possible that we may go again, because they want us back, but the pockets are low.

"We always focus on the problems that the low-income people meet."
                                                                —Cyrene Stephenson

Sistren takes up most of my time now. Sistren mean a lot to me because it gives me more strength. I mean it shows me a way that I can put myself out and do something for myself, right? It teaches me to meet people. Because sometime when I'm in the country, I would just close myself. But now that I meet a lot of people, I have to socialize myself.

We always focus on the problems and the suffering that the low-income people meet: the women have a lot of kids and maybe they go and sell themself, or them go and see a man and the mother kick them out. And they end up having a baby what them don't even want. The man leave them and gone; the mother have to take over again. If you'd ever been to any of our workshops, you'd know that we teach the low-income people how to help themselves—not only depend on other people but how they could help themselves and take care of their kids. We try to show the mother that when the child make a mistake, just take the child and sit with the child and teach the child. Talk in a quiet form that the child can understand instead of going around and beat and curse the child.

When we have a workshop, we talk with the people and they involve themselves. And through that, we always use their problem to show them through the skit. Like when we put on a skit at a workshop in Claredon, a lady stand up and said, "Who tell you about me problem?" And when we finish, you see the difference in them before they leave. Even the men. When we went to the prison, a guy in the prison said how he was going to come out and hurt the woman who let him reach there. But when we finish the skit, he just come around and—well, I don't know if he really did that once he outside—but at the moment, he came around to our thinking and forget his own.

My boyfriend, he's an ignorant person, and it's hard to even tell him anything really. I try, but he's very hard to deal with. He's not employed all the while, because that kind of work that he doing—building—there's a lot of people doing the same thing. Maybe he get a house two times a year—maybe two houses a year! So most of the time he's not working. And Sistren has helped me, because sometime I would just get ignorant, too, and step out and forget certain things. Instead of just walking out on a person, you try to help the person. I myself, get mad at my kids. And they say to me, "What the use going up there and teach other people, and you can't teach yourself!"

We are trying to show women that they must not depend on a man alone, and they must not say women can't do certain things. They must always go out and try to do what they want to do. Some people think mechanic work is for man, plumbing is for man, and all those work. But if you decide that you want to do something, just go and do it.

If we had more schooling, we could manage then. Sometime we go abroad and people say they don't understand us when we talk. Our English-wise is not good; we most use patois. I even have production now doing and I have to be trying my best to talk in the right way, because this woman is supposed to be a very high—you know—an aristocrat. What I would like is us going back to school, doing English, math, and a little history too.

"All I need is a little training to put me straight."

—Lana Finnikin

I was born on the 19th of January, 1954, in St. James. My childhood years were very interesting because it was a big family—with brothers, cousins, aunties, uncles—and everybody used to live together. There were 10 of us. I was the only child from my father, and I didn't live with my mother: I grown up with my grandparents, right? So I was a spoiled child.

My mother got me when she was taking her local examinations. When she was entering for the third year, she get pregnant with me. My grandmother took me from her and tell her to go back to school. She go back and get pregnant with the second sister that dies. After that they still encourage her to go back, but she leave and come to town. Nobody knew nothing about her: she didn't write and everybody was worried.

I was six when she came back to the country. She have three more children, and she leave them with my granny. At the same time, my father came back from England and was asking in the district for me. One morning I was getting ready to go to basic school, and I see this gentleman come up and ask if my granny inside. And I said, "Yes, sir." I run inside and say, "Ooo! A big black man coming." I remember he give me a pair of white shoes and a piece of cloth. My granny said if I want it, I must take it—she not taking it. I take it from him and she make a skirt. The Sunday after, I remember I wear the skirt and a blouse and the shoes to Sunday school. I was bragging the whole Sunday to the smaller children, saying that my father come back, and I see him for the first time. After that, I never see him again. I'm 28, going 29, and I don't see him after that.

I leave St. James and come to town when I was 11, going 12. It was like I was the head of the household, because my mother do domestic work and have to come in late and leave out early. At that time, it was five, six of us; and everybody have to go to school. We would get up in the morning and tidy up the house, then come back in the evening, cook and wash, and go to bed. When Mama come in, she always say she was proud of us.

I remember when I was 17 and started to go to school for typing and things like that. One morning in class the headmaster give us some newspaper to read. There was some big girls from, you know, as you look at them you can see them come from a middle class family. The headmaster at them you can see them come from a middle class family. The headmaster handed *them* this morning's *Gleaner* and give *us* the old newspaper to read. So I say, "I not reading the old news. I read it last week. I want something new to read this morning." And he take me out of the classroom and carry me down and take a piece of rubber tire and give me about six lickings. When I look at my body, it was like if the natural blood stand up inside. And I took up my books and went home until Mama come home. She ask me what I'm doing there, and I show her my underclothes—I couldn't wash out anything. And we went to the doctor, and the doctor say he going to give her a certificate to take to the police for her to either prosecute the teacher or charge him with something. The doctor say that teacher shouldn't have any right to use a rubber tire: should use a cane or something else. I tell Mama, "I'm not going back there."

Here at Sistren we have teams—secretarial team and PR team and finance team. Each team have three members. I work with the accounts for four years now. I didn't have any training in accounts. I just took up Sistren account and started doing it. We have an accountant come in and show me what to do and how to put the books together and things like that. She came in the other day and check the books, and she said that they are okay. All I need is a little training to put me straight. If I get that qualification, I don't need for no more accountant to come in and audit the books. But the problem is that rehearsals and things like that take up the time, and we cannot find any time to do schooling. I am also stage manager for the group: it is very time-consuming and responsible work, because you sometimes have to play the role of director. I already say, "Next year, don't count me in the work. I'm going to school to get some G.C.E. —General Certificate—and some courses in accounts."

"We start in from the bottom of the ladder and just climbing gradually."

—Pauline Crawford

I was born in Kingston. At the age of about three months, my father take me from my mother and bring me to his wife, and his wife grew me until I was about three. Then she take me to the country to live with her mother. When I was about 11, sickness take her, and I had to come back to town and live with my stepmother and my father. My father is a simple man, you know—things that my stepmother do, he wasn't really that concerned. And my stepmother didn't like me all that much. She would beat me. I run away from home when I was about 12.

At first I say I was going to look work, and I stay with a woman awhile, but she tell me I can't stay there anymore. Luckily, when I pack up and was leaving, I look into the *Gleaner* and see a "on premises" work in

Kingston. I go there and work until I about 17 or 18. Then my stepmother come for me and me start to live back with them.

When the Impact Programme come in, my stepmother get the work, but she tell me, "Go and do it!" And being under her roof, I have to go. My friends, they laugh: it's me working and have to give the money to her because I working under her name. So I change the name to mine, and then one night I didn't carry her any money. She say me can't stay and put me out after 12 in the night.

I work now with Sistren and all my income is from Sistren. After *Bellywoman Bangarang,* the government change and they say they don't see us fit staying in schools as teachers' aides—so we lose that work. Right now we get a small allowance of about $200 (US$67) a month. Each month when I check up, 40, 50 dollars spent on bus fare, right? And you *see* this area that I live in. That's why I even move here—because the rent is cheap. I would like to live in a nicer area, but that would be about $100 a month just for rent alone; and with the allowance that I get, I can't pay rent, can't buy clothes. But I'm grateful in the sense that I can eat and drink—not much—but I can eat and drink from the group.

Sistren itself, we start in from the bottom of the ladder and just climbing gradually. That is the illustration I can use with the people I know. I tell them that before we start, we never even dream of traveling; we never dream that we could be getting a small allowance from it; we never dream that it could even continue for so long. Togetherness is the key. Sometime the going get rough, you know. But it's good that a group of 13 women can really come together and through all this struggling and problems—you know, home and children—still stay together all the five years. Most of the workshops, we don't get any pay. We not thinking about the money. Deep down it's like we satisfied with what we do.

Right now we doing textiles. If we could get a market for the textiles, that would be additional income. We not getting any government assistance at this time. If Sistren get more financial aid and more recognition from our country—if the government could really look on our side—I can foresee we moving ahead. Because we have a message out there.

"You don't have to be teacher and nurse to be important."
—Jasmine Smith

When I was having those children, when I'm not working, I just sit at home. I don't have anywhere to go, unless I can afford to pay two dollars or so—then I would go to the movie. After I get this employment and we came together as a group, I was glad because I don't have to sit at home anymore. I was also afraid: I face certain problems and I think I was the only person facing those problems. But when we came together and start to talk to each other, then you find that people like you face similar problems.

In our productions, we talk about the relationship between a mother and a daughter, and how we don't relate to our daughters properly. For instance, in *Goddie and Yvonne,* Yvonne is having her first period and Goddie is trying to tell her that she mustn't go out—and in a difficult way that is hard for her to understand. We should notify our daughters beforehand. I tell my two girl children—one is 8 and one is 13—from way back. So that if it come upon them, they can deal with it, and that they are not frightened. And we talk about how girls are being raped by men and how the public, like the church, try to ban the girl from society because she's been raped, and it is no fault of her own. That is the part that I play when I play Marie, who's being raped by some boy. I play also a girl that my mother don't want me and just leave me with this woman. And this woman, the only place that she allow me is go to church. And so I am not aware of the things happening round me. It is easy for me to perform these roles, because I have experienced many things like that.

What would I say to all women? You don't have to have many certificates; you don't have to pass exams to be on top; you can work your way up by doing something that is worthwhile. All of us want our children to pass exam, and we want them to be a nurse and teacher, but you don't have to be teacher and nurse to be important. You can be important in your own way. I know that the work we are doing now is very important. I would encourage all women to keep up and do something that is worthwhile. And you will be on the forefront.

"Now I have somebody to talk with."

—Mae Thompson

I was brought up by my mother alone; she was my only source. I use to tend her business. She have a farm, in St. Catherine, with cane and banana and yam and all those things. I used to collect the money for the cane and banana. Just the both of us live together. She sent me to technical school and I did basic subjects: a little English, science, and a little dress designing. When I was 16, I got pregnant and have to leave school. My mother felt upset, being that she was looking for me to really come out with something. She turn me out.

I use to wait until she go into the bush; and then I just run in and thief some of the money, because I use to know where the money is. And I thief some food. One time she have a pot of mutton soup on the fire, so I just go in and take out the pot. But it was hot and drop from me and she coming through the door and saying, "Thief! Thief!" Then it happen that people talk to her and she take me back.

I have a boy, and even that child grow up without a father: my mother never want his father to come to the house. So I leave home after a time and my son stay with my mother. In Kingston, I took evening classes; I didn't work because my mother use to support me. When I was pregnant with the second child, she give me everything, you understand? That really touch me because she took sick. She send a telegram to call me, say she could die any moment. I say, "I will come tomorrow." But she die. She took out a tooth and it gave her a hemorrhage and the hemorrhage kill her.

After the little girl, my third child, I get a little work. My mother always said to me: "When a woman work for herself, she can stand up and grow. But when you have to depend upon a man, you have to be worried." My boyfriend have a job then, but still I want my own money. So when I start the Impact Programme, I work my little money, and I buy what I want—I buy my little furniture and things. I have three children; but the second one, a boy, he was killed by a car. And my first, who is 16, he gone by himself. The girl is with me.

Right now my thinking is too weary. I'm doing this drama here right now, and sometime I worry. My baby's father oppose me. He say, "You up on stage now. You soon gone with another man." Sometime when I leave from home, I don't cook the food because it will go cold. So I wait until night to prepare food, and he become angry with me sometimes. First time him reach home before me, he say, "Don't do that again." So generally now, my little daughter, she's quite helpful. I make sure and put the food what I want to cook on the table, and when she comes from school at two o'clock, she helps me.

Why I appreciate and I glad to be in Sistren is my first coming together working with women, coming in contact with so many different people. Because it was only me and my mother alone. She use to say, "Keep yourself from women. Women are some people you not to trust or deal with too much." So now that I come to Sistren, I have somebody to talk with. And sometime people in the group will say, "You must cheer up. You must be confident within yourself."

It was a dread scene for me the first time I'm going on stage and see so much people look at me. Man, I tremble sometimes! When we went on stage, I use the cardboard that say "Strike!" to put in front of me because I was shaking. Now I feel when I go up on a stage, I can master myself. I feel confident. I wish for the group that we may continue to work with each other as long as the group continue to grow.

NOTE

This article originally appeared in *Grassroots Development* (Vol. 7, No. 2, 1983).

5

Recapturing the Old Ways: Traditional Knowledge and Western Science Among the Kuna Indians of Panama

•

MAC CHAPIN

In the early 1980s, the Kuna became the first indigenous group in Latin America to mark off a large chunk of virgin rain forest—approximately 60,000 hectares—within their territory and set it aside as a wildlife reserve. This project fell neatly in line with growing worldwide concern over deforestation in the tropics and was widely applauded by conservation groups. In 1983, with substantial combined funding from the Inter-American Foundation (IAF), the Agency for International Development (AID), the Smithsonian Tropical Research Institute (STRI), and the World Wildlife Fund (WWF), the Kuna formally launched the Proyecto de Estudio para el Manejo de Areas Silvestres de Kuna Yala (PEMASKY).

The project center at Nusagandi, located at the point where the El Llano–Cartí road cuts across the Continental Divide and begins its descent to the Atlantic coast, started receiving biologists interested in carrying out studies in the area. The indigenous staff soon grew to some seventeen people, including half a dozen park guards and seven members of a technical team. The project was organized and managed by the Kuna, with initial assistance from outside advisers brought in on a contract basis. During the first years, the Kuna worked with enthusiasm and energy. They set about writing a management plan for the park, putting up buildings at Nusagandi, demarcating the border of their legally recognized homeland (the Comarca of Kuna Yala),[1] and publicizing their efforts among their own people in the islands. They also made contact with conservationists throughout the world and traveled to conferences and workshops as far away as England, Belgium, the United States, and Brazil. As a result, the "Kuna park," as it is generally known internationally, is perhaps one of the most talked-about undertakings of its kind in the world. This is not to say that it is well known. Aside from having a few cursory details and a sense that the Kuna are attempting to save a piece of rain forest, few outsiders know much about what is going on at Nusagandi.

One of the most intriguing aspects of the enterprise is its mix of modern scientific and traditional Amerindian elements. From the outset, the Kuna project staff had little problem integrating ecological concepts such as "ecosystem" and "watershed" into their thinking; on the surface, at least, the traditional elders living in the communities along the coast were more than open to notions that stressed the interrelated, systemic character of the world. There was no need to make arguments for the importance of biological diversity; the Kuna depend in a fundamental way on nature's variety and know a good deal about it. Even the idea of setting aside a section of rain forest as a park was in line with their thinking.

This rapport initially seemed so neat that many of those associated with PEMASKY, Kuna and non-Kuna alike, began talking of the natural fusion of traditional wisdom with modern concepts of biology, especially for the program component dealing with environmental education. The Kuna technical staff, all educated at the university level in Panama or abroad, began speaking of the elders in Kuna Yala as great conservationists and men wise in the ways of the natural world. In fact, they said, many of the ecological concepts now being put forward by biologists were far from new: The elders already understood notions such as ecosystem and biosphere from both a practical and theoretical perspective, albeit in a language different from that of Western science. Indeed, in its own special idiom the traditional Kuna worldview preaches a strong conservationist line: respect for nature and the need to care for the earth and its living creatures. The elders, for their part, had no objections to the programs being outlined in such detail by the youngsters, and they agreed universally on their goal of demarcating and patrolling the border of the Comarca.

Unfortunately, attempts to bring together the traditional and modern scientific bodies of knowledge have not extended much past the initial discussion stage. Despite the best of intentions, the technical team never managed to ingest much of the substance of the old view of the cosmos, and the elders never took much of an interest in Western biology.

In this chapter I discuss some of the reasons this fusion has not taken place in anything more than fragmentary fashion and reflect on the loss of traditional knowledge and ritual in general. To give substance to the discussion, I summarize the main lines of Kuna oral tradition and then highlight Kuna theories of how the universe functions, with special reference to concepts dealing with nature and resource management. I then attempt to place this traditional belief system within the present context of rapid social and cultural change that has been an increasingly persistent characteristic of Kuna Yala over the past fifty or so years. Central to this analysis is the introduction of Western education in the region, for it is in this arena that the worldview of the elders comes in contact with Western scientific thought.

THE TRADITIONAL KUNA WORLDVIEW

The largest group of Kuna live in the Comarca of Kuna Yala, a 200-kilo-meter-long strip of jungle extending along the Atlantic coast from the region of Cartí as far to the west as the village of Armila, just short of the Colombian border. The Comarca comprises a thick band of rain forest stretching from the ridge of the Continental Divide down to the coast and encompasses more than 300 tiny coral islands a mile or so offshore. More than forty of these islands, along with twelve mainland villages, accommodate a population of between 40,000 and 50,000 people. All of the villages are strategically situated near the shore to facilitate access to the interior, where agriculture is practiced and where vital resources such as fresh water, firewood, building materials, and so forth are procured.

The Kuna have enjoyed geographical isolation since Europeans arrived in the New World and have managed to maintain an exceptional measure of political and cultural autonomy into the present. They were granted Comarca status in 1938, and because of the absence of roads into the area the Kuna have remained relatively insular. The only non-Indians living in Kuna Yala are a handful of schoolteachers, Colombian traders, and religious missionaries. In this environment, the Kuna political system, as embodied in an institution called the "gathering," has continued to give order and reason to Kuna life.

The gathering sessions are held nightly in most Kuna communities.[2] They are presided over by a governing body consisting of at least three chiefs, a handful of official interpreters, and a varied collection of village elders and politically active younger men with a strong voice in community affairs. It is here that village business is discussed and resolved, community members are lectured on matters of morality, and the Kuna worldview is taught. Much of this is accomplished through long narrative chants (part of a tradition called "the way of the Father") that chronicle the collective history of the Kuna people and depict in lavish detail the workings of the cosmos. The chants constitute basic texts in history, morality, natural science, and civic behavior, and they are supplemented with often lengthy discussions by the "interpreters" that relate their content directly to the audience and the problems of the contemporary world.

The Kuna learn about the natural world by listening to the historical chants in the gathering sessions, by participating in ritual ceremonies of various types, and by discussing, in less formal contexts, all manner of knowledge about the spirit world and its inhabitants. The philosophical underpinnings of the Kuna system are supplied primarily by community leaders and ritual specialists; the practical aspects of this system are filled in by the Kuna's interactions with the natural world in the jungle and along the coastal reefs and mangrove swamps. The daily visits of the men, in particular, to the mainland to farm, fish, hunt, gather building materials and firewood, and carry out a variety of other tasks give them a thorough knowledge of their environment, which in turn provides substance for the oral traditions. The chants describe real places in the jungle and along the coastal estuaries; they describe the physical appearance and behavior of animals, the germination and growth cycle of plants, and a myriad of other phenomena that would be nothing more than abstractions were not the listeners experienced participants in the world about them. In this sense, the chants are reassuring: They catalogue familiar things, reaffirming a coherent and satisfying way of life, and this is a good part of their meaning for the audience. Without this experience in the common routine of "traditional" activities, the chants would have a hollow ring, describing a reality far removed from daily life. Not surprisingly, the elders consider this worldview, as it is expressed in the sacred lore, to make up the core—or, as they put it, the "soul"—of their identity as Kuna.

THE KUNA COSMOS

According to Kuna tradition, the earth is the body of the Great Mother, and in the beginning she came naked.[3] The Great Father joined in sexual union with the Great Mother, and she gave birth to all of the plants, animals, and humans. When they arrived, both the Great Mother and the Great Father were thinking far into the future, and they set about preparing their creation for the appearance, far into the future, of the "Golden People," the Kuna. The world at this time was pure spirit, and all of the children born of the Great Mother were likewise spiritual.

The children of the Mother were given names and informed of their duties on earth, as the Mother herself had been counseled when she first arrived. The medicinal plants were advised about their role in curing illness; certain animals were told they were to be used by the Kuna as food; a number of hardwood trees were given instructions for their use as construction materials in house building; and so forth.

As the initial creation came to a close, the Great Mother gave birth to a spirit named Muu (literally "grandmother" or "midwife") and installed her in a large house along the bank of the River of the Mists. Another spirit couple—a man named Olobenkikiler and his female companion, Olokekebyai—was brought forth and placed in the Region of the Trees, near Muu's domain. The Mother and the Father then abdicated their reproductive duties, leaving Muu with the task of siring all of the future animals and human beings. The spirit couple residing in the Region of the Trees was given the ongoing task of reproducing all of the earth's plants.

The world in the beginning was a paradise. The Mother, clothed with jungle vegetation, lived alone on the bank of a huge, gently flowing river and took care of all her creations. Her name during this age was Olodililisobi, and her body—the earth itself—was as soft as that of a newborn baby.[4] The trees were without tough bark, their wood was soft and easy to cut, and their sap ran sweet and exuded delicious fragrance. There were no plants with thorns. Edible plants produced their fruit every four days. Peccaries were as harmless as their domestic cousins, and curassows were as docile as chickens. Whenever the Mother was hungry, she only had to say, "I want to eat peccary," or "I want to eat agouti," and the animal whose name she mentioned would wander into her patio. She would then dispatch it with her machete, quarter it, and roast it over her fire. To obtain fish, she merely placed a basket on the river bank, and the fish would oblige by jumping into it.

There was no misery, no suffering, no illness. The river currents ran at a tranquil pace. The sun shone softly, like the tender rays of the moon. Rain fell gently upon the soft earth. Serene breezes laced with sweet fragrances ventilated the jungle. There were no noxious insects, nor were there poisonous animals. The spirits causing illness were absent from the earth, and death was unknown.

It was into this utopian setting that the first humans—a man named Piler and his wife, Pursobi—made their appearance. They produced five sons, each of whom was a powerful shaman, and they all sired a host of children who were what the Kuna call "animal-men." These beings were not literally animals, but they possessed physical and behavioral traits that linked them with particular creatures in the forest. Among those who came into being at this time were tapir-man, jaguar-man, agouti-man, spiny anteater–man, snake-man, wasp-man, and so forth. One of the sons of Piler and Pursobi was the father of a series of virulent spirits that caused paralysis, tumors and boils, rotten vomiting, "yellow sickness," and a host of other ills. Another son was the father of cold and violent winds.

As the animal-men proliferated across the surface of the earth, corruption became prevalent and began to spread. The inhabitants of the world at this time often staged drunken feasts in which they pitted their strength against each other, brawling indiscriminately and causing havoc with their chaotic magic. Tapir-man delighted in crazed wrestling matches with manatee-man in which they would plunge through the walls of houses and snap trees in half. The father of cold brought forth cyclones and freezing blizzards for no other reason than to show off his skills. And the father of sickness spread suffering and death as a form of personal entertainment. The venom of wasps was lethal. Snakes merely had to stare at their victims to bring on fits of trembling and death.

The corruption that had tainted the inhabitants of the earth brought about a fundamental change in the nature of things. The mother's name changed to Olokwatule.[5] Her flesh became hard, and life on earth turned harsh and tenuous. The trees and bushes grew tough and fibrous, and their sap ran bitter and burned the skin. Foul smells permeated the jungle. Thorns appeared, and the edible plants became more niggardly with their fruits. The animals of the jungle were transformed into wild and dangerous beasts. The rivers swelled into violent torrents at the rainy season, and the sun's rays burned the skin. In general, nature shifted from its benign and protective stance to become unpredictable and treacherous. It was also during this time that the spiritual essence of the earth became overlaid with substance.

The Great Father, growing concerned, sent successive waves of "good men" with instructions to counsel the wrongdoers and bring them back on the moral path. These emissaries traveled far and wide, speaking and chanting in the villages of the earth, warning of impending punishments from the Great Father if they refused to correct their profligate behavior. But the villagers refused to listen. They answered the emissaries that they were fully aware of what they were doing, that they had arrived on the earth first, and that they were the direct descendants of Piler, who was the son of the Great Father and the Great Mother. Respect had dropped to such a level that chants in the gathering hall were often disrupted with loud farting.

Seeing that his attempts to turn the tide were futile, the Great Father sent cyclones and earthquakes to castigate the people. He caused the surface of the earth to turn over, and everybody was plunged to the fourth level of the cosmos, where they still reside in spiritual form. The cosmos came to have eight levels. The Great Father had his domain on the eighth level, where he cared for the spirits of the "good" people after they died on the surface of the earth; Muu continued her reproductive functions from the fourth level, as did the couple in charge of germinating the earth's plants. Indeed, the fourth level became the locus of all reproduction on earth. It also became fixed as the source of the rain, the rivers, and the sea.

Again the population of the earth increased, and with it came more corruption and disorder. The Great Father sent another man, named Mago, to counsel the wayward inhabitants. Two of Mago's children, a boy and a girl, had incestuous relations, and from their union were born eight children. The most prominent of these was Tad Ibe, who was the first great Kuna culture hero.[6] Tad Ibe and his siblings set about learning all of the principal curing chants and medicines, and with this knowledge they were able to reduce the terrible power of the evil spirits of the earth to a pale shadow of what it had been before their time.

After spending their lives combatting evil, Tad Ibe and his siblings retired to the heavens, and the history of the earth continued unfolding. Four times the earth was populated and then swept clean of the corruption that welled up and ran unchecked: first by violent winds, next by fire, then by darkness, and finally by a massive flood. When the waters of the flood subsided, the Golden People appeared. Shortly afterward, the second great culture hero, Ibeorgun, and his sister, Olokikadiryai, were sent by the Great Father to educate the new inhabitants. The Kuna at that time knew nothing of their history and lived in a state similar to that of the animals. They wandered about seminaked, knew no ceremonies, were ignorant of kinship ties, and left their dead to rot on the ground near their villages. Ibeorgun and his sister traveled over a wide range, visiting all of the Kuna villages and teaching the people their culture.

Much of what they taught the Kuna was knowledge that had been discovered by Tad Ibe and his siblings in the distant past but had been lost during the successive disasters. With their mission complete, Ibeorgun and Olokikadiryai left the surface of the earth, and nine powerful shamans arrived to continue their teachings. It was during this period that the white-skinned foreigners from a place called *Yurup* made their appearance in Kuna Yala from their home across the ocean.

THE KUNA SPIRIT WORLD

The world as it exists today has a dual nature: It is composed of what is termed "the world of spirit" and the "world of substance." The world of spirit is invisible to the waking senses yet surrounds and resides inside every material thing. Human beings, plants, animals, rocks, rivers, and villages all have invisible "souls" that are spiritual copies of the physical body.[7] The world of spirit underlies the world of substance and gives it its vital force. At the same time, it extends out in all directions through the eight levels of the cosmos, which have no material counterparts. These levels are a different order of reality, in which familiar points of reference no longer exist and human spirits can easily become disoriented and confused. Few Kuna ritual specialists allow their spirits to journey into this realm unless absolutely necessary, and only then after taking careful preparations and erecting safeguards.

The spirit realm is constantly impinging on the lives of the Kuna as they go about their daily routine. Spirits periodically attack the weak and defenseless, causing illness, deformity, and death. They roam through Kuna villages under cover of darkness, startling lonely passersby in the unlit streets and abducting their souls. Children, especially infants, are extremely vulnerable to spirit attack and must be guarded carefully day and night. Men alone in the jungle meet spirits head-on and are forced to flee for their lives. On balance, however, life is relatively benign for those who behave themselves in moral fashion and take the necessary precautions.

The spirits generally respect those who follow the rules, which are recorded in and reinforced by Kuna tradition.

According to Kuna tradition, certain places beyond the perimeter of the village are designated sanctuaries of spiritual animals, plants, or "demons." There are communities of spirits living in the hills and mountains on the mainland; in "whirlpools" found below the surface of the ocean, lakes, rivers, and swamps; and in clouds floating through the sky. The mainland domains are often described by the Kuna as "corrals" full of terrestrial animals; whenever the numbers of certain species become depleted in the jungle, their "guardians" replenish the supply by releasing a fresh inventory from the corrals. In similar fashion, during the months when the rivers flood and the seas become unruly, fish, turtles, and all manner of marine creatures are being expelled from the whirlpools of the earth. And the giant clouds that billow and roll across the mainland at the height of the wet season carry jungle animals that are discharged into the forest with rain. It is through the collective medium of liquid—the menstrual blood of the Mother—flowing from the center of the cosmos toward the surface of the earth that the jungle and the sea are continuously being replenished with living things.

Underlaid and animated by a realm of spirit, the Kuna earth is a living being, the source of all life. It is the body of the Mother, who carries on her never-ending task of regenerating the planet with newly born plants and animals from her womb deep in the bowels of the cosmos. The thick mantle of rain forest covering the mountains and valleys constitutes the Mother's "green clothes." The rivers are simultaneously seen by the Kuna as the Mother's vagina, for their reproductive function, and as her breasts, because they nurture her creatures with her milk. She provides the Kuna with food, building materials, firewood, and countless other materials they need to survive; and Kuna leaders, in the nightly gathering sessions, constantly admonish their people to treat her and all of her things with respect.

THE KUNA AND CONSERVATION

This worldview constitutes the philosophical basis of what might be termed the Kuna "conservationist ethic." The crucial thread running through it is respect for the earth and the need for humans to care for its natural endowment. In fact, the Kuna have personalized nature in such a way that animals, plants, and spirits are dealt with as if they were human beings. They must be treated with respect, flattered, and negotiated with. For example, Kuna medicine men initiate the gathering of plant medicines by approaching the plants and explaining the reason for their mission. They then follow strict etiquette in cutting off pieces of the plants, wrapping them in leaves, and placing them in fiber baskets for the journey home. Once the medicines have been prepared for use, the medicine men "counsel" the souls of the plants regarding the behavior expected of them within the patient's body. All of this is performed in the most civil manner; even when dealing with illness-causing spirits, Kuna ritualists behave with courtesy and deference.

The idea of creating the Nusagandi preserve as a "botanical park" came from the Kuna belief in "spirit sanctuaries" in the forest that are the exclusive domain of colonies of spirits. Although these sanctuaries are often situated on choice agricultural land within easy distance of Kuna villages, they may not be cleared of their natural vegetation. Certain of the larger trees, in particular, must not be taken down, for it is in their branches that the spirits string their clotheslines. When these areas are violated, either consciously or unwittingly, the resident spirits commonly rise up in rage and retaliate by unleashing epidemics and pestilence on the community of the transgressor. However, these spirit territories can be safely visited for the purpose of collecting plant medicines, an activity that is carried out with respect. The area of the Nusagandi park along the Continental Divide, although not a known spirit sanctuary, was explicitly viewed by its founders as a natural refuge and botanical garden in this same tradition.

CRACKS IN THE OLD BELIEFS

The Kuna worldview, although constantly evolving and incorporating new elements throughout the march of history, has maintained its coherence in large part because the Kuna have enjoyed unusual geographic isolation from the rest of the world, a circumstance that has allowed them to keep their social and political institutions intact. The gathering sessions lie at the heart of a cultural system that has socialized generation after generation into the Kuna way, maintaining continuity and coherence. However, pressures coming from inside and outside of Kuna society during the last decades have greatly eroded this insularity, to the point where the Comarca is now something of a patchwork of communities running from the highly acculturated to the staunchly traditional. Whatever the stance of any particular community may be, accelerated change has become a central fact of life throughout the region. Perhaps the best way to understand this process is by focusing first on the role of Western education.

WESTERN EDUCATION IN KUNA YALA

In 1904, the community of Narganá, located approximately six hours by motorboat to the east of Cartí, elected an acculturated Kuna named Charly

Robinson to the position of first chief. Robinson had been raised by an English family on the Colombian island of Providencia, and when he reached adulthood he returned to the island of his birth with the mission of "civilizing" his people. Shortly after becoming chief he made an arrangement with the Panamanian government to send seventeen village boys to school in Panama City, and in 1907, on the urging of the Catholic Church and the government, he accepted a priest named Leonardo Gassó to preach the gospel and run a community school. Although there were mixed feelings about this development on the island of Narganá and on nearby Corazón de Jesús, without exception all of the surrounding Kuna communities reacted with strong opposition. The threat of violence rose to such a height that in 1908 Robinson asked the Panamanian government for and received a shipment of guns and ammunition to defend the island from attack.

Over the next three or four decades, Western education alternated among several religious missions, yet it grew steadily amid conflict and periodic flare-ups. It expanded its sphere of influence gradually at first, then more rapidly, until by the 1960s it had become implanted in virtually every community in the region. Whereas the communities near Narganá and Corazón de Jesús were at first strongly against the penetration of Western education, they eventually fell firmly into the grip of the school system. Today it must be said that although teachers in the more traditional holdout communities are still fighting a rear-guard battle with community elders, the effect of Western education on the greater part of the Comarca has been significant, and its range is steadily expanding.

All healthy societies must adapt to changing conditions, and it is evident that Kuna culture has been modified considerably through time. It was only during the nineteenth century, for example, that the Kuna began living on the coral islands off the coast, and at some point during this time the women started sewing the reverse appliqué blouses called *molas*. The use of steel, introduced by the Spaniards, certainly ushered in a revolution in the way the Kuna exploited the mainland jungle, and the arrival of crops such as bananas, plantains, coconuts, and rice—all of which are now staples among the Kuna—transformed their agriculture in a fundamental way. These changes no doubt provoked profound adjustments in Kuna life, but they could be and were incorporated into the Kuna worldview; because the Kuna managed to hold on to their autonomy, they maintained control over the process of change.

However, the introduction of Western education in this century has set off a process of change that is essentially different from the change the Kuna experienced in the past: It has begun to alter their minds, making a direct hit on their worldview. In many of the more highly acculturated communities, all school-age children are obliged to attend classes through the sixth grade; as a result, the school has taken over a large portion of the socialization functions previously exercised by the family. This regulation effectively takes all of the boys out of the jungle at precisely the time when, under the old system, they would have been accompanying their fathers to the mainland and learning how to farm, hunt, gather firewood, and carry out other traditional activities. Students are not expected or encouraged to expend their energies on manual tasks, and when classes are finished in the early afternoon they can be found roaming about the island, visiting with friends, playing basketball, or studying. On the islands with schools up to the ninth grade (such as Ustuppu and Narganá), many boys reach the age of eighteen or twenty with no experience in the activities that had been standard for all Kuna men in the past. They have no knowledge of the jungle or the sea, they know nothing about farming, and they have no particular interest in ever gaining such experience. The girls, for their part, spend little time learning women's activities. In the eyes of a Catholic nun who taught for more than two decades in Kuna Yala after her arrival in the 1950s:

> Most of those who have received only elementary education (through the 6th grade) continue cultivating laziness and do not cultivate the land. Their families complain about this situation and say that when the old men, who are the ones who presently are interested in agriculture and have not attended school, die, hunger will come to the tribe because of the laziness of the youth; and they throw the blame on modern education, on Western Civilization, which has caused these changes.[8]

Perhaps the saddest aspect of this pattern is that in the most acculturated communities the majority of the young people no longer learn much of anything from their parents. In the eyes of the youth, the wealth of skills and experience possessed by the elders have become largely irrelevant.

The degree to which Western education has penetrated and even come to dominate Kuna culture was not foreseen by many of the elders who promoted it in the early years. Nele Kantule, perhaps the most important Kuna chief of this century,[9] was leader of the community of Ustuppu, located roughly at the midpoint of the Comarca, from the early part of the century until his death in 1944. In the 1920s, Nele recruited two Kuna teachers who had been educated by the missionaries at Narganá and established a small school on his island to teach basic skills in reading and writing. He envisioned Western education as a two-pronged weapon: On the one hand, the Kuna could use it to learn the skills of the Panamanians and confront them on their own terms; on the other hand, it would allow them to write down the words of the chants, copy the ancient histories and keep them in books, and in this way guard against cultural loss. At the same time, he was aware of the dangers of this strategy and constantly preached against perversion of the newly introduced system. Beyond this, he recruited Kuna teachers rather than non-Kunas.

Yet, try as they might, the Kuna were unable to control and direct the force they had unleashed. By the 1940s, the Ustuppu school had grown to a building made from imported wood planks housing six grades. By the mid-1970s, the school had become so large it had to be relocated to a sprawling cement structure on an adjacent island. It had an enrollment of over 1,000 students between kindergarten and the ninth grade and was taught by a squadron of forty Kuna teachers.[10]

The growth in school size and number has been steady and rapid since the 1960s, and the effects of the spread of Western education have been pervasive. It must be said that Nele was a prophet in foreseeing the importance of education as a defensive weapon on the national level. By comparison with other Indian groups in Panama, the Kuna have proved themselves extremely successful in competing in the arena of Panamanian politics. They have among their number lawyers, doctors, agronomists, biologists, sociologists, economists, and anthropologists who have attended universities in Europe, the United States, and Mexico, as well as in Panama; one Kuna, a medical doctor, reached the position of Vice-Minister of Health in the mid-1980s. The school system in Kuna Yala is staffed almost entirely by Kuna teachers. All of this expertise, combined with the Kuna's innate sense of cohesion and organization, has allowed them to develop institutions that operate with relative effectiveness in the dangerous waters of the Panamanian political scene.

However, Western education brought side effects that neither Nele nor his colleagues were able to hold at bay. Nele apparently pictured the accumulation of reading and writing skills as something useful yet minor, something extra and discrete, akin to a lamination that would add to the whole without invading and blending with the traditional Kuna core. At no time did he entertain the notion that his people should have their cultural identity eroded away, leading them in the direction of becoming Panamanians, or that modern education would drastically transform their minds. Yet this is essentially what has occurred. Although they have picked up useful skills, the younger Kuna in the areas of deepest penetration of Western education have been socialized into an alien value system, with all its accompanying prejudices and biases, to the point where they are fundamentally different from their parents. In these communities, there is not only a generation gap between the elders and the youth but also a cultural gap; the children have been educated with a different worldview through the medium of a foreign language (Spanish). Beyond this, the alien culture has been promoted as superior to the old ways. For years, students in the schools have been told that the Kuna language is a lowly "dialect" and that education will prepare them for a life that is considerably more "civilized" than that of their parents, who are simple farmers. Traditional history and ritual have been seen as primitive and therefore amusing at best. In a community study done by the students at the Ustuppu school in 1973, beliefs relating to curing are called "superstitions." The authors of this study go on to explain that the old belief system is disappearing: "Through education one succeeds bit by bit to change this traditional mentality that in part affects them. The teaching of science makes them recognize their error."[11]

Although this degree of repudiation of the traditional worldview is not yet found in the more remote communities, it is advancing on them inexorably and has spawned varying degrees of confusion and ambivalence among those who have been run through the educational system. The students on the most acculturated islands are not like their parents in many ways, but they are still Kuna; they may speak some Spanish and they have learned to read and write, but they are not Panamanians. It is common for the older men in the more acculturated communities to accuse the youths of not being "genuine Kuna" because they have no understanding or knowledge of traditional history and ritual and no sense of what or who is "important" in the traditional scheme of things. Their identity as "genuine Kuna" is fragmentary, and their identification with Panamanians is even more tenuous. In a very real sense, the youths who find themselves in this state are neither fish nor fowl.

ATTEMPTS TO RECAPTURE THE PAST

Since the early 1970s, many younger Kuna from acculturated communities—and especially those with a high school or university education—have been making attempts to rediscover their cultural roots and reclaim their status as "genuine Kuna," giving birth to an incipient revitalization movement. Individuals throughout the region are giving Kuna names to newborn babies (instead of Spanish and English names, which had been the custom for years), and communities are drafting official legislation to make participation in select rituals mandatory, erecting special buildings for ritual purposes, and introducing traditional history as an integral part of school curriculum. Among the most substantial projects have been the taping and transcribing of ritual chants and the creation of artwork depicting mythological themes. Kuna youths have established a number of *centros* in Panama City and on several of the larger islands dedicated to the study of Kuna culture, and some of the members, many of whom have university training, are actively involved in learning the more esoteric of the traditions.

The PEMASKY project was conceived as a receptacle in which the old culture would be mixed with Western science to create some sort of synthesis. Since the beginning, personnel from PEMASKY have been key actors in the Centro de Investigaciones Kunas (CIK), a small research group staffed mainly by Kuna social scientists. In the early and mid-1980s, the CIK managed to initiate several community studies and carry out

research into traditional hunting and agroforestry systems, and PE-
MASKY's presence drew it toward the conjunction of indigenous culture
and natural resource management. Kuna ethnobotany was eyed as a crucial
area of investigation, one that could be meshed with Western scientific
botany. By the same token, there was considerable internal discussion of
how to coordinate the Kuna understanding of the animal kingdom with the
zoology of scientists working through the Smithsonian Tropical Research
Institute. Kuna ritual specialists were to be brought to the park area to
identify and label plants, and there was talk of holding seminars and
courses in traditional knowledge.

THE FALTERING REVIVAL

Unfortunately, very few of the items on PEMASKY's agenda have received even cursory treatment. Outside of a few broad statements about
the importance of traditional knowledge, nothing substantial ever came of
their endeavors to work it into their operational program. No texts of
chants or stories relating to nature were collected, and no scheme was developed to bring traditional specialists to the park area to accompany
members of the technical team. There was a short foray into the study of
traditional agroforestry systems, but that fizzled rapidly, and nothing followed the initial (and very superficial) studies undertaken by one member
of the technical team and an English agronomist from the Centro
Agronómico Tropical de Investigación y Enseñanza (CATIE) in Costa
Rica. In 1987, work was begun at Nusagandi on a small botanical garden
of bushes and trees labeled with Kuna and scientific names, but this effort
was abandoned after a short time.

By the same token, virtually all of the projects of PEMASKY and
other *centros* over the last fifteen or so years to tape and transcribe oral
histories and produce books and pamphlets have been either inconsequen-
tial or ineffectual. Attempts by community leaders in highly acculturated
areas to reinstitute the yearly round of festivals and rituals and make participation mandatory have consistently met with failure. As a general rule,
in communities where a heavy erosion of traditional life has already occurred, programs designed to roll back the clock and recapture the past
have not been successful. Where tradition remains strong, there is no perceived need to preserve esoteric knowledge; the people simply continue
practicing their rituals and submerging themselves in the oral histories,
nervously watching the advance of Western culture on the periphery. The
process of displacement marches forward.

In the most acculturated communities, as well as in Panama City,
some young Kuna have made attempts to recast the old knowledge in a
new mold through the production of plays and poetry. These works are

quite interesting in that they contain bits and pieces of the oral traditions but are decidedly Western in structure and emotional tenor. The chants and the public speaking of the gathering sessions are filled with intricate and highly colorful metaphors and images and marked by a characteristic stoic cadence (see Howe, 1979). By contrast, the creations of the youths are superficial in their traditional content, display a distant relationship to the jungle (although it is invariably a central element), and introduce themes and emotions that are more common in Panamanian culture than among the Kuna. (For example, youthful love between the sexes is often expressed in a florid romanticism that has no fit in traditional Kuna culture.) However well done these pieces may be—and the plays are generally popular among both Kuna and non-Kuna in Panama City—they have little resemblance to the old traditions. They are made out of mostly new cloth and cut to a new pattern.

All attempts to revive and revitalize the traditional oral histories and the rituals have fizzled, and I would like to suggest a few explanations. These attempts have met with heavy resistance for reasons intimately related to the factors at play in the steady decline in ritual knowledge in general. First, attempts to record and transcribe the chants have been marred by a lack of coherent methodology and coordination. One aspect of this incoherence is the fact that no standard alphabet for Kuna, an unwritten language, has yet been decided upon.[12] In 1975, a linguist with the Ministry of Education attempted to organize a group of young teachers at the Ustuppu school for the purpose of developing a bilingual-bicultural program for all of Kuna Yala. This effort lasted less than a week, becoming mired in a battle over the proper orthography to be used as well as general confusion among the teachers over methodology. Verbal battles erupted between generations over the sacred character of the traditions, and in the end the elders voted in the gathering to have the linguist removed from the island. Clearly, the inability of the Kuna to agree upon an official alphabet involves much more than mechanical linguistic considerations.

Perhaps most important, however, is the fact that the youths regard the traditional histories and curing chants more as curious museum pieces than as practical knowledge they might utilize in the context of daily life. Whereas Kuna elders treat the oral histories as living documents that describe, elaborate upon, and interpret the world, the youths perceive them as exotic narratives describing a foreign realm, much in the same way that present-day Europeans regard the "fairy tales" of the brothers Grimm.

The acculturated youths are not willing to spend much time in the community gathering hall listening to long hours of chants to learn the traditions. They are even less willing to learn the curing professions because all of the chants—which contain the most secret and profound knowledge of the Kuna symbolic world—are performed in a ritual language that is so different from colloquial Kuna as to be unintelligible to the uninitiated.[13]

The youths want to receive the traditional histories and theories of how the universe functions in abridged form in a book or a magazine that they can pull off the shelf and read when the urge takes them. They are primarily curious because they believe that the chants will tell them something about what it means to be a "genuine Kuna," but the chants hold little meaning for them beyond this. They are not interested in becoming ritual specialists like their fathers, nor are they anxious to become chanters in the gathering hall. In other words, traditional knowledge has a fundamentally different meaning for the elders and the acculturated youths, and the ways in which they deal with it are very different.

Second, in order to understand the substance of traditional views of the world, a young Kuna male must have a thorough knowledge of the jungle. He must know how to identify plants and animals. He must know how particular animals behave, how the rivers and the jungle change during the yearly cycle, where spirits live and what the names of their domains are, and a whole series of things that can only be learned through intimate and sustained contact with the mainland, the coastal estuaries, and the offshore reefs. Without this knowledge, learned firsthand through years of work and study in the jungle and at sea, the chants are next to meaningless. Medicines and materials used for a variety of domestic tasks cannot be found, and animals cannot be identified, much less hunted. Unless the youths become farmers like their fathers, any attempt to recover the past through the study of ritual knowledge will be both futile and hollow.

Third, even those youths who express interest in relearning the oral traditions often see no particular value in what they are doing beyond what they can personally gain, and this is limited. Years ago, ritual specialists never expected monetary remuneration for their services. Instead, they were seen as social servants and accorded special status in the community, which was considered reward enough. In the more acculturated communities, however, the prestige value of ritual has declined steadily over the last few decades, and most specialists now charge modest fees for their services to keep in line with the cash economy that has so thoroughly permeated the region. Because ritual professions demand long and arduous training and no longer bestow either much money or prestige upon their possessors, few youths are interested in embarking on ritual careers. In the present scheme of things, there is little incentive to learn ritual knowledge either as a specialist or a layman. It simply lacks the social meaning it formerly had.

Fourth, demographic patterns have altered to such an extent over the past fifty years that people in many communities can no longer find the time to become ritual specialists or even to participate in ritual events such as the puberty and mass exorcism ceremonies. In the 1930s, many Kuna households contained twenty or more people and had five or six adult men providing for the subsistence needs of the members. The labor force was large and well organized around household needs, and food, by all accounts, was generally abundant and varied. Because all of the subsistence fronts were so thoroughly covered and money was not yet involved in the food economy, it was possible for virtually every household to support one or more ritual specialists within their ranks, and there was always time to participate in ceremonies and festivals.

Today, with massive out-migration of the adult male population to urban centers in Panama, household size has diminished to as much as a quarter of the earlier figure, and it is common to find a single adult male—often a man over the age of fifty—serving as the sole provider of the wide selection of staple products from the mainland jungle. In many communities fewer than half of the men of productive age are involved in agriculture, and although some cash generally filters back to the community from members working in Panama City or Colon, procurement of food is a constant problem. Given this situation, it is no longer realistic to allow potential providers to spend extended periods learning rituals, gathering medicines in far-off corners of the jungle, or making lengthy preparations for ritual events. Even participation in the ceremonies, some of which may last for up to eight consecutive days, puts too much of a strain on things. Quite simply, virtually everybody is absorbed with productive activities, leaving them little time for anything else—especially when that "anything else" no longer holds the prestige it had in the past.

All of these obstacles have been magnified for the members of PEMASKY's technical team, for the park project is physically located in what amount to three geographically and culturally separate worlds: Panama City, where the project's main office is located; the Nusagandi site, perched in quiet isolation on the crest of the Continental Divide; and the island communities of Kuna Yala. Travel among the three sites is difficult and time consuming. The journey from Panama City to the islands involves a small plane to one of the sand and gravel airstrips along the coast; travel among the islands, which are strung out over 200 kilometers of coastline, must be made in motor-driven dugout canoe. The Nusagandi center can only be reached from Panama City after a three-hour trip in a four-wheel-drive vehicle over a precipitous mud and gravel road, and travel from the center to the Kuna Yala coast is a very treacherous undertaking. Consequently, project staff have never been able to move easily back and forth among the three sites, and few of the elders have shown interest in hiking the twenty-one kilometers along the road leading from the coast up through the foothills to the Continental Divide. Consequently, members of the technical team have ended up spending most of their time in Panama City, where their families live.

After all, Panama City is the stage for virtually all of PEMASKY's contact with agencies supplying technical and financial assistance; the bulk of the meetings, paperwork, phone calls, and other diplomatic and bureaucratic work is done there. In this realm, the Western worldview holds overwhelming sway. The common language is Spanish. The staff has been working steadily since the project's inception to produce large numbers of technical documents, and most of their work has had to follow guidelines dictated by the non-Kuna world. One example of this non-Kuna orientation is a comprehensive management plan that is structured largely on a model offered by CATIE. This document is a requirement to gain the designation of "biosphere reserve," which the Kuna have been seeking since 1985.[14] Given this situation, it is not surprising that in the project as a whole, the Western scientific side of the supposed equation has received far more treatment than has the traditional knowledge of the older generation of Kuna Yala.

THE FUTURE

As the Kuna confront the coming decades, they stand at a crucial transitional stage in their evolution. The old world is passing out of existence in some villages and hanging on for dear life in others, while the new world, with its concomitant values and beliefs, is stepping in to fill the spaces left empty. Non-Kuna influences have reached virtually every corner of the region in ways that Nele Kantule never could have understood.

Many observers have spoken of the Kuna's vitality and instinct for survival, noting the remarkable way in which they have adapted and retained their identity in a changing world that each day embraces them more tightly. It may well be that the Kuna will manage to preserve their social, political, and economic autonomy for some time to come and endure as a group. Even if this occurs, though, they will emerge with a greatly altered social system, rendering much of the old worldview anachronistic and irrelevant. The old traditions are so intimately bound up with the old way of life that as the old way of life changes, so must the belief system that explains it and gives it symbolic importance. A new synthesis will surely emerge. But the core of the Kuna's rich, expressive culture, encompassing the collective history of the tribe and the complex of beliefs relating to the way in which the universe operates, can only be retained in a traditional setting, and this is disappearing rapidly.

One crucial question relating directly to the work at Nusagandi remains: If the traditional belief system described in this chapter disappears and is no longer a living part of their culture, will the Kuna continue to treat the earth and all of its creatures with the same respect? Will the new ecological ethic of the Western scientific tradition be able to perform anything approaching the same function?

NOTES

The ideas in this paper have gained substance from lengthy discussion, stretching over the last 20 years, with James Howe. Both of us agree that the discussion is far from finished.

1. The name Kuna Yala means "Kuna territory" in Kuna. Just recently, the Kuna have chosen this term in preference to "San Blas." This latter term is still used by most Panamanians and is found in virtually all of the literature on the Kuna.

Peter Herlihy defines the Panamanian concept of comarca as "an Indian homeland with semiautonomous political organization under jurisdiction of the federal government." See "Panama's Quiet Revolution: *Comarca* Homelands and Indian Rights," *Cultural Survival Quarterly*, Vol. 13, No. 3, pp. 17–24.

2. The most comprehensive discussion of the "gathering" as the heart of Kuna political life is found in Howe 1986.

3. The bulk of this discussion comes from Mac Chapin, *Pab Igala: Historias de la Tradición Kuna* (Centro de Investigaciones Antropológicas, Universidad de Panamá, 1970), and *Curing Among the San Blas Kuna of Panama* (unpublished Ph.D. thesis, University of Arizona, 1983), together with countless conversations with James Howe.

4. The word *dilidiligwa* means "soft, bland"; as one Kuna ritualist told me, "like the flesh of a newborn baby."

5. From the word *kwa*: the heart of a tree, thus hard.

6. Tad Ibe was the sun. His most important brother was Puiksu, the morning star. His other brothers—Olele, Puutule, Kwatkwatule, Olowagibipilele, and Olosuignibelele—were stars, as was the only female of the group, Olowai-ili.

7. The Kuna word *purba* has many related meanings and can be translated in different contexts as "soul," "spirit," "shadow," "image" (e.g., "face image" equals "photograph"), "menstrual blood" (red *purba*), "semen" (white *purba*), and "secret," among others. It can be taken to mean the underlying essence of material things.

8. L. Soto, Sor Rosa Maria, *La Estructura de la Familia en la Tribu Cuna* (Disertación a Licenciatura en Misiología, Pontificia Universidad Urbaniana, Roma, 1973), p. 175.

9. Regina Evans Holloman, *Developmental Change in San Blas* (unpublished Ph.D. thesis, Northwestern University, 1969), pp. 437–454; Chapin, *Curing Among the San Blas Kuna*, pp. 444–467.

10. Chapin, *Curing Among the San Blas Kuna*, p. 469.

11. Ibid., p. 478.

12. Several systems have been proposed over the years. The Baptists have translated the bible with an orthography later approximated by the Swedish linguist Nils Holmer (1951). Holmer's system was adopted by Sherzer, Chapin, and James Howe (*The Kuna Gathering: Contemporary Village Politics in Panama*, University of Texas Press, 1986.) However, I have since dropped this orthography because it is misleading for the general reader (eg. "k" has a soft [voiced] "g" sound, whereas "kk" has a hard [unvoiced] "k" sound), and the Kuna themselves generally reject it. Kuna attempts over the years to standardize their script for the purposes of bilingual education have all met with violent debate, and no resolution has been reached.

13. Joel Sherzer, *Kuna Ways of Speaking: An Ethnographic Perspective* (Austin: University of Texas Press, 1983), pp. 21–71; Chapin, *Curing Among the San Blas Kuna*, pp. 179–206.

14. The biosphere reserve designation, sponsored by the Man and the Biosphere (MAB) program, carries no legal weight, but it would enable the Kuna a certain amount of protection for their park because of international recognition.

6

Black Poetry of Coastal Ecuador
•
Juan García Salazar

Born in 1944, Juan García Salazar grew up in a small village near the mouth of the Santiago River in Ecuador's Esmeraldas Province. His mother, a local woman, was black; his father, a refugee from the Spanish Civil War, was a Spaniard. When Juan was five, his father died, and his mother sent him to live with a doctor from a nearby island who promised to take care of the boy in exchange for his labor.

Forced to leave school early to earn a living, Juan is largely self-educated. He learned Italian while studying at an orphanage run by Italian priests, and he learned French while living with a French-speaking family. He has an extensive knowledge of African poetry written in French and has studied source materials on the slave trade from French West Africa. He learned research skills and anthropological techniques while working as a field assistant for several scientists. Along the way, he also acquired some English.

Since early childhood, Juan has held one job or another. As a boy, he sailed with his mother throughout the local island estuaries as far as Tumaco to trade rice for clothing. Later, he learned carpentry. He operated a small factory in Bogotá for several years before eventually returning to Esmeraldas as a volunteer social worker and schoolteacher in the black communities along the Santiago River.

After his return to Esmeraldas, Juan became increasingly disturbed by the rapid and widespread dissolution of traditional black culture. At the heart of the tradition were *décimas,* an adapted form of Spanish poetry, and the *decimero,* the person who recited memorized poems and/or composed new ones. The personal and group experiences of generations of black Ecuadorians were embedded in this rich oral lore. Now, those voices were being drowned out by radio and television and by standardized school curricula. Since neither Ecuadorian nor foreign anthropologists had taken much interest in studying or recording this oral tradition—and since illiteracy among blacks was high—Esmeraldas' past seemed about to disappear without a trace. So, using a tape recorder, a camera, his notebook, and his skill as an interviewer, Juan launched a one-man campaign to collect, catalog, and study examples of Afro-Ecuadorian culture.

In 1978, he received a small grant from the Central Bank of Ecuador, which helped support him while he collected décimas. A grant from the Inter-American Foundation has assisted Juan's work since 1980 on a more extensive project that includes the studying of rituals, myths, folk medicine, music, and household artifacts in Ecuador's two major black communities—Chota and Esmeraldas—and researching archives on slavery.

Beyond his own studies, Juan has worked hard to promote and publicize Afro-Ecuadorian culture to all of his countrymen and to blacks in particular. He has lectured at the Banco Central in Quito, at the Military Academy, at universities, cultural centers, schools, and in peasant communities. He has also provided materials to schools and has directed a thesis, Slavery in Ecuador. In 1979, he gathered a group of about 15 black university students and professionals together in Quito to found the Afro-Ecuadorian Study Center. The center recently published the first of a forthcoming series of Cuadernos Afro-Ecuatorianos (Afro-Ecuadorian Pamphlets) to disseminate information about black-Ecuadorian culture to urban and rural blacks.

●

Black slaves sailed to America with the first Spanish explorers, traveling with their masters on expeditions throughout the New World. But until 1517, when the slave trade between Africa and America began, those blacks were born in Europe and had been Christianized. Africans were not permitted in the Americas out of fear that their religion might "contaminate" the Indian population.

After the traffic began, of course, colonists were usually contemptuous of their new slaves and their traditions, characterizing Africans as so dull-witted that there was no point in educating them or their children. In the Spanish colonies, in fact, it was illegal to teach blacks to read or write, and oral instruction was limited to religion and work-training.

The ability of blacks to preserve their ancestral traditions depended not only on the moral and legal codes of their European owners, but also on the attitudes of native Indian populations, on geography, and on climate. Ecuador was a relatively benign area for the Africans, and its black communities were able to sustain much of their African heritage. African culture was also preserved by *cimarrones,* or runaway slaves, who started independent communities far beyond the reach of any owner (although in these clandestine and isolated societies, ancestral traditions were fragmented since the cimarrones came from different tribes). Finally slaves were permitted to entertain themselves on certain feast days; and the music they played, the stories they told, their drums, dances, riddles, and oral poetry fused into the new syncretic culture of black America.

When slaves did maintain some of their African traditions despite the diaspora, those practices were ridiculed by other Latin Americans and were even forbidden by law. Black freedmen frequently tried to improve their status by assimilating Spanish culture, forgetting their slave past, and denying their African heritage. Those efforts to rise socially and economically usually failed, and blacks remained in the poorest, most-deprived class. Any use of African tradition in the literature of the day was seen as proof of poor taste, and both writers and critics tried to erase all such traces. Blacks with even a rudimentary education copied the European models adopted by the local ruling class.

The Negritude Movement, which began in Paris during the 1930s among black students from the French colonies of Africa, paved the way for acceptance of black poetry by educated Latin Americans. Black poetry was also promoted by a shift in Latin American literature that took place during the late 19th century. Many writers began to search for national identity and a "continental awareness" to protest the social injustices that were inherited from Spanish colonialism. The fate of blacks came to be seen as an integral part of the history of that oppression, and the new attitude helped legitimize black literature as an art form.

The literature of black Ecuadorians has centered on oral poetry. It has been given the Spanish name of *décima*, although its form is very different from the classic composition created by Vicente Espinel in the 16th century. The Spanish décima is a stanza with 10 lines of eight syllables each and a strict rhyme scheme of *abbaaccddc*. The American décima found in Ecuador is a poem that begins with a *redondilla* (a four-line stanza) that is composed of the last lines of the four 10–line stanzas that follow. Generally, rhyme and meter are looser in the American version.

The American décima is a child of both African and Hispanic culture. Of course the language is Spanish, as is the original form, and Christian motifs frequently appear in the poems. But it is Africa which provided the framework that explains why these poems have been so important to Ecuadorian blacks. In Africa, there were two kinds of poets: chroniclers and storytellers (or balladeers). In both cases the poetry was oral. The poet was required to memorize poems that had been handed down and also to compose new ones. The chronicler was a highly respected person who knew by heart the genealogy of the village or clan chief, recounted heroic deeds, and recorded the customs of the group. Chronicles often stretched back to the creation of the world, and chroniclers were consulted as though they were living libraries. The balladeer, or storyteller, on the other hand, was known for his wit as well as his memory. Balladeers preserved the proverbs, the stories, and the anecdotal history of the group. They also performed in public literary duels that tested each poet's ability to compose spontaneous, sometimes barbed, verse.

In Ecuador, the *decimero* (the reciter of décimas) is both chronicler and balladeer. A decimero may compose his own poetry or the décimas may be handed down, but the language is highly figurative and rhythmic to make memorization easier and to display artistic mastery. The style feels African, and traditional African themes are often used.

Basically, there are two kinds of décimas: those that deal with the "human" and those that deal with the "divine." *Décimas a lo divino* have their roots in Catholicism, the only religion the slaves could safely practice. Catholicism not only promised the slaves a better world to come, but by devoutly embracing their masters' religion, slaves gained their masters' confidence. Even today, decimeros receive special status for their knowledge of the Bible. The subjects of divine décimas range widely: from tender evocations of Jesus, to meditations on original sin, to speculations about the end of the world.

Décimas a lo humano range across the whole social life of coastal blacks. In these poems, the poet can interpret and narrate his community's experience. Many décimas recount historical events—often the community's only historical record. Other poems are satirical—pricking pompous politicians, Hispanic culture, or local attitudes. Some décimas are simply good stories—flights of fantasy.

Ecuador's black poets also engage in *argumentos*, or poetic duels. The duels use the décima form, and also focus either on the divine (*argumentos a lo divino*) or the human (*argumentos a lo humano*). One decimero recites a poem, and the next poet must respond. Grounded in spontaneity, these literary faceoffs challenge the competing poets' verbal dexterity, their wit, and their knowledge of the Bible and secular subjects (even such unlikely ones as mathematics). Argumentos are full of flash and thunder, and they provide a forum where younger poets can also display their talents.

For the past seven years, I have been tape recording and transcribing décimas. More recently I focused my research on Esmeraldas and Imbabura Provinces, which have the two largest black populations.

Since there is no living decimero tradition in the Chota Valley of Imbabura, my field assistants and I did our actual décima-collecting in Esmeraldas. We divided the province into two sections that we visited for 10 months each. The northern zone ran from Rio Verde in the south to San Lorenzo in the north and included the Santiago and Onzole Rivers. In this area we studied seven key communities: La Tola, Limones, San Lorenzo, Playa de Oro, Izquandé, Río Verde, and Chontaduro. These communities are about 20 kilometers from each other. Some are located on the coast while others are situated along the rivers. The northern region is very difficult to reach, and the influence of modern culture is less apparent. As a result, the old ways are more purely intact. All of the decimeros we found who also composed their own poetry came from this area.

The southern zone extended from Rio Grande in the north to the Muisne River in the south and included the Quinindé River. Here there were larger towns, such as Esmeraldas and Quinindé, and more modern forms of communication. The area is a center for commerce and tourism. Not surprisingly, authentic traditions are being lost more quickly here, and there are no more decimeros who compose their own work. We visited many settlements but found decimeros who could recite the older décimas only in Esmeraldas, Quinindé, Atacames, and Muisne.

As soon as we heard of a decimero in either the north or south, we would visit him. First we would chat and ask about his background: his age, place of birth, job, and so forth. Then we would ask him to talk about his work as a decimero. Did he compose or only recite? Where had he learned his décimas? Where was he known? Finally, the decimero would recite some of the work he knew so that it could be recorded on cassettes. We could not ask the poets to write down their décimas since almost all of the reciters were illiterate.

Once the material was collected, décimas had to be transcribed while taking care to preserve the idioms, the metaphors, and the new words coined by each decimero. Afterwards, it seemed like a good idea to prepare a glossary so that the poems would be more accessible to the general reader.

Altogether, we collected about 300 décimas and interviewed about 20 decimeros. A representative anthology of these poems and an analysis of the tradition were recently published by the Banco del Ecuador, which will make the work more available to the Ecuadorian public. Ironically though, even as we began making a written record, the end of the tradition seemed nearer. We found only about half-a-dozen young decimeros, and the radio is displacing oral poetry in even the remotest areas.

I do not believe that my collection of décimas will reverse or stop any of these trends. Preservation of the past, however, has opened up some new possibilities for the future. A wealth of information has been gathered which has, in turn, spawned books and even dissertations on black culture in Ecuador. Some of the décimas may be used by the Ministry of Culture as basic educational material in the schools and in adult literacy programs. The décimas can also be used more informally by small study groups that form around an interest in black culture. Even the radio, which thus far has been a negative force, could play a part in maintaining oral traditions. There are cultural programs that need suitable materials to broadcast, and the décimas are there, waiting to be used. Finally, black Ecuadorians now will be able to refer to their own established and written record of a legitimate tradition of literature. Pride in past accomplishments strengthens self-respect and lays the groundwork for future development.

"Complaint Against the Railroad"
There's a complaint before the judge,
the judge of the circuit court:
the train has killed some boys
along the railroad track.

"Come here, Mr. Railroad,"
His Honor called aloud,
"Why did you kill the boys
who were only walking around?"
"Oh sir, I don't kill anyone,
they make me—it's the truth.
The boys just ask for trouble,
they always look for death,
and I don't care if people
complain before the judge."

There's a brakeman on the train,
you'd think he'd look around
for guys standing on the track
so he won't run them down.
He should stop the train right away
and not just let it race,
for the life of any man
is worth a lot to the state,
and this complaint's been brought
before the circuit judge.

If this is true then I
can save Railroad some strife;
nobody is to blame
if a man throws away his life.
The railroad runs along
its track in a race against time;
and if the brakeman wanted to,
he just couldn't stop on a dime.
The train just couldn't stop
along the railroad track.

"Let's All Get Together"
Let's all get together
all of us in Limones
and ask the Health Department
to get rid of the rats.
People are in trouble:
a huge army of rats
eats up all our food
and even scares the cats.
No animal is as smart
as the wily, clever rat.
No trap can catch him
and he's growing very fat.
All of us in Limones
let's all get together.

One day a woman said
"I've lost a bar of soap."
Later she found out that
it and a rat eloped.
A perfumed bar of soap,
what could they want it for?
They can't eat the soap,
and never wash, I'm sure.
Let's all get together
all of us in Limones.

I bought a basket of corn
and left it out alone.
The next day—not even husks—
the kernels were all gone.
Everything was eaten;
the rats had made their meal
right there in the basket.
Get rid of the rats. That's all!
Let's ask the Health Department.

I haven't finished telling
my story without end.
Rats swarm throughout the world
you can't get rid of them.
By day the coward-rat hides,
he goes inside a cave;
he only comes out at night—
that's when a rat is brave!
Let's ask the Health Department
to get rid of the rats.

    "The Cow Flew in a Plane"
The cow flew in a plane
to the Port of Buenaventura
because here in Tumaco
the poverty was so bad.

She left for Panama
on yet another plane
and had them pull a tooth—
she couldn't stand the pain.
She had pains 'round her heart,
she wanted an examination.
They couldn't find a cure,
she wanted an operation,
and for these mysterious reasons
the cow flew in a plane.

She went with the idea
of finishing what she began,
of finding out about
the Korean War if she can.
For many of the creatures
are having a time that's rough,
only the rich can play
and rest and eat enough.
But for the poor cow,
the poverty was so bad.

When she was healthy again
and we thought she was back to stay,
she wanted to take a trip
to the U.S. of A.
to see what she could see
in that cold place far away.
She wanted to talk to the priests
and to the Chief of State,
and for these mysterious reasons
the cow flew in a plane.

"The Black Goat"
Between la Tola and Limones,
from Limones to Borbón,
there's a black goat walking
and his title is Esquire.

Every Christian knows him,
every man in the place
knows Señor Eloy Lara.
One quick look at his face—
you'll know how bad he is.
His mean and evil ways
glare in those cold hard eyes,
this snake with his devil's gaze
between La Tola and Limones.

Back in 1900
someone paid his bill—
just when the sucker forgets it
he gets another bill.
The snake takes ten percent interest,
he pushes your back to the wall
and says to you "My friend,
I want my money, that's all."
And he walks, as I was saying,
from Limones to Borbón.

How many poor unfortunates
have paid their lives away,
the wretches have lost their shirts
to this serpent without shame!
That's how he treated Valencia
and poor Severo, the clod,
and that's why Quintero said
"We can only leave him to God."
And with his rapid step
there's a black goat walking.

I wish that God were willing
to send a tidal wave
that would sweep the snake out to sea
and drown him, the dirty knave.
Everything he does is evil,
no man would feel any grief
because nobody has any love
for that shyster lawyer thief
who mistreats everyone of us.
And his title is Esquire.

"The Black Man's Question"
Like the ignorant man I am
I really have to ask:
if the color white is a virtue
why don't you whiten me?

It's no insult to be black,
don't let it give you the blues,
even society ladies
wear their shiny black shoes. . . .
and black eyebrows and black lashes
and beautiful long black hair.
Let anyone here explain,
my question is very fair.
I really have to ask
like the ignorant man I am.

I ask without hesitation,
it's something I don't understand:
when the Lord who made us all
mixed His water and sand,
what color clay did He use
to give father Adam shape?
And if you want to shut me up
first answer—I'll shut my trap.

Like the ignorant man I am
I really have to ask.

I ask (because I want to)
if being black is a crime.
I've never seen white letters
since the beginning of time.
Christ's holy cross was black,
that's where our Savior died,
and Mother Mary wore black
when Her Son Jesus died.
I really have to ask
if the color white is a virtue.

The black man with his blackness
and the white man with his white,
all of us come to our end
in the tomb as black as night.
Then, the beauty of white ladies
will end from pole to pole,
and the critic will be finished
and the man as black as coal.
If the color white is a virtue,
why don't you whiten me?

NOTE

This article originally appeared in *Grassroots Development* (Vol. 8, No. 1, 1984).

7

Self-History and
Self-Identity in Talamanca
•
PAULA R. PALMER

In tourist brochures and school textbooks, Costa Rica is presented as a white, homogeneous country. For the most part it is; yet 9,000 Indians and 35,000 blacks also live there. Few in number, geographically isolated, and poor, Costa Rica's Indians and blacks have carried on lives beyond the sight of the dominant, white society.

Until the 1950s life had changed remarkably little for the Bribri Indians in the canton of Talamanca in southern Limón province. Some 3,000 Bribri lived in thatch and palmbark dwellings scattered through river valleys and mountain forests. At home they spoke their native tongue. They cultivated plantains, beans, cocoa, and corn. Each family was self-sufficient, except at harvest, when work was done communally, farm by farm. Although the government formally abolished the kingship of the Bribri, *sukias* (healers skilled in herbal medicine) continued to provide local leadership as well as health care. Even the United Fruit Company failed to disrupt the stable community life of the Bribri. When the fruit company arrived in 1910, the Bribri moved inland. By 1930 the fruit company was gone, and the Bribri returned.

The pattern of cultural survival was similar for Talamanca's blacks. During the second half of the 19th century, West Indians established fishing and farming villages along the coast. A hundred years later those communities were still largely unassimilated—black, Protestant, and English-speaking. Every family cherished its Broadman Hymnal and its West Indian Reader. Community life revolved around cocoa and coconut agriculture and such Jamaican-English pastimes as cricket, baseball, calypso, and quadrille dancing.

The isolation of Talamanca diminished in the 1950s, when Costa Rican citizenship was first offered to the black, West Indian descendants. The government sent teachers from the inland *meseta central*; primary schools were built; and the younger generation began to speak Spanish.

113

Based on interviews—such as this one—with Bribri elders, a group of indigenous students from an agricultural technical school produced a series of publications on the history, culture, and development problems unique to Costa Rica's Talamanca Coast. (See CR-042 and CR-103 in the Appendix.)

Influence from "the outside" has increased dramatically over the past two decades. In the Bribri area of Amubri, the first residential Catholic mission was established during the 1960s. The Talamanca Indian Reserve, administered by a commission in San José, was established during the 1970s. By 1980, petroleum explorations had begun within the reserve. Since the Indians are not allowed to own private property in the reserve, mineral rights are held by the Costa Rican government. Many fear the outcome of new mining projects that are planned in the area.

The black coastal communities also face growing pressure from the outside world. Cahuita National Park was established in 1970, depriving scores of black families of legal titles to their farms—all the more painful since the Parks Service, which technically administers the land, lacks the funds to compensate residents. In 1976 a road was completed that linked Talamanca with the Atlantic port of Limón. Government community organizers arrived and imposed their ways on people who were accustomed to taking care of themselves through their own organizations—lodges, Protestant churches, English school boards, and the Jamaican Burial Scheme society.

The most serious threat to coastal life began in 1977 with the passage of the Beachfront Law (Ley Marítimo-Terrestre) which eliminates private property rights within the first 200 meters of the seashore. Coconuts planted along the beach by the early Talamanca families became the state's "natural resources." Urban development planners from San José are currently preparing zoning blueprints for Talamanca villages, which would remove all residences and farms from the 200–meter "tourist zone"—with perhaps one exception, a "typical coastal residence" to be preserved inside the national park as a tourist attraction!

How have the people of Talamanca responded? Alphaeus Buchanan, a second-generation cocoa farmer and the first manager of Coopetalamanca, the local agricultural cooperative, says:

> We're not against progress. We are a progressive people. When our grandfathers came here, there was nothing. They planted farms; built houses, schools, and churches; organized sports clubs; built roads and bridges—everything we have here, we made with our own sweat and intelligence.
>
> We want a better life for our children. We want modern conveniences—why not? We want our children to have choices we didn't have. Maybe they can be lawyers, mechanics, journalists, scholars. The ones that want to be farmers, they must be better prepared than we are, because agriculture has to be more technical in the future.
>
> We can learn a lot from the teachers and technical experts that come in, but we can't learn from them how to defend what is ours. We have to learn that from ourselves. They will teach our children Spanish and typewriting, and science and the history that they know, but *we* have to teach our children our history. *We* have to defend our property and our way of life.

Mr. Buchanan and the 110 members of Coopetalamanca use their cooperative as a base to fight for the rights and the needs of their people. Economic development is their primary goal, but to achieve that, they believe they must attack barriers that are rooted in education and culture. People who never see their experience reflected in the media, school curricula, or government institutions are ill-equipped to use those media or to negotiate with those institutions to improve standards of living and to defend their rights.

During the late 1970s, Coopetalamanca board members identified several needs for their education committee to consider. First, Costa Ricans needed to be educated about Talamanca so that government programs

could be more responsive to local realities. Second, the people of Talamanca had to be inspired to organize themselves to defend their rights. Finally, Talamanca's youth needed a strong, positive sense of themselves, of
their cultures, and their history.

•

I first became involved in these problems through my work on an oral
history of the Talamanca coast. Since 1974 I had been teaching in a locally organized English school in Cahuita. I had begun tape-recording
stories from the town's oldest residents in order to create reading material
for my students. Eighty-three-year-old Mr. Johnson's stories of turtle
fishing, sailboat commerce, tapir hunting, and snake doctoring were fascinating reading for the children of Cahuita, whereas "Tip and Mitten"
were incomprehensible. The local English stories became so popular that
the board of education encouraged me to edit them chronologically, add a
description of contemporary problems and aspirations, and publish the
collection as a local history. Something powerful happened during the interviews for that book, *'What Happen': A Folk-History of Costa Rica's
Talamanca Coast*. The speakers, aware that their personal experiences
would be published, began to reappraise the importance of their experiences. They began tying events together and drawing new conclusions.
For example:

> When the banana company came in we cut down our cocoa and planted
> bananas. Then the company left. They were going to take up the tram-
> lines, but we made them leave them there, and we built little tramcars and
> pulled them with mules, and for the first time we had public transporta-
> tion along the coast. *We did all that ourselves!*

I, too, was changed by these conversations. A bond formed between
the speakers and myself, and with it came a mutual sense of power and responsibility. I came to believe that the young people of Talamanca needed
to experience this bonding to know themselves and to carry on building
their communities. Young people had so much to be proud of, and they did
not know it.

"Mr. Gavitt's Calypso"
Cahuita National Park

National Parkers are going around,
Into my farm they love to walk,
Telling everybody all around the town,
They say, "This is National Park!"

They want to get a full detail,
How long I own this piece of land?

"No tell no lie or else you going to jail!"
That's what they made me to understand.

They want to know my mother's name,
From whence she went and whence
   she came,
What kind of fellow was my father?
How long since he married to my mother?

They want to know about my grandmother,
They want to know about she religion,
What kind of fellow was my grandfather?
All of this they say they must understand.

I say, "Your question is hard for me,
Give me a chance and I will see,"
Finally I came to a conclusion,
"I find an answer to your question."

My grandmother was an Anglican,
My grandfather was Jonathan,
They got a little boy, he was very bad,
   I say,
When the fellow dead, they were more
   than glad.
Me mother was Rebecca, an Israelite,
Me daddy was Willie, an Amalekite,
When it come to me, I don't got no land,
I'm a true-born Calypsonian.

The idea for an oral history project at Talamanca's agricultural high school took shape during 1980. We are indebted to the high school students of Rabun Gap, Georgia, who publish *Foxfire* magazine, for their successful example of oral history as an educational process. *Foxfire* provided the model which the people of Talamanca adapted to their own situation. Our idea was to teach students oral research skills and photography, take them to interview local residents, and then use that research to tell Talamanca's story by publishing a magazine. For Coopetalamanca, the magazine project promised a way to unite people—young and old, Indian, black, and Hispanic—in search and celebration of their identity. By distributing the magazine locally and nationally, they would extend their message to larger communities.

In 1980 Coopetalamanca received a grant from the Inter-American Foundation to launch the project. Local high school staff and the Ministry of Education personnel were receptive. For several years the ministry had talked vaguely about "regionalizing" the curriculum, without specifying how. Students in Talamanca are sent instructional materials produced in the *meseta central*. Nowhere in those texts do they encounter photographs of blacks or contemporary Indians. There are no wooden houses on stilts, no mothers cooking with coconut milk, no fathers fishing with *pejibaye* spears. The oral history project offered the Ministry of Education an experimental model for bringing regional characteristics vividly into the classroom.

Thirty-seven Talamancan tenth and eleventh graders participated in the project in 1981 (48 in 1982) under the supervision of two teachers, a photography instructor, and myself, the project coordinator. We began by discussing what we knew about Talamanca's history, how we had learned it, and from whom. Working groups were formed around topics of mutual interest: the old ways of the Bribri Indians, the evolution of transportation, the history of specific communities, the use of herbal medicines, the petroleum explorations, and the sea lore of coastal fishermen. Each group practiced using tape recorders and cameras, and refined questions for interviews. When the students felt ready they chose informants among their family members and neighbors, people who had lived the history and could voice their own experiences.

Nearly every weekend groups of students set out in the project's orange jeep—wherever and as far as Talamanca roads go, up into the Indian Reserve, down to the Panama border at Sixaola, along the Caribbean coast. At roads' ends we walked, toting camera bags, tape recorders, and lists of questions.

One of the first year's most memorable experiences was an overnight trip to Amubri in the Indian Reserve. The parents of an Indian student took a group in the family's motorized dugout up a series of rivers to the grandparents' home. Of six students and three teachers, only the Indian student, Ana Concepción, had been there before. Her parents, don Tranquilino and doña Donata, motored and poled the canoe up the tributaries of the Sixaola River, recalling their childhoods in the High Talamanca and teaching us how to greet our hosts in Bribri: *is a shkéna* (good morning).

That afternoon and the next day, Ana's parents were our guides and translators during visits to the thatch and palmbark homes of a very old man, a very old woman, and a sukia. We learned about the customs and ceremonies surrounding birth and death, the training of sukias, and the scarcity of young Indians who want to learn the herbal cures. We heard of the conflict between more traditional Indians who seek out the sukia and object to petroleum explorations, and the "modern" Indians who use the mission health post and welcome the oil company's roads.

Fascinated, students listened for hours to conversation and laughter in a language they had never heard. When the old woman, doña Apolonia, laughed from her hammock, the students, too, broke out laughing. And when she improvised a song in Bribri, dedicated to our visit, the students were spellbound.

Later, in the classroom, pupils played the tape of doña Apolonia's song over and over. A Mennonite linguist helped them translate the lyrics, and they learned what doña Apolonia was telling them:

So sad, sad, sad, I tell you.
The Spaniard, the white man, is here on
the mountain.
My hut is in the mountain, where he
came and spoke.
When I first came to the mountain, I
sang proudly.
Now we don't have this, don't have that.
Now even the words have gone.
We can't speak. . . .
How can we sing? No one understands
us.
It's so sad, our silence is so sad.

As a result of the Amubri experience the students asked the high school director to let them form a class in the Bribri language. Although the course is not yet organized, because of scheduling problems, the director and the ministry have agreed that it will be offered.

The students who visited Amubri later transcribed their tapes, selected photographs, and wrote an article for the first edition of *Nuestra Talamanca, Ayer y Hoy* (Our Talamanca, Yesterday and Today). Students sent photographs and complimentary copies of the magazine to all of their informants and hosts. They followed up articles with in-depth interviews with other informants on topics broached in their first talks: burial ceremonies, the controversial petroleum explorations, the history of the Catholic missions among the Bribris. After the first issue appeared, they received two letters: one from an Indian man who offered to take them to ancient burial sites, another from an Argentine writer who sought permission to use phrases from doña Apolonia's song as the epigraph to his novel-in-progress.

During the two years of the project, other students wrote about the histories of their home towns, Indian crafts, the dangers of deforestation, snakebite cures, traditional recipes, and calypso songwriters. When students are asked to describe what they have learned through their participation, they point to improvements in their oral and written skills, their new familiarity with cameras and tape recorders, and the value of knowing and appreciating their own history.

During 1981 and 1982, Talamanca students published three 1,500-copy editions of *Nuestra Talamanca, Ayer y Hoy*. Most of the magazines were sold inside Talamanca. University journalism students who helped with the final editing of the articles also sold the magazine in San José.

Small groups of students went to the capital for the publication of each issue. They gave interviews about their work to national newspapers, radio, and television, and gave talks at high schools in Limón province and in San José. The students' enthusiasm and involvement in their little-known region attracted money from several private donors for projects at the high school.

In October 1982, the Ministry of Education invited the students to give three full-day presentations about their oral history project to social studies teachers in Limón province who were discussing regionalization of the curriculum. The teachers then urged the Ministry of Education to reprint and distribute the three issues of the Talamanca magazines as text material for all schools and high schools in the country; extend the oral history project to all Limón province high schools in 1983; and publish the future oral history work of Limón students either in a magazine or in national newspapers.

In response, the ministry print shop is now republishing the three issues of the Talamanca magazine for use as social studies texts. Whether a province-wide oral history project will be implemented depends on ministry resources and the dedication of area teachers. One Limón teacher who participated in the seminar wrote:

> The work that you have done is really quite extraordinary. It is a model for other institutions in the country. Speaking for myself, it has sparked an enormous interest to begin working with my students in a similar way.

Although grant funding expires in early 1983, Talamanca's oral history project will continue, under the supervision of teachers trained during the past two years. Printing costs prohibit further editions of a typeset magazine, but profits from the sale of the three printed editions will finance future mimeograph editions for local distribution. For a wider audience, Talamanca students will rely on the Ministry of Education and national newspapers.

The long-term impact of this kind of learning on local attitudes and national policies cannot be measured. But we who have participated know that it has enriched *our* lives. When a brawny, 16–year-old boy asks for a picture of doña Apolonia to put on his bedroom wall, when a child who lives in a thatch-roof house receives a thank-you letter from the Minister of Energy and Mines for photographs, when a shy Indian girl becomes indispensable to her classmates because only she can translate Bribri, when a 17-year-old who speaks Spanish as a second language stands in front of 40 teachers and explains why a piece of national legislation is unjust to her community . . . then something significant has happened.

NOTE

This article originally appeared in *Grassroots Development* (Vol. 6:2–7:1, 1982–1983).

8

Reviving Crafts and Affirming Culture: From Grassroots Development to National Policy

•

BRENT GOFF

"Twenty-five years ago, not many people were even aware that Colombia had a national tradition of artisanal production, much less that it was on the verge of being lost." Cecilia Duque, executive director of the Museo de Artes y Tradiciones Populares in Bogotá, speaks with quiet resolve. She is sitting in her office at the museum, surrounded by stunning examples of Colombian arts and crafts, many of them no longer being produced. In playing a leading role to revitalize those traditions, she is determined that the museum will not be simply a repository for prized artifacts, but also a center for reviving the artisan communities and popular cultures that bring those artifacts into being. Nevertheless, she knows the outcome of this struggle is far from certain.

Throughout Colombia, and in much of Latin America, craft traditions are being undermined by a variety of factors, among them urbanization and the increasing popularity and availability of low-cost manufactured goods. On one level, factory products can simply be a better buy: Cheap plastic buckets and assembly-line shoes can be as functional and as long-lasting as more costly ceramic pots and handmade sandals. On another level, factory goods are more attractive because they evoke the desire for modernization while craft goods reflect an archaic past. Artisans, who are typically unorganized, poorly capitalized, and cut off from regional, national, and international markets, find it hard to compete with manufactured goods without lowering product quality. Items incorporating traditional standards of craftsmanship and high aesthetic values are being replaced by shoddy goods, such as neon-colored ashtrays and stamped-out replicas of Incan gods, made explicitly for the tourist trade. These factors undermine not only traditions of craftsmanship but also the living, breathing culture of which crafts are an expression. If artisans cannot make a

Photo: Miguel Sayago

The Fundación para la Investigación y el Desarrollo de Sucre (FIDES) trains youth from several dozen Colombian communities to play traditional musical instruments, thereby strengthening the cultural identity and ethnic pride of local people. (See CO-403 in the Appendix.)

living from their work and do not enjoy the respect of their community, then their children will not follow in their footsteps. When a craft tradition dies, the community and the nation lose a vital link with their past and a portion of their identity.

The general trend may be irreversible, but there are hopeful signs of improvement in Colombia. At the center of that change is the Asociación Colombiana de Promoción Artesanal (ACPA), a unique institution that has developed a comprehensive strategy for reviving craft traditions during the past two decades. ACPA first concentrated on informing the Colombian public of its cultural heritage through the Museo in Bogotá, hoping thereby to increase demand for quality handicrafts and create broad support for artisanal production. A second stage involved working directly with local artisanal groups throughout Colombia to help them revive and preserve their craft traditions and improve their socioeconomic well-being. A third level of activity is now taking place as ACPA is joining with the Ministry of Education and other public and private institutions to design and implement an innovative program of rural education grounded in local and regional culture. This article discusses each of these three phases and describes how it was eventually possible to scale up ACPA's approach.

LAYING A FOUNDATION

ACPA was the offspring of an earlier private voluntary organization, Unidad Femenina, which brought upper- and middle-class women's associations from throughout Colombia under one umbrella to address some of the country's pressing socioeconomic problems. Although Unidad Femenina dissolved in 1966, its crafts committee continued to function and soon reorganized itself as the Asociación Colombiana de Promoción Artesanal.

As Cecilia Duque makes clear, ACPA had unique organizational advantages from the start. "Our strength came from the regional committees that had been organized earlier. We knew it was important to call the nation's attention to a part of its culture that was on the verge of vanishing before it could even be recorded. It was decided to hold exhibitions in Bogotá, and the regional committees made that possible. They documented the artisanry of each department, and scoured the countryside for older artisans who still practiced traditional techniques and might be able to teach others. They raised money from local governments and commissioned works for display and sale in Bogotá. In this way, they hoped not only to preserve the country's cultural heritage but also to create employment."

The exhibits were a resounding success. During the next three years, several were held at various sites in the capital, including the Museo del Chico, the Museo Nacional, and the Caja Agraria. Participants recall these occasions almost as festivals. At each, crafts from a featured department were displayed, and many of rare beauty were offered for sale. To emphasize that these were products of a living tradition, artisans were invited to demonstrate how their work was made, and folklore groups performed dances and songs. The exhibit openings were attended by Colombia's first lady, the governor of the featured department, and many local notables. Media coverage was extensive and enthusiastic. As Berta Llorente de Ponce de León, a founding member of ACPA and president of its board of directors, notes, "For the first time, people began to see the crafts as art."

Soon the search was on for a permanent exhibition site to consolidate that success. With enormous volunteer effort and the support of the Colombian government, ACPA acquired and restored a decaying 18th-century convent in Bogotá's colonial district and transformed it into the Museo de Artes y Tradiciones Populares. Opened in 1971, it is an architectural gem, a national treasure, and the premier museum of arts and crafts in Colombia. Through permanent displays and special shows it promotes public awareness of traditional crafts in the context of the customs and daily life of the communities that produce them. The museum store provides an outlet for artisans to sell their products, and the staff refers interested buyers directly to master craftsmen.

Although the museum soon became a focal point for artisans throughout the country, Duque and her board of directors began to realize that a new level of involvement would be needed if the facility was not to become a reliquary. Supporting a few master craftsmen by preserving and marketing their work did nothing to broaden the base of production so that craft traditions would not die with this aging generation.

PUTTING RESEARCH INTO ACTION

From the beginning, ACPA believed it was important not to become "just another buyer" of handicrafts. For one thing, Artesanías de Colombia, the government crafts organization, was already trying to stimulate the crafts sector as a whole by purchasing large quantities of goods for resale both domestically and abroad. For another, ACPA had begun to wonder if the creation of artificial demand was the right medicine for the country's ailing crafts traditions. The commercial approach of the government program did not ensure the preservation of traditional techniques and designs, and in making scattershot purchases from only a few artisans in each locality, it tended to further fragment already divided communities.

Consequently, ACPA decided on a radically different approach. It would try to use its limited resources to maximum advantage by organizing communities of artisans to help themselves. "We decided," Cecilia Duque says, "that the crisis in crafts production was deeply rooted, and finding an answer meant focusing first on the artisans themselves rather than on what they produced." Beginning in 1977, with grant support from the IAF, ACPA launched an intensive program to help artisan communities create their own development programs. Three criteria were used to target assistance to artisanal groups: the lasting aesthetic and cultural value of a given craft tradition, the danger of its disappearing without outside assistance, and its potential for economic viability. ACPA's previous experience documenting crafts traditions helped it identify likely candidates for assistance and provided invaluable contacts within the communities to begin organizing.

The first phase of ACPA's program is one of applied research in conjunction with the community itself. "You can't go into a community and expect to find answers unless you are prepared to listen," Duque notes. "But this is active listening, geared toward helping people uncover what they can do to improve their situation." Duque emphasizes this work is not for disinterested academics, but people capable of evaluating information in terms of community promotion. The research teams must blend a composite of skills: an instinct for human relations, some knowledge of social science methodologies, and a familiarity with craft techniques.

After clearing the project with municipal authorities, ACPA's outreach team visits local artisans in their homes to gather data on income, health, production techniques, output, raw materials, relations with buyers, and other pertinent economic and social conditions. "It's important for these initial contacts to be informal, almost conversational," Duque says. "This stage requires great patience and tact. People who feel like they are being looked at under a microscope aren't likely to be inspired by the person at the other end to feel greater confidence in themselves or their craft." The conversations usually include the entire family. Craft production is typically a family enterprise, and by giving everyone a voice from the beginning, Duque stresses, it is much more likely that benefits and decisions from future participation in a community action program will be shared by the family as a whole.

This initial phase can take six months or longer. Then the seeds begin to sprout. A series of community meetings are convened in which artisans can discuss problems in common. To stimulate discussion at these meetings, ACPA has developed an extensive library of booklets and audio visual materials that target key issues for craft communities. Once the ice is broken, however, field workers are careful not to impose solutions. "We are very aware of the danger of paternalism," says Álvaro Chaves, a noted anthropologist and member of ACPA's technical staff. "We have to remind ourselves that we are not here to teach. We are invited into communities to learn something from them."

The airing of common problems at community meetings is a powerful impetus for organizing common solutions. Most artisan communities are highly fragmented, sometimes because of family or political disputes, but often because artisans are competing on unfavorable terms for access to markets. In most cases that situation is exploited by intermediaries, who buy crafts on consignment or in return for a little cash and enough raw materials to keep production going. Organizing as a precooperative, which entails fewer legal requirements than a cooperative, is one way to remove some of these bottlenecks and increase production. By pooling resources together in a credit fund, a precooperative can buy raw materials in bulk, providing members with a steady, economical supply of inputs to increase production. Sometimes ACPA agrees to buy a group's first inventory, either to encourage the formation of a precooperative or to help it capitalize its production fund. This first inventory might be sold through the museum in Bogotá. In general, though, ACPA helps groups develop their own strategy for direct marketing in order to provide higher rates of return for members and encourage the group's independence. The precooperative is typically run by a board of five officers, elected annually.

ACPA's degree of direct involvement in the new organization varies, depending on the history and capabilities of the group. At the beginning, ACPA may exert considerable influence over group policies and activities, usually through elected officers to the precooperative board who agree to consult with the association and represent it within the board. "We maintain very close relations with each community," Cecilia Duque explains. "We put capital into a fund for the new organization when it forms, usually as a loan, but on occasion as a grant if the group shows itself responsible but remains strapped for cash. Our representation on its governing board gradually tapers off to one member. The group should be mature after five years. After 10 years, the group is expected to be independent."

To help a new organization improve its management skills, ACPA arranges for training courses in bookkeeping, marketing, human relations, and other relevant topics. ACPA's technical director, Ligia de Wiesner, organizes workshops to improve production methods, materials, and designs. Although the association is committed to preserving craft traditions, it is not purist in the sense of rejecting all changes out of hand. "Crafts evolve naturally," de Wiesner explains, "and modifying a design or production technique to improve quality should be encouraged. Sometimes those changes involve a return to prior, higher aesthetic standards, and other times they involve updating an item to appeal to modern tastes. The tension between maintaining tradition and meeting market demand does not have to be destructive; handled the right way it can also spark creativity." As an example, she cites the hemp weavers of Guacamayas, who for generations produced beautiful *alpargatas*, or sandals, and small weighing baskets for hand-held scales. Although both were remarkable products, the market for them was vanishing. So ACPA technicians suggested using the same traditional production techniques to weave larger baskets. The new products caught on, reviving the tradition and the prospects of the artisans simultaneously.

Not all crafts are preservable, however. "Some traditions inevitably disappear," de Wiesner says, shrugging her shoulders. "Before intervening, one must weigh various factors—the artistic value of a craft, its practical uses, whether it is marketable. Sometimes the best intentions cannot save a craft, but even then we can at least document the tradition so that it does not vanish without a trace." To that end, ACPA is compiling detailed descriptions, drawings, and photographs of craft technologies and products for an archival center at its museum in Bogotá.

THE BARNIZADORES OF PASTO

Since 1977, ACPA has assisted nine artisanal groups, with varying degrees of success. Perhaps the most notable have been the *barnizadores* of Pasto. This relatively small group, primarily men, practices a unique craft whose roots extend back to pre-Columbian times. Using a complicated process, craftsmen convert the gum of the *mopa-mopa*, a tropical shrublike tree, into paper-thin sheets of dyed material, or *barniz*, which are applied with freehand artwork to wooden trays, boxes, animal figures, and other articles. The resulting products look something like Japanese lacquer ware, but are in fact unique.

When ACPA began its assistance in 1979, the barnizadores were in dire straits. "Of all the groups we've worked with," says Duque, "this one seemed least likely to make it." It is commonly remarked that "Pastuzos eat Pastuzos"—meaning that the people of Pasto tend to undercut each other habitually—and the barnizadores were no exception. An attempt to form a cooperative in the early 1970s had already failed, rubbing salt in old wounds and inflaming traditional rivalries. Several craftsmen had been able to sell their work through Artesanías de Colombia, but most were at the mercy of a few local middlemen who commissioned cheap curios for the tourist trade that were a pale reflection of past standards. The barnizadores also suffered from unsteady supplies of mopa-mopa gum, the crucial raw material for their craft. The only source was a relatively small area of the Putumayo jungle, a 12-hour bus ride from Pasto. Prices fluctuated wildly, in part because intermediaries occasionally tried to corner the market. A better supply system was necessary to ensure the barnizadores' survival, but for that they needed to organize and build up a capital fund, neither of which seemed likely.

For three years ACPA's team of specialists worked patiently with the barnizadores, listening to their troubles and looking for ways to bring people together. A turning point came when de Wiesner commissioned works from several craftsmen for presentation at a group meeting. The one requirement was that the work had to express each artisan's creativity. Freed from the restraint of producing for traditional intermediaries, many of the barnizadores made objects of striking beauty. Asked to comment on each other's work, men who looked past one another in the street began to express feelings of grudging admiration that soon gave way to questions about how a certain effect had been accomplished. A meeting became a workshop.

In 1982, the workshop became a precooperative of 18 barnizadores. With a grant from the IAF, the new organization took its first step toward regularizing access to raw materials. A fund was established to ensure a steady supply of mopa-mopa gum from the Putumayo. The group also made arrangements with local woodcarvers, and opened its own woodworking shop, to obtain a dependable supply of objects for decoration. Each member received inputs free of charge, but finished work had to be submitted to a quality control committee for payment. When a piece was accepted, 5 percent of the payment would be deducted for the precooperative's capital fund. Another 5 percent would go to the group's solidarity fund, from which interest-free loans can be withdrawn for medical or family needs. The product was then marked up in price by 60 percent to cover the costs of raw materials and administrative overhead, and put up for sale.

With ACPA's help, the group attacked the marketing problem next. Several members traveled to craft fairs in Colombia and abroad, and a brochure was prepared detailing the group's history and promoting the artistry of its products. In 1986, the group used a loan from ACPA to buy an old colonial house in central Pasto to provide office and meeting space, a gallery, and a store for retailing finished goods. After a year of renovation, the Casa del Barniz opened its doors for business. The Casa's store has become the precooperative's primary source of income, and sales have been brisk. Artisan income has risen commensurately—nearly quadrupling in the eight years the group has been together. In 1988, per capita earnings were around 80,000 pesos monthly, or about US$250—more than three times the national minimum wage. Several barnizadores earn considerably more.

Asked how their lives have changed, members are quick to note improvements. "Things are better now, no doubt about it," said a young barnizador as he hunched over his work, deftly adding layers of gold barniz to a handsome jewelry box. "A few years ago most of us would have discouraged our children from taking up the trade. Now I want my two sons to learn it."

Over a meal at a local restaurant, another member in his mid-40s summed it up this way: "Today we feel more secure. I used to resist the idea of organizing, of training and working on human relations. Now I see I was blind, that working together is the key to getting ahead."

Most members now own their own houses; they work shorter weeks but have an assured source of income; and they can tap a solidarity fund for assistance if someone in the family gets sick, has an accident, or dies. But most of all, what you sense is a fierce pride in their work, in their skill at turning ordinary woodcarvings into objects of intricate and dramatic beauty.

Although these accomplishments are real, and the group has been celebrated by both local and national media as a model for artisan organizations, there are troubling signs about the durability and extent of that success. The fault lines of personal and professional differences run deep, and tremors are still felt periodically. Although members are required to market their work through the precooperative, some continue to trade with outside intermediaries, giving rise to recriminations. More troubling, some artisans have left, and the group has actually shrunk in size to 16 members. Many other barnizadores would like to join, but the group is reluctant to admit them, fearing that production might outstrip demand, or that new members would undermine solidarity and production standards. This impasse cannot persist indefinitely, however, since Colombian law limits the lifespan of precooperatives, and becoming a full cooperative requires at least 25 members.

In assisting the formation of artisan organizations, ACPA hopes not only to preserve dying craft traditions but to generate jobs. Although quality production has been revitalized by the barnizador precooperative, it remains unclear whether or not the overall market has in fact expanded enough to support more than a few artisans. In that case, ACPA's best intentions would only have succeeded in winnowing out the winners from the losers, creating a guild rather than a cooperative business.

A second, unintended result may also be occurring. The barnizadores have traditionally prospered by adding value to the products of local woodcarvers. As the barnizador precooperative has grown more affluent, resentment has developed among a local group of woodcarvers that prices for their primary products have not kept pace. Agreements between the two groups have broken down, and the woodcarvers fear that the barnizadores hope to bypass them altogether by setting up their own expanded woodworking shop. The barnizadores contend that the new shop will assure a steady stream of low-cost materials and give regular work to "interested" woodcarvers at the same time.

THE POTTERS OF RÁQUIRA

The limitations and ambiguities of trying to revive craft traditions through artisanal organization are also apparent among the potters of Ráquira, in the department of Boyacá. ACPA began working there in 1982 to preserve some of the traditional styles of ceramics, such as the fabled *caballitos*, or clay horses, that were disappearing. Ceramics production in the region can be traced back to the pre-Columbian Muisca culture, but the thread has frayed during the past two decades. The hills that rise above the town have been stripped of trees to expand wheat production and to feed the small kilns that sit behind many of the houses. The mode of craft production has progressively shifted toward larger, coal-burning ovens equipped to handle masses of standardized planters and animal figures, principally pigs, that have been stamped out in molds suited to the specifications of middlemen from Bogotá. Some 30 small ceramics factories have sprung up around the town, casting a pall of coal-black smoke over the valley.

"When we came to Ráquira and began talking to potters about the possibility of reviving some of the older designs, people were stunned," Duque recalls. "Producers of traditional pottery were at the bottom of the ladder in the community, and their children were often ashamed to admit their parents worked with clay. But once we convinced artisans that we were there to help, they began to open up and talk about their needs. With time, we even saw children begin to take up the craft again."

Just as in Pasto, the potters of Ráquira suffered from being unorganized. Dependent on marketing through middlemen who often only took pottery on consignment at cut-rate prices, the potters found it ever harder to keep pace with the rising cost of raw materials. Strapped for cash, they steadily sank deeper into debt. ACPA's technical team realized that formation of a precooperative similar to the one in Pasto was the obvious answer to lowering the cost of raw materials and gaining direct access to consumer markets.

Unfortunately, the artisans of Ráquira are even more divided than those of Pasto, primarily because of politics. During the 1940s and early 1950s, Colombia was shaken by La Violencia, a period of protracted conflict between supporters of the Conservative and Liberal parties. The region around Ráquira was deeply scarred, leaving a bitter legacy of feuding among local families that has yet to heal. ACPA realized that the level of personal animosity, complicated by the differences between small and large producers, was a gap too great for a cooperative to bridge. Instead, the association decided to open a small museum as a neutral space where potters could meet, learn more about their own ceramic traditions, and hopefully begin to discover common ground for mutual action.

The museum is housed in an unobtrusive, colonial-style house on the town's main square. Photographs of local potters and texts describing their work grace the walls, and display cases hold examples of ancient and more current styles of traditional pottery. There is a small store, a stockroom that sells ceramic materials at cost, and a studio for holding workshops and demonstrations. Changing exhibitions of local work and periodic juried competitions have made the museum a point of informal contact for potters, and it has fostered closer ties between town residents and those in the surrounding countryside. The exhibitions and workshops have encouraged local potters to be more creative by exploring new techniques and designs. A new form of popular art has emerged—tiny human and animal figurines set in typical village scenes—for which there is a growing market.

Although the museum represents a step forward for local artisans, instilling greater pride in their work and even renewing interest in some traditions, such as the previously mentioned caballitos, it has not put food on the potters' tables. The high cost of materials and the low prices for finished goods make small-scale production nonviable. As one potter put it, "What I do is more like a sport than a job." ACPA continues to look for alternatives that would lower production costs, such as finding ways to convert kilns to handle a more economical mixture of coal and wood. But even that modest step seems thwarted, since many artisans are reluctant to add to the foul air already choking the valley. More tangible economic progress awaits the time when the potters are able to overcome their differences and organize effective methods for working together.

The complex intertwining of development and cultural issues that ACPA has encountered during its efforts to assist artisanal communities, such as those in Pasto and Ráquira, has fostered the realization that self-help programs, even when they can tap able promotional and technical support from a concerned NGO, are only part of the solution in reviving craft traditions and making them economically viable. As a result, ACPA has tried to broaden its impact by seeking out partnerships with other public and private agencies such as universities, government ministries, and the Federación de Cafeteros, an influential network of coffee growers.

One early effort that helped set a precedent for this pattern involved the Cholo Indian woodcarvers of the Chocó rain forest. This group faced an array of development issues that made collaboration with a number of organizations essential. For that reason, ACPA worked closely with the Cholos' own tribal government, as well as with teams from the Universidad Javeriana and the Ministry of Health.

Another, more recent example is a joint project to help the barnizadores gain access to steady supplies of the mopa-mopa gum. Many of the trees that produce this resin are now old and have become less productive, and the zone in which they grow is plagued by guerrilla activity and drug trafficking. For some time the barnizadores have tried to gain support for the creation of a preserve in which the cultivation and harvesting of this tree would be controlled. Until recently, the idea had met with little success. Now, however, a consortium backed by several important Colombian institutions—including INDERENA, the government natural resources institute—has been created to tackle the problem. ACPA played a vital role in facilitating this effort.

SCALING-UP AND THE CRAFTING OF KNOWLEDGE

Over the years, ACPA has come to realize that its community development programs might contain the seeds for a more systematic approach suitable for adaptation by others. To digest what it had learned and to devise more effective ways to aid craft communities, ACPA in 1984 began a project called the Center of Artisan Studies. An umbrella effort, bringing together old staff such as Ligia de Wiesner with new people, the center forms temporary research teams tailored to pursue specific lines of inquiry, including research on particular types of artisanal production, on marketing and promotion, and on the underlying conditions that contribute to the success or failure of craft organizations. These studies not only feed data to ACPA's ongoing community development programs, they are increasingly being used to influence government policy toward the crafts sector. For example, ACPA has presented the departmental government of Tolima with a plan for constructing gas-burning kilns in the ceramics community of La Chamba, where deforestation is rampant, and with a proposal to remodel the crafts workshop at the penitentiary in Ibagué. In Quindío, it has recommended opening a craft school to revive local handicrafts production and boost employment. And in Bolívar, it has proposed creation of a crafts microenterprise in the Free Trade Zone on the Caribbean Coast. ACPA hopes that recent changes in Colombian law that provide for the direct election of mayors and delegation of greater budget authority to local levels will allow increased cooperation and dialogue with municipalities.

The center has also expanded ACPA's educational role and the services it can provide to artisan groups. Specialists have developed training programs geared to the needs of artisans, and booklets and manuals have been produced dealing with ways to streamline production and improve marketing, management, and financial record-keeping. In addition, the center's audiovisual unit has produced numerous videos, slides, and tapes on Colombian craft and folk traditions. It is the only facility in the country devoted to producing this kind of material, and it has received numerous contracts and grants from domestic public and private institutions, as well as from the Organization of American States. Productions have included a 12–part, prime-time television series on traditional culture aired in 1989; a series of national radio programs on the oral history of various regions in Colombia; and a series of audio tapes on the traditional songs and games of Colombian children. The Instituto Colombiano de Bienestar Familiar has found this last production an invaluable tool for linking cultural awareness with early childhood education, and has distributed the tapes through Madres Educadoras, a network of community day care centers located in poor barrios throughout the country.

Perhaps the most significant expansion of ACPA's activities, however, involves its decision to work through the national school system. In the early 1980s, Cecilia Duque approached the Ministry of Education with a proposal to incorporate elements of traditional popular culture into school texts and curricula. ACPA's work with artisan communities had yielded abundant examples of the native genius of Colombia's craftsmen, knowledge that could help forge a stronger sense of cultural identity among schoolchildren. "Working with artisans has been important," she says, with a rueful smile, "but we felt we had to reach young people to have a chance of really preserving these traditions for future generations."

There is a story told at ACPA that illustrates the depth of the problem that must be overcome. Some years ago at a pottery exhibit at the museum in Ráquira, several of the potters were disconcerted when their coffee was served in locally made clay mugs. Shaking their heads, they announced a preference for factory-made cups instead. Duque and her peers had founded the Museo de Artes y Tradiciones Populares nearly 20 years before to dispel the blindness that had prevented so many people from seeing that Colombia possessed a rich national crafts tradition until it was almost lost. Yet this was a cultural blindness so pervasive it afflicted even the people who produced crafts, preventing them from seeing the beauty they had made with their own hands.

The initial response of the Ministry of Education to Duque's proposal was negative. "No one had thought of combining popular culture and education before, only elite culture," says Vicky Colbert, vice-minister of education at the time. After several years of effort, however, and with Colbert's backing, an agreement between ACPA and the ministry was finally signed in 1984. ACPA assembled a team of technical specialists and, with the support of an IAF grant, began to develop curriculum materials for a rapidly expanding national education program known as Escuela Nueva.

Escuela Nueva had been started in 1976 to revitalize the nation's rural school system by making it more flexible and relevant to the needs and interests of its students. Nearly 40 percent of Colombia's rural schoolchildren have to stay out of school at least part of the time to help their families with farm work. Previously, these students were often held back and not promoted. Under the Escuela Nueva program, which mainly involves primary schools, the grade system is fluid and students are allowed to proceed at their own pace. Strong emphasis is placed on classroom interaction rather than learning by rote, and the school extends itself out into the community. Traditional subjects, which once bore little relation to the daily lives of students, are placed in their local and regional context. Students are encouraged to actively investigate the world around them, to understand how local stories and legends can be examples of history and literature, and to recognize crafts as forms of popular art. In short, the program is designed to help young people see their own communities as worthy classrooms for study, and to find within them the seeds for community development.

ACPA's first task in developing the cultural components of the program was to prepare materials for an area where the Escuela Nueva was already well established—the stretch along Colombia's Pacific Coast with its rich heritage of black culture. ACPA's technical team spent months gathering information on the region's music, dance, plastic arts, rituals, folktales, and dress that could be adapted into multimedia classroom materials. These materials were then tested in the schools and revised based on feedback from teachers and pupils. This procedure has since been extended to other parts of the country, and ACPA is in the process of creating comprehensive standardized packets—of books, pamphlets, audiovisuals, and games—that can be used nationally, in combination with specialized materials targeted regionally.

Grounded in popular culture and pragmatically oriented, the curriculum of the Escuela Nueva is designed to promote involvement and to nurture the sense of self-worth and identity that is the keystone of community development. Students begin by working with the concepts of culture and personal identity, then move on to manual skills—such as the making of crafts. Children are encouraged to think of the family as a productive unit, as a *microempresa*, and they are urged to contribute to or help start small family businesses. The program culminates in the establishment of a

Museo Vivo, a "living museum" in which students and their parents can create displays that highlight local crafts, customs, and traditions.

The Escuela Nueva program is now in place in over half of the nation's 26,000 rural schools, reaching approximately half a million students. Although ACPA's materials have yet to reach them all, initial results have been encouraging. "The response has been tremendous, from students, teachers, parents," reports Marina Solano, coordinator of ACPA's curriculum project. "People are discovering that culture is all around them, not just in museums or concert halls, and that it is the very stuff of life."

Since the introduction of this curriculum on the Pacific Coast four years ago, teachers there have reported improved attendance and greater interest and self-confidence among students. Even the teachers say they take greater interest in local culture. The program has won praise and support from the World Bank, UNESCO, and UNICEF, and has been studied by officials from 46 nations around the globe. By all indications, the program will continue, and with it, ACPA's involvement. According to Vicky Colbert, "You can expect to see an even greater marriage between ACPA and Escuela Nueva in coming years. The scaling-up of this project is assured because it works, and the government knows it."

Despite this growing influence over national policy, ACPA's directors are aware that their organization has traced a circle in the course of its evolution. They remember how their goal of preserving craft traditions by raising public awareness led them to develop strategies to help the artisans themselves, and how the knowledge they have accrued in the process has deepened the nation's understanding of what needs to be nurtured. "We are not going to abandon our earlier work," says Cecilia Duque, "because success depends on integrating where we have been with where we are going. We will continue to work on both levels—assisting local groups and developing a process of national education—because both are needed if either is to succeed." ACPA's challenge at the local level is to help create strong organizations, self-empowering and self-sustaining. Its challenge at the national level is to help people understand that this vitality echoes the nation's heartbeat.

NOTE

This article originally appeared in *Grassroots Development* (Vol. 14, No. 1, 1990).

9

Taquile's Homespun Tourism

•

KEVIN HEALY & ELAYNE ZORN

The island of Taquile, a remote speck on Lake Titicaca in southern Peru, is a land of stone walkways, thatched huts, mountain vistas, vivid color, and ancient customs. Life there had changed little over the centuries until the island was recently discovered by a new breed of tourists, rugged young travelers looking for the "unspoiled." But Taquile has become no ordinary tourist paradise. Unlike the inhabitants of most other Developing World communities that attract visitors, the Taquileños have managed to develop their own facilities to exploit tourism. Until now, they have controlled the tourist trade themselves and have reaped its economic benefits. Yet success—even the relatively limited success of Taquile—is not without cost and risk.

Taquile, located on the high Andean plateau, or "altiplano," is an improbable place for tourism. In the 1930s it was briefly famous as a site for political prisoners, including a deposed president, Sánchez Cerro; but otherwise the island passed centuries in obscurity.

About three miles long and less than a mile wide, the tiny island twists like a fish's tail at its southern end. The landscape is rocky and steep, with earthen-colored huts and a few eucalyptus trees and bushes. Paths wind around Inca-style terraces, potato fields, and stone walls and lead up to ancient burial towers on the mountaintops. The eastern side faces out over forty miles of crystal clear, deep blue water. On the horizon, under a vast dome of azure skies and majestic clouds, are the snow-capped mountains of Bolivia. At night sparkling stars fill the Andean sky, and the glow of a silver moon occasionally shimmers on Titicaca's waters.

The inhabitants of Taquile are Quechua-speaking Indians, subsistence farmers who for countless generations have grown potatoes, barley, and broad beans in private plots on terraced mountainsides. Traditionally, the island has been divided into six "suyos," or sections. Each "suyo" contained a single crop that was rotated through a six-year cycle. Taquile's farms produced small surpluses, and the island's modest stores stocked few goods. Unlike other Andean communities, the islanders owned few

135

At the Smithsonian Institution's Festival of American Folklife, in Washington, D.C., Alejandro Flores Hu-
atta, from Peru's Taquile Island in Lake Titicaca, discusses the meaning of the precolumbian symbols
on a hand-woven belt. Preserving the traditional artisanry of Taquile is crucial to both the local
economy and for maintaining ethnic pride and identity. (See PU-093 in the Appendix.)

animals as insurance against crop failures. The poorest Taquileños eked out a living by fishing from reed boats on the deep waters of Lake Titicaca. For cash, the men worked seasonally on coastal farms, in the southern copper mines, and at odd jobs in nearby cities.

On the west coast of the lake is the nearest large commercial center, the port city of Puno, with a population of about 60,000. To reach it, islanders traveled eight to twelve or more hours in wooden sailboats. Each boat was owned by ten or twelve families whose male members took turns navigating. Although residents of other lakeside communities began changing to motorized boats in the mid-1960s, the Taquileños were too poor to make the change. Timid, speaking faulty Spanish, and wearing baggy Western clothing over their traditional costumes when they came to town, the Taquileños were emblematic of Peru's rural backwaters.

Yet despite its acute poverty, Taquile was not without resources. The Peruvian anthropologist José Matos Mar has documented how the community ingeniously began to mobilize savings during the 1930s to purchase the island over the next two decades from its "hacendados," or "landowners." And in the 1940s, the Taquileños mobilized to construct wooden sailboats.

Moreover, the superb quality of Taquile handweaving was equaled by only a handful of communities. Everyone—men, women, and children— knew how to weave. The men knitted elegant stocking hats (ch'ullus), while the women used horizontal ground looms to weave belts (chumpis), bags (ch'uspas), shawls (lliqllas), carrying cloths ('unkhuñas), ponchos, and scarves. Men and boys also wove cloth that they sewed into shirts, vests, skirts, and pants. Weavers bartered for alpaca and sheep's wool from the herdsmen around the lake. Trained since childhood, Taquileños spun ceaselessly—in between other tasks—everywhere on the island.

Taquile was one of the few local communities where both women and men wore—as well as wove—traditional clothing. Their red, white, and black costumes were brilliant against the rocky landscape. Their dress and weaving techniques linked the faraway styles of medieval Spain to their Andean heritage. Although Taquileños occasionally sold textiles to travelers in Puno, they had little experience with organized textiles sales. In 1968, with the assistance of coauthor Healy, then a volunteer in the U.S. Peace Corps, the islanders created a cooperative, based on the structure of traditional leadership, to market their weaving. The community trust for this venture came begrudgingly. Only after a successful Peace Corps–led rat control campaign were the islanders willing to embrace this local development idea. "Jilakatas" (elders who are the island's traditional authority figures) collected new and used weavings for trial sales in Cuzco, a day's trip by train or bus from Puno. These articles were sold on consignment in a Peace Corps–sponsored store that was set up to sell goods from southern Peru's many artisan cooperatives. When the trial sales produced $150, distributed among approximately seventy people, a commercial "boom" began and islanders started commuting regularly to Cuzco on sales trips.

Since the Peace Corps store charged only a modest administrative overhead and the remaining profits went directly to the artisans, the islanders learned the market value of their work. The sales demonstrated that their everyday weavings were attractive to outsiders, especially tourists, and could produce regular cash income.

Unfortunately, three years later the Cuzco retail outlet collapsed. A local manager had embezzled funds, and the Taquile artisans suffered a big loss when many of their weavings held on consignment vanished as the store closed. Yet not everything was lost. The islanders had discovered Cuzco's rapidly expanding tourist market and knew that their weavings were among the best in southern Peru. Taquileños who formerly only delivered products to the cooperative store began to use their market knowledge to sell weavings directly to tourists on the streets of Cuzco. They also found buyers and export distributors in the southern city of Arequipa and in the capital city of Lima. By the mid-1970s, foreign buyers and Lima exporters were selling the red "chumpis" and "ch'uspas" of Taquile to sophisticated consumers in Western Europe and the United States.

Despite its beauty, Taquile remained outside the tourist circuit and was overshadowed by the area's main attraction: floating reed islands that were populated by a dwindling Indian population and located within a twenty-minute motorboat ride of Puno. The only way to reach Taquile was aboard one of the collectively owned wooden sailboats. Only the most adventurous travelers were willing to get off the afternoon train from Cuzco and then spend an entire night sailing a cold, windswept, and often rainy lake. All of that changed, however, when in 1976 the *South American Handbook*—a widely read tourist guide—described Taquile as an out-of-the-way, unspoiled island in Lake Titicaca. Foreign tourists began arriving at the dock at Puno, trying to book passage to Taquile. Several Puno and other private boat owners soon added the island to their tourist run on the lake. (About ten years later articles about Taquile's tourism appeared in the *New York Times*, the *Washington Post*, and the *Boston Globe*.)

By 1977, the Taquileños had pooled their savings and bought second-hand truck engines to power their sailboats. Travel time between Puno and the island dropped from twelve to three and one-half hours, and the tourist traffic increased. In early 1978, new sailboat cooperatives were formed, with groups of thirty to forty families ordering vessels from Taquile's two shipwrights. Although still rustic, the new boats had cabins and were safer, more attractive, and larger than the older craft. They could comfortably carry as many as twenty tourists. A grant from the Inter-American Foundation, a U.S. group that supports small-scale development activities in Latin America, enabled the Taquileños to purchase spare parts and boat motors for six groups. The Peruvian Coast Guard and the Ministry of Tourism licensed the Taquileños to carry travelers and issued regulations and set fares.

The islanders proved to be competitive with the private boat owners at Puno. Eventually, the islanders displaced the Puno boat owners and obtained an officially sanctioned monopoly. By 1982, the number of cooperative transport groups had expanded to thirteen.

In November 1982, the round-trip fare between Taquile and Puno, which is set by the Peruvian Coast Guard and the Ministry of Tourism, was approximately U.S. $4.00. Since the costs of spare parts, fuel, maintenance, and the replacement of motors and wooden boats are high, the boats have operated at a narrow margin between slight profit and slight loss. Yet local control of boat traffic produces benefits other than cash income. It also subsidizes the cost of transport for Taquileños who travel to and from Puno. In 1982, 435 people, representing virtually every family, shared ownership and management responsibilities for one of the thirteen boats. Now every family has access to cheap transportation, and Taquile's trade and communications with the mainland have improved substantially.

The increased boat traffic has also provided new personal income and on-the-job training. The three members of the crew on each Puno round trip now receive regular payment for their work. New boats have meant more hulls and fittings to be produced by the island's boat builders. During the last fifteen years, crew members have acquired valuable skill in engine repair and maintenance—sometimes at the tourists' expense, as when crews have fixed mechanical breakdowns in the middle of the lake.

Yet Taquile's environment is hospitable for only the hardiest of travelers. The island has virtually none of the standard tourist services: excursions, shops, medical facilities, or motor vehicles. There is no electricity or plumbing. There are few beds on the island—nothing even approaching a third-class hotel. Most visitors are backpackers in their twenties and early thirties who are traveling on a limited budget. They soon learn that "rustic" on Taquile can mean rugged.

The island is more than 13,000 feet above sea level, an altitude to which few visitors are accustomed. After making a three and one-half hour boat trip, travelers must make a forty-five-minute climb up the side of a mountain on a winding stone stairway. At the pinnacle, a "campesino" reception committee greets the new arrivals and registers them by age, duration of stay, and nationality. The committee describes the physical layout of the island, its principal attractions—for instance, some archaeologically interesting burial towers—and assigns accommodations with a local family in an adobe hut. Like the Taquileños, the tourists sleep on "tortora" (lake reed) mats on earthen floors or on raised stone platforms.

In 1978, 68 families were authorized by local authorities to take in overnight foreign guests. By August of 1982, the number had risen to 207 families—in effect, every family on the island—and in the same month a record 1,800 people visited the island. Tourists come from North and South America, Australia, New Zealand, Japan, Israel, and especially

Western Europe. Community records show that 5,300 tourists visited Taquile between January and August of 1982, an average of more than 750 per month. Most visitors stay for only two or three days. Although the growth of tourism has been steady, weeks can pass with few visitors.

Taquileños manage tourism through an array of committees, for example, housing, weaving, food, and transportation. Special tasks such as construction or public maintenance are handled in a traditional manner by volunteer work groups set up by the committees. In the past six years, the islanders have established rules and prices that they and the tourists are expected to honor.

The entire community meets weekly in informal Sunday assemblies in the village square. As is common in the Andes, Indian and Spanish systems are mixed in Taquile. The island elects both traditional authorities and modern political officials; but traditional leaders such as the "jilakatas" have increasingly lost power to the government officials. The community "ancianos" (elders) are expected to advise the various authorities and the community as a whole.

During the first tourist season, two privately owned restaurants were opened by Taquileños who had returned from many years in Lima. Seven restaurants are currently in operation on the island. Each is owned and managed by community groups or families and is located in the "urbanizing" village square. Restaurant fare is slightly more varied than the food in peasant households—omelets, pancakes, and fish in addition to soup, potatoes, and herbal teas. Traditionally, most islanders have not been active fishermen, but the tourists' demand for fish has stimulated the formation of two fishing cooperatives, consisting of twenty-one and fifty members. Fish are also purchased from fishermen in nearby lakeside communities.

Potential and actual tourist income has encouraged such household improvements as extra rooms, tables, benches, tablecloths, kerosene lanterns, washbasins, and simple bedding gear such as reed mats and factory-made woolen blankets. These improvements are approved by an island commission. Nearby stores furnish toilet paper and beer. These products are novel to Taquile and are generally considered to be the maximum in allowable creature comforts consistent with an "authentic Andean experience." Each approved household directly receives the tourist income from lodging and in most cases from meals. An overnight stay in April 1983 cost thirty cents; a fish dinner fifty cents.

During the late nineteen-eighties, the Taquileños added new physical infrastructure to various public places. There has been a mini–community construction boom in outhouses and archways. Made from rock and cement and standing approximately 12 feet in height, the eight odd archways (at last count) reinforce the island aura of an ancient and mysterious civilization. Taquileños similarly have used their communal labor skills to construct a stone walkway several meters wide over an unkept dirt path previously strewn with stones and assorted debris. This has become a form of "main street" which cuts across the width of the island between the village square and toward one of the principal docks. In the square itself, restaurant owners have set up outdoor stone tables and chairs for tourists to chat and bask in the Andean fresh air and sunshine. Public buildings on the square also have been relocated and rebuilt to refurbish the image of local community government.

The increased income saved from boat transport also paid for "modern" Taquile infrastructure on the mainland. For various generations, unable to afford the cheapest hotel, the islanders turned their sails into tentlike covers for overnight accommodations in their boats at the Puno dock. The islanders constructed a nearby office with adjoining dormitory rooms. A major acquisition for the office is the private telephone, which carries great symbolic and practical value for entering the Puno tourist trade competition.

When Taquile's tourism began in earnest in 1976, textile marketing changed as well. Most local crafts had been sold by Taquile's middlemen in Cuzco, Arequipa, and Lima; now, goods could be sold on the island itself. Taquile's weavers eventually formed a community-run artisan store, where they could sell their diverse and increasingly numerous products. With middlemen eliminated, craftsmen received higher incomes.

An elected committee administers the store while the island's men take turns working as unpaid sales clerks. The crafts committee meets weekly to set prices based on the quality of workmanship and the amount of labor. The labor force is the same as in the premarket Taquile of the 1960s. Every man, woman, teenager, and child over eight earns money by producing crafts.

In recent years, store sales have averaged roughly $2,500 per month, rising as high as $5,700 during the peak tourist months of July and August. In addition, since August 1982, the island has held a widely publicized annual two-week crafts fair. Tourists visiting the island for only a few hours of one day buy several thousand dollars' worth of weavings at these fairs.

Thirteen years of experience with markets and tourists have affected what is produced in Taquile. Responding to demand, the Taquileños have created new products that have evolved from their traditional clothing styles. At present the community store stocks numerous shirts, vests, and pants of homespun cloth in natural colors and in a variety of weaves. "Peasant" shirts are particularly popular among the island's youthful tourists. Male weavers have adapted the techniques and designs used in stocking caps to produce a new kind of vest (chaleco músico) with rows of bright, fanciful, multicolored patterns. Women continue to weave extraordinarily fine bags and belts of varying widths, colors, and motifs. One tourist-related innovation in bags and belts is more extensive use of natural colors. Despite rates of return that are normally much less than a dollar a day, textile output in Taquile and nearby communities has mushroomed in recent years. One reason is that even with the low rate of return, weaving and knitting can be done during spare hours when there are no cash-producing alternatives. Many Taquileños stay up all night to work by kerosene lamps. The Taquileños have also begun to farm out some weaving tasks to people in nearby towns and to market textiles from neighboring Amantaní and Capachica in the island's cooperative store.

Although the quality of some textiles woven in Taquile has undeniably declined since marketing began in earnest, the drop is less than might be expected from the experiences of other communities. True, the widespread use of commercially spun and dyed yarn lowers the quality of the products. And men now knit "ch'ullus" (stocking hats) with less detail than in the past; their designs are larger, with more empty space. But the knitters now rely far less on repetitive motifs than they once did, and they incorporate a wider range of themes drawn from local culture and daily life. Moreover, the stocking hats retain their soft texture, their rich color combinations, and their beauty even though knitting machines are beginning to be used on a minor scale. The women have adopted similar measures to reduce production time for belts and bags, but their weavings are still superb despite inferior yarn quality.

The steady flow of tourist traffic encourages Taquileños to advertise their weavings by wearing them. While tourism encourages cutting corners, it also reinforces local pride in dress, workmanship, and native traditions. Taquileños still save their finest weavings for their own wear and use in festivals. All in all, the quality of both tourist and traditional weavings is probably still among the highest in Peru.

With the assistance of coauthor Zorn, a weaver and anthropologist, Taquileños organized a community museum to preserve and display their older, better textiles. To help retain examples of Taquileño weavings within the community, the Inter-American Foundation contributed to a fund to purchase fine old pieces owned by Taquile families. However, the rustic museum idea did not take hold until a group of Taquileños had returned from a visit to Europe sponsored by a European cultural organization where they had seen South American exhibits in ethnographic museums.

Taquile's style of tourism stands in sharp contrast to the experiences of other Third World communities where benefits are trickle-down at best and are offset by outside control, the erosion of cultural integrity, and the disruption of traditional lifeways. Taquile's six years of self-operated tourism demonstrate that a community can set its own terms for tourist development and capture the lion's share of the benefits.

From the outset of the community's attempt to manage its own tourism, the Taquileños had certain advantages—an unforced friendliness, colorful and highly visible folk practices, a thriving crafts tradition, and a spectacular landscape. The island's greatest previous handicap—its isolation—

became a dual advantage. First, Taquile's remoteness attracted tourists who enjoyed a challenging trip and savored the island's authenticity. But more importantly, Taquile's isolation allowed the islanders to keep outside entrepreneurs at arm's length while the community itself developed facilities and management skills.

The Taquileños have been fortunate. In several important ways, tourism has reinforced rather than undercut traditional life-styles. Weaving, for example, has flourished. The islanders enjoy making and selling a product that symbolizes traditional culture and values. This craft can be practiced between other tasks throughout the day, raising the value of otherwise marginal time. Rigorous childhood training in weaving and knitting continues, and the local esteem for quality textile production remains intact.

Boats in Taquile have always been owned cooperatively rather than individually. Tourism has built upon this tradition and produced diverse benefits. First, control of the motorboat traffic allows the community to regulate the flow of tourists, distributing them equitably among individual homes. Second, the newer and larger vessels give Taquileños more comfortable, reliable, and frequent access to the mainland. Third, management of boats has taught the islanders much about business administration and the operation and maintenance of machinery. Finally, boat building has evolved into a mini-industry. Local craftsmen now design and build all the large motorboats, and they have trained new and younger boat builders. Many neighboring lake communities now order their boats from Taquile.

On the other hand, women have not reaped a fair share of benefits from the tourist boom nor has their relative status on the island improved. The new decision-making committees that manage the island's various enterprises exclude women. Most of the popular and more profitable artisan products are made by men, and significant female labor may be displaced as the market shifts from products made by women to those made by men. However, times may be changing. Alternate educational programs primarily for women are now being offered by a local Catholic Church program.

Agriculture on Taquile's rugged terrain has always been difficult. With the growth of tourism, agricultural production has been boosted, and more cash is available for agricultural intensification. Taquileño farmers offer produce directly to consumers, earning income that normally goes to middlemen. Moreover, money from tourism provides a safety net against the risks from periodic drought, hailstorms, and frost. This cushion enables the farmer to weather seasons of heavy crop loss, such as the severe drought that afflicted the "altiplano" during 1982–1983.

Yet the productive capacity of traditional agriculture on an arid and overused landscape may be nearing its limits. Not only are there more tourists, there are also more Taquileños. Since the early 1950s the population has nearly doubled, increasing from about 640 to 1,250. Expanding economic opportunity has also encouraged a reverse, urban-to-rural migration. Many Taquileños are returning to their native island from the cities, bringing urban-learned skills and consumer tastes. If local food production cannot keep pace with new demands from islanders and tourists, traditional agricultural self-sufficiency may well give way to dependency on imports.

The traditional egalitarian character of Taquileño society emerged, in part, from shared poverty. To buy the island from the "hacendados" in the 1940s and 1950s, the islanders had to pool capital and act collectively. Similarly, forty years ago no individual commanded the necessary capital and labor to operate a sailboat, so families joined together and formalized rules to protect individual rights within groups.

Tourism has both reinforced this communal tradition (through boat cooperatives, for example) and undermined it. With new kinds of economic opportunity, social stratification has increased. Restaurant and store owners, textile middlemen, and some individual boat owners have developed specialized services. As they prosper, their needs and obligations tend to diverge from those of the rest of the community. So far, however, the rules of social behavior have acted to regulate competition, and Taquile continues to distribute economic benefits with remarkable equity. Everyone— young and old, male and female, the poorest and the better off—has benefited to some degree from tourism. Without question, there is a widening gap between ideal and actual behavior, but Taquileños continue to attach great importance to the common good.

Today's Taquileños walk a narrow path between holding to tradition and accepting change. Tourism is a powerful force that pushes in both directions. To date, there has been a kind of balance, but the flow of tourists has been relatively modest.

No one knows what the limits of accommodation may be before cultural destruction sets in. Foreigners are now practically a part of the landscape. In the evening they gather to play musical instruments and to drink in the restaurants, a scene reminiscent of a European pub or coffeehouse. Tourists with clicking cameras congregate at all the major rituals and religious festivals. Community life continues, but at what point will the local rituals and fiestas become simply spectacles for tourists? When does a community become merely a stage?

Taquile's life has already been altered. Fifteen years ago, locked doors were unknown, and strong controls were exercised over social drinking. The past six years have witnessed incidents of tourist-related theft and drunkenness, as well as trampled crops, nude bathing, and drug use. More people, more consumption, and more waste have meant a growing garbage disposal problem.

Many residents have acquired consumer goods—wristwatches, record players, radios, cassette players, and binoculars. Even a few battery-operated television sets appeared in a local restaurant. Yet at the same time, health and nutrition problems remain severe. Maternal death in childbirth is high and so is infant mortality. Children continue to suffer from undernourishment, gastroenteritis, and diarrhea.

Services that are created for the tourists do not always carry over to the community. The town's seven restaurants collaborated with local officials to install the island's first potable water system, but so far service has not extended beyond the restaurants. When asked recently about the island's lack of electricity, one leader responded, "An electric generator would make too much noise and therefore spoil the tranquility the tourist seeks."

The people are poor and the temptations great. "How to please the tourist" has become a major preoccupation. After a few hours with a Taquile family, foreign tourists regularly receive requests of "compadrazgo" (godparenthood) in an opportunistic attempt to hitch up a family to affluent "gringos."

Yet at the same time, the islanders are learning about countries and customs from all over the globe. Lasting friendships are not uncommon. Visitors sometimes send gift packages containing household utensils, publications, and medicines; and many Taquileños receive postcards, letters, and photos from friends around the world. To top it off, during the late 1980s, Taquileños made sojourns to the North. Eleven islanders traveled to Paris, representing Peru in a folkloric dance festival. They sampled French wines and numerous cheeses and gazed at European urban life from the heights of the Eiffel Tower. Two other islanders traveled respectively to London and Kansas (U.S.A.) to organize exhibits and give talks on Taquile's ethnic art. Six others traveled to Washington, D.C. for the American Folklife Festival. In 1990, the first telephone was installed on the island, widening further its connection with the outside world.

The island continues to acquire greater worldwide fame for its textiles and tourism after centuries in international and national obscurity. Television producers from exotic places such as Brazil and Japan have filmed programs on Taquile and student groups from as far away as the northeastern United States take excursions there to observe Andean peasant life and community-controlled tourism.

Looking to the future, however, the community must confront two main challenges. First, can it continue to adjust to, and benefit from, tourism without being swallowed up by the influx of outsiders? Can a strong culture continue to build on its strengths, and will that future community continue to be proud of itself?

The second challenge may be even greater. Tourism is still controlled by the community, but as the stakes rise, that control cannot be taken for granted indefinitely. Experiences in recent years demonstrate what the Taquileños are up against but also how they can respond when acting together.

An intriguing struggle between Taquile and outside entrepreneurs and government officials has been under way for some three years. Incursions by private boat owners in collusion with government authorities had undermined community control over boat transport. A small circle of local Puno elites from the government tourist ministry, the coast guard, local tourist agencies and an association of private boat owners had collaborated to undercut Taquile's established role, giving private boat owners the major share of tourist transport to Taquile. This allowed, for example, a single private boat company during the peak tourist season to employ three speedboats to transport some seventy tourists a day to Taquile, creating a big leak from the island's income flows. Also this mode of boat transport has increased day travelers to Taquile who may buy textiles but do not stay overnight. This is a problem because room and board payments make up a major portion of the islanders' income. In addition, the boat owner frequently insulted the Taquileños, calling them "brutes" and "indios" or "Indians."

To enlarge their Taquile-bound transport business, the association members had the advantages of mestizo (mixed blood) status and Spanish-speaking skills in the urban cultural milieu of Puno. Since boat tickets are sold on trains, in hotels, and through travel agencies, Taquileños as stigmatized Indians encounter barriers for tapping such markets. For example, the mere entry through the doorway of a tourist hotel can be a risky and humiliating undertaking. A specialized practice locally referred to as "jalando gringos" (pulling gringos) enabled young mestizos, often students hired by the competing boat owners, to sell ticket packages for the non-Taquile boatmen.

In April 1989, to reverse the declining conditions of their transport business, the Taquileños called a strike and blockaded the four docks on the island to prevent the private boats packed with tourists from landing. Hundreds of Taquileños, including children, mobilized. Women stood in the forefront brandishing long wooden poles to keep the boats away. This burst of female courage was perhaps the most remarkable behavior of this collective protest action, apparently a result of the Catholic Church's consciousness-raising educational programs on the island. Men holding slings assembled across the hillsides above the dock. The throng would race from dock to dock at scattered island locations to block each successive landing attempt. Several days later, they allowed the tourists to deboard and enter the island while forcing the boat owners to leave, thus recovering the return trip business for themselves.

Subsequently all private non-Taquileño boat traffic has been suspended to the island, putting the transport control back in the hands of the islanders. Taquile invoked the "ley de comunidades" as the legal argument for their action. Peruvian law grants their community absolute control over the soil and subsoil rights (save mineral resources), which for the island includes the dock areas. With assistance from a lawyer from the Catholic

Church, the Taquileños sued the boat owner's association while simultaneously beginning the paperwork in the capital city of Peru to obtain *official recognition* as an "indigenous community."

The private boat owners' association meanwhile retaliated against the original strike/blockade by filing suit against the top authority on the island as an "agitator" out to destroy its legitimate business interests. This legal effort fizzled, however, within several months. In July 1989, big challenges still lay ahead with a new tourist season beginning in July and a lack of response from the Peruvian government bureaucracy regarding their indigenous community status. Nonetheless, at least for a time, the islanders had regained control over a major part of their income-producing activities and had become more integrated with Peru's national tourist industry through formal agreements with the local tourist agencies.

In the meantime, the tourists arrive and leave—more each year. The Taquileños have shown that tourism, at least on a small scale, need not be managed by outsiders or be culturally destructive. Although the islanders' future is far from certain, they continue to build a community industry based on popular participation and the equitable distribution of benefits.

NOTE

This chapter is an updated version of an article that first appeared in *Grassroots Development* (Vol. 6:2/7:1, 1982–1983).

10

Work and Tradition

•

MARÍA CHUMPÍ KAYAP, MIGUEL JEMPÉKAT,
CARLOS MORENO & CHARLES DAVID KLEYMEYER

The connection between work and cultural expression is central to the betterment of human welfare. This relationship is also important when the loss of traditions, inevitable or not, has a negative impact on people's capacity to perform their work or on the quality, appropriateness, and usefulness of the product.

In this chapter we will examine two groups of people—the Shuar and the Quichua. These groups have broad similarities—both are Indian, and both are located in Ecuador—but they have differences as well. The Shuar case demonstrates the connection between work—women's farming and men's hunting—and oral traditions that are dying out. This loss of tradition involves both cultural penetration from without and change from within, as is mentioned by María Chumpí, and is very similar to the challenge faced by the Kuna (Chapter 5). The Quichua live 8,000 to 12,000 feet higher than the Shuar, and by necessity are more likely to maintain the traditional work form described here. Their case demonstrates how traditional work forms in communal farming and public works projects are reinforced by cultural expression—indeed, are forms of expression themselves.

SHUAR ORAL TRADITIONS

The Instituto Normal Bilingüe Intercultural Shuar is a bilingual teacher training school in the heart of Shuar territory in Ecuador's Amazon region. In 1985, the school added a cultural preservation program to its curriculum. Students who return for vacations to their distant jungle villages take a simple tape recorder and collect all forms of oral traditions from their elders. These tapes are processed for publication and for use in the Shuar bilingual radio school, for which many of the students will one day work.[1]

Later in this chapter, Miguel Jempékat, the Shuar rector of the Normal School, offers an eloquent justification for such cultural preservation activities. Following his statement, María Chumpí Kayap, who compiled this

149

For centuries, Andean communities have used mingas, or communal work days, to increase agricultural production and improve local infrastructure. Here, villagers from Quererani in Oruro, Bolivia, weed onions in a community-owned plot. The minga tradition is reinforced in such settings by other traditions having to do with food, dress, stories, riddles, and songs.

collection of sacred chanted songs, or *anents,* explains women's central role in Shuar agriculture and how these songs have historically been vital to carrying out that role. Implicit in her presentation is a reaffirmation of the relationship between traditional vocal music—content and form—and work. Neither writer pretends to prescribe what stance the Shuar people should take regarding the future use of these songs. They are simply preserving this form of Shuar oral tradition and "returning it to the people." In the end, it will be up to the Shuar people as a group to address the questions of whether and how this and other manifestations of their cultural heritage can be kept alive.

In highland Ecuador, and throughout the Americas, grassroots groups use music, dance, and other expressive forms to generate the cultural energy that draws people, time and again, to meetings and other events and keeps them involved and optimistic about achieving necessary change.

QUICHUA WORK FORMS

In the Andean context, the importance of traditional collective or reciprocal work forms—the *minga, ayni, randinpac, uyari,* and *maquita mañachi* —cannot be overstated. If these work forms were to vanish over the coming years, the impact on economic and civic life in the Andes would be substantial. The contributions made by campesinos to their own socioeconomic well-being by means of these work forms far outweigh contributions from national or international development programs. Thus, these work forms should be preserved and their role should be expanded, not only for indigenous communities but also for other populations who might adopt these forms. In Ecuador, for example, non-Indian groups have adopted collective work forms such as the *minga,* even utilizing that term to describe them.

The strength of these work forms comes from their cultural roots (dating back to pre-Incan times), which are replenished and reinforced in part by necessity and opportunity and in part by active, contemporary manifestations of cultural expression, including music, dance, stories, food, and dress. This reinforcement is observably mutual: Traditional, collective, or reciprocal work forms such as the *minga* both perpetuate and are perpetuated by the various forms of cultural expression that surround them.

Many anthropologists and other observers have described and analyzed these work systems and their historical roots in the Andes. Development practitioners, however, and especially cultural activists possess a unique perspective on this phenomenon and how it fits into the larger context of Andean development. Carlos Moreno, who has lived and worked all his life in the central Ecuadorian Andes, has observed and participated in hundreds of *mingas* and related work parties. He has also been an educator and cultural activist for more than twenty-five years, drawing often on these work forms in the execution of programs ranging from literacy training and reforestation to the establishment of community bakeries and artisan workshops. He was a founder and leader of the Feria Educativa, the Servicio Ecuatoriano de Voluntarios–Chimborazo, and the Unidad de Educación para el Desarrollo.[2]

—*Charles David Kleymeyer*

•

ANENTS: RELIGIOUS EXPRESSION OF THE SHUAR INDIANS

There are things that life demands of us that are hard to accomplish and that we endure because we must, but there are others that fit us like a ring on a finger. The monograph required to qualify for the baccalaureate at the Shuar Bilingual Intercultural Institute could have turned out to be so much drudgery but instead was more than we could have dreamed of.

We Shuar have unfortunately had no time to reflect on our culture, much less to write down our reflections. Contact with other cultures makes us feel subjected, and it is scarcely possible for us to go on thinking and feeling as Shuar. As a result, although a considerable amount has been written about us, there is very little that we can present as the actual authors.

Shuar students have now succeeded in becoming writers of our own culture. We have done real works of research, completely original works, demonstrating our sense of identity and self-awareness, which in the past we have failed to appreciate simply because of lack of knowledge. Surely there is no better work to be done by a Shuar than this.

In this spirit, we have sent all of our students to their home *centros* (this is what we call our communities) to confront themselves as well as their elders. Difficulties and problems have abounded, and we have discovered how far we have strayed from our culture, doing things that are not us, under the pretense of integration, civilization, and education.

In the end, we have come up with a document of eighty to one hundred pages. These are simple things, just as life is simple. Perhaps they are not expressed so well in English, but they are facts, and that is what matters.

Now comes the second part: returning to the people what the people handed over to us. We want these ideas to reach the hands and hearts of the Shuar so that they will read them and start to face up to, and affirm or deny, what their brothers and sisters are saying. That has been our reason for starting to publish some of these works, and our primary hope is that they will be most read in the homes of Shuar families.

It is then that we will be able to say that we are not out of touch with our people after all, that the Intercultural Bilingual Normal Institute *is* the Shuar people, serving the Shuar people.

—*Miguel Jempékat,* excerpted from María Magdalena Chumpí Kayap, *Los "Anent": Expresión Religiosa y Familiar de los Shuar,* Instituto Normal Bilingüe Intercultural Shuar de Bomboiza and Ediciones Abya-Yala, Quito, 1985

•

We, the young, no longer sing anents. In their place, we have chosen to appreciate Western music.

We, the young of today, have turned our backs on the Shuar culture, for there is no longer communication between the bearers of the pure traditional culture and the present generation.

The subject was unknown to me, and I resolved to seek out the reasons why the anents were sung, and at what times and places.

In researching this paper I [María Chumpí Kayap] was able to speak with elders such as Rosario Putsum, Teresa Chinkiamai, Pedro Awak, and Juana Ipiak, wonderful people and carriers of the lore, and to them I wish to express my appreciation, admiration, and respect. I regard this work as incomplete and hope that other young people will make it more significant by extending and deepening it as part of a living culture that must be acknowledged and maintained by all of us who call ourselves Shuar.

The anent is a prayer through which the Shuar communicates with the divine world; it is a literary composition in verse or prose accompanied by music, the content of which expresses what the singer wants to acquire spiritually.

There are other compositions that the Shuar use to express human feelings; for this we use not the anent but the *nampet,* which is in a different musical style. The anent, then, is a sacred chant.

Today we Shuar still have a fairly extensive repertoire of nampets but have almost completely forgotten the anents and *ujajs* (pronouncements that give strength and courage to the warrior). This is why I focus so heavily on anents in this research.

An anent is a prayer to the spirits for aid. The important thing is not so much the literal content as the spiritual attitude it is able to induce, especially the forces it unleashes that enable the Shuar man or woman who sings it to make what the anent says come true.

Anents of the Vegetable Garden and the Woman's Role

The woman has a well-defined number of tasks to do herself, but she also helps the man in certain tasks, such as removing branches and clearing away slashed brush. Women provide *chicha* and food to men who are engaged in heavy labor or setting off on hunting expeditions, and to everyone at feast days.

The primary area of woman's work is the garden. The woman plants all the crops but corn, plantains, *orito* bananas, and other things a man can plant. She also does the weeding and harvesting.

The anents presented below are directed to Nunkui, the superior being who taught women to cultivate garden plants and who makes them grow and multiply. The name "Nunkui" means "earth"; it is the seed that gives life to plants from the depths of the earth. It is a mysterious force that quickens all seeds.

This is why women place little Nunkui stones—called *nantar*—in the garden; they sing prayers so that this mysterious creative force will give life to vegetables and food to humans.

Nunkui is regarded as a harvest spirit. It is believed that Nunkui is responsible for pushing the crops up through the ground—in other words, for making them grow. Without Nunkui's help a woman cannot expect success, and so she tries in every way to attract Nunkui into her garden and make it stay.

These practices spring primarily from a belief in two main demands that Nunkui makes on the Shuar: that it be given a place to dance, and that it be given children.

If the woman in charge of the garden fails to clean it properly, Nunkui will withdraw deep into the ground and move away to the cleaner plot of another woman, taking the crop along and causing the weeds to suddenly grow more thickly in the garden that it left. This is why the garden has to be cleaned with great care.

In the following anent for planting, the woman sings a chant of propitiation to Nunkui to ensure that it will not sink more deeply into the ground:

> "Nunkui" (earth)
> Because I am a woman, Nunkui,
> I am calling the food,
> gently planting,
> I am planting;
> From out of the dark
> I call the food.
> Because I am a woman, Nunkui,
> in my clean garden,
> standing in the dark,
> I call all foods.
>
> I go along, placing the seed,
> because I am a woman, Nunkui.
> I call the food;
> I call all foods.
>
> With my cold hands I go, placing the seed;
> I cover it with earth.
> In this way I plant
> the sweet potato of the Shuar woman,
> throwing the bad seed away.
> I call the food;
> I call all foods.
> Every morning
> in this fertile earth
> with my cold hands I go
> placing the seed.
> (Rosario Putsum)

This anent is sung as the seeds are planted in the garden, so that they will develop well during their growing period:

> "Shukém" (boa)
> Like the tail of the boa,
> entwine, entwine,
> entwine to great length
> within the earth.
> Like the thickness of the boa's head
> I come calling;

> I call all foods,
> because I am a "sajino" woman,
> I come calling in shouts.
>   (Rosario Putsum)

Keeping the garden clean of weeds is woman's work, which she does with a machete, removing the weeds by the roots. She does this every day in the morning. The children help throw away the trash. The woman goes to the garden before sunrise. When the sun starts getting hot, she returns home to prepare food and chicha for her husband. This anent is sung so that the weeds will not grow rapidly:

> "Jempe" (hummingbird)
> Being alone,
> I, hummingbird woman,
> being alone,
> I blow on the plants.
> Because I am a woman, Nunkui,
> I blow on them.
> I am hummingbird woman.
> Because I am hummingbird woman,
> I blow on the plants.
> For I am a woman, Nunkui.
> Being alone,
> I, hummingbird woman,
> blow on the plants.
>   (Rosario Putsum)

This anent is sung standing in the garden when plants there die or do not produce well. Nunkui is asked to remove the pests that attack the plants in the garden and make new plants come up:

> "Paki" (sajino)
> Because I am "sajino" woman,
> I call the food.
> Because I am "sajino" woman
> I come calling in shouts
> from among the wilted plants.
> Because I am a woman, Nunkui
> from hill to hill I come.
> Because I am "sajino" woman,
> and from among the dry leaves
> I call the food,
> from the piles of dry leaves
> I come calling;
> I call all foods.
> Because I am "sajino" woman,

I come calling in shouts.
                    (Rosario Putsum)

This anent is sung to ask Nunkui for plentiful food:

"Nunkui" (earth)
Because I am a woman, Nunkui,
I call the food.
Here I stand calling,
being all alone,
calling the food.
Together with the man Shakaim
I am calling
the food.

You, man—Shakaim—
you call the food, too.
Don't be afraid of me;
call the food.
All my children,
yours too,
call the food.
Don't be afraid of me.
Because I am a woman, Nunkui,
I am calling the food;
being alone,
I call the food.
                    (Teresa Chinkiamai)

Anents for Domestic Animals

Most of the domestic animal species were introduced not too long ago by contact with other peoples, as can be seen from their Quichua and Spanish names: *atash* (*atillpa*, or hen), *patu* (*pato*, or duck), *popuu* (*pavo*, or turkey), *kuchi* (*cochino*, or pig), *cuy* (guinea pig), and *waka* (*vaca*, or cattle).

This anent is sung so that newborn chicks will grow and not die. They are likened to partridges:

"Las Gallinas" (hens)
My partridge hens
make sounds, breaking little sticks.
My partridge hens,
my little partridges
which don't usually die,
make sounds, breaking little sticks.

> My chicks have grown hard;
> my partridge hens
> which don't usually die,
> make sounds like little sticks.
> My little partridges
> which don't usually die,
> make sounds like little sticks.
> (Rosario Putsum)

This anent is sung for raising pigs, especially when there are young piglets. The anent likens them to a type of plant, *chirishri,* so that they will multiply like weeds spreading over the ground.

> "Los Puercos" (pigs)
> Like chirishri plants,
> my dear pigs,
> like chirishri
> that multiplies in the same place
> where the seeds fall,
> multiply right here
> as chirishri does;
> multiply right here,
> my dear little pigs.
> (Rosario Putsum)

Anents for Hunting and Hunting Techniques

When there were no more birds, Etsa (the sun) created them anew. Puffing through his blowgun, he vanquished and killed Iwia. Etsa is invincible: at the end, his victory was total and final. Etsa was represented as a man of divine descent. In the duel, the one with divine strength was Etsa, who would be victorious and instruct the Shuar on the life they must lead on this earth.

The people gradually adapted to the jungle and overcame the immense difficulties that nature threw up in front of them. It is believed that Nunkui gave the Shuar the dog for hunting. It is also believed that the presence of a woman, through her association with Nunkui, will help the man have better luck. In addition, she constantly sings to Nunkui so the man will be able to find quarry and so the dog will be protected from snakebites and other misfortunes.

Hunting is exclusively man's work. Two days before leaving, he prepares his gear. He carefully cleans his blowgun (*uum*) with cotton (*umch*) and a long cord called a *japik.* He prepares his darts, spreading poison on the tips of some of them and not on others. He puts a store of cotton silk in his *tunta* (quiver).

The dogs are given a drink of *malicoa* (*maikiwa*), which prepares them well for the enterprise. In addition, the *chankins* (baskets) are prepared, the machete is sharpened, and the flame (*jii*) is gathered up for making fire and smoking meat.

The preparations completed, the men set out for the place where they have decided to hunt.

This anent is sung when the hunters strike off into the forest with their blowguns, so that luck will go with them and their aim will be good when they find forest birds. When singing this anent, one must liken himself to a hawk:

> "Los Pájaros" (birds)
> The trilling birds
> come in flocks.
> I, likening myself to a hawk,
> crouching I approach them.
>
> Because I am a little boy,
> I have gained power from Etsa;
> crouching among the branches, I go.
> I have an immortal soul,
> and that's how I really am;
> I am the son of Shakaim,
> because that's how I am.
>
> My arrows are infallible,
> taking aim I go;
> I go alone into the jungle,
> Holding up my blowgun, I go.
> (Pedro Awak)

This anent is sung on departing for the hunt, so that snakes will not hurt the dogs:

> "Los Perros" (dogs)
> I protect from danger,
> my satam dogs;
> because they are very good hunters,
> I have given them malicoa to drink.
>
> Dear brother-in-law snake,
> do not bite my dogs;
> if you hurt them, I will take your life.
>
> Do not bite my dogs;
> I am taking my dogs to the hunt;
> Together with them, I go,
> protecting them from dangers.
> (Pedro Awak)

This anent is sung when going to hunt with dogs, so they will find quarry and not run into bad luck:

"Los Perros"
To my satam dogs;
Loose the dogs.

You, who are a woman, Nunkui,
loose the dogs;
I will go, calling.
Let us head to that mountain,
my satam dogs;
I go, calling
my satam dogs.

You, who are a woman, Nunkui,
think and pray with your song,
that I will not have bad luck.
I go calling the dogs.
You, who are a woman, Nunkui,
carrying your chankin
on your head,
come behind me
I go calling the dogs,
my satam dogs.

Let us head to that mountain.
You, who are a woman, Nunkui,
carrying the banana in the chankin,
carrying it, come along,
come behind me.
(Rosario Putsum)

The traditional songs that survive today are only the nampets, or secular songs. The anents are now disappearing.

If we were to lose them completely, a large gap would be left in our culture. The elders composed those anents to move the gods to grant their wishes.

There are anents for all the different activities that are carried out, and they are expressions that pray for the success of the act performed. We, the Shuar youth, no longer sing them; we are losing this ability to communicate with the divine powers through the anents.

The elders sang the anents with intense fervor; they believed in what they said in the anent, just as one feels today when one prays or talks to God. It is true that, as a result of the evangelization imposed on us by colonizers, we Shuar now regard the anent as inferior to their prayers.

May my effort, though incomplete, serve to encourage other Shuar youth to start practicing and rediscovering those important and formative cultural expressions, which enlivened every moment of our elders' lives.

—María Chumpí Kayap

●

THE POTATO DIG AT LLINLLÍN

In the corner of Chimborazo Province known as Columbe, there is a small town that was founded in the first decades of the Spanish conquest. This town lies south of the canton of Colta and is surrounded by forty Indian communities. The region has one of the largest Quichua populations in Chimborazo, an Ecuadorian province with more than a thousand Indian communities.

In pre-Incan times, the Columbe was the seat of one of the Indian districts in the kingdom of the Puruháes. One of its principal communities is Llinllín, which took the name of a common tree of the area. Few places kept their original names when the Spaniards divided among themselves not only the land but also the lives of the Indians that lived on the land. Most places received new Spanish names as part of the aggressive colonization effort.

History tells of resistance by the Llinllín Indians, who did not escape conquest by the Incas, from whom they took their customs and even their language. Working on communal property, Llinllín Indians established social bonds that kept them alive for generations. They succeeded in preserving their ancestral customs, their ethnic distinctiveness, and their indomitable will to work. The Spanish masters, having extracted the ready wealth of these peoples, decided to divide up their lands, ushering in the era of the *encomienda*. By 1709 the Llinllín hacienda emerged as the property of General Bernardo Dávalos. Legend has it that to cross this estate from one end to the other took two days on horseback. On this basis, it is asserted that the hacienda originally had an area of some 20,000 hectares. Since then, its lands have been gradually pared away, until today 4,500 hectares remain.

For centuries the Indians of Llinllín, like those of other haciendas around the town of Columbe, served their masters under laws and regulations in place since the time of the encomiendas. The Indians had no right to a wage and had to serve their masters in exchange for a piece of land, called *huasipungo*, for their subsistence. If a hacienda were to be put up for sale, the notice would read as follows: "Selling, 5,000 hectares with 1,000 Indians." Although Indian families or individuals could leave if they wished, their only viable alternatives were to move to urban slums, where they faced social isolation and other hardships, or to move to similar highland haciendas.

In these semifeudal circumstances, a series of conflicts flared up on the Llinllín hacienda in the 1970s when the Indians presented several complaints to the owners and requested an adequate wage and recognition of certain civil rights. Repeatedly refused their requests, the Indians finally laid down their tools and plows and refused to work. At the owners' request, the hacienda was placed under siege by local authorities. After considerable hardship and violence, and through a long process of strengthening themselves as a grassroots organization, the Indians of Llinllín finally succeeded in getting the more progressive national government to intervene. Shortly thereafter, the Ecuadorian Institute of Land Reform and Colonization (IERAC) bought up the lands and awarded legal title to the 1,050 Indian families of the Llinllín community.

One might think that a people that had been subjected to centuries of inhuman exploitation could have lost its cultural values, but now that the people of Llinllín are free and once again owners of their land, we find that their cultural values have persevered. During the era of their servitude to masters, these values were encouraged only if the masters wished it as a means for improving the Indians' work output. But now these traditions are taking on new life, and the ancestral customs are once again coming into their own, in practically every aspect of the people's lives. From peons they have become landowners, and after having worked collectively for the sole benefit of a single family of landowners, they are now developing a social mode of production based on the solidarity necessary to benefit the entire group.

For those of us who have been close to this community for many years, it is very easy to observe the difference between how the people worked when they were peons, always subjected to a master, and the present level of group participation in all tasks, as decided upon by the community leaders. One example of this change is notable during the process of planting and harvesting potatoes in Llinllín. It is clear that work is no longer imposed by whip and insult; there is no longer a foreman or overseer (who was often an Indian like themselves) representing the landowner and riding around, whip in hand, to punish anyone he chooses. In the potato digs, campesinos were always being caught concealing large, prize potatoes in their clothes to take home as a *guanlla,* for which they were harshly punished. Similarly, the gleaners—generally the wives and daughters of the peons, who had the job of picking out the potatoes left behind in the earth—were even subjected to pawing by the overseer or master on the pretext of recovering stolen potatoes that they suspected the women had concealed.

This is an example of the feudal form of exploitation under which the Indians of Llinllín lived for centuries. Today, despite the surviving traces of a colonial mentality and a stereotypical image of the Indian, the situation is different, and we have found that, despite all they went through, the Llinllín Indians either never lost their dignity or their pride or are now recuperating these feelings.

At a potato harvest today, no one polices anyone, yet everyone works—without the pressure of a master over them. Some dig the potatoes out of the ground; others carry the filled bags and pile them on a large mound, from which several persons select those potatoes that will supply seeds for the next planting and those that will be distributed and sold.

One very interesting fact accurately reveals the new attitude of the people. By a previous, spontaneous agreement, each family is entitled to a *guanlla* of the very best potatoes—up to a 100-pound bag per day—something they were once punished by the master for taking. Asked why they are allowed to carry off so many potatoes, one of the leaders said, "All our lives we were mistreated for taking just one potato. Now that the land is ours, the crop is ours, we have that right in compensation for so much suffering."

The potato dig on the Llinllín hacienda—and in many other communities of Chimborazo and elsewhere in the country—is almost a rite. This is the time when many cultural expressions emerge. Because all human affairs are bound up with the vital processes of the earth, the dig is timed to certain events such as the phase of the moon, and when it starts, there is always a ceremony to give thanks to God—better stated, the people thank mother earth, *Pachamama,* in the name of God. Then, during the dig itself, a whole series of expressions and actions emerge, vestiges of the people's culture, which, despite their past circumstances, they never forgot.

For the Indians of Llinllín, work and cultural expression make up a single whole—a shout, a song, a whistle, a gesture, and the throwing of a potato at an unmarried girl all are expressions of their culture that purge their work of aspects of sacrifice or ordeal and make it instead an act of joy. Though the work is hard, it is no longer degrading but an act of solidarity. The harvest is theirs, because the land is also theirs.

Actually, we are witnessing a process that started with the recovery of the land and is now generating events of high significance for the Indian social system. These events add up to a genuine recovery of cultural values that for centuries were subordinated to the interests of the dominant colonial groups. As they profited from the work of the Indian, these groups did not care if the *minga,* the traditional communal workday, lost its proper meaning of participation in all kinds of public works, not strictly production, and became part of the white man's authoritarianism.

For the people of Llinllín, the minga is no longer an imposition of authority by the master but an almost spontaneous expression of reciprocal solidarity among themselves, actuated by their communal interests and without distortion of its native symbolism, which has nothing of the sense of unpaid labor to which the white man had reduced it. Thus, in Llinllín, the minga attains its true meaning and establishes the direct relationship between contemporary culture and the Pachamama (mother earth) of the Puruháes, which rewards the unified effort of all people who come together for a single purpose—the common good.

Consider, for example, how the people act out various expressions of their culture during the minga for the potato dig—especially now that master and overseer are no longer around to prevent the young man from wooing the *guambra* (girl) of his dreams by throwing at her either a stone or the biggest potato for her to keep as guanlla. Or consider the community meal—one of the most ancient expressions of local ancestral culture, in which each family contributes the food it has brought from home. These acts, all symbols of what the earth can produce, embody the blend of work and recreation that is part of the people's essence and their way of being.

It is also common at a minga to hear a reed flute intoning an improvised melody or children singing a song as they tend their family's animals. Similarly, women tending livestock will improvise a song with words that generally tell some story from their own lives; meanwhile, they weave a *shigra* (bag) or spin sheep's wool to make flannel cloth or a poncho for their husband. As we can see, in Llinllín there is a symbiosis between work and artistic and recreational activity. This is not to say that work is neglected or given lesser importance. On the contrary, in their amusements the people find stimulus and the energy needed to transform their hard work into an act of gaiety.

During the potato dig, forms of cultural expression emerge that reveal in their variety what it is to be an Indian. For example, during the barley or wheat harvest, on an extensive tract of land, the Indian laborers sing the *jahuay,* a traditional song once heard in virtually all Indian districts in the Andean highlands. This is a choral song sung in Quichua by all the people involved in the harvesting. One man, the *paqui,* sings by himself a stanza that narrates events from his own life, and all the others repeat the refrain in a resounding, gleeful shout.

Many times we have heard in this song verses that conveyed lamentation, pain, anguish, and rebelliousness, all in response to oppression. One could speculate that it is the origin of the Andean song of social protest. Even so, this song is never without a verse dedicated to woman, to love. The following are some verses by way of illustration:

"Jahuay"

Cunanca caparishun
urqucunan chimapuragta,
tucui cuna jahuaynishun
cebadata cutshichashpa.

Now let's shout
till the high meadows hear us;
we'll all cry jahuay
as we harvest the barley.

Jacu Jaculla huambrita
Jaculla cebadita cuchunamunhai.

Let's go, let's go, little girl;
let's go harvest barley.

Ay jahuaihua jahuaihua!
Ay jahuaihua!

Ay jahuay, jahuay!
Ay jahuay!

Huasquitata aparingui huambrita
umintaitulla apari huambrita.

Carry the rope, little girl;
carry the sickle, little girl.

Ay jahuaihua jahuaihua!
Ay jahuaihua!

Ay jahuay, jahuay!
Ay jahuay!

Muru manquita aisangui huambrita; huira machquita agara huambrita.	Bring along a clay pot, little girl; bring along the barley-meal roasted in lard, little girl.
Ay jahuaihua jahuaihua! Ay jahuaihua!	Ay jahuay, jahuay! Ay jahuay!
Cunanca cebadata parvajcaj runa marcharisha ucu urita singuita caparichy.	Now let's shout, until the man who piles the barley for the threshingfalls to the ground in a fright.
Ay jahuaihua jahuaihua! Ay jahuaihua!	Ay jahuay, jahuay! Ay jahuay!

Unfortunately, these ancestral customs have been fading away because of the presence of religious sects that regard the jahuay as a heathen song that Christians may not sing. However, in some places they have started to sing the jahuay again during the wheat or barley harvest or as a folklore number performed at festivals.

In Llinllín, as in many other communities of Ecuador, there are other cultural forms that link the expressions of daily life to the production process—that is, to work. Some of the principal cultural manifestations associated with work are *randinpac, uyari,* and *maquita mañachi.*

Randinpac

Though *randinpac* means literally "for buying," the appropriate definition here is that the members of a community join together to build a house, for example, especially one for newlyweds. All contribute to the construction in different ways in exchange for food and an invitation to the housewarming party, known in Quichua as the *huasipichay.*

The *randinpac* is an act of solidarity, reciprocity, and free giving. If, sooner or later, everybody is to have a house built, then the benefit will eventually be for all.

In olden days, while the roof was being placed on the house, there were musicians who lightened the work by singing and playing traditional music in Quichua. Here once again it is seen how in Quichua culture, expressive entertainment and work go hand in hand, whereas the mestizo and white cultures believe that the two should not be mixed.

Uyari

When the Indians had to work all day long on the hacienda, they had to find alternative ways, in the little time left to them, of working in common to benefit their friends, neighbors, and the members of their families. *Uyari* involves participation in small tasks on a strictly voluntary basis, but with the expectation that some day the beneficiary will reciprocate. As a rule, uyari was provided to help plow some small plot of land, to help in sheep shearing, or to aid in a small potato dig or the harvesting of barley, which normally had to be done outside of working hours on the hacienda. Thus, it was common for people to rise at five in the morning for their uyari work so that they could be at work on the hacienda at seven. In any case, the master's work never failed to get done because of the uyari, but the Indians always found ways to make the necessary time to help one another.

Maquita Mañachi

When there was any emergency work to be done—for example, fixing a road damaged by a landslide, harvesting a small barley crop before the rains came, or repairing a house that was on the verge of collapse—it was quite common for people to ask friends to help out.

In the old days, this work was done, as in the other arrangements, with the tacit understanding that it would be reciprocated in kind. But the influence of feudal domination degraded these cultural processes and forced the payment for maquita mañachi to be made in produce or animals. Today the practice of maquita mañachi survives as a cultural act of reciprocity.

In sum, we can say that in the Quichua world, particularly in the Llinllín community, work and cultural expression are completely interwoven. One could even posit in such cases that work is dependent on cultural expression and that expression depends on work. Even if this is not so, it cannot be expected that community work will be duly accomplished in the absence of the cultural practices discussed here, which transform this labor into an act of joy and faith by a group of people who have been bound to the land for centuries and who feel compelled to render to it gratitude for their survival.

A striking difference between work in the Quichua world and work in the Western world lies in this blending of cultural expression and production in the one case and the separation of "recreation" and work in the other.

Singing during work is a favorite form of cultural expression among Indian people, and many writers have thought their songs sad. This perception entirely misses the mark, for both the music and the lyrics of their songs are more than anything a cultural expression of homage to the earth, of homage to themselves, sung in such a manner that they become hymns of the undying faith and hope of these people.

—Carlos Moreno M.

NOTES

1. See Appendix, EC-148.
2. See Appendix, EC-053 and EC-165, and Chapter 3 in this book.

11

Living *with* the Land:
Ethnicity and Development in Chile
•
Alaka Wali

In the small village of Rulo Gallardo, tucked into a fold of gently rolling
hills in southern Chile, a group of Mapuche men and women have assembled in the committee meeting house to talk with an anthropologist about
how traditional values and customs affect their lives. The awkward silence
is broken by a young man speaking Spanish, who tells the story of his
early days at public school, the humiliation that followed whenever he
spoke Mapundungu, the Mapuche language. It is a story shared by other
young people in the room; one by one they put aside their inhibitions to recount the hazing from teachers and other children that finally made them
give up speaking in their first language. Hearing the pain in their children's words, the old women in the room softly lament, in a mixture of
Spanish and Mapuche, at not having steadfastly transmitted their ancestral
language. Feeling the rush of loss, people in the room at first deny that traditional culture counts for much anymore, but slowly the threads of another story emerge that exemplify the religious beliefs and conceptions of
good and evil that make these people Mapuche.

Almost 1,200 miles to the north, in a vastly different setting of rugged
snow-capped mountains and high barren plateaus, a group of Aymara men
and women gather a few weeks later to discuss their culture. Reticent
about their own beliefs and traditions, they inquire curiously about the culture of their visitor (herself from India), and in the process of exchanging
stories, open a window into what it means to be Aymara.

The Mapuche farming their lush green fields in the south and the Aymara astutely exploiting "eco-niches" in the high Andean reaches of
Chile's Norte Grande have little in common save their centuries-long
struggle to retain control over resources in the face of a national society
exerting its dominion through legal decrees, forced acculturation, and
military conquest. In recent years, the battle over resources has been
framed as a debate about development. Many of Latin America's efforts to

Indigenous children learn traditional music in a program run by Folil-Che Aflaiai, an organi-zation formed by Mapuche Indians living in Santiago, Chile. These Mapuches face the daunt-ing task of trying to maintain their sense of group identity in a modern metropolis. (See Ch-398 in the Appendix.)

modernize since World War II have focused on homogenizing populations, on the theory that this would grease the wheels of economic growth. This scenario visualized local cultural and social differences as obstacles to be overcome, not opportunities to be seized.

The shortcomings of this approach, exposed during the past decade of economic and environmental crisis, have led some theorists and practi-tioners to search for alternative methods that would spur "sustainable de-velopment." They have posited the thought that long-term growth depends more on careful resource management than on more-intensive resource ex-ploitation. Increasingly, policymakers think the key to designing and im-plementing effective resource management means not only permitting local differences, but fostering them to tap local systems of knowledge. Considerable evidence indicates that indigenous peoples have successfully protected and managed fragile ecosystems for hundreds of years while achieving relatively high standards of living. This has given rise to the hypothesis that organic forms of local social organization are prerequisites to successful development.

This hypothesis rests on two assumptions. First, patterns of local social organization, influenced by shifting economic and political contexts, form the core of ethnic identity. Ethnicity, then, is not just the outward difference in clothes, music, dance, and even language: It is forged as communities respond through their social institutions (such as patterns of exchange, kinship relations, and religious systems) to the problems of adaptation. Second, effective local participation in a development project can occur by preserving and building on this ethnic identity. If participation is sought through the imposition of nonindigenous cultural strategies, the project endangers community control over local resources.

Among the Mapuche and Aymara, this hypothesis about sustainable development is being tested by two IAF-supported nongovernmental organizations (NGOs). Although working in very different contexts and facing different problems, both NGOs use strategies that reinforce ethnic identity, and the results in both cases are higher production *and* greater local control of land and resources.

Success in two projects, however laudable, is not a blueprint for simple replication elsewhere. The NGOs working with the Mapuche and Aymara have unique programmatic emphases that make them different from each other. A closer analysis of the projects' activities and methodologies, however, reveals three common factors in the success of both that are transferable to other programs. Community autonomy, acceptance, and responsibility each works in its own way to reinforce group identity, enhance self-esteem, and empower project participants.

THE COMMUNITY IS IN CHARGE

The success of the Sociedad de Profesionales para el Desarrollo Rural (SOPRODER) in working with the Mapuche and the Taller de Estudios Rurales (TER) in working with the Aymara is in no small measure due to their common strategy of permitting communities to define the agenda and set the pace for development. Their variation in implementing that strategy is a product of two NGOs with different institutional backgrounds interacting with two different indigenous cultures, each with its own history.

Today's Mapuche are descendants of a fierce but loosely organized nomadic people who stopped the Incan empire in its tracks and resisted the Spaniards for 300 years before finally submitting to "pacification" in the mid-nineteenth century. Subsequently confined to *reducciones*, or mini-reservations, that were titled to *caciques* who were heads of extended families, the Mapuche were forced to abandon their lives as hunter-gatherers, to become herdsmen of cattle, and finally to take up the plow.

Life on the reducciones, while difficult, offered a measure of autonomy. Indigenous religious beliefs persisted, and new forms of social organization emerged based on mutual obligations to kin and community. The communities, which were named after a local geographical feature such as a river, often included several reducciones. It was these communities that shaped ethnic identity, making the Mapuche distinct from the Chileans rapidly settling the countryside around them. By the turn of the century, within the boundary of their communities, the Mapuche lived in dispersed households, with no main streets or village plaza. Some houses eventually incorporated outside building materials such as wood planks or tin roofing, but many had walls of cane or tree bark and thick thatched roofs. Pasturage was held in common, and though each nuclear family had usufruct rights to individual parcels of land, plots could not be bought or sold. While the Mapuche now buy and sell goods in outside markets, reciprocal exchanges of resources and labor prevail within each community. These indigenous forms of cooperation help the Mapuche redistribute resources and protect fragile lands. The relationship between community and land, in turn, reinforces identity.

A century of systematic discrimination and encroachment on their land base has left the Mapuche mired in poverty. Overuse has depleted the soil, and the shortage of arable land has forced the young to migrate. Over half of the 900,000 Mapuche in southern Chile now live in urban areas, where they are poorly assimilated and in danger of becoming a permanent underclass. In 1979, a law was enacted that forced each family to register its own deed, privatizing community land and transforming it into a cash commodity. This law proved the most dangerous threat yet to the Mapuche community because it caused increased migration and unraveled the intricate web of mutual obligations that defined ethnic identity.

The year before, an interdenominational group called DIAKONIA, in an effort to counteract the poverty and out-migration, started a project among the Mapuche around the city of Temuco that helped tap the latent power of ethnicity by strengthening the community. SOPRODER is a non-denominational NGO that grew out of this effort; three of its ten-person staff have been working with the Mapuche for more than a decade, helping organize local committees to implement project activities; three of the staff are Mapuche themselves. Each committee, which may represent more than one Mapuche community, holds biweekly meetings and usually is visited each week by a SOPRODER technical team.

Each committee sets its own goals within an integrated program designed to improve subsistence levels, increase family incomes, and resolve domestic and social problems. The committee for the community of Rulo Gallardo, for example, is composed mostly of older women, and their emphasis has been on the development of artisan crafts, such as sewing and weaving, and on a health project. Yet the participants have also, over the years, adopted many of the agricultural techniques promoted by SOPRODER's extensionists, leading to a dramatic increase in wheat and lentil production. Now, instead of persistent shortages, households actually have surpluses. By contrast, the community of Leufuche, which recently joined the program, was unable to take advantage of the agricultural program initially. Leufuche's land committee has instead emphasized social work to help combat the area's high incidence of alcoholism, broken families, and emigration by young people.

SOPRODER's willingness to let the community set the pace of development has given Mapuche participants a sense of control over the direction of change. Rather than being told what to do when, they decide which elements of the program best suit their needs. Among people who have lost control over so many aspects of life, regaining a sense of autonomy has been a key step in reinforcing the identity and integrity of the community.

This can be seen in Rulo Gallardo, where the committee faced the task of selecting a monitor to participate in a new health program that combined training in basic first aid with the collection and prescription of traditional herbal remedies. As the discussion unfolded, the committee's first impulse was to select a young person who was literate. No such person was readily available, however, and the feeling slowly emerged that older women on the committee had been excluded from active work. An older woman then volunteered to be the monitor if others agreed to help with the parts of the job requiring literacy. The committee recognized the value of her knowledge about herbal medicines, and committee leaders agreed to help her with written materials. In the process of choosing a monitor, the committee balanced the value of literacy with the need to preserve traditional knowledge, reaffirming the ability of elders to contribute to their communities and the relevance of oral traditions in modern times.

The program carried out by TER among the much more scattered Aymara communities of northern Chile has, from the outset, had as its primary goal the preservation of indigenous ethnicity. Most Aymara live in the Andean regions of Ecuador, Peru, and Bolivia, with fewer than 30,000 residing in the Norte Grande of Chile, which was seized a century ago from Peru and Bolivia during the War of the Pacific. Tensions still exist in the region, and the government has exerted itself to "Chileanize" the region through education programs, civic crusades, and tight border controls.

The mining boom in guano and nitrate that followed the war fueled rapid growth in the coastal towns of Iquique and Arica and profoundly altered life among the Aymara. The patterns of exchange that prevailed in the region began to break down as the Aymara farming the lower valleys became integrated into the new market economy and lost their language and customs. The highland Aymara, who were primarily llama herders, lost ready access to maize and other food crops produced at lower elevations, and many began to emigrate in search of better livelihoods.

Those who remained in the altiplano retained their language, social structures, and kin affiliations into the 1970s. The basis of Aymara ethnicity rests on religious beliefs reflecting strong ties to the environment, close attachment to local villages, and the concept of *ayllu*, a lineage system that allocates the distribution of resources and labor. However, when the government of Augusto Pinochet created a free trade zone in Iquique in the mid-1970s and interest in mining intensified, new pressures were exerted on the altiplano. Communities became increasingly stratified as some Aymara men began to haul cargo full-time for merchants shipping imported goods from Iquique across the highlands to Bolivia and Peru. In order to buy a pickup truck, these men sold off their herds, gradually severed their obligations to their communities, and became more and more urban. At the same time, the downhill stream of young Aymara continued unabated, until as many as 70 percent of all Chilean Aymara had settled in urban areas.

TER emerged from a group of social scientists studying the highland Aymara under the auspices of the Universidad de Tarapaca in the 1970s. This group soon saw that their research needed practical application. TER's current staff of ten professionals with diverse skills is convinced that the survival of the environmentally fragile altiplano as a productive region depends on the survival of the Aymara as a people. Consequently, TER selects its development projects not only for their ability to increase production but for their ability to knit communities together.

In order to enhance the sense of autonomy of the high valley communities, most of TER's projects have concentrated on improving infrastructure, including the building of two model irrigation canals and two dip baths for llamas. Current plans call for another canal and water storage tank, a windmill and canal project, and a school. While the projects are not technically novel, the degree of community control over them has been unusual, and central to their success.

For instance, the community of Chapicollo clearly needed to produce more diversified crops to replace those it could no longer obtain from farmers at lower elevations. TER staff thought the obvious solution would be to modify the ancient low-valley technology of canals the Incas built out of sand and stone for transfer to the highlands where risky rain-fed methods predominated. Rather than imposing this solution by offering to build the structure, TER used the idea of a canal to spark a community discussion that would pave the way for stronger local organization.

The first step was to hold regular community meetings in which every aspect of the project was aired: the route of the canal, the division of labor, the types of building materials. A number of disputes soon arose. Some Aymara families had begun to migrate seasonally to the lower valley, fanning there for part of the year while maintaining their llama herds in the altiplano through a complicated set of sharecropping, land rental, and kinship relationships. These families resented the demand for communal labor mandated by ayullu since it came at a time when their fields in the lower valley required considerable attention. The most likely site for the canal also seemed the most controversial, reigniting land disputes between the people of Chapicollo and their neighbors in Inquelga and Aravilla that had smoldered since a titling process was instituted by the Chilean government at the turn of the century.

As people resolved these conflicts and reached compromises with their neighbors and relatives outside the community, they not only realized the continued utility of indigenous methods of working together, they also gained confidence in making their own decisions and implementing them. By facilitating the discussions and carefully watching from the sidelines as they moved to fruition, the TER staff reinforced local social organization. Eventually relatives living in squatter settlements in the lower valley decided to return and pitch in. Residents from neighboring villages also decided to help build the canal, some because they had claims by marriage to fertile land in the area, others because they expected that the people of Chapicollo would one day help them build their own canal.

Because of the protracted nature of negotiating these arrangements, canal construction took more than three years. TER confined itself to providing cement to supplement the sand and stone gathered locally, facilitating transport, and giving technical guidance. By the 1988 growing season, the canal was ready for use by some residents. Families used the water to raise their yields of potatoes and *quinoa*, a high-protein grain grown throughout the Andes, and for the first time harvested garlic and other vegetables that had never grown in the altiplano. TER was confident now that indigenous forms of action that strengthened community autonomy were also compatible with modified traditional technology.

THE COMMUNITY MUST AGREE

When SOPRODER and TER insisted on putting the community in control of the pace of development, they implicitly limited themselves to techniques and technologies that were acceptable to the community.

SOPRODER only introduces easily adaptable technologies. Some of these new methods are modified versions of indigenous practices. It recommends cultivation techniques such as composting and new methods of planting and harrowing; technologies such as a new time-saving plow, the *arado sincel*, whose three blades are angled to avoid churning the topsoil and help conserve nutrients; and inputs such as organic fertilizers that are simple, inexpensive, and easily applied. As a result, Mapuche farmers have reduced their need for expensive agrochemicals while increasing production.

In each case, the new technique was thoroughly discussed with farmers, modified by their suggestions, and tested on a small scale before being widely introduced. The new harrowing technique is one example. Staff members Ana Mella and Augusto Gallardo experimented on the SOPRODER model farm with a method that involves extensive harrowing of wheat fields when the new plants are about three inches high and weeds are just taking root. Although the weeds are uprooted, the technique appears to be foolishly counterproductive since the wheat is plowed under. But two weeks later the wheat reappears, more robust than ever. To allay farmers' fears, SOPRODER demonstrated the technique on small sample plots in communities, hoping that people would be inspired by the results to plant larger fields. Some farmers, however, remained wary.

Such was the case in the community of Calof where a farmer had volunteered to let his field be harrowed in the new way. A few days before the scheduled demonstration, a government extension agent visited him and counseled against the procedure. Instead, he urged the farmer to accept "free" herbicides. The farmer was torn between his loyalty to the SOPRODER program and his reluctance to offend the government or refuse free inputs. Rather than make the farmer choose, Mella suggested that half the field be treated with the government herbicides while the rest was maintained with the new harrowing method. This would allow local farmers to judge the results for themselves before locking themselves into a weed control method. Mella realized that the new technique offered the possibility of making the Mapuche less dependent on outside resources, but she also realized that independence would be hollow if the Mapuche could not be trusted to make their own decisions. As a result of this experiment, most farmers in the area are using the SOPRODER harrowing method.

TER's work with a textile project in three Aymara communities underlines the importance of community acceptance in building the self-confidence and self-esteem required for taking another step in development. The project is designed to preserve traditional weaving techniques and increase household incomes by involving women in spinning wool and making textiles for sale. The women own the enterprise and, with the help of TER staff member Lucila Pizarro, are learning how to run it.

The women of each community elect leaders to coordinate production, which is marketed in a small shop, rented by the project, in the city of Iquique. The store is staffed by young Aymara women who have migrated to the city. They earn additional income by using wool spun in the altiplano to knit some of the sweaters they sell in the store. While the store serves as a museum for educating tourists and cityfolk about Aymara weaving techniques and the meaning of designs, it has also inspired a minirevival in the altiplano. The women of the village of Cotasayal for instance, have turned to their mothers to deepen their knowledge of traditional weaving patterns.

Motivated by the prospect of getting higher prices for their spun wool and textiles, Aymara women are taking better care of their llama herds to ensure higher quality fleece. This has increased support for TER's program of improved livestock management and led to demands for antiseptic dip baths. In this instance, community acceptance of one project has led to acceptance of another. Like the Mapuche, the Aymara are finding that gains in production are related to growing self-esteem.

THE COMMUNITY IS RESPONSIBLE

SOPRODER and TER have managed the process of development assistance in ways that have given Mapuche and Aymara communities the desire, confidence, and ability to take greater responsibility for their own destinies. Indigenous peoples are increasingly identifying their own problems and trying out their own solutions.

SOPRODER's primary technique for accomplishing this has been the training of monitors. Selected by local committees, monitors receive specialized instruction in a particular skill such as wheat production, horticulture, animal husbandry, or health. Monitors are then responsible for training others in their new specialty.

This program has had several positive effects. Monitors are encouraged to travel to other communities to offer technical assistance; they hold seminars to exchange information; and they have become a beacon for Mapuche pride and self-worth. The latter is particularly important because the systematic erasure of Mapuche ethnicity from the public schools has deprived the Mapuche of indigenous role models who not only understand sophisticated technologies, but are able to teach their own people how to use them.

A recent committee meeting in Leufuche is illustrative. Two SOPRODER staff members attended, accompanied by two monitors from other village committees. As part of the meeting, SOPRODER planned to set up a demonstration plot to see which of five wheat strains performed best in the area's microclimate. SOPRODER extension agent Ricardo Sánchez opened the session by holding up each variety and briefly describing its characteristics, but he quickly stepped aside in favor of one of the visiting monitors, Francisco Curiñir, a wheat specialist. The monitor then led a spirited discussion, distinguishing the varieties in detail, explaining the care required by each, and listing the possibilities for crossfertilization. Meanwhile, Sánchez quietly slipped away to hoe the demonstration plot for tilling. And off to the side, the other visiting monitor,

Mercedes Curimil, who specializes in orchards and animal husbandry, was busy discussing the latest information on fruit horticulture with her counterpart from Leufuche. The subliminal impact of SOPRODER technicians voluntarily taking a backup role to Mapuche "experts" was visible to anyone familiar with grassroots projects.

The confidence these experts have developed from working with each other and the knowledge they have gained about the common problems facing the Mapuche have led them to form Rayen Koskulla, a pan-community organization independent of SOPRODER, although formed under its auspices. The two monitors who visited Leufuche are the president and secretary of this organization. Initially, Rayen Koskulla, the Mapuche name for the *flor de Copigue,* a common Chilean flower, was only a coordinating body with no source of funds and no agenda of its own, although its board was controlled and elected by all the committee members. Both the leaders of Rayen and the committees themselves grew dissatisfied with this limited role and began to press for more autonomy. In early 1988, Rayen attained legal status as an *asociación gremial,* which is similar to a rural cooperative. It hopes to exert more control over the revolving credit fund now managed by SOPRODER and to set up a marketing network to obtain higher prices for cash crops.

Among the Aymara, TER has been active in promoting both intra-community and pan-community seminars that incorporate technical training with more wide-ranging discussion of the nature and goals of development and their relation to the community's needs and problems. The pan-community *encuentros* were the first general gatherings of representatives in many years to discuss common problems and explore the meaning of Aymara identity.

This series of three-day meetings, many of which focused on ways to strengthen local organization, eventually gave birth to Aymar Marka, or "the Aymara people," an umbrella organization dedicated to defending Aymara ethnicity through the promotion of its culture and the provision of services to altiplano communities. Recently Aymar Marka has embarked on a legal battle to protect community rights to water and land from renewed claims by mining companies.

Both Aymar Marka and Rayen Koskulla face grave problems as Chile returns to democratic rule. First, the constituents of both groups remain largely the project beneficiaries of SOPRODER and TER, only a fraction of the much larger Mapuche and Aymara populations. If either organization is to succeed in its goal of combining ethnic preservation with economic development, it must broaden its membership substantially. This may be difficult for Rayen since the committee structure on which it rests is an invention of SOPRODER and has yet to attract participation by caciques and other community leaders. Aymar Marka has made some progress, however, through its participation in a federation of Aymara organizations in the north.

Second, the centuries of systematic oppression and forced assimilation have so eroded the native forms of social organization that their original shapes are barely perceptible. The attempts by SOPRODER, TER, Rayen Koskulla, and Aymar Marka to renew those forms are significant, but in the end may come too late.

Finally, both of the indigenous organizations and their NGO progenitors are aware that considerable internal stratification exists among the Mapuche and the Aymara. No one yet knows if reliance on indigenous social institutions and practices that stress egalitarian modes of resource use will be able to prevent further stratification as increased production leads to tighter integration into the national market economy. The NGOs, too, face problems because both rely heavily on dwindling international donor funding.

GUIDEPOSTS FOR THE ROAD AHEAD

It is unlikely that either the Mapuche or the Aymara will be able to maintain their ethnicity if they are forced to alter their fundamental relationship to the land. For the Mapuche that means finding new ways to counteract the pressure toward individual rather than community landholdings. The Aymara must protect their water rights and find a way to preserve the fragile ecology of the altiplano from outside pressures to exploit the area's resources. Chile itself has a stake in these struggles. If the rural Mapuche lose their land and their identity and flock to cities where they are not welcome, they may create an underclass that is a permanent burden on the national society. If the Aymara are unable to protect the ecology of the Norte Grande, the source of water for the lower valleys and coastal cities in this arid region will also be endangered.

Fortunately, the return to democracy has created a new opportunity to expand the accomplishments of SOPRODER, TER, and the organizations that have emerged among their beneficiaries. The Chilean government has recently moved to establish a decentralized corporation called Condición Especial de Pueblos Indígenas (CEPI) to handle indigenous issues and funnel loans and resources to local communities. Funds have yet to be appropriated, but CEPI is headed by José Bengoa, an anthropologist who has worked extensively with the Mapuche and was an IAF consultant for the SOPRODER project. CEPI's mandate includes working closely with NGOs to formulate policy toward indigenous people.

The return to democracy also may allow for closer cooperation among indigenous populations and the NGOs that assist them, allowing one group to learn from the experience of others. TER, for instance, could benefit from the technical know-how SOPRODER has developed in increasing agricultural production. Now that Aymara communities are receiving irrigation from their new canal for the first time, they will be farming more intensively and may need access to credit and extension services, which TER is not equipped at present to provide. SOPRODER, on the other hand, might benefit from making explicit some of the unexpressed ethnic components underlying its program. Systematic applied research along the lines pioneered by TER might allow SOPRODER to develop a more penetrating view of Mapuche ethnicity beyond the maintenance of cultural forms such as dress, music, and art. Most grassroots organizations experience difficulty in making the transition toward greater autonomy from the NGOs that help give them birth, and Rayen Koskulla and Aymar Marka are no exception. But in responding to the organizations' demands for greater control over project resources, SOPRODER and TER have the opportunity to help Chile's indigenous peoples form organizations that give traditional values a new shape. This is occurring within the context of a new political awakening among Chile's indigenous peoples that has led to the formation of their own political party, Partido Tierra e Identidad (PTI).

No one suggests that any of these hopeful signs are panaceas. The process of maintaining ethnicity by fostering community autonomy, acceptance, and responsibility clearly results in a slower pace of economic development than some theorists would find acceptable. It also may involve higher commitments of staff time and resources by NGOs. Yet these projects have harnessed the opportunity to continue growing in sustainable ways because they have been responsive to community norms and elicited community participation. They suggest that other indigenous groups can also find their way in a changing world if they are empowered to explore the potential of their own technologies and social institutions and mold them to the needs of development. The benefits will be not only a greater richness and diversity in national cultures, but a better chance of preserving the resources of an ever-shrinking planet.

NOTE

This article originally appeared in *Grassroots Development* (Vol. 14, No. 2, 1990).

12

From Failure to Success: Tapping the Creative Energy of Sikuani Culture in Colombia

•

XOCHITL HERRERA & MIGUEL LOBO-GUERRERO

The women ignore us. They don't want to sweep their houses or boil drinking water. The grandmothers say they never boiled the water and it hasn't killed them yet.

When someone is seriously ill, people in the community say the promoter should pay the cost of transporting the person to town and feeding him, that that's why we earn good money.

They don't believe us when we talk about parasites and microbes; they think diseases are caused by witchcraft.

These were some of the reluctant responses that finally emerged during our first meeting in December of 1984 with a group of indigenous community health promoters. We had come from the Fundación ETNOLLANO to the small village of Cumaribo—one of the centers for the settlements of Sikuani Indians scattered throughout the eastern lowlands of Colombia—at the request of the Regional Health Service to help find a remedy for its disappointing efforts to assist the Sikuani people. As a first step, we were holding a 10-day seminar with the health promoters, of whom much had been expected but who seemed to have accomplished little.

Although our first question—"What are the most serious problems you face in working daily with your communities?"—had seemed an obvious one, the uneasy silence we met from the 15 young promoters indicated that they did not find it so. Perhaps it was the first time they had been asked. Or perhaps each felt that those daily obstacles were caused by his own shortcomings, which should be hidden from outsiders.

We should not have been surprised at the tension and discomfort our question had provoked. The young men before us were among the 34 Sikuanis who had been selected by their local communities for training by the Regional Health Service of the territory of Vichada. The earliest trainees had studied at the urban hospital in Puerto Carreño, the territorial capital, while the newest promoters had been trained around Cumaribo, a newly settled town along the middle reaches of the Vichada River. The syllabus that formed the basis of their studies followed principles set by the national ministry of health and were based on the urban and peasant milieus of the Colombian heartland. The rigid emphasis on nursing techniques, basic pharmaceuticals, the installation of latrines and water systems for public sanitation, and the promotion of dietary regimens appropriate for highland Colombians made it difficult, if not impossible, for the Sikuani promoters to question the origins of the health problems they would encounter in their own remote lowland communities. Basic health education received scant attention in their coursework, and when it was prescribed, it was to be carried out according to formulas drafted in Bogotá.

That is why the first responses to our question on that December morning were so timid, affirming that all was well, that the communities were happy and that their only needs were for more advanced training in nursing, more drugs and equipment, better transportation, and panels for the tin roofs of local health posts. How was this to be reconciled with the misgivings of the Regional Health Service itself, which on several occasions had expressed concern over the high dropout rate—nearly 60 percent—among its indigenous promoters and had begun to wonder if those who stayed on did so only for the salary, small as it was?

At that point we realized that our objective—to achieve true community participation in solving local health problems—was too ambitious for the moment. Instead, we would have to focus on the promoters themselves, finding ways to reconcile their conflicting roles as members of an indigenous community and as government officials within that community. The problem before us was to remove the barriers that kept the promoters from unleashing their creativity to work as Sikuanis as well as representatives of a government agency.

So we proposed that they take all the time they needed to think about the question we had asked and that they discuss the problem in their native language. We were in no hurry, and could wait as long as necessary, provided that someone from the group would translate the discussion for us. Immediately the atmosphere was transformed, and although the intense discussion that followed seemed incomprehensibly chaotic to us, by noon we had the first answers describing the real problems that promoters faced in their daily work. The broad outlines of the participatory research program we would undertake with them during the next two years emerged from those answers.

We had reason to believe that such a program might provide the key to developing a new kind of training program for indigenous promoters, one that would integrate them into the community by forging links with the *cabildos*, or representative councils of local officials, who had begun to consolidate their authority with the support of the Organización Nacional Indígena de Colombia (ONIC), and that would not only emphasize curing the ill but would also emphasize promoting health. Our preliminary research convinced us that the declining health among the Sikuani was related more to recent ecological and sociocultural changes than to strictly medical factors.

A CULTURE UNDER STRESS

The Sikuani, one of some 70 indigenous groups in Colombia, number nearly 20,000 people living in small villages scattered among the savannahs of the Orinoco River Basin, mainly in the department of Meta and territory of Vichada.

Until the 1950s, the Sikuani, like many other Amazonian and Orinocan tribes, were able to maintain their traditional way of life. Their seminomadic lifestyle enabled them to withstand, with relative success, the military offensives of the Conquest and the colonial era, the attempts of the Jesuits to convert and permanently settle them, and the incursions of the indigenous Caribs, who in the seventeenth and eighteenth centuries roamed the area in search of slaves to sell to the Dutch in the Guianas. The Sikuani sustained themselves by hunting, fishing, gathering edible roots and insects, and by slash-and-burn farming, primarily of *yuca amarga*, or cassava. They built houses from palm fronds and made clothes out of tree bark. Primarily self-sufficient, they supplemented their production by trading with other indigenous peoples in a network that linked the Andes to the Guianas and the Amazon Basin, and that had its own currency made of polished shells, or *quitipa*. Their mobility also enabled the Sikuani to survive the epidemics of measles, smallpox, and influenza brought by the conquistadors and later settlers, diseases that wiped out the more settled tribes, once numerous and vigorous, such as the Achaguas.

During recent decades, however, colonization by peasants displaced from other parts of Colombia and in search of new farmland has combined with the activities of Catholic and Protestant missionaries to form a tightening noose around the Sikuani. Fleeing the frontiers of settlement, the Sikuani moved ever eastward, only to find settlers from Venezuela moving westward up the Orinoco and blocking their escape. As their territories shrank, the Sikuani were forced to reduce their mobility and defend the few areas of savannah and jungle left to them.

One immediate consequence of reduced mobility was an impaired diet. The Sikuani were cut off from many of their traditional sources of protein—the game, insects, roots, nuts, turtle eggs, and wild fruits that were vanishing along with their habitat. And as a new generation of Sikuani passed through mission boarding schools, tastes began to change. In those communities where nutritious traditional foods such as the palm grub and freshwater snail were still plentiful, the younger Sikuanis came to regard them as fit only for savages and to prefer pasta and rice, which are less nutritious and were not always easy to obtain. The result has been an increasingly limited, lower-protein diet based on cassava consumption.

The effects of malnutrition have been compounded by exposure to new diseases through contact with whites, while concentrated settlement in villages has facilitated the spread of contagions once they are introduced. The formation of permanent villages has also led to other problems. The accumulation of human waste and garbage, and the feces of increasing numbers of domesticated cattle, chickens, pigs, and dogs have polluted the streams that provide water for household use, making them primary sources of disease. The final result of all these factors has been high rates of intestinal parasites, tuberculosis and other respiratory illnesses, malaria, and skin infections.

At the same time, the Sikuani have been replacing traditional practices that promoted health—such as breast-feeding, the use of medicinal plants, and a diversified diet based on local foods—with products—such as infant formulas, pharmaceuticals, and canned goods—that make cash-poor villagers ever more dependent on a market economy. This trade-off not only has often been for the worse, as we have seen in the case of dietary changes and will see in the case of bottle-feeding infants, under the present terms of exchange it tends to further weaken a culture that is already under severe stress, undermining the bedrock of identity that is an important source of individual health and well-being.

Fortunately, despite the changes of the past 30 years, the roots of the Sikuani culture are still intact, particularly among the older adult population, which did not attend missionary boarding schools. The Sikuani still practice traditional medicine, still speak their native language, still maintain their oral history, and still practice traditional rites. In recent years, the cabildos and indigenous organizations in the region have launched a creative process of cultural reaffirmation aimed at strengthening the moral, spiritual, and material values of Sikuani society in order to defend tribal lands from outside colonization. The shamans, or traditional healers, have played an active role in this process.

Unfortunately, the promoters trained by the Regional Health Service have not. Indeed, it seemed that the values they had learned in childhood from their parents and relatives had been erased after three months of training as paramedicals. The concepts of "microbes," "bacterias," and "viruses" seemed to have entirely displaced the spirits of the water and land, and the spells and ritual devotions that invoked or appeased them. Many of the newly trained promoters lost interest in supporting themselves through agriculture, hunting, and fishing, and preferred to wait at health posts in their homes—day in, day out—for a patient to come in and ask for a drug. As salaried employees of a government agency they were in danger of being transformed into an indigenous elite with little connection to the communities that had selected them. This widening gap provoked complaints by the *capitanes*, or village leaders, who in some cases even confiscated promoters' salaries to finance community projects.

BRIDGING THE GAP THROUGH PARTICIPATORY RESEARCH

Our preliminary research and our first meeting with the Sikuani promoters convinced us that the successful strategy that we had previously used to assist the neighboring Arauca people—preparing a culturally sensitive health manual for use by indigenous paramedicals—would not work here. The greater cultural isolation and the remoteness of the area required greater community participation simply to identify local health problems, and then to define appropriate and effective strategies for coping with them. As a first step it was necessary to integrate the Sikuani health promoters into the cabildos' development projects so that they could identify again with their own communities.

It might have been easier to begin the program from scratch with new trainees, but that seemed to waste the training that the health promoters had already received, and as it turned out, those promoters themselves would prove to be a necessary bridge between the Western and the traditional Sikuani medical systems. To retrain the promoters to see their work from the perspective of the community rather than that of a government agency, we based our program on participatory research, a methodology that involves the community in every phase of the process—from formulating the problems and identifying resources and strategies, to interpreting results and taking corrective action. Participants not only benefit from the concrete results of such research, they also learn how to analyze and solve their own problems. Financial and in-kind support would be provided by the IAF, the Regional Health Service of Vichada, the Apostolic Prefecture of Vichada, Colsciencias, the Fundación para la Educación Superior (FES), ETNOLLANO, and the community itself.

Since the community provides the foundation for training, our first task was to win the support of the cabildos and local organizations. After several meetings, an acceptable formula was hammered out. Research would focus on aspects of Sikuani culture and traditional medicine, but the cabildos could stipulate which topics not to investigate, because they might expose tribal mysteries. Three specific areas were selected for analysis: the history and current situation of the community, Sikuani medicine, and the traditional diet.

The program would evolve through a series of seminars with 15 health promoters, who would gather information from their communities on selected topics and analyze the data in cooperation with project anthropologists and the staff of the Regional Health Service. Based on those findings, projects, primers, and educational materials would be developed to improve community health. Periodic meetings with the communities and the cabildos would ensure that the program met perceived needs and expectations.

At first, it was hard to change old habits. The promoters still thought of training in terms of formal courses taught by doctors and nurses who, quite naturally, were accustomed to being the teachers. But a role reversal began to take place as the seminars focused more tightly on the history, customs, and traditional medicine of the Sikuani communities. Clearly the promoters were the only ones in a position to know about these matters, and it was up to them to teach us. The promoters became the central figures in the meetings, and the important discussions were conducted in Sikuani, which one of the promoters would then translate into Spanish. Often, after several days of discussing a topic, the promoters would decide that they had to return to their communities to interview other people— women, elders, shamans—who were in a better position to know. The doctors, nurses, and anthropologists listened and learned, and tried to fuel the process by suggesting ideas or techniques that might be helpful.

Curiously enough, the topic that proved to be pivotal in defining the direction of the program was Sikuani history, and several meetings were devoted to it. The promoters began by asking people in their communities several basic questions: Was the community healthier today than 20 years ago? Did people eat better before? What changes had occurred in the way people lived? How had those changes affected health and diet? Piece by piece a historical and social overview of disease began to emerge, which was complemented by summaries that project anthropologists presented of the writings of travelers and ethnographers who had visited the area in the past.

At the end of the process, each promoter prepared a profile of his community that not only summarized its history, but also contained an appraisal of the general state of health, perceived morbidity rates, and local peoples' opinions about their problems. The reports were read at community meetings and discussed, sparking lively debates about which problems were most urgent, how they were caused, and what could be done to solve them.

From the outset of the seminars, we had stressed that the Sikuani had a great wealth of cultural resources that was being lost and that must be recovered if efforts at autonomous development were to succeed. In their research, however, the promoters uncovered several examples that cast doubt on our point of view. Were we suggesting that the Sikuani should once again use the *casas mosquitero*, or mosquito-proof communal houses built of thatched palm fronds, which anthropologist Gerardo Reichel-Dolmatoff had described in 1945 and which the elders remembered as a thing of the past now that most palm trees had been cut down and families lived in their own homes? Were we saying that people should become nomads again to find new palm trees and to avoid certain diseases and clean up the rivers? This led to long discussions about the concepts of progress, tradition, and paternalism, not in the abstract, but related to the changes in Sikuani life-style that the promoters were documenting in their research. We wanted to reduce morbidity and mortality rates by promoting actions that were consistent with the needs and values of the community, incorporating new technologies only if the community could control and use them properly. The question was: Did health practices have to be traditional for communities to appropriate them?

CLARIFYING "TRADITION" AND "PROGRESS"

A project to provide clean drinking water helped clarify how the old and the new could be linked effectively. The history the promoters were reconstructing clearly showed that the pattern of concentrated settlement in permanent villages, which had become prevalent in the past 20 years, had led to the pollution of the primary sources of water for domestic use. Streams in the area had become dangerous sources for parasites and pathogens, and diarrheal illnesses had become chronic, especially among children.

The Sikuani saw nothing odd about water being a major cause of sickness, although their reasoning was different from that of Western doctors. "Many diseases are caused by water that has not been properly cleansed," one promoter told us, explaining that in their journeys the Sikuani never drink water from another river without first ritually purifying it.

The promoters raised the water problem during our early seminars and began reflecting on ways to solve it. As the various technical alternatives were discussed, it became clear that resources would have to come from outside the community. To install wells, which seemed the best alternative, hand pumps, piping, and other materials would have to be purchased.

Since the villagers lacked the cash for these purchases, the promoters had to learn to formulate a project proposal—complete with justifications, objectives, and activities—in order to obtain outside financing. Hours were spent drafting the proposal, which was modified and expanded in response to community suggestions that were collected between our sessions.

Women in the community became an important source of support for the project, quickly realizing that community wells would reduce the burden of having to travel every morning to a stream—often an hour away—to fill water jugs that they would carry balanced on their heads, on the long walk home. But did the women really want to stop going to the stream every morning? Wasn't this daily chore also a good pretext for meeting, chatting, and matchmaking? In the end it was decided that the wells would provide enough clean water for drinking and cooking, while bathing and laundering would continue at the stream.

The communities had many things to consider before decisions could be made, and the promoters took the lead in the discussions. Should the well water be ritually purified? Should there be rituals for the hand pumps as well? After such questions were raised and resolved, it was finally decided that the communities would not only contribute their labor to the project but would raise their own funds to buy tools and spare parts to maintain the system.

The remaining challenge was to obtain the funds for purchasing and installing 36 manual pumps, and for training two members of each community to maintain and repair the wells that would be built in the 30 villages served by the promoters. The Sikuani already had the most important thing: a written project proposal that had been extensively discussed and analyzed in the communities. Enough money was obtained from the Centro de Cooperación al Indígena (CECOIN), a nonprofit foundation that provides technical assistance to indigenous communities, and the official agency for land reform, the Instituto Colombiano de la Reforma Agraria (INCORA), to begin implementing the project at 18 sites. The remaining pumps would be installed during the next dry season.

While well construction was under way, the promoters began implementing an educational campaign on the water problem, using posters in Sikuani that they prepared during our meetings. As the communities learned how to use, repair, and maintain their new water systems, they made the project their own. It was now clear to the promoters and to us that the important thing was not whether health resources were traditional or modern but whether or not they are controlled by the communities. Technological innovations can be assimilated when they are sufficiently discussed beforehand.

The lack of discussion and local control also helps explain why government medical services in the area have been so underutilized, even though professional medicine has resources that could significantly benefit indigenous communities. That is, health posts, pharmaceuticals, diagnostic equipment, doctors and nurses, and paramedicals are often wasted precisely because the local population, despite its obvious need, lacks the framework for understanding how they work, and the opportunity to reflect how such resources can be appropriately incorporated into local development. The surveys and interviews conducted by promoters in 30 communities revealed that people usually sought care only after the quarterly or semiannual delivery of pharmaceuticals to the health post, or in the advanced stages of a disease that the shaman could not cure and often too late for either the promoter or his supervising doctor to treat successfully.

The promoters also kept case histories during this research period that made it possible to identify specific situations in which medical recommendations were ignored by patients. Treatments for tuberculosis were not followed because a patient thought the symptoms of the disease were caused by witchcraft. Dietary regimens to counteract illnesses caused by nutritional deficiencies were ignored because they contradicted the thinking of the shaman. The oral rehydration and breast-feeding campaigns conducted by the promoters for years appeared to have made no impression on mothers. The conflict between traditional medicine and the provision of state health services that seemed to lie at the heart of such problems was the next issue that the program would explore.

CLASSIFYING DISEASES IN TERMS OF TRADITIONAL MEDICINE

A 1981 regulation of the national ministry of health that sets guidelines for providing services to indigenous communities urges the coordination of traditional and modern medicine. In practice, such attempts have often failed because health professionals believe that traditional medicine divides diseases into two classes—those with natural and those with supernatural causes. Natural diseases are regarded as those that require treatment based on cause-and-effect relations, understood in terms of the scientific logic of Western medicine. Supernatural diseases are those attributed to spiritual causes that require treatment by magic or witchcraft.

In their participatory research project, the 15 Sikuani health promoters challenged this view, spending several months working out the rationale and internal logic of the medical practices and beliefs that they had learned, as children, from their parents and grandparents. The work became truly exciting when the promoters began to realize that the knowledge in traditional lore could be organized into many categories. Traditional medicine ceased being a disjointed collection of names for diseases or a series of seemingly arbitrary treatments based on antiquated customs, and became, instead, a complex organic system whose structure and dynamics arose from the present and past history of the Sikuani people.

Before that could happen, however, it was first necessary to understand the very notion of "classification," which emerged gradually as a product of their work. First they compiled a long list of all the Sikuani names for diseases. Then they played what they called "the game of the little boxes," in which they identified those diseases that could be subsumed by other diseases. Little by little, broader categories were identified, until an approximation of the Sikuani system of classifying diseases emerged. The promoters then took their charts back to their communities for discussion before returning to our next meeting to make corrections. The promoters spent long hours collating the information they had gathered and discussing the concepts behind each category before finally assigning a disease to its given box.

The medical personnel of the Regional Health Service, who always attended our meetings, were visibly impressed by this process. A short time ago in Cumaribo, the rural doctor told us: "My image of traditional medicine was transformed. I always thought that indigenous peoples were superstitious, that their medicine was no more than herbal remedies and spells. Now we should understand each other better because I'll be able to appreciate the diagnoses patients offer when they come in for exams."

The nurse's aide expanded the point. "This work has helped me see why patients are sometimes so reluctant to come to the health post, or why they take off in midtreatment to see the shaman. Before, I would scold the promoters because I thought it was their fault when things went badly. Now I don't think it's a simple problem. Instead, I should support them so they can work better with traditional medicine."

These comments, and others like them, were made at an evaluation meeting with medical personnel that led to concrete proposals for ensuring better communication between medical personnel, the promoters, and the community. The promoters now give doctors, with each referral, a bicultural case-history form detailing the Sikuani diagnosis of the disease and the way the patient has been treated in the community, by both the promoter and the shaman. And charts now hang on the wall at the health center in Cumaribo and at health posts in outlying villages so that medical personnel can better understand patients and prescribe treatments that respect the practices of traditional medicine.

This joint effort by promoters and medical personnel consolidated the participation of promoters in the program. Promoters, aware of the essential knowledge they had as Sikuanis, gained the confidence to be more open with supervising doctors and nurses. Many of the problems that were cited before the program began were not problems of "laziness" or "vagrancy" at all, but misunderstandings that cleared up when the promoters were able to speak up and be understood.

The promoters now realized that representing a medical institution did not require losing faith in their own traditions. Nor was it a question of becoming traditional healers. Rather, they were the indispensable mediators between Western and traditional medicine. In learning to analyze the differences between the two systems, they were in a position to find the best options for adapting the services of the national health system to the needs of their own communities.

As their role clarified, we noted a direct relationship between increased participation by the promoters and a shift in the contents of the research program toward the specific problems that they faced in their daily work. This became apparent when the promoters tried to explain the traditional concept of a disease known in Sikuani as *amibeje*.

DECISIONMAKING SPARKS CREATIVITY

Promotion of breast-feeding is a priority of the national ministry of health, and rural health promoters have been chosen as the best-qualified group to spread the word in local communities. As we would later learn, Sikuani women did not share that assumption.

At the outset of the research program, surveys by the 15 Sikuani promoters of mothers in 30 communities revealed troubling data on the nutritional intake of small children. Children are weaned, on average, at six months of age, and bottle-feeding often commenced just two days after birth. When the situation was discussed at our first meetings, the promoters explained that women thought the bottle was more convenient. We supported the doctor and nurse when they underlined the urgency of showing mothers the economic and sanitary disadvantages of bottle-feeding, which was, moreover, alien to traditional culture. The promoters were instructed, during several lectures, in ways to convince mothers to change their behavior. To monitor the success of these efforts, the promoters were also given the task of keeping records on the number of women who stopped breast-feeding before their children's first birthday.

Several months later, when the task of systematizing traditional medicine was the focus of attention, discussions about the category "amibeje" raised the issue of breast-feeding once again. At last, the promoters felt able to formulate the question they had long wanted to ask. "What can we do when women insist on bottle-feeding? We *have* spoken with them, but we can't force them to violate the advice of the shaman. They have their reasons, and we understand them."

The program then zeroed in on the promoters' need to reconcile their work with the community's values, resulting in a diagnosis—developed by all the promoters working together—of a problem that transcended the usual difficulties of implementing a simple educational campaign on breast-feeding. Previous campaigns had failed because they ignored how the changes that had occurred in women's work, the shifting relationship between Sikuani men and women, and the traditional explanation for the origin of many childhood illnesses interacted.

When the Sikuani maintained a seminomadic lifestyle, women walked to their fields in 15 or 20 minutes. Today, settled in permanent villages and raising livestock, the Sikuani often have fields two or three hours away, making it difficult for women to bring young children along, especially when it is necessary to make the return trip home loaded down with produce. The bottle, then, has been a great convenience, enabling mothers to leave young children at home in the care of a grandmother, aunt, or other relatives. Infant formula, however, is costly so it is often diluted with stream water, which as we have seen is contaminated with pathogens. Even with the advent of wells, a poor understanding of hygiene and the importance of sterilizing bottles poses grave risks of transmitting gastrointestinal infections.

A shift in the traditional rules governing the relationship between men and women has occurred alongside the change in work patterns. Schooling and the learning of Spanish have given women a greater freedom in their relationships with both Sikuani and nonindigenous men, provoking increased jealousy and sparking lovers' quarrels.

This, in turn, was linked to the way the Sikuani explain the rise in infant mortality from diarrhea and vomiting as an increase of the disease called amibeje, which can be roughly translated as "bewitched breast" and which affects children through a poisoning of the mother's milk. It occurs when a man who has been wounded by love touches a woman's breast and casts a spell. Any future child who suckles at her breast will grow ill and die. Amibeje, then, not only defines the nature of many childhood illnesses and explains the new practice of early weaning despite the high rate of gastrointestinal infections associated with bottle-feeding, it also acts as a social control, reinforcing traditional mores. The danger of transmitting sickness becomes a mechanism for culturally limiting the disorder in sexual relations caused by social changes that outstrip the ability of people to absorb or assimilate them.

Analysis of the problem vividly demonstrated how formidable the obstacles are to linking traditional and modern medicine. The promoters understood this and sided with the community saying, "For now we need to learn to properly handle the bottle so we can teach mothers how to protect their babies when breast-feeding is not possible."

That decision transformed the breast-feeding campaign into a study of nutrition that would provide mothers with the information they needed about the relationships between infant mortality, food hygiene, and family economy. Written and audiovisual materials from other programs in Latin America, Africa, and Asia were reviewed to give the promoters ideas about preparing appropriate materials for their own communities. A study of the traditional Sikuani diet was also begun, in the hope that ways could be found to diversify local diets that had lost much of their nutritional content as a result of cultural change.

AN EVOLVING FRAMEWORK FOR PROBLEM-SOLVING

Two years after the program of participatory research began, it was clear that the promoters were no longer the passive students we met for the first time on that sullen December morning in 1984. They were no longer isolated from the cabildos, who had invited them to explain their work and to propose ideas about how health programs could be carried out in the communities. And at the beginning of one of our final program meetings, the promoters told us that they had established, with the support of the cabildos, their own organization—La Organización Promotor de Salud Rural Indígena del Vichada (OPROSRIVI)—to continue the process of participatory research. In February 1988, the Consejo Regional Indígena del Vichada (CRIVI) was organized to defend and promote the interests of the indigenous people in the area. OPROSRIVI joined CRIVI to form the Comité Permanente de Salud. The Comité has drafted a proposal, with the help of personnel from the Regional Health Service, to research the prevalence of malnutrition and the growth and development patterns of Sikuani children. And at the invitation of the Health Service, they are helping to train a new group of health workers in participatory research.

Despite these favorable signs, it is difficult to know how deeply the attitudes of the nonindigenous medical personnel working in the area have changed. But when a nurse puts aside the booklets on hygiene that were produced in Bogotá and asks her students at the local school to gather medicinal plants in order to ask their parents about the uses of those plants, then certainly something has changed.

As for the communities themselves, much remains to be done. The attitude that it is up to the government to solve all of the problems of indigenous peoples, that only the government has the power to do so, is deeply ingrained. Since the training program was focused on the promoters rather than directly on the communities, and because of the slow pace of unearthing, evaluating, and restoring what has been hidden for so long, the promoters have not been able to accomplish all of their goals within the communities. Not only are the promoters searching for appropriate ways for male promoters to provide care for women without arousing the jealousy of husbands and the disapproval of grandmothers, but they are wondering how to more directly involve the shamans—who are usually their elders—in their work.

And there is a myriad of practical questions that remain to be answered, many of them requiring resources beyond the reach of the community. How can transportation of the seriously ill to the health center be improved? Considering the remoteness of the region midway along the Vichada River, can the health center in Cumaribo be staffed with a resident physician, and can drugs be delivered in a timely fashion to outlying hamlets and villages?

The promoters, however, remain undaunted. In recovering their traditions, they have developed the confidence to make decisions and stick by them. The fact that communities have recovered their health promoters opens a way for the Sikuani to renew themselves through participatory research and action.

NOTE

This article originally appeared in *Grassroots Development* (Vol. 12, No. 3, 1988).

Part 3

•

Conclusions

13

Cultural Expression and Grassroots Development

●

CHARLES DAVID KLEYMEYER

"Culture is like a tree," says Mariano López, a Tzotzil Indian leader from the municipality of Chamula in Chiapas, Mexico. "If the green branches— a people's language, legends, customs—are carelessly chopped off, then the roots that bind people to their place on the earth and to each other also begin to wither. The wind and rain and the elements carry the topsoil away; the land becomes desert."

More than 2,000 kilometers to the south, along the lush green coast of northern Ecuador, black folklorist Juan García Salazar echoes this urgency and offers a solution. "Cultural rescue," he says, "is impossible without development at the community level. And the converse is also true."

Many in the development world have overlooked this linkage between culture and development, between tradition and change. When the resource base fueling the world industrial economy seemed inexhaustible, it was possible, as David Maybury-Lewis points out in the preface to this volume, to think of "development" in mechanistic terms, as a problem of scale rather than value. Technology was a skeleton key for unlocking the wealth of nations, and both capital goods and the institutional framework for using them were presumed to be one more set of consumer products for export, pouring off an assembly line in the North. By the late 1960s, that optimism had dimmed, and many development theorists blamed the lack of progress on backward-looking traditional cultures.

In Latin America, as anthropologist Alaka Wali notes in Chapter 11, this criticism was frequently internalized, particularly in countries with sharp ethnic divisions dating back to the conquest. Cultural homogenization that expressed the values and needs of the modernizing urban elite was thought to be a precondition for greasing "the wheels of economic growth . . . [and] . . . local cultural and social differences [were visualized] as obstacles to be overcome, not opportunities to be seized." Whether capitalistic or socialistic, modernization was a good to be imported from abroad and imposed from above.

Joel Corneille, a young Haitian from Port-au-Prince, uses traditional techniques to make baskets from banana and palm leaves. Comité Artisanal Haïtien, a local grassroots support organization, assists him with credit, quality control, and marketing of his wares for sale and export.

As Wali adds, the limitations of this approach have been exposed during the past decade by the debt crisis crippling the economies of developing countries and by a looming worldwide environmental crisis. A search is now underway for alternative methods to spur "sustainable development," in which long-term economic growth is presumed to depend on more careful management rather than on more intensive exploitation of resources. This approach requires a new way of thinking about problems, one that emphasizes diversity and seeks to tap the strengths of indigenous cultures, regarding them as rich repositories of knowledge accumulated from centuries of "living with the land."

In examining alternative development programs among the Mapuche and Aymara peoples of Chile, Wali identifies two urgent reasons for supporting indigenous local cultures. First, when people such as the Mapuche in southern Chile are uprooted from the countryside by ill-considered public policy, they lose not only their land but also their cultural identity, that mixture of values, social relationships, and skills that forms the bedrock of their productivity. They are likely to flock to cities, where, unequipped to support themselves, they are in danger of becoming a permanent underclass, further burdening a society already unable to provide basic services to its urban population. Second, indigenous people may be the most effective stewards of the fragile ecosystems they often inhabit. When the Aymara in the Norte Grande range of the Chilean Andes struggle to protect their agricultural water rights from the encroachments of nitrate mining companies, they are affirming their intention that the land remain livable long after its mineral riches are exhausted. By insisting on this longer-range view, they are protecting not only the livelihoods underpinning their way of life but also the watershed that supplies the lower valleys and coastal cities of this arid region.

Generations of social and economic oppression have made it unlikely that either the Aymara or the Mapuche will succeed in their uphill struggles to save their land unless they receive outside assistance. Wali emphasizes that development programs cannot succeed among indigenous populations unless they build upon and strengthen the patterns of community organization that form the core of ethnic identity. The community must be given options that allow local people to set the agenda for their own development and to select technologies that strengthen rather than undermine community cohesion.

Nowhere, however, has the hopeful identification between the fate of indigenous culture and the environment been more pronounced than among the Kuna of Panama. Chapter 2, "Identity and Self-Respect," concludes with the observation that the creation of a park for scientific research demonstrates the Kuna's ability to "pick through the wares of Western culture, select those ideas and techniques that seem useful, and then tailor them to their own conditions." The park, which began as a roadblock to prevent colonists from encroaching on tribal land, evolved into an ambitious proposal for decoding Kuna lore in order to discover methods of sustainable agriculture appropriate to the tropical forest. Author Patrick Breslin remarks that it is the Kuna's secure sense of cultural identity—their knowledge of who they are and where they come from—that permits such an experiment to go forward, and he offers their experience as an example of the self-confidence required in *any* successful grassroots development project.

It is disturbing, then, to learn from Mac Chapin in Chapter 5 that traditional Kuna culture may be vanishing despite one of the most energetic and self-conscious efforts by any Indian group in the hemisphere to control the process of change. The introduction of new skills needed to coexist with Panama's political system and cash economy has slowly unraveled the connection between education and traditional work patterns, disrupting the transmission of beliefs to the young and undermining the traditional view of how the world works and where humans fit in. The Kuna began setting up Western-style schools more than half a century ago and now include within their ranks university-educated lawyers, biologists, and other professionals. Some of these professionals helped establish the research park. According to Chapin, they envisioned the project as a receptacle in which the old culture would be mixed with Western science to create a new and stronger alloy. Yet their plans to catalog the community's rich oral tradition, to bring Kuna ritual specialists to the park to identify flora and fauna, and to have these elders work alongside project technicians to study the scientific basis for traditional forestry systems have not come to fruition.

Part of the reason for the lack of progress is logistical: The park headquarters is far removed from the coastal communities in which most tribal elders live and from Panama City, where most of the young project team is located to coordinate technical assistance and funding with outside agencies. Yet this geographical separation also mirrors a generational rift among the Kuna about the nature of culture itself. To the elders, Kuna culture is a body of inherited knowledge that is renewed through each generation's intimate contact with the reefs, estuaries, and jungle of the San Blas region; it is the sap of a living tree. To the acculturated young, culture is a clue to what it means to be a "genuine Kuna," a solution to the riddle of self-identity posed by modernization; it is the immense and inert heartwood that holds a tree upright in a gale.

The limited success of the research park reflects the narrowness of the generational consensus. The park's primary purpose was not to serve as a crucible for forging a new identity but to form a coalition with sympathetic outsiders that would lessen the imminent danger that the land would be ravaged by other outsiders. Some temporary breathing space has been secured, but Chapin wonders what will happen if the Kuna are unable, by way of this project or some other, to renew the spirit of the old culture before it is reduced to an elaborately carved ornamental bowl. Can some variant of Western ecology still emerge to fill the bowl with something nourishing, or will it simply reflect the emptiness that comes from being neither Panamanian nor Kuna? The answer is far from certain, and that poses an even thornier riddle. If one of the few indigenous peoples in the hemisphere to survive into the twentieth century with its culture, identity, and political and economic autonomy relatively intact cannot weather the buffeting of modernization, what are the prospects for culture-based development anywhere?

One clue comes from the Quichua of highland Ecuador, as described in Chapter 10. The Quichua draw strength from the *minga* tradition of communal labor, a practice that has in turn been strengthened through development programs that depend on it to prepare fields for planting crops and to reforest barren hillsides. Another clue comes from the Talamanca coast of Costa Rica, as illustrated by Paula Palmer in Chapter 7. Palmer's students, borrowing techniques from their peers in the Appalachian region of the United States who produced the *Foxfire* series of books (see the Bibliography under Wigginton), began to document the vanishing past of their unique region, tapping the cultural energy of the entire community and setting the stage for future development projects.

Mexican Nobel Prize winner Octavio Paz has said that the essential quality of modernism is change, and its dynamo is a critical deconstruction of the immediate past that requires the reinvention of identity (Paz, 1974). This "identity crisis" is a chronic condition, and it afflicts nations as well as individuals. When Breslin noted the ability of the Kuna Indians of Panama to "approach Western culture like careful department store shoppers rather than awestruck primitives," he was describing an essential modern survival skill. Chapin's essay develops this insight by suggesting that survival also requires the ability to shop wisely through one's own past. That is, the only antidote to the corrosive self-doubt that accompanies modernization is constructive self-criticism.

Cultural activists use cultural expression not only to spark social action but also to provide a mirror with which people can examine their culture from within. This process can take the form of sociodramas enacted by the Feria Educativa in Ecuador (Kleymeyer and Moreno, Chapter 3), or the efforts of indigenous paramedics to map out the deep logic of traditional medical systems. In Chapter 12 Herrera and Lobo-Guerrero chronicle how this rise to consciousness through participatory research gave the Sikuani people a powerful tool for problem solving that unleashed the latent creativity in their own heritage and provided a means for reconciling tradition with progress. The Sikuani have now institutionalized this process that regards myth as a data base, teaching a second generation of paramedics how to guide their communities in applying participatory research to solve other problems. This effort has paralleled the rise of a representative political organization to defend Sikuani interests vis-à-vis the outside world.

The same process is under way among other ethnic groups elsewhere in the hemisphere, including the Shuar and Quichua of Ecuador described in Chapter 10. It should be emphasized that this cultural activism is not a romantic quest to restore an ideal, perhaps imaginary, past. Nor is it an attempt to enshrine "the primitive" in developing-world societies, a concept that may reflect the West's nostalgia for its own vanished past. Rather, it is an attempt to make explicit what is implicit in every grassroots project—the linkage between culture and development that Juan García Salazar referred to at the beginning of this chapter.

The cases in this book show how that linkage works: Cultural expression generates cultural energy, which in turn mobilizes individuals, groups, and communities to social action. This cultural energy gets people to lock arms and join in a group effort, to come out to meetings night after night. It keeps them working long hours on a community project as unpaid volunteers. It stirs their imaginations and their longing to transform their lives; and it shores up their confidence and courage to face the challenges that lie ahead.

Cultural energy helps people to reach deep down and find strength and resolve they were not sure they had. When the gospel choir bursts into song, when the panpipes blend with the high valley wind, when the actor triumphs over adversity with a clap of the hands, when the drum rhythms roll, people feel inspired, affirmed, bonded to other members of their group, and capable of going to the edge of their dreams and beyond.

Cultural energy is generated by common people through everyday creative expression—in work and in what Westerners call "entertainment" (a distinction many non-Westerners do not make). But it is also generated by the concerted efforts of cultural activists who are part of grassroots initiatives. The cases in this book demonstrate that such activists consciously tap into this energy source and direct it toward social and economic goals—ideally, constructive ones. Although their work is difficult to measure precisely, it can be readily observed and palpated. The ability of these persons to sustain their activism is crucial to many types of development efforts.

In short, what we have learned is that cultural energy can make the difference between whether a development effort gets launched or not, is sustained or not, produces an impact or not. Cultural energy can be a powerful force in the creation and strengthening of group solidarity and commitment, organizational efficacy, participation, and volunteer spirit.

Cultural expression, then, is a prime source of energy that can be tapped and harnessed for human development. The individuals and groups described in this book not only demonstrate its power and effectiveness, they also show that it is part of, not separate from, real life. It is embedded in the melody, lyric, rhythm, motion, image, design, and color of a song, dance, legend, poem, theater script, textile, or mural. What is more, the cultural energy that is thereby generated is renewable; it not only drives action, it is replenished and increased by action. As people expend cultural energy to achieve goals, they become aware of this source of power within themselves as individuals and as a group. Instead of being depleted, the store of cultural energy therefore tends to increase with use, and people practicing this approach find themselves *energized through effort*.

Nevertheless, in modern times, traditional forms of cultural expression are in constant danger of being lost, distorted, or expropriated. It follows, therefore, that the generation of cultural energy—and the ensuing components of successful development efforts—are equally in danger. The case materials in this book argue for strengthening the link between cultural tradition and social change, supporting cultural activism and tapping and harnessing cultural energy as an integral part of grassroots development efforts.

The linkage between culture and development has been compelling even in grassroots projects that began as archival efforts. Although the full impact of García Salazar's own work compiling the folklore of Afro-Ecuadorians awaits the response of future generations, García Salazar's presence has already proven crucial to the consolidation of numerous small-scale fishing cooperatives in his native province of Esmeraldas, culminating in the precedent-setting emergence of a federation of these cooperatives. Los Masis, the Quechua musical group described by Breslin in Chapter 2, not only has revitalized traditional Andean music in the Sucre region of Bolivia but also has begun to help a Tarabuco Indian community tackle the problems of rural poverty and development. Paula Palmer's work, which inspired young people to investigate the cultural diversity of an isolated section of Costa Rica and harness a "technology of self-respect," preceded the efforts of a local group to start experimental tree nurseries to diversify food and cash crop production among the area's black, Bribri Indian, and mestizo communities (see Carroll and Baitenmann, 1987).

Most of these efforts, however, have existed in geographic and cultural isolation from one another, and it would be misleading to say that they, or the 215 projects briefly described in the Appendix to this book, constitute the basis for a definitively integrated or orchestrated cultural approach to development.

Ironically, the clearest indication of how cultural recovery can begin to have a national impact comes from an institution—the rural school system—that cultural activists have often viewed most skeptically as an instrument of sociocultural oppression. Many of the teaching materials used in the Escuela Nueva program (which serves nearly half of Colombia's 26,000 rural schools) have their roots in "participatory research" and are intended to inspire students to apply the same techniques to their own lives and communities. As Brent Goff describes in Chapter 8, the curriculum is "grounded in popular culture and pragmatically oriented . . . to promote involvement and to nurture the sense of self-worth." Abstract concepts such as culture and personal identity are given concrete form through hands-on activities such as the making of crafts. Students learn through investigating the world around them that popular crafts have traditionally been rooted in family enterprises, offering a model for production that they are encouraged to join or help start. The community itself becomes "a worthy classroom for study, within . . . [which one finds] . . . the seeds for community development." Audiovisual and written materials geared to regional cultures are being combined with standardized packets for national distribution, offering the next generation of citizens a vision of how they can create a Colombian blueprint for development.

The program has attracted widespread interest and support from international funders, including UNESCO, the World Bank, the Inter-American Foundation (see CO-306 in the Appendix), and others. It has been studied by officials from forty-six other nations as a promising new model for rural education. This level of interest in a culture-based development project is highly unusual, and it suggests two things—a growing realization of the need for a new development paradigm, and the general lack of knowledge about what common techniques might make the model work.

The fact that large-scale development institutions know so little about the process is in itself revealing. The cultural component of the Escuela Nueva program in Colombia has taken nearly two decades to evolve, and it happened with minimal outside support. Like the many other projects detailed in the Appendix to this book, it began with local voices responding to local needs. The fact that so many disparate groups from all corners of the hemisphere have adopted this strategy despite the general lack of outside support suggests that there is a common source of energy driving grassroots development. There is an urgent need to record these experiences, to find an analytical framework that fits the contours of what is being lived, so that knowledge can be shared and refined and passed on, so that vital lessons will not be limited to those who live within range of a project's voice, so that lessons will not die when a project dies. What all of these efforts have in common is their capacity to generate cultural energy and harness it to propel grassroots development. In sum, the cases presented in this book demonstrate that cultural energy is the force needed to produce the effort, sacrifice, and adaptation called for in social change efforts at the grassroots level.

ISSUES AND PROBLEMS

One of the major strengths of the culture-based approach to grassroots development is its local, bottom-up nature. Typically shaped by the disadvantaged themselves or by the development practitioners who work with them, it is not the latest fashion to be exported from the developed world. It offers an alternative to the belief that development equals modernization, which equals Westernization. This different approach suggests that there are many valid paths to development and that each society must discover its own. Change may be desirable, but it also disrupts. When people participate in determining the form, direction, and rate of change, when it comes from inside them rather than being imposed, it is more likely to be constructive and enduring, to be accepted by the people themselves.

Some people suggest that cultural traditions and social change are mutually exclusive, if not diametrically opposed, and that marginalized groups must choose one or the other. As this book illustrates, cultural activists believe that tradition and change are in fact inextricably linked and mutually reinforcing. Moreover, the absence of a cultural facet can lead to debilitating tensions between a given development program and its projected beneficiaries, a fact that should give pause to pragmatists.

All cultures develop and survive by borrowing from other cultures, as well as by reforming and reinventing their own legacy. The real issue, then, is *who has control* over change, not whether or not change should take place at all. Will it be instigated and driven from without or within? Answering this question poses potential problems in the design, financing, and implementation of cultural action programs.

The case studies in this volume show that timely and appropriate outside assistance is often required for a besieged group to collect itself and mobilize its own resources for development. Although ethnic peoples are best able to identify what must be preserved and what must change, no one should view traditional ways as necessarily benign or inviolate. After all, some groups have customarily practiced wife burning, female circumcision, or the indiscriminate killing of endangered animals for their body parts. Sometimes tradition and cultural identity entail denigration or hatred of other people. These cases are relatively clear-cut and unlikely to win or deserve outside support. But what about cultural decisions where value judgments are relative, where gain and loss are measured by shifting points of view? When is it wise for ethnic peoples to put aside or transform their traditional ways? to obtain employment? to receive the benefits of Western knowledge of health and illness? to increase agricultural yields or introduce cash crops to generate desperately needed income? There are no easy answers for most of these issues, nor is there even agreement upon which ones are key.

As Chapin illustrates in his discussion of the Kuna (Chapter 5), change often happens *to* groups, in spite of their best efforts to control the process. The jury is still out on whether cultural rescue and maintenance will be viable over the long term. Cultural expression deals with meaning within *living* societies. Sometimes an entire genre of cultural expression no longer represents that living reality, necessitating invention of new meanings and forms of expression to fit the new situation.

In the early 1980s, Ariel Dorfman visited a number of the cultural projects included in this study. He wondered if they could hold their own in a time of financial scarcity and if these individual voices, noble as they were, would ever be heard above the din of the mass media (Dorfman, 1984). This is a crucial question, because neighborhood or community "self-help" can seem futile if the only images of successful people one sees are North American or European actors on syndicated television series, or if the solution to problems is portrayed only in terms of mass consumption. Only a handful of projects—such as Radio San Gabriel in Bolivia and Radio Latacunga in Ecuador (EC-136)—have gained access to the airwaves to broadcast culture-based, nonformal education programming to widely dispersed rural communities. Their experience suggests that the same modern technologies that threaten to undermine traditional cultural forms can be harnessed to preserve and renew them.

Juan García Salazar argues that radio and television have done more damage to black culture in his native Esmeraldas in the past 30 years than slavery did in 300. Yet he is one of the first to recognize that new technologies can also be tools of survival. He and other cultural activists have skillfully employed low-cost tape recorders and cameras and readily available print technology, such as presses, offsets, mimeographs, and photocopiers. The potential for participatory, interactive uses of these technologies is great and needs to be explored further.

Some critics claim that such investments are not justified in a time of scarce development resources because cultural action projects have very limited benefits compared with projects concentrating on so-called basic human needs such as food, housing, and health care. However, marginalized people have a broader view of basic needs and deprivations. They understand well the anger, diminishment, and paralyzing shame that comes from negative social stereotyping. Reversing that process can transform a group's culture and provide the foundation upon which firm structures can be built to meet basic needs. Although relatively small in number, the cases forming the heart of this book involve projects that emerged spontaneously from the grassroots throughout the hemisphere. In each case, low-income people chose to allocate their own scarce resources (time, materials, money, and energy) to cultural activities. The diversity and breadth of this experience suggest that grassroots development is best built on a foundation of strong identities and group pride, which are in turn fed by the cultural energy that springs from creative expression.

At a time when theorists of all stripes agree that high levels of local participation are needed to maximize new development resources, this linkage is too often overlooked. The degree to which culture is integrated into a project can offer funders a vital clue about the level of real participation. The degree to which elements of popular culture are manifest in development projects provides a thumbnail measurement of whether or not local people have been enabled and allowed to bring themselves to the project.

In spite of its many strengths, however, a culture-based approach is not a panacea for the ills of disadvantaged people or for societies beset by deep-seated ethnic or sectarian tensions. To portray it as such is a mistake, because doing so suggests that marginalized people alone can overcome powerful historical and socioeconomic forces that require structural solutions within the larger society. Although a culture-based approach cannot cause such tidal changes by itself, it does prepare the way and complements other efforts—as demonstrated by the Feria Educativa. The culture-based approach is a worthwhile item to include in the development worker's toolkit; its usefulness will depend upon the skill of the craftsperson and the magnitude of the problem at hand. Its effectiveness should not be exaggerated, but neither should the approach be tossed aside as obsolete, nor archived as an antique.

If misused, cultural action can further divide people. Some critics argue that it inevitably reinforces separatism, or "Balkanization," or encourages reverse racism by fostering an attitude of "us vs. them." It is important to remember that separatism and racism have long histories that are deeply rooted in the underlying political economy. Cultural action can either alleviate or exacerbate these structural foundations of conflict, but it does not *cause* the conflict.

None of the many cases scrutinized for this study condoned separatism or reverse racism. Indeed, when there has been conflict, it has often been a result of project success. When governments or other authorities have taken such activities as a challenge to their power and closed a play, whitewashed a wall mural, or banned a protest song, it has been because of the project's effectiveness *as* cultural expression.

The link between cultural expression and development often does not need to be forged; it already exists, although it may be in danger of being lost. In such cases, cultural rescue and revitalization strategies come into play. Survival techniques that have worked successfully for generations are discovered anew, and constructive change becomes a process not of moving into something different but of moving back on course.

Perhaps the most difficult cultural activities to justify are those with an intrinsic interest and value but no certain practical purpose—at least in the near term. For example, the traditional stories and oral poetry collected in the 1980s among Afro-Ecuadorians led by Juan García Salazar may not be fully appreciated or utilized until the next generation. But if these materials had not been collected when they were, they would have perished with their speakers. This newly anthologized oral literature is an invaluable part of the patrimony of all Ecuadorians and will be crucial to the maintenance of a strong identity among Ecuadorian blacks, the bedrock on which their future development efforts will partially rest. Its present role may be minimal in comparison with a future one that cannot be predicted at this time.

Whether their goals are immediate or long-term, cultural expression efforts typically confront the same challenges that grassroots development projects in general do: strengthening the organizational base; furthering democratization; setting long-term priorities; and teaching lessons and providing training in necessary skills in management, bookkeeping, and marketing. They face the same kinds of problems and pitfalls in maintaining group continuity and cohesion; resolving internal conflicts; addressing leadership and management shortcomings; warding off outside interventions and dependencies; facing the challenges of economic self-sufficiency and marketing of products; and overcoming social or geographic isolation.

Although some of these problems are unique and require special solutions, most point to the need for training, technical assistance, participatory evaluation, experience in self-management, and networking—in short, human resource development and organization building. Other problems, such as systematic ethnic discrimination and political harassment, call for solutions on the societal level and are largely beyond the reach of local groups.

In the end, support for a culture-based approach to grassroots development requires an uncommon level of trust and respect for disadvantaged peoples on the part of governments, financial institutions, and private development organizations. Such entities must be willing to give up control and respond to bottom-up initiative and management. The examples in this book foreshadow what might be accomplished if the effort is more systematically nurtured.

ACTION AGENDA

The case material and analysis in this book point to a number of ways in which culture-based grassroots development could be strengthened. The following agenda is recommended for action by those wishing to facilitate the consolidation and advancement of this alternative approach to the challenges of development:

Increase direct support for cultural expression activities. Ways must be developed to distribute resources more widely and fairly among cultural activists and their organizations, delivering those resources directly into the hands of the practitioners themselves whenever feasible. Funding should be done in a judicious and appropriate fashion. Whereas any amount of money can cause intragroup conflict, too much money can overwhelm a group, distort it, and produce inefficiencies. Likewise, donors must have realistic goals for their support, neither exaggerating project objectives nor withdrawing just when a group is poised to consolidate its gains. And although all agree that intervention and paternalism are to be avoided, so must the opposite extreme of laissez-faire. Thoughtful monitoring of funds is healthy for all sides and can lead to increased efficiency and effectiveness, as well as richer learning. Giving constructive support is an art and must be approached with care and sensitivity.

When considering where to give support for cultural efforts, it is wiser to take a broad and eclectic approach than to pursue the handful of ideas or methods currently in vogue. Similarly, it is all too common for one or two groups in a region to become the darlings of the development world and receive assistance (some of it superfluous) from all sides. It would be preferable for donor support to be as multifaceted and broad-based as the pluralism it frequently professes to nourish.

Those involved in cultural activism are, not surprisingly, some of the most imaginative and articulate project designers in the world of grassroots development. There is no need to generate ideas for them. Several of the categories of activities they often propose are particularly worthy of support. One of these is preservation of ethnic heritage through what is often called "cultural rescue" (e.g., collection and recording in the field) and "cultural maintenance" (e.g., storing and performance). The next step, "cultural revitalization," entails activities such as the recuperation of expressive forms that have been lost or are being lost, as well as efforts to use traditional forms in new ways and develop entirely new forms to express reality. This act of "cultural re-creation" calls for appropriate ways to introduce change without undermining the core values of community identity.

Many of these activities require only minimal outside support; they are carried out largely through the donated labor of dedicated volunteers, the majority of whom are part of the group or community. Sometimes, though not always, support is needed for full-time coordinators' salaries, raw materials, transportation for cultural exchanges and presentations, and publications and other forms of dissemination. Keeping in mind the risks inherent in modern technologies (particularly in the mass media), many of the simpler technologies can be put to use by cultural activists to carry out their cultural rescue, maintenance, and revitalization activities. Examples are tape recorders, photography and video equipment, mimeographs and offsets—items that are financially beyond the reach of many groups.

Provide other forms of support through intermediary institutions or associative networks. It would be useful to expand efforts to strengthen the self-reliance—financial and otherwise—of both the intermediary support groups (often called "nongovernmental organizations") and the grassroots networks that are involved in cultural activism. Supporters must accept that most of these groups—just like the prominent cultural centers of the industrialized world—will never be completely self-sustaining. Many will need some monetary aid for as long as they are active. To encourage autonomy and efficiency, it is important to funnel services into the kinds of human resource development and organization building discussed earlier in this chapter, especially to improve leadership, management, and self-assessment skills.

One of the greatest risks inherent in external support for a cultural approach to grassroots development is that outsiders will set priorities and strategies, manage their implementation, jealously broker all forms of aid, and perhaps even supervise the distribution of benefits, relegating the cultural action group itself to a cameo role. Well-intentioned attempts to "help" ethnic groups maintain their culture or use cultural expression for development may end up primarily benefiting outsiders, including commercial and political interests, academics, and funders themselves, ironically reinforcing old modes of paternalism and dependency.

Often, the best that an outside institution can do is to find ways to enable grassroots cultural activists and their organizations to carry on their own work for their own purposes and on their own terms. Such institutions can do so by providing timely access to necessary resources—financial, material, and human. They can also lobby authorities to change laws and policies and to uphold the human, economic, and cultural rights of disadvantaged peoples. But sometimes an enabling approach simply calls for staying out of the way and encouraging others to do the same, leaving culture-based projects the "social space" and the time they need to be effective.

One particularly effective way of supporting cultural activists is to enable them to form and strengthen informal networks and formal associations at the local, national, and international levels. Such coalitions facilitate those most closely involved in preservation, revitalization, and other activities in setting their own agendas, design their own strategies, and carry out their own efforts to support and enable one another. This implies a partnership approach on the part of supportive institutions—which need to look beyond the labor-intensive, short-term costs to the long-term rewards that flow from sharing experiences, concepts, and methodologies.

Develop clearinghouses to serve cultural activist organizations in fundraising and networking. One of the most difficult aspects of the culture-based approach is finding financial support. Cultural activists are commonly handicapped by their remote locations and their inexperience in "grantsmanship." They would benefit from clearinghouses to put them in touch with sources of grant monies, bibliographical materials, data on similar projects, and other resources. Two existing organizations that are playing such roles are the Paris-based International Fund for the Promotion of Culture, an official body of UNESCO, and CULTURELINK, the Network of Networks for Research and Co-operation in Cultural Development, sponsored by UNESCO and the Council of Europe.

Such institutions might eventually evolve into retailers of grant funds, channeling support from wealthier funders convinced of the importance and efficacy of cultural action but lacking the staff and experience to scour the countryside and urban neighborhoods to identify the most promising groups and monitor their performance and changing needs. Clearly these umbrella institutions would have to be nongovernmental (or multilateral), nonprofit, and free of any political or religious agenda.

Clearinghouses also have the potential to promote improved networking among cultural action groups, counteracting pervasive geographic and sociocultural isolation. Often, the simple awareness that a similar organization exists elsewhere gives a group heart and the renewed energy to face its own challenges. Networking can also facilitate cultural exchanges and the transfer of skills among different disadvantaged groups, some of them historical rivals, as was the case in the First Ecuadorian Festival of Amazonian Folklore (see EC-082 in the Appendix). It can even lead to formal federations of cultural action groups (see also EC-082). Festivals, workshops, field visits, and performance tours are all viable mechanisms for promoting networks and sharing information. All require resources not often readily available to financially strapped cultural groups.

Develop mechanisms to assure that ethnic peoples control their cultural property rights. A critical, unaddressed issue is the question of ownership of cultural forms—intellectual as well as material property rights. Native peoples of Latin America and the Caribbean have seen their cultural property expropriated freely over the past five centuries—from traditional medicines, crafts, and food crops to songs, designs, and antiquities (not to mention land, water, and mineral rights). In one case, leaders of an effort to revive traditional weaving designs in Bolivia (see BO-222 in the Appendix) had to turn to European collectors who possessed rare pieces that no longer could be found locally, even in museums.

This frequently overlooked issue of cultural property rights is full of complications and ambiguities. Can anyone simply expropriate a song, an herbal cure, a design, a seed variety, or an antiquity and market it for profit? At the local level, who has the right to use these forms for their own benefit? Can it be any insider, or must it be the collectivity? What about special outsiders, such as dedicated professionals or the members of other ethnic minorities? And who has the right to decide how the forms will change? Should it be limited to a local cultural elite, often self-appointed, to choose when to rewrite a song or dramatize a folktale or transform a traditional dance or festival? It is too easy to say that "the people will decide." Which people? Who speaks for the people in these instances?

In some cases, such as that of the Shuar-Achuar Federation in the Ecuadorian Amazon region, a representative body—the federation leadership—certifies some cultural groups and efforts and bans others. Other Indians in the hemisphere, such as the Kuna in Panama and the Taquile Islanders in Peru, are attempting to increase their economic and legal influence over local handicrafts and tourism (see Chapters 5 and 9). Nevertheless, in most cases there is no barrier to prevent the expropriation of culture and no system of copyrights to funnel profits back to indigenous groups.

Official national and international bodies can call for respect and forebearance but are hard pressed to enforce it. Their jurisdiction tends to be limited to cross-border disputes involving tangible cultural artifacts—e.g., smuggled antiquities, but not songs, symbols, tourism, and handicraft techniques. As complicated as the task would be, such bodies should meet with representative ethnic groups to broaden the concept of cultural property. Viewing the problem pragmatically, in today's world a cultural patrimony should be seen, among other things, as a resource owned by a certain group, and limits should be placed on how and to what extent outsiders can unilaterally exploit it. The preservation and sustainability of such a rich resource will depend largely on seeing that the economic rights to it remain with its traditional creators.

This issue has special urgency in the case of indigenous peoples in endangered tropical forests. A considerable portion of the modern pharmacopoeia derives from the knowledge of flora and fauna embodied in the ethnoscience of native peoples, yet there is no payment for the use of this intellectual property. If fair compensation were made, forest peoples would have a better chance of surviving and of protecting the habitat that still possesses untapped renewable resources.

Enhance access of cultural activists and groups to national and international entities. A factor impinging on each of the previous recommendations is the need for improved and increased access, on the part of cultural activists and their organizations, to key societal institutions, such as ministries of education, human rights organizations, agencies of the United Nations and other multilateral bodies, and even agrarian reform agencies, national and international media, and world lending institutions.

Simply gaining more access is not enough. Cultural activists must be able to reach out beyond already sympathetic funders and other supporters if they are to have a lasting impact on sociocultural impoverishment and promote broad-based development among the poor. The barriers preventing such progress include the imposition of monocultural/monolingual education methods on ethnic minorities, social discrimination and human rights abuses, loss of land rights and environmental degradation in ancestral territories, appropriation of cultural forms, and official negation of history. These are all issues of overwhelming significance for cultural survival. At their core they speak to the already well-articulated need for self-determination and self-governance on the part of all peoples, not just ethnic minorities. Achieving this, as we know too well, is no simple matter. Unless their voices are heard by the national and international entities that determine priorities and strategies of poverty alleviation and development, ethnic minorities and the poor in general will be relegated to the role of supplicants, clients in need of intermediaries, and objects of development (or impoverishment); they will not themselves be significant actors in shaping the process and allocating its benefits. Yet they often have key information and techniques for solving local problems and tapping into local resources and therefore should be involved at every step of the way.

Support efforts to broaden and strengthen processes leading to cultural pluralism. Building societies that are truly culturally pluralistic requires self-determination and self-governance by minority peoples to ensure their long-term cultural survival. It also requires efforts to increase intergroup tolerance, respect for the civil rights of all ethnicities, and general knowledge and appreciation about the cultural roots, contributions, and history of all groups in society. As many cases in this book demonstrate, cultural expression can be an effective tool that ameliorates social atomization, alienation, and conflict and helps create a healthy pluralism.

Among other things, a vision of increased cultural pluralism holds out the prospect—worldwide—of genuine nation building based on consensus rather than exclusion. When characterized by autonomous participation and mutual tolerance, enhanced pluralism can lead to more workable democracy, improved internal and cross-border relations, and reductions in animosity and violence at the national and international levels. As we come to the end of this century, we are painfully aware that few of the many challenges we face have greater importance for human welfare and survival. Relations among ethnic groups, as the world media report every day, are vital components of several of these challenges. Interethnic disharmony can be a major obstacle to achieving progress toward development goals.

Step up research and evaluation of culture-based development. Having established the efficacy of a culture-based approach, the time has come to refine existing knowledge about its methods and disseminate the lessons more widely. As in all areas of grassroots development, this process requires far more research and evaluation than has been carried out to date— fewer than 10 percent of the projects in the Appendix to this book, for instance, have been formally evaluated.

For such research to be useful, better indicators must be developed to measure impact and demonstrate cause and effect. Given the nature of cultural action, indicators and measures will necessarily be more qualitative than quantitative, and refining them will require alternative ways of looking at development. The search begins with rethinking the concepts of deprivation and well-being. Many cases in the public eye today demonstrate that it is just as significant for a group to be culturally and socially deprived as to be deprived in a material sense.

This new search for knowledge, and especially for causal relationships, must be pursued through direct, balanced collaboration with cultural activists and ethnic artists and artisans rather than through obtrusive, self-serving studies by outsiders working alone. Collaboration provides external analysts with an insider's view and reflective practitioners with new techniques of measurement and evaluation.

In many instances, disadvantaged peoples are already carrying out their own research and self-assessment, on their own terms and for their own purposes. With increased resources and opportunities, they could deepen the process. Frequently they are the most innovative and probing analysts of their own circumstances and skilled disseminators of the knowledge they distill. Sometimes, of necessity, that means departing from the orthodox researcher's dependence on the written word and communicating their findings through graphic arts, popular theater, song, and storytelling.

Here are a few of the areas in which further study is needed:

The impact of cultural action. What cultural strategies and methods work best and under what conditions? Which are most likely to fall short or be counterproductive? What are the major pitfalls, and how can they be avoided? What are the characteristics and causes of internal vs. external impact of cultural action on groups?

The proper role of outside organizations in facilitating cultural preservation and revitalization. What are the potential problems and caveats when outsiders become involved (including middle-class urban professionals from the same country)? How is the insider-outsider relationship best managed, and what are the implications of its being collaborative and mutually beneficial versus vertical and utilitarian?

The political implications of culture-based development. When and how do cultural expression programs become hot potatoes, burning practitioner and funder alike? How do such activities threaten established centers of power, and how inevitable is this threat?

Official cultural policies. What has been the impact of modern national cultural policies? What are the implications of more active or intrusive policies (such as those enacted in Jamaica and Mexico) and ones that are less so (such as the one in Ecuador)? How do countries vary in their policies in accord with their different political and economic structures, and what are the comparative strengths and weaknesses? What have been the results of official efforts to increase cultural pluralism?

The policies and strategies of ethnic movements. Can ethnic movements indeed achieve "integration without assimilation," in the words of Shuar leader Ampam Karakras? How do they deal with the charges and risks of reverse discrimination and separatism? How do they collaborate with (or fend off) external cultural activists and government agencies? What are the best ways of supporting and facilitating bottom-up cultural movements? What are the prospects for achieving multiculturalism from below?

If these and other areas of research are actively pursued, future culture-based development efforts will be conceptually better grounded. Better information about the outcome, including the side effects, of past actions will provide guides to future policies and strategies.

Disseminate experience about culture-based development. One of the strengths of cultural efforts—their innovative and sometimes unconventional approaches to social problems—can be easily misunderstood. Cultural practitioners face the challenge of better communicating the breadth and depth of their experience to critics and potential allies, locally and abroad.

In addition to those in Latin America and the Caribbean, there are myriad cases from Africa, Asia, and other parts of the developing world—and the industrial world as well—where culture-based grassroots development has been tried. Scores of these cases are documented in publications listed in the bibliography of this book and in several UNESCO bibliographies on culture and development (the most comprehensive one being Luce Kellerman's *The Cultural Dimension of Development: A Selective and Annotated Bibliography*, published in 1986 and updated in 1991). But most cases remain undocumented. Practitioners and observers alike should disseminate information about culture-based development projects more widely, not only by writing about them but also through photography, film, video, audio tapes, and face-to-face exchanges.

This exercise in development education will require investment and open-mindedness from funding institutions. Without a doubt, the potential rewards are great. Cultural expression groups have the vitality to inspire similar development programs among the poor and to show the peoples of the industrialized world that investing in the grassroots development efforts of disadvantaged peoples can pay dramatic dividends.

The culture-based approach to grassroots development deserves more attention and support than it has had to date, but its advocates must avoid romanticizing either disadvantaged peoples or the past. Each culture is a living process, one tree in a forest. It is a vibrant, evolving forest, not a petrified one. There is no single cultural approach that has the answers for all people. Development is bound to vary by place. And it is not the result of a set of answers but of a set of questions.

As we weigh the effectiveness of a culture-based approach to grassroots development and consider its unique techniques, we should above all maintain our focus on the *central* issues confronting our global community: the need worldwide to improve quality of life and reduce suffering by enabling all peoples to reach their full potential as productive contributors to their societies. Doing so requires equal respect for their political, economic, social, and cultural rights.

Scientists and ecologists are making a persuasive case for preserving the world's endangered environments—from oceans to tropical forests—in order to protect the planet's biological diversity and our resource base. Preserving cultural diversity may be equally important for maintaining access to the storehouse of information and creativity accumulated by previous generations. And its link to environmental preservation goes both ways.

This crucial and difficult set of challenges requires a multifaceted response that summons up all the ingenuity, imagination, and strength we can muster. The grassroots development efforts described in this book represent a vital first step in generating and harnessing the cultural energy and will necessary to meet such challenges.

Appendix:
Cultural Expression Projects Supported by the Inter-American Foundation, 1973–1990

●

Caryl Ricca & Charles David Kleymeyer

The project descriptions that follow were adapted from Inter-American Foundation public statements and project histories. These descriptions emphasize those aspects of a given project in which cultural expression is either a means to a development end, a development end in itself, or both. In numerous cases, a project's cultural component complements other activities such as production, organization building, education and training, etc. The descriptions reflect the original project designs unless records reveal significant changes during the course of project work.

The list includes 215 projects that entailed cultural expression, funded over the course of seventeen years for a total of $20,880,236. The median-size grant was for $63,740. Dollar amounts can be deceptive, however, because in some cases only a small percentage of the funds were designated for cultural expression per se, whereas in other cases virtually all the funds were directly related to cultural expression activities. We have chosen to record the total amount obligated for each project, because the cultural component plays an integral and vital role in all of them.

Note that for those projects active after September 30, 1990, termination dates and dollar amounts are subject to change in some cases, as the grants are subsequently amended for more time or funds.

ARGENTINA

ACT—Asociación Cultural Taiñi: 9/90–7/92; $25,700 To expand the involvement of twelve Wichi communities in cultural expression and preservation—through workshops to train Indians in dance, drama, and music, and through at least three public performances in the region. The objectives of this project were to increase understanding and appreciation of Wichi culture among non-Indians in the region and to strengthen intercommunity ties among twelve Wichi Indian villages through nonformal education using traditional songs, dance, and oral histories. (*AR-280*)

BARBADOS

Yoruba House: 9/74–10/77; $70,880 To assist this cultural foundation for the creative and performing arts in constructing a stage and establishing a printing press, to employ youth, and to generate income for Yoruba House itself. A dance company was organized and a number of other cultural activities were conducted, including arts and crafts programs, television shows, lectures, and publications. Stressing self-reliance and community action, Yoruba centered its performances and work on African and black identity themes. (*BA-005*)

BUT—Barbados Union of Teachers: 8/80–8/81; $3,770 For a three-week workshop on the use of drama techniques to facilitate learning, designed for teachers and community development workers from six Caribbean countries. (*BA-012*)

BAHAMAS

Institute of the Arts: 6/80–8/80; $10,060 To carry out a six-week pilot program called "Takin' the Arts to the People," consisting primarily of workshops in Bahamian drama and music. Emphasis was given to participation by grassroots groups from Nassau and, on a limited basis, by artists in the Family Islands. (See also BAH-005.) (*BAH-003*)

Institute of the Arts: 8/81–9/81; $6,000 To implement its second summer arts training and performance program on the theme "A Natural High," using drama, music, and discussion sessions on such topics as family life and drugs. (See also BAH-003.) (*BAH-005*)

BELIZE

TMCC—Toledo Maya Cultural Council: 6/88–5/92; $25,000 To hire two men—one Mopan and the other Kekchi—to carry out activities in the Toledo District creating greater awareness and understanding of the broad Mayan community and its self-help development possibilities. (*BE-081*)

COIP—Caribbean Organization of Indigenous Peoples: 9/89–3/90; $13,000 To sponsor a conference in Belize for delegates from national indigenous communities of St. Vincent, Dominica, and Guyana to exchange experiences, provide information and insights about how to interact with majority groups, and prepare a self-help development agenda for indigenous peoples of the Caribbean. Representatives were to visit indigenous communities in Belize to exchange cultural information and document language, music, and craft forms for later circulation throughout the Caribbean. (*BE-086*)

BOLIVIA

Ayni-Ruway: 9/74–3/78; $133,555 For an incipient organization in Cochabamba and two rural communities to undertake a culturally sensitive rural development project managed by local leaders known as Kamachis. Activities included Quechua-language theater, artisan production, small enterprise development, and utilization of traditional barter systems. Ayni-Ruway also worked with a well-known Bolivian filmmaker to produce a documentary of its experiences. (See also BO-063.) (*BO-026*)

Ayni-Ruway II: 6/78–1/81; $239,700 To strengthen Ayni-Ruway's access to the wool supply so as to increase the profit margin on exported artisan goods. Ayni-Ruway also established outlets in two major Bolivian cities for the growing volume of artisan products. It opened an exchange and cultural promotion center in Salta, Argentina, to incorporate local Quechua-speaking, highland peasants into its expanding network of production/exchange and cultural revitalization groups. In addition, funds allowed Ayni-Ruway to research and apply traditional technologies in order to increase production of wheat and potatoes and to organize a health services program integrating traditional medical practices with Western medicine. (See also BO-026.) (*BO-063*)

Teatro Runa: 2/80–7/83; $130,896 For this community-oriented educational theater group to expand its outreach and educational program, principally by offering workshops to students preparing for teaching careers. Through these workshops rooted in Andean traditions, Teatro Runa hoped to spark imagination and creativity in an educational atmosphere often dulled by rote memorization and emphasis on conformity. (*BO-078*)

Centro de Promoción Cultural Campesina, "Ayni": 5/80–5/83; $52,698 To produce a daily fifteen-minute radio program on Aymara culture, disseminating folk stories contributed by local campesino communities and reaching more than one million altiplano listeners. Ayni also gave a number of courses to campesino women on tailoring, seamstress work, crafts design, and Aymara culture. (*BO-086*)

Centro Cultural Masis: 6/80–12/90; $265,775 To conduct workshops in folklore, music and dance, cultural research, arts, and radio in an effort to influence the public school curriculum. The objective was to introduce creative mechanisms to stimulate curiosity about the past and about the region's social and cultural problems. (*BO-087*)

Centro Cultural Guaraní-Quechua: 9/81–9/86; $111,361 To organize a number of meetings between traditional Guaraní and Quechua authorities as a forum for analyzing regional problems and exploring possible solutions. In addition, the Centro offered training programs on handicrafts, preventive medicine, rural carpentry, tanning of hides, and nutrition, and it produced numerous publications to complement its educational programs and convey indigenous cultural values. *(BO-119)*

Pedro Ovio Plaza Martínez and Juan de Dios Moya: 6/81–10/81; $5,000 To enable two of Bolivia's most outstanding sociolinguists to attend a linguistic institute at Cornell University. They participated in a variety of workshops and courses concerning the use of indigenous languages in bilingual education programs. *(BO-121)*

Joven Teatro: 6/82–12/84; $68,701 To set up a cultural center in a marginal barrio of Santa Cruz where Joven Teatro could produce plays and give instruction in other artistic activities designed to increase community awareness of common problems. *(BO-138)*

CIDAC—Centro de Investigación, Diseño Artesanal y Comercialización: 9/82–6/85; $81,504 For work with three traditional artisan communities, to improve and diversify traditional crafts products (hammocks, palm leaf hats, ceramics) and to expand existing sources of raw materials and markets in the city of Santa Cruz. *(BO-155)*

TIFAP—Taller de Investigación y Formación Académica y Popular: 8/85–7/92; $167,550 To assist local community leaders with special expertise in topics such as agriculture, health, and cultural revitalization to document their knowledge and disseminate the information to other Bolivian groups concerned with grassroots development. *(BO-209)*

ILCA—Instituto de Lengua y Cultura Aymara: 2/85–1/88; $117,280 To continue ILCA's educational program designed to help low-income teenagers improve their reading and writing proficiency in Aymara, and to encourage greater appreciation of the language. The program includes the training of rural school teachers and other leaders in bilingual education techniques and in the preparation of appropriate educational materials. *(BO-210)*

THOA—Taller de Historia Oral Andina: 9/86–5/91; $72,135 To expand and consolidate a research and educational program involving the collection of oral histories in Aymara rural communities, the organization of an oral history archive, and the dissemination of these materials through simple publications and experimental radio programs. The principal objective was to reinforce a positive sense of ethnic identity among the Aymara and to encourage democratic forms of organization based upon the Andean community tradition. *(BO-213)*

ACLO—Asociación Cultural Loyola: 9/85–7/90; $242,425 To develop a training program to encourage the production of high-quality traditional weavings among low-income women in the impoverished northern provinces of Chuquisaca. *(BO-222)*

El Taller de Música Arawi: 9/85–6/91; $77,879 To conduct a training and technical assistance program in traditional Andean music for representatives of community centers and music groups in low-income urban neighborhoods of La Paz. The training was to help develop greater Andean cultural pride and to strengthen the role of local organizations in a wide range of community development activities. *(BO-225)*

CIC—Centro de Investigaciones Cerámicas: 8/86–7/88; $41,560 To consolidate and expand CIC's training, technical assistance, and laboratory analysis services for indigenous potters and to offer courses in such areas as kiln construction, raw materials analysis, improvements in pottery methods, and pre-Hispanic ceramics techniques. *(BO-237)*

Casa de la Cultura "Raúl Otero Reiche": 9/86–12/90; $83,460 To expand the Casa's library network and training program for five low-income neighborhoods in the city of Santa Cruz. The objectives were to make practical educational materials accessible to students and the public in order to contribute to cultural development and improve learning skills. *(BO-238)*

CIDDEBENI—Centro de Investigación y Documentación del Beni: 9/87–4/91; $45,950 To undertake a study of the cultural traditions and conditions of poverty of the indigenous Moxos population, a quasi-nomadic group of several thousand persons in the eastern jungles of Bolivia who undertake messianic migrations that force them to seek refuge in jungles and other inhospitable regions, where they confront a harsh survival existence. The study will assist outside agencies in designing and implementing basic development programs that address the health, income, and housing needs of these isolated, impoverished peoples. *(BO-247)*

Proceso: 7/88–5/90; $83,300 To conduct an extensive training program in Santa Cruz for members of neighborhood youth organizations and field workers from nongovernmental development agencies, including the Unión de Grupos Culturales. The training utilizes theater, puppets, dance, and other forms of expression and communication (such as pamphlets, audiovisuals, newsletters, radio scripts, and cassettes) to upgrade nonformal education skills in group dynamics, community organizing, analysis, and social communications. *(BO-259)*

HISBOL—Historia Boliviana: 2/90–12/91; $15,500 To publish and distribute a series of inexpensive pocket-sized books for development practitioners and a wider public on issues of women and culture in development, ecology, agriculture, and peasant-controlled development organizations. *(BO-292)*

BRAZIL

LABORARTE—Laboratório de Expressões Artísticas: 7/75–7/76; $24,800 To support this association of youth groups promoting the expression of folk culture in São Luis and Maranhão. LABORARTE purchased equipment and supplies to document and disseminate various native forms of art, music, and playacting that are gradually disappearing from the traditional neighborhoods and rural villages. (BR-176)

Grupo Olorun Baba Min: 10/76–6/77; $15,935 To present Afro-Brazilian music and dance in theaters and neighborhood centers of Rio de Janeiro in order to help people experience the drama of their own history, inform the population about the contributions of blacks to Brazilian culture, and stimulate neighborhood groups to develop their own expressions of their cultural identity. (BR-275)

MAEC—Movimento Amador de Expressão Cultural: 10/76–12/77; $24,608 To enable this local association of over twenty neighborhood artistic and theatrical groups to purchase equipment and a truck to mount a mobile theater. The purpose was to encourage folk art and cultural expression among the poor residents of urban São Paulo. (BR-299)

Grande Escola de Samba Quilombo: 12/76–6/77; $20,000 To purchase sewing machines for production of costumes and school uniforms in order to generate income for the group, and to purchase a printing press for production of pamphlets on popular culture. This social and cultural organization seeks to preserve and provide a setting for the celebration of Afro-Brazilian religious and cultural traditions as expressed in music and dance in their own neighborhoods. (BR-314)

Instituto de Pesquisa das Culturas Negras: 4/77–4/78; $82,000 To purchase office space and audiovisual equipment for this volunteer organization providing research services, educational programs, visual aids, and technical assistance to community groups and individuals from the poorer communities of Rio de Janeiro. The objective was to enable black communities to appreciate their own history and achieve more effective participation in development. (BR-315)

Mini Comunidade Oba-Biyi, Terreiro Axe Opo Afonja: 5/77–7/78; 10,000 To establish a children's multicultural learning center and organize a program of formal education that emphasizes Afro-Brazilian origins and customs. This enabled the community to deal with the process of cultural absorption. (BR-341)

Antônio Morais Ribeiro: 7/77–7/78; $3,000 To equip and support this scholar to study Afro-Brazilian history, religion, music, and cuisine, and to disseminate his findings in the form of publications and programs conducted in schools, study centers, and other community organizations. (BR-358)

CAT—Corporação dos Artesãos de Tiradentes: 6/83–9/85; $42,540 To enable this nonprofit corporation to expand handicraft production and establish new marketing channels, while preserving artisan traditions dating back to the eighteenth century. (BR-501)

FGT—Fundação Gaúcha do Trabalho: 9/83–12/85; $144,400 To enable this educational and cultural service organization to expand its handicraft development program by establishing a marketing and raw materials supply center in Porto Alegre, and by opening eight local centers for the production of high quality goods made of leather, wool, plant fibers, cattle horns, and clay. FGT bases its work on traditional culture and skills, while providing new production and marketing mechanisms designed to generate higher and more stable incomes for artisans. *(BR-505)*

FUNCARTE—Fundação Casa do Artesão: 7/83–9/84; $20,000 To expand FUNCARTE's handicraft development program in the area of wicker furniture production as a means for economic and cultural development in the State of Maranhão. *(BR-506)*

CARDI—Cooperativa Regional Artesanal de Diamantina, Ltd.: 6/83–9/84; $25,000 To increase the production of *tapetes arraiolos*—seventeenth-century handwoven Portuguese rugs—an important colonial artisan tradition. *(BR-507)*

Cooperativa Central de Produção Artesanal Potiguar, Ltd.: 6/83–12/84; $68,500 To expand the cooperative's marketing and raw material supply services, facilitating increased production of traditional handicrafts made of local materials such as palm leaves, sisal, clay, wood, fiber, colored sand, and stone. *(BR-509)*

FRM—Fundação Roberto Marinho: 2/85–8/87; $30,000 To enable the FRM to carry out research and documentation of artisans in the state of Rio de Janeiro and then develop a training and marketing program designed to increase the family incomes of traditional artisans. The FRM sponsors a wide variety of cultural programs fostering appreciation of Brazilian artistic expression and stressing the preservation of Brazil's cultural heritage. *(BR-567)*

CEAEC—Centro de Estudos de Apoio às Escolas da Comunidade: 8/86–9/89; $77,532 To develop a community schools methodology, design an art education curriculum, and conduct a survey of the cultural activities of four communities in low-income areas of Recife and Olinda. *(BR-624)*

CLF—Centro de Cultura Luiz Freire: 5/87–10/90; $243,487 To provide technical assistance, training, and financial support to community organizations involved in nonformal education for schoolchildren and illiterate adults in Recife. The CLF began as an organization that produced cultural events and later expanded its focus to include broader development activities. Throughout its history, however, it has emphasized the use of traditional culture (particularly Afro-Brazilian culture), and the electronic media, in achieving educational and development goals. *(BR-644)*

CARIBBEAN

UWI—Department of Extra-Mural Studies of the University of the West Indies: 12/75–4/76; $3,500 To hold a four-day conference in St.

Lucia for approximately 25 dramatists from the eastern Caribbean. As a direct result of the conference, the Theater Information Exchange was established. (See also CAR-034, CAR-053.) *(CAR-019)*

TIE—Theater Information Exchange: 3/78-12/79; $43,006 To enable Ken Corsbie—Guyanese-born dramatist, playwright, and journalist—to continue efforts to formalize an association of Caribbean dramatists. TIE evolved into a network of concerned artists who use various forms of drama to reflect on societal issues and dilemmas facing Caribbean people. (See also CAR-019, CAR-053.) *(CAR-034)*

TIE—Theater Information Exchange: 10/80–6/81; $16,250 To cover partial costs of the Third Conference of Caribbean Dramatists, held in the U.S. Virgin Islands. Approximately fifty dramatists from throughout the region attended the fifteen-day event, and a forty-five-minute videotape was produced to document the experience. (See also CAR-019, CAR-034.) *(CAR-053)*

IOJ—Institute of Jamaica: 3/90–2/91; $14,900 To develop, in collaboration with the University of the West Indies and the Smithsonian Institution, an educational module on Caribbean history and culture to be distributed to public schools throughout the countries of the English-speaking Caribbean. *(CA-088)*

CHILE

ICECOOP—Instituto Chileno de Educación Cooperativa: 2/77–2/79; $305,200 For producing radio broadcasts, newspaper publications, and pamphlets that disseminate technical, marketing, cultural, and educational information. This served as a forum for representatives of peasant organizations to discuss activities of the cooperative federations, air peasant concerns, and preserve the voice of the campesinos as well as their rural culture and values. *(CH-071)*

Los Comediantes: 12/76–3/79; $22,000 To assist the actors of this popular theater group, who live and work in local communities, to identify important problems in the daily lives of barrio residents. These issues were then presented in the form of sociodrama, followed by discussion sessions that served to raise consciousness about the problems reflected in the play and to pose possible solutions. *(CH-075)*

IER—Instituto de Educación Rural, and the Comunidad de Alto Chelle: 6/78–12/83; $276,716 To assist Alto Chelle in establishing a family school firmly rooted in the life and culture of their rural community. The methodology entails students alternating between classroom and farm home at intervals corresponding to agricultural cycles. While at school, students study a basic curriculum and choose practical research topics that they will investigate upon returning home. *(CH-109)*

CENECA—Centro de Indagación y Expresión Cultural y Artística: 12/79–11/81; $131,114 To help eight theater groups and twelve popular music groups develop their art as an authentic expression of Chilean culture. Workshops focused on networking among the groups, strengthening ties with the community, neutralizing official censors, minimizing individual self-censoring, employing forms of artistic expression that reflect the Chilean people, and developing more effective channels of dissemination. (See also CH-220, CH-403.) *(CH-170)*

CADA—Colectivo Acciones de Arte—Chile: 11/80–3/81; $4,500 To enable a CADA member to travel through North America and Europe visiting artists, cultural groups, and funding agencies, so as to explore possibilities of funding a museum of Chilean art and popular culture. *(CH-200)*

TIT—Taller de Investigación Teatral: 1/81–7/81; $5,000 To finance a portion of the travel expenses for a three-month international tour of the play "Tres Marías y Una Rosa," directed by Chilean playwright David Benavente. The play, based on interviews in local barrios, investigates the changing role of working women as it is shaped by economic and social factors including their husbands' temporary layoffs and chronic unemployment. (See also CH-229.) *(CH-207)*

CENECA—Centro de Indagación y Expresión Cultural y Artística: 9/81–7/83; $138,150 To analyze the state of artistic and cultural expression as it had emerged in Chile in the 1970s, and to train schoolteachers, parents, and organizational leaders in understanding and using communications media for educational and cultural development. (See also CH-170, CH-403.) *(CH-220)*

TIT—Taller de Investigación Teatral: 3/81; $1,500 To cover theater rental expenses for the international tour of the play "Tres Marías y Una Rosa." Ten performances were given in New York to capacity crowds. (See also CH-207.) *(CH-229)*

FREDER—Fundación Radio-Escuela para el Desarrollo Rural: 9/82–10/85; $98,815 To undertake a community development program benefitting thirty-five Huilliche Indian communities, and to sponsor twenty-four courses on agricultural production, handicrafts, community organization, and Huilliche language, culture, and folklore. Funds were also used to provide legal assistance related to land titles and boundaries. *(CH-270)*

Casa Kamarundi: 5/82–5/83; $5,000 To support a program to train forty slum children in theatrical basics, including facial and body expression, public speaking, mime, acting, theater history, and group dynamics. The purpose was to promote education, group organization, and cultural revitalization. *(CH-273)*

ADMAPU—Asociación Gremial de Pequeños Agricultores y Artesanos: 6/82–11/82; $2,000 To enable this Mapuche Indian organization —which promotes unity and cultural awareness among the Mapuche people—to send four representatives to a conference sponsored by the

Consejo Indígena Sud-Americano (CISA). At the conference, delegates discussed and posed solutions to the loss of cultural identity and the dissolution of social structure among South American indigenous groups. (See also CH-278.) (*CH-277*)

ADMAPU—Asociación Gremial de Pequeños Agricultores y Artesanos: 9/82–11/83; $36,596 For selecting eight of ADMAPU's best promoters to work full-time to provide or arrange for agricultural technical assistance and training in handicrafts, community organization, health, education, and housing among the Mapuche population in south central Chile. This project was designed to provide a viable alternative to Mapuche families who have been forced to sell their lands and migrate to urban centers, a process that has contributed to the loss of Mapuche patrimony and a disintegration of Mapuche social structure. (See also CH-277.) (*CH-278*)

Comité Coordinador de Talleres Femeninos de Coyaique: 6/82–6/83; $9,935 For purchasing equipment and hiring instructors to offer courses in handicrafts, food preservation, and family health and hygiene for the members of affiliated groups. Seminars in women's organization, workshop coordination, and leadership training were also held, and many new women's groups were formed in the area as a result, including theater and folklore groups that keep alive the cultural traditions of the people. (*CH-279*)

Comité Artesanal, Cooperativa Campesina Nueva Esperanza: 2/83–12/84; $28,300 To address scarcities of raw materials, the major limitation on increased output of woolen handicrafts that are produced and sold by women as a traditional export of the local economy and constitute a large portion of the average monthly family income of Isla Maillen. (*CH-316*)

Vicaría de la Solidaridad: 5/83–10/90; $379,140 To carry out community development and income-generation activities among some 320 community organizations in Santiago, and to enable the Vicaría's workshop unit to assist numerous mutual-aid (*solidario*) groups in craft marketing and production. The famous Chilean *arpilleras* (appliqué panels) with their graphic social themes are a product of these *solidario* groups. (*CH-324*)

Instituto de Antropología, Universidad de Tarapacá: 9/84–12/86; $66,798 For carrying out field research in three indigenous communities of the Chilean altiplano, to determine the population's perceptions and expectations regarding primary education. This analysis was designed to contribute to the development of a new educational curriculum incorporating the cultural heritage and traditions of the local Aymara population. (*CH-359*)

Vicaría Zona Norte: 9/85–12/90; $177,740 To assist thirty local groups of parents and neighbors to carry out recreation and child-development programs for some 5,000 young people in low-income areas of northern Santiago, utilizing the dramatic and graphic arts to express democratic culture. (*CH-384*)

Sociedad de Tejedoras de Putaendo, Ltda.: 9/85–12/88; $68,770 To purchase raw materials and open a sales outlet in Santiago, for the production and marketing of traditional crochet weavings. The objectives were to generate employment, enhance Chileans' knowledge and appreciation of important local crafts, and demonstrate the value of cooperative action by women in raising household incomes and developing local, self-managed organizations. *(CH-387)*

Cooperativa Campesina Chonchi, Ltda.: 9/86–6/89; $35,400 To improve members' sheep herds and wool production, and to reactivate the production and sale of traditional Chilote handicrafts. This pilot project was the first peasant-controlled effort to improve sheep herds in this part of Chile. *(CH-388)*

SOPRODER—Sociedad de Profesionales para el Desarrollo, Ltda.: 9/86–2/93; $341,165 To improve the subsistence levels of Mapuche Indian families, strengthen a second-level Indian association, Rayen Koskulla, and preserve Mapuche culture. Activities include providing farmers with credit and technical assistance in agriculture and small enterprise, training local leaders, and encouraging the strengthening of Mapuche organizations through participatory community development projects. *(CH-397)*

Folil-Che Aflaiai, Organización de Mapuches Residentes en Santiago: 3/87–2/91; $29,589 To reaffirm Mapuche culture while providing members with social and economic skills needed to adapt to urban life. Activities included: courses in language, history, folklore, and crafts; technical training in urban gardening, sewing and tailoring, literacy, and health; and artistic presentations, seminars, and the production of a bimonthly publication. *(CH-398)*

TER—Taller de Estudios Regionales: 4/87–4/89; $40,186 To support TER's work with four highland Aymara Indian communities in northern Chile. Specific project objectives included: improved crop production through expansion and rehabilitation of simple irrigation systems; training and technical assistance in water resource management, and agricultural production and marketing; promotion of independent, democratic Aymara organizations at the village and regional levels; preservation of Aymara culture and ethnic identity; and sharing of project experiences with other Aymara communities. *(CH-402)*

CENECA—Centro de Indagación y Expresión Cultural: 8/87–8/89; $72,670 To carry out in six regions of Chile an applied study of low-income handicrafts producers of three types—traditional, ethnic, and contemporary. This study was designed to analyze marketing, organization, quality control, and the cultural significance of Chilean crafts. Plans included publishing a crafts manual and a series of short instructional pamphlets for distribution to participants. (See also CH-170, CH-220.) *(CH-403)*

Taller Imágenes: 12/87–7/89; $48,717 This independent audiovisual production firm headed by Patricia Mora Barros will make and distribute a fifty- to sixty-minute color documentary film on issues affecting Chile's

Aymara community, featuring the perspective of the Aymara women. *(CH-407)*

IPES—Instituto Profesional de Estudios Superiores Blas Cañas: 4/87–2/88; $81,250 To research and document Chilote culture, devise formal and nonformal educational programs to disseminate the findings on the island, and instruct school promoters on the culture of Chiloé. Additional activities included implementation of small experimental economic enterprises in five rural communities, focusing on traditional craft production, music, dance, and legends; these activities were designed to test the commercial potential of Chilote culture while protecting its uniqueness and values. *(CH-413)*

Vicaría Zona Centro: 10/87–12/91; $105,184 To train more than 600 poor women, jobless youth, and leaders of neighborhood-level mutual-aid groups in administration, management, marketing, and job skills, utilizing various forms of cultural expression. *(CH-417)*

TEC—David Benavente/Taller de Comunicaciones: 3/89–8/90; $37,400 To enable Chilean film and video producer David Benavente to produce a forty-five minute color educational video in conjunction with the participants in two grassroots development projects aiding Chile's two principal indigenous minorities, the Mapuche and the Aymara. *(CH-433)*

CEDEM—Centro de Estudios para el Desarrollo de la Mujer: 9/87–8/90; $68,505 To assist Mapuche women in the Temuco area to improve the value of their spun yarn and traditional woven goods through specialized training, thereby contributing to the maintenance of Mapuche culture. (See also CH-456.) *(CH-434)*

CORDILLERA, Programa para el Desarrollo Comunal: 5/89–3/91; $70,684 To provide training and technical assistance to forty-five neighborhood councils in five predominantly low-income boroughs of Santiago in organizational management, budget analysis, and planning and execution of local community-development projects, and to establish cultural centers for the preservation and dissemination of local culture. *(CH-448)*

CEDEM—Centro de Estudios para el Desarrollo de la Mujer: 5/90–5/92; $67,080 To train a six-person indigenous team to manage the production, marketing, organization building, and educational operations of the Mapuche Women's Project in Temuco. The project assists thirteen base groups, including 170 Mapuche women artisans, in the preservation and marketing of traditional Mapuche crafts. (See also CH-434) *(CH-456)*

TEA—Taller de Estudios Aymara: 5/90–5/92; $62,053 To assist in the improvement and expansion of artisan production by ten rural and four urban groups of Aymara women, so as to increase sales of artisan products, prepare artisans to take over the management of marketing operations, and preserve traditional techniques and forms. TEA activities also include reinforcing traditional agricultural products and practices among Chile's highland Aymaras. *(CH-459)*

TER—Taller de Estudios Regionales: 5/90–12/91; $69,544 To provide technical assistance in production, organization building, and cultural revitalization among the Aymara Indians in the Camiña-Colchane altiplano and valley and in the city of Iquique. *(CH-460)*

Comisión Regional Huilliche de la Junta General de Caciques: 9/90–9/91; $5,930 To hold meetings and field sessions with membership organizations to prepare proposals for sociocultural and economic development, and cultural preservation, in response to the Chilean government's announcement of prospective legislation and policies regarding the social, cultural, and economic situation of Chile's indigenous minorities. *(CH-465)*

COLOMBIA

Teatro Identificador: 2/74–2/76; $213,262 To enable Manuel and Delia Zapata to extend their efforts to preserve the black cultural heritage of Colombia. Researchers made lengthy visits to remote villages documenting cultural expression in the form of tales, legends, dances, ceremonies, myths, and traditions. This material was then turned into dramatic presentations, as well as acted out in improvisation by local people. The researchers also produced a library of tapes, slides, and manuscripts—a rich and constantly used resource. *(CO-046)*

USEMI—Unión de Seglares Misioneros: 6/74–8/83; $821,684 To develop literacy programs and nonformal education strategies that respect indigenous values and culture. Some of USEMI's many outstanding achievements include: the provision of the first written form of the Kogi and the Arahuaco languages; publication of over twenty works on cultural and historical aspects of the Kogi and Arahuaco; development of bilingual education programs subsequently adopted by the Colombian Ministry of Education; training of local indigenous teachers and health-care workers; and assistance in the drafting and implementation of an indigenous education reform law passed in June 1978. *(CO-048)*

Cabildo Kamza: 6/76–10/86; $127,236 For the Cabildo to work with 350 Kamza families to secure property rights to several thousand acres of tribal lands and put them into production. The Kamza received training in cooperative management, accounting, and marketing, and worked at restoring patterns of communal production in order to reaffirm tribal roots. The Cabildo also sponsored the efforts of a tribal elder, trained in anthropology, to collect and publish Kamza folktales, legends, and ceremonies for use in local schools. *(CO-072)*

Fundación Colombiana de Investigaciones Folclóricas: 2/77–8/85; $127,014 To fund a broadcasting facility in northern Cordoba that would serve as a forum for an ongoing radio dialogue among marginal rural communities, drawing on local culture as a source of program content and focusing on current issues from a campesino perspective. *(CO-098)*

ACPA—Asociación Colombiana de Promoción Artesanal: 9/77–1/85; $371,789 To enable ACPA to initiate a broad educational program, planned in conjunction with traditional rural handicraft producers to fill needs that these artisans identify. ACPA helps lay the foundations for organization by means of which artisans may improve their economic standing and focus attention on social problems. Activities concentrated on weavers, *barniz* workers, hammock-makers, woodcarvers, basket-weavers, Cuna mola appliqué workers, potters, and straw hat makers. (See also CO-306.) *(CO-121)*

Fundación Cultural "Teatro El Local": 9/78–12/83; $93,500 For partial funding of salaries and the construction of a cultural center housing a theater, a coffeehouse, a bookstore, and a place for aspiring artists to exhibit their work. This would allow El Local members more time to provide training and assistance to theater groups in the barrios surrounding Bogota in an attempt to tap creative strengths, bring social issues into focus, and add vitality to community action efforts. *(CO-127)*

Fundación Cultural Teatro Taller de Colombia: 3/80–6/82; $79,544 To purchase and renovate a bus as a means for carrying socially conscious theatrical productions and training to outlying urban barrios and remote communities throughout Colombia. In addition, Teatro Taller purchased a modest locale to house workshops for itself and other local theater groups, and it offered special outreach programs to orphans, steet children, deaf people, and the ill. *(CO-180)*

Cine Mujer: 9/81–4/85; $105,954 To produce a documentary film depicting the personal strength and character of a peasant woman artisan who wove baskets to supplement family income. She became recognized as a leader in her community and was given special recognition by Artesanías de Colombia for her craftsmanship. It is hoped that other women who see this film may identify with her and learn from her experiences. *(CO-194)*

Grupo Precooperativo Artesanal, Casa del Barniz de Pasto: 9/82–3/86; $47,333 To assist this group to raise the standard of living of its members through improved production and marketing techniques, as well as to preserve the integrity of their traditional craft. These highland artisans, known as *barnizadores*, are named for a unique process of overlay design that has been practiced in this area of the country for several centuries using a resin from the lowland tropical *mopa mopa* tree. *(CO-233)*

Drs. Nina S. Friedemann and Jaime Arocha: 8/82–7/85; $27,720 To conduct a study of Colombia's black population, the major purpose of which was to provide Colombian blacks and the society at large with accurate and objective information regarding the artistic, literary, cultural, and economic contributions that blacks have made to Colombia's development. The final results of this study are considered to be among the most significant materials produced on black culture in Colombia—*Un Siglo de Investigación Social: Antropología en Colombia* (1984), *Carnaval en Barranquilla* (1984), and *De Sol a Sol: Génesis, Transformación y Presencia de los Negros en Colombia* (1986). (*CO-236*)

Grupo Precooperativo Centro Artesanal de Morroa: 6/83–9/86; $63,740 To enable this group to strengthen its hammock-making enterprise, provide health services to members and to the community at large, and construct an artisan center. Inspired by the historic and cultural importance of their craft, the group has been tenacious in its struggle for a fair share of the economic benefits of their labor, while serving as an example to other artisan groups embarking on similar self-help initiatives. (*CO-257*)

ACPA—Asociación Colombiana de Promoción Artesanal: 9/84–9/90; $378,500 To establish a Center of Artisan Studies as part of ACPA's program to revitalize handicrafts production in Colombia, concentrating on the well-being of the artisans themselves. The center was designed to concentrate on the technical, cultural, and economic problems facing producers of selected traditional handicrafts and their communities. A long-term goal was to formulate concrete recommendations to private and governmental organizations seeking to improve conditions and production levels of Colombia's artisans. (See also CO-121.) (*CO-306*)

ETNOLLANO—Fundación para el Etnodesarrollo de los Llanos Orientales de Colombia: 9/85–2/91; $125,163 To enable ETNOLLANO, an applied research organization, to design a training model for native health promoters working with communities of Sikuani Indians in the Department of Vichada. This program will assist native extensionists working with the local Ministry of Health in designing and implementing community-based health programs adapted to the social and cultural characteristics of Indian groups in the region. (*CO-323*)

Fundación para el Desarrollo Infantil: 9/85–9/87; $42,000 To collect and edit approximately fifty children's stories for use in public schools in the Department of Valle. These stories were gathered from members of rural and urban communities, and are based on aspects of community life which are culturally relevant to young readers. (*CO-325*)

Asociación Cultural de Fusagasugá: 4/86–4/90; $187,600 To provide programs to teenagers entailing creativity and culture within a broader effort involving early childhood education, primary health care, environmental sanitation, civic education, and adult literacy. (*CO-334*)

Fundación PEPASO: 6/86–12/91; $232,140 To further its literacy and community development programs in over thirty *barrios* of Bogotá by helping organize neighborhood groups around music, theater, and dance, as well as carrying out a series of major festivals of urban popular culture. (*CO-335*)

FIDES—Fundación para la Investigación y el Desarrollo de Sucre: 6/89–12/90; $23,800 To establish five schools for the preservation, instruction, and dissemination of *gaitas y tambores* music (traditional flutes and drums) in five communities in the department of Sucre. *(CO-403)*

AJUSAN—Asociación de Juventudes de Santander: 1/90–12/91; $48,200 To carry out a training and organization program to develop youth leadership, an economic program to create income-generating opportunities for young people, and a cultural and sports program to promote autochthonous cultural expression and constructive activities for some 2,000 youths in eighteen municipalities of the Department of Santander. *(CO-419)*

Fundación Habla/Scribe; 4/90–4/92; $80,800 To broaden an unconventional literacy training and popular communication methodology by employing the collective production of graphic arts materials in poor black and Indian communities in four regions of western Colombia. The project includes production of a pictorial dictionary for use in reading classes, emphasizing local scenes and cultural symbols, and it entails unprecedented and innovative exchanges among Colombia's black and Indian populations. *(CO-422)*

Resguardo Indígena Emberá de Guangui: 6/90–5/93; $45,000 To build a community center, study and preserve the Emberá language, improve health conditions through traditional and preventative medicine, and upgrade housing and sanitation facilities, thereby benefiting 115 extended families of Emberá Indians. *(CO-426)*

COSTA RICA

COOPETALAMANCA—Cooperativa Agropecuaria y Servicio Múltiples de Talamanca, R.L.: 9/80–8/83; $75,410 For this farmer's cooperative on the Atlantic Coast of Costa Rica, to sponsor an effort with the local agrotechnical high school (coordinated by folklorist Paula Palmer) to conduct a community research project to investigate and analyze the region's history, culture, and contemporary problems and to disseminate this information in a magazine format. (See CR-103.) *(CR-042)*

Asociación Indígena de Costa Rica: 9/81–3/84; $137,190 To enable this indigenous association to hire a small staff to coordinate the implementation of programs in leadership training, technical assistance, cultural appreciation, and project planning. The association is a national federation comprising seven indigenous groups in Costa Rica and was formed to create economic opportunities, promote the cultural and social values of the Indian communities, improve leadership skills at the local level, and foster solidarity among Indian peoples. *(CR-046)*

Paula R. Palmer: 4/84–3/86; $18,680 To update, expand, and translate Palmer's 1977 book, *"What Happen": A Folk History of Costa Rica's*

Talamanca Coast, the first comprehensive oral history of the region. Palmer coordinated the oral history project that was carried out by students from Talamanca's high school and sponsored by the major producers' organization in the area, COOPETALAMANCA, whose leadership felt that cultural identity was crucial for future development prospects in the region. (See CR-042.) *(CR-103)*

ACPATP—Asociación de Conservación y Promoción de las Artes y Tradiciones Populares: 9/88–9/90; $57,566 To establish an artisan training program targeting fourteen rural communities throughout the country and providing artisans—including members of Indian and peasant women's groups—with technical assistance in design and production technology, financing of craft production, and marketing through a San José store and international contacts. *(CR-239)*

DOMINICA

PAT—People's Action Theater: 12/79–6/80; $17,250 To support activities carried out in response to the needs caused by widespread hurricane damage. Funding was provided to cover travel expenses of a performance tour that would disseminate information on conditions in Dominica and raise money to restore PAT to performance capacity, and to produce and broadcast a dramatized radio serial on reconstruction issues. PAT is an organization of actors, writers, and musicians formed in 1970 to promote education and social, historical, and cultural awareness throughout Dominica. *(DO-048)*

MCL—Management Consultants Limited: 1/82–5/83; $17,480 To send two Haitian craftspeople, skilled in the art of banana fiber crafts production, to Dominica for six months to transfer their skills to Dominican craftspersons on the Carib Reserve. *(DO-074)*

DOMINICAN REPUBLIC

Casa de Teatro: 3/79–11/88; $152,250 To carry out a fundraising campaign, training programs for local artisans and cultural groups, research programs on local culture, and a "Cultural Expansion Program" in the poorer and more isolated areas of the country. The Casa de Teatro is a cultural education institution, organized by a group of professional educators and artists as a center for the collection and dissemination of materials related to the Dominican cultural heritage. *(DR-040)*

Ballet Folklórico Dominicano: 3/80–8/81; $16,000 To help the ballet cover the general expenses of making two records of folk music and one book reviewing a variety of Dominican folk forms. This cultural organization is concerned with the investigation and dissemination of Dominican culture through dance and music, and is composed entirely of children and young adult volunteers from poor urban barrios. (*DR-044*)

ECUADOR

CEPTEL—Centro de Producciones para la Televisión Latinoamericana: 6/75–11/78; $333,356 To produce and distribute an alternative soap opera for television, depicting realistic life situations and relevant social issues such as agrarian reform, migration, the social relevance of the church, and machismo. By presenting these topics to the general public in an artistic and entertaining way, CEPTEL hoped to stimulate thinking and action on some of the basic social problems facing Latin America. (See also PU-033.) (*EC-023*)

UNIDAD—Departamento de Educación Popular Permanente de Chimborazo: 9/79–10/86; $625,540 To support UNIDAD's educational, economic, and social promotion activities serving over 1,000 rural indigenous communities in Chimborazo Province. These activities included literacy training, community bakeries, artisan workshops, community forestry, and the strengthening of local organizations at the village and federation level. As a key element in this broad development program, UNIDAD expanded the scope of its *Feria Educativa* program, which promotes cultural revitalization through presentations of music and dance, and through sociodrama encourages campesino participation in discussions of pertinent socioeconomic and cultural themes. The *Feria* serves as an initial entrée into local Indian communities, and ultimately as a motivator for campesino participation in UNIDAD's development efforts. (See also EC-165.) (*EC-053*)

Programa de Antropología para el Ecuador: 3/80–12/81; $66,455 To enable a group of actors to establish a popular theater workshop in a Quito *barrio*, produce socially conscious dramas, and evaluate the experience in written form. Based on anthropological research, productions were created that identified cultural roots and explored potential solutions to difficult social problems. (*EC-069*)

Etnopublicaciones: 12/80–12/86; $99,230 To support an Ecuadorian folklorist to collect and anthologize rapidly disappearing traditional black cultural forms in the Esmeraldas and Chota provinces. The goal was to preserve and revitalize the local black heritage, including stories, poems, myths, rites, musical instruments, tools, and household items. (*EC-074*)

Vicariato Apostólico de Esmeraldas: 9/81–12/83; $14,400 To enable the Vicariato's Committee for the Promotion of Esmeraldas Culture to expand its educational center/reading room by acquiring additional materials related to the historical, social, cultural, and economic context of black and Indian inhabitants of Esmeraldas Province. This complemented the Vicariato's other activities, which include organizing conferences and seminars, sponsoring studies and publications, preparing radio programs, and collecting rare, unpublished, or out-of-print books and documents. *(EC-076)*

Cooperativa de Producción Agropecuaria "San Pedro", Ltda.: 9/81–6/87; $48,370 To support this beef-producing cooperative's renowned cultural group, Los Yumbos Chahuamangos, in its efforts to revive and maintain the important cultural forms of the lowland Quichuas, including music, dance, dress, traditions, oral histories, and hunting and fishing techniques. The Yumbos demonstrate these forms to both Indians and non-Indians in Ecuador, while assisting emerging cultural groups in the region to carry out similar activities. *(EC-082)*

Sociedad de Sordos Adultos "Fray Luis Ponce de León": 3/83–8/89; $83,550 To codify Ecuadorian sign language, prepare the first sign language text for the country, institute leadership and vocational training, and organize a theater for the deaf. The long-range objective was to enable the deaf to become better integrated into the cultural and economic mainstream of Ecuadorian life. *(EC-116)*

Mundo Andino: 4/84–1/91; $68,900 To research, publish, and distribute culturally appropriate educational materials adapted for post-literacy learning efforts of campesino adults in the highlands. More than two dozen booklets were produced using language and illustrations from everyday life to treat topics such as agricultural and artisan production, traditional beliefs and practices, local history, and family and community organization. *(EC-124)*

Radio Latacunga: 8/85–1/91; $160,650 To improve radio programming and transmitting by hiring Quechua-speaking announcers, purchasing better equipment, and obtaining technical assistance in equipment maintenance and radio education. Efforts were also made to increase grassroots participation by expanding campesino-produced programs and Radio Latacunga staff outreach into communities being served. Radio Latacunga's activities complement local development efforts by improving bilingual radio programming in the areas of agricultural production, environmental protection, public health, organizational development, and cultural revitalization. *(EC-136)*

Sociedad Salesiana del Ecuador: 9/85–8/88; $80,000 To strengthen bilingual education and skills-training programs for preschool children and adults in forty-six highland peasant communities of Cotopaxi Province. As part of this effort, the project team collected and disseminated local and regional folk history, legends, and oral traditions, for use in classrooms and the formal curriculum. *(EC-146)*

Instituto Normal Fisco-Misional Bilingüe Intercultural Shuar de Bomboiza: 11/85–5/90; $89,100 To support the institute's programs that train teachers to work effectively in a bilingual radio education system (Shuar/Spanish), and to strengthen a new effort in which Shuar students collect information on the cultural history of their own villages for dissemination through improved educational materials. (*EC-148*)

José Chávez Morales: 9/85–9/89; $15,160 To collect the folk traditions of Chávez's native Imbabura Province, publish them in Quechua and Spanish, and provide low-cost printed bilingual materials to institutions that promote local education, adult post-literacy training, and cultural revitalization. (*EC-150*)

Federación de Cabildos Indígenas de la Parroquia Cacha: 4/86–3/92; $79,800 To assist this organization of eighteen indigenous peasant communities located in the highland province of Chimborazo to increase its organizational capacity, agricultural productivity, and off-farm income. Efforts were also made to maintain the rich cultural heritage of the local Indian population through such activities as collecting folklore, organizing regional festivals, and teaching music, dance, and handicrafts production to local youth. (*EC-159*)

CONFENIAE—Confederación de Naciones Indígenas de la Amazonía Ecuatoriana: 4/86–9/92; $185,500 To establish a pilot program offering bilingual-bicultural basic education to indigenous students in the Amazonian region of Ecuador, utilizing in part local traditions and symbols. (*EC-160*)

UNORSAL—Unión de Organizaciones Campesinas de Salinas: 7/86– 6/91; $52,300 To assist this federation in promoting employment and income-generating activities appropriate to both the cultural and environmental settings. The main thrust of the current project is the promotion of ecologically sound food production enterprises, expansion of a reforestation effort, and the establishment of a program to preserve the cultural heritage of the region by collecting local folklore and artifacts of traditional production techniques. (*EC-163*)

SEV-CH—Servicio Ecuatoriano de Voluntarios—Chimborazo: 9/86– 11/89; $384,790 To implement a program in Chimborazo consisting of nonformal education and training, strengthening of peasant organizations, technical assistance, and reinforcement of traditional culture. As part of its cultural revitalization activities, SEV-CH collects and publishes local songs, stories, and oral histories, and organizes annual music and dance festivals. Much of this work is carried out by its cultural action group, the *Feria Educativa.* (See also EC-053.) (*EC-165*)

Comuna y Cooperativa Indígena San Rafael: 5/87–12/88; $20,500 To enable this group of subsistence farmers to restore and expand the old manor of the former Hacienda San Rafael, so as to offer local organizations a meeting room, a training center, a community store and offices, a carpentry shop, a knitting and weaving room, and a music workshop where young people learn to play traditional Indian instruments manufactured by the community. (*EC-177*)

Grupo de Danza, Teatro y Música "Angara Chimeo": 9/88–6/91; $14,550 To carry out a program of preservation and dissemination of the black cultural heritage of highland Chota Valley, entailing a range of activities: improving the cultural center that Angara Chimeo helped establish in the town of Chota; obtaining technical assistance and training for members in areas such as cultural maintenance techniques and project management; and expanding the group's capacity for collecting and performing cultural material in three program areas—dance, popular theater, and music. (*EC-198*)

CONAIE—Confederación de Nacionalidades Indígenas del Ecuador: 3/90–10/91; $81,460 To collaborate with the Federación Awá, a member of CONAIE, and the Ecuadorian government's Unidad Técnica del Programa Awá (UTEPA) in the implementation of bilingual and environmental education programs for 5,000 Awá Indians living in northwestern Ecuador. The project includes the establishment of educational centers in seventeen Awá communities, production of culturally and ecologically appropriate curricula and educational materials, training of Awá individuals as bilingual instructors and ecological guides, and provision of basic education to Awá adults and children in both Awapit and Spanish. (*EC-205*)

AINAIS/TAIS—Asociación Interprofesional de Artesanos Indígenas de Salasaca and Trabajadores Artesanos Indígenas de Salasaca: 9/89–3/91; $13,050 To enable two artisan organizations in Salasaca, Tungurahua, to implement a training and technical assistance program to improve and diversify their production, marketing, and organizational capacity. This includes operating a working capital fund to purchase raw materials, and gathering and reproducing historical and cultural information for distribution among the Salasacas and eventually for better marketing their artisanry. (*EC-206*)

Pre-Asociación de Educación Artesanal: 9/89–3/91; $28,820 To enable this organization of rural educators from thirty-five communities in the Department of Chimborazo to create employment opportunities by expanding production of clothes, weavings, and musical instruments, as well as to teach crafts to local artisans and to foster cultural awareness by sponsoring a music festival. (*EC-215*)

EL SALVADOR

Asociación de Empresarios Circenses: 9/87–9/90; $104,560 To establish a rotating loan fund enabling thirty small, traveling circuses to maintain, upgrade, and replace the tents, materials, and equipment necessary for their performances, thereby increasing the viability of these struggling performing troupes. (*ES-056*)

Patronato Pro-Patrimonio Cultural: 2/88–1/91; $144,744 To train 400 volunteers and hire four full-time cultural promoters, in order to elicit, identify, preserve, and share the traditions, customs, folklore, music, dance, and other forms of cultural expression that foster the reclamation and affirmation of national identity and promote national development in the areas of Nahuizalco and Caluco, in the state of Sonsonate, El Salvador. To this end, the Centro planned to assemble equipment and materials for a traveling exhibition to make forty-five tours over three years, reaching approximately 70,000 beneficiaries. (*ES-061*)

GUATEMALA

ARTEXCO—Federación de Cooperativas de Producción Artesanal: 6/77–9/79; $94,086 To establish a rotating loan fund for ARTEXCO's member artisan cooperatives to purchase raw materials in bulk, and to establish a guarantee fund to provide advance payment for the products of local cooperatives. ARTEXCO was the first federation of artisan cooperatives in Guatemala that produce traditional handicrafts. (*GT-054*)

Cooperativa "Estrella de Occidente", R.L.: 9/80–10/81; $3,000 To assist indigenous artisan weavers to produce and market their traditional clothing, and raise member incomes by providing additional working capital to purchase raw materials. (*GT-100*)

PLFM—Proyecto Lingüístico Francisco Marroquín: 3/83–3/84; $26,866 To assist efforts to increase literacy and bilingual skills among Guatemalan Indians by carrying out the following activities: editing dictionaries in the Mayan Indian languages of Mam, Cakchiquel, Kanjobal, and Kekchi; computerizing information gathered on other languages; editing materials for literacy programs; microfilming previously completed linguistic surveys; and charting the geographical distribution of Guatemala's Indian languages. (See also GT-137.) (*GT-133*)

PLFM—Proyecto Lingüístico Francisco Marroquín: 7/85–1/87; $26,500 To continue efforts to increase literacy among Guatemalan Indians through research and preparation of bilingual educational materials. Specifically, the PLFM computerized data collected on several dialects; edited dictionaries in Ixil, Kanjobal, and Kekchi; prepared a linguistic map for the Cakchiquel language; and designed and produced bilingual educational materials in Kanjobal, Quiché, and Chorti. (See also GT-133.) (*GT-137*)

AEMG—Asociación de Escritores Mayances de Guatemala: 3/87–3/91; $68,400 To enable AEMG to provide Guatemala's indigenous population with new ideas and production techniques through collection and publication in Quiché of traditional stories and legends, as well as documents on civil law, the Guatemalan constitution, health, and nutrition. (*GT-160*)

Asociación de Artesanos "Aj Quen": 1/90–12/90; $56,475 To develop and carry out a market strategy for artisan production, including organizing an educational program to promote, both nationally and internationally, a better understanding of the varied ethnic/cultural expressions of Guatemalan weaving. *(GT-207)*

GUYANA

St. Cuthbert's Craft Centre: 1/82–8/84; $15,340 To enable this association of over sixty Amerindian artisans to complete construction of a facility to house its handicrafts training and marketing programs. Ancillary activities included outreach to incorporate other Amerindian communities in the Craft Centre program, and experimentation with the cultivation of the wild tibisiri palm, a critical raw material for Guyanese Amerindian craft production. *(GY-008)*

HAITI

CEH—Conference Episcopal d'Haiti: 9/85–7/88; $561,650 To assist CEH in sponsoring a national, five-year program aimed at helping up to three million Haitian adults become literate in Creole, Haiti's national language. Funds were used to cover partial costs of personnel, teacher training, creation of pedagogic materials, equipment purchase, and administrative overhead. *(HA-094)*

HONDURAS

ASEPADE—Asesores para el Desarrollo, and Rafael Murillo Selva: 9/79–3/81; $85,814 To enable ASEPADE to carry out project activities with Garífunas, black Caribs living along the northern coast of Honduras. Project objectives included heightening awareness of the socioeconomic problems faced by Garífunas, promoting respect for and preservation of the Garífuna cultural patrimony, and facilitating exchange between Garífunas and other sectors of Honduran society. ASEPADE researched Garífuna legends and folklore, compiled these in a text, and with the participation of Garífunas, collectively wrote and staged a "Theater of Identity," presentations of which were followed by open discussion. A film and videotape were made to document the experience. (See also HO-075.) *(HO-046)*

Rafael Murillo Selva: 6/82–7/82; $5,000 To cover the travel and per diem expenses of the artistic director of Asesores para el Desarrollo, as he showed the videotape of the Garífuna "Theater of Identity" to educators, theatrical groups, and public audiences throughout the Caribbean basin region and the United States. (See also HO-046.) *(HO-075)*

Pre-Cooperativa de Tejedores Intibucanos: 9/82–5/86; $19,200 For providing training in administration and bookkeeping to strengthen this emerging cooperative's management capability, and for purchasing equipment and materials to increase production of its woven products. The group is made up of indigenous weavers who have revived an artisan skill that had virtually disappeared from Honduras. (*HO-078*)

OFRANEH—Organización Fraternal Negra Hondureña: 12/82; $5,000 To organize a national-level OFRANEH meeting, in an attempt to foster organizational consolidation of Garífunas. Traditionally, the Garífunas had lived in scattered villages, enjoying something approaching loose social cohesion, but were unable to consolidate themselves politically. In the face of this disorganization, the Garífunas have been relegated to a marginal ethnic status in Honduras, and few government social programs have reached them. (*HO-081*)

JAMAICA

MRR—Mystic Revelation of Rastafari Community Co-operative and Cultural Centre: 3/77–3/78; $60,407 To enable the musicians and cultural workers in this group to use their talents and resources to stimulate development in their urban community. Funds were granted to expand the music school, and to establish a cooperatively owned and operated recording studio, the revenues of which would be used to support other community development projects. (*JA-034*)

Jamaica School of Dance/Institute of Jamaica: 2/77–1/85; $147,400 To develop and establish a three-year Dance in Education diploma course to prepare twenty graduates to work as cultural agents in the Jamaican school system and in programs for out-of-school youth. Funds also financed the publication of a book entitled *Caribbean Cultural Identity: The Jamaican Case*, by Rex Nettleford, the director of the institute. This work is regarded as one of the best sources on Caribbean culture and its implications for socioeconomic development. (See also JA-061, JA-062.) (*JA-037*)

Sistren Theatre Cooperative: 7/79–9/80; $8,500 To enable Sistren to expand its performances in poor urban and rural communities, secure better theater facilities, and strengthen its organizational and financial capability through government-sponsored training courses in drama, general education, and cooperative management. Sistren, a popular theater collective organized in 1977 by thirteen working women from low-income urban communities, is dedicated to encouraging women to reflect on their conditions and search for positive ways of becoming involved in the resolution of social and economic problems. (See also JA-057.) (*JA-047*)

Sistren Theatre Cooperative: 4/81–9/84; $40,988 For establishing a textile design and silkscreen workshop to develop an additional source of

income and employment for the members of Sistren. (See also JA-047.)
(JA-057)

Jamaica School of Drama/Institute of Jamaica: 9/81–10/84; $104,035
To support a three-part program for increasing the use of drama in community organization and school curricula, while strengthening the Jamaica School of Drama's outreach capacity and repertory as a means for attaining institutional self-sufficiency. The Jamaica School of Drama has been experimenting with theater as a practical medium for learning, not only in the usual curricula of formal schooling but also in the training of grassroots development groups. (See also JA-037, JA-062.) *(JA-061)*

Jamaica School of Arts/Institute of Jamaica: 9/81–9/82; $9,038 To finance the publication of *Jamaica Maddah Goose*, a bilingual book of folktales and nursery rhymes in the Jamaican dialect and standard English. This book provides a unique educational tool for enhancing the cultural identity of the Jamaican child, and its sale to foreign tourists is hoped to foster appreciation for the popular tongue and the culture of Jamaica. (See also JA-037, JA-061.) *(JA-062)*

LATIN AMERICA

TOLA—Theatre of Latin America: 4/79–3/80; $126,000 To facilitate the participation of Latin American groups and individuals in the first hemispheric conference on theater, organized by TOLA. Tola is a private organization that attempts to foster social and cultural development by sponsoring programs that disseminate important aspects of Latin American thought, criticism, and creativity to both Latin American and North American audiences. The conference entailed presentations of contemporary drama of the Americas, and a full week of workshops on theater and its role in society. (See also LA-052.) *(LA-046)*

TOLA—Theatre of Latin America: 2/80–12/82; $141,225 To allow TOLA to support a network of regional centers dedicated to the exchange and dissemination throughout the hemisphere of knowledge, skills, techniques, and information regarding theater. The grant helped support these efforts through a documentation center, a library, and seed money for a translation center. TOLA also organized workshops, performances, and exchanges focusing on cultural forms as creative forces in social change. (See also LA-046.) *(LA-052)*

OAS—Department of Cultural Affairs, Organization of American States: 7/81–11/81; $5,000 To help fund the planning conference for a project being developed by the OAS, entitled "Kindred Spirits: The Art and Science of Blacks in the Americas." This project was designed to disseminate information about and promote a new understanding of the largely nonwritten cultural tradition of blacks in the Americas. The main objective of the conference was to plan the scope and nature of an interpretive traveling exhibit that would explore the cultural affinities of blacks with other peoples of the Americas, through their visual art, crafts, and technologies. *(LA-070)*

MEXICO

IMDEC—Instituto Mexicano para el Desarrollo Comunitario: 12/73–9/76; $16,931 To enable IMDEC to extend its urban communications project to four additional slum areas in Guadalajara. IMDEC developed activities that included community theater, wall drawings, a newspaper, and fiestas in order to portray problems and issues affecting the community, promote a stronger sense of identity, and foster creative cultural expression. *(ME-015)*

Instituto de Asesoría Antropológica para la Región Maya: 10/74–10/75; $17,585 To establish an applied anthropology center for the Mayan region of Mexico, so as to offer anthropological training to personnel, promote collaboration among development workers in Chiapas, and lay the groundwork for a sociocultural evaluation of the development work being carried out in the Mayan area. *(ME-031)*

Diócesis de San Cristóbal de las Casas: 10/74–11/74; $1,185 To enable a linguist and an educator to analyze a series of meetings and a statewide congress promoting unification and solidarity among the Mayan Indians of Chiapas. The purpose was to share this experience with other Indian groups in the hemisphere. *(ME-033)*

Asociación Cultural de Bachajón, A.C.: 9/77–8/80; $23,068 To strengthen, expand, and assure marketing outlets for a Tzeltal Indian women's cooperative producing traditional tapestries. Activities entailed: training programs in cooperativism, including administration of a revolving loan fund; social promotion; purchasing of materials and marketing of the tapestries; construction of workshops and warehouses; and improvement of skills, such as development of new designs and use of new color combinations. *(ME-078)*

PRADE—Proyecto de Animación y Desarrollo, A.C.: 9/77–9/80; $114,400 To support PRADE's work among the Nahuat Indians of Puebla by financing the following activities: establishment of a small coffee processing plant and a carpentry shop; initiation of beekeeping activities; development of an experimental program to train young community members to be development agents; introduction of potable water and bathing facilities; construction of a health clinic and training of a number of residents to serve as nurses and paramedics; and research and collection of sociocultural aspects of Nahuat community life. (See also ME-164.) *(ME-086)*

Casa de la Cultura de Tlacotalpan: 6/78–12/78; $7,800 To enable twenty-three Mexicans to participate in the "Mexico Today" Symposium and the 12th Annual Folklife Festival held in Washington, D.C. and other U.S. cities. The Casa de la Cultura is dedicated to the documentation, teaching, and dissemination of the local cultural heritage of Veracruz. *(ME-106)*

Sociedad de Artesanía Santa Lucía de Tenejapa: 7/79–5/80; $43,255 To construct a multipurpose building to serve as a regional weavers' museum, tourist store, weaving workshop, storage area, day care center, and overnight sleeping quarters in the Indian community of Tenejapa, Chiapas. *(ME-138)*

Comunidades Indígenas de Capacuaro y San Lorenzo: 10/79–12/80; $20,500 To develop a carpentry workshop and two musical bands in the Indian communities of Capacuaro and San Lorenzo, located in the Sierra Tarasca region of the state of Michoacán. *(ME-141)*

PRADE II—Proyecto de Animación y Desarrollo, A.C.: 7/81–7/88; $155,415 To establish a center to evaluate PRADE's regional development program among Puebla Indian communities, in an effort to test alternative approaches and techniques that may benefit Indian communities more directly. PRADE also published books and pamphlets on methods for teaching, reading, and writing in Nahuat. (See also ME-086.) *(ME-164)*

Fomento—Fomento Cultural y Educativo: 1/83–3/86; $102,120 To continue an educational radio program for peasant residents near Huayacocotla, Veracruz, the content of which included folklore, regional music, news, agricultural information, analysis of current events, and the sharing of organizational experiences among different rural communities. An underlying theme of the radio program has been the recognition of the value of campesinos, their communities, and their organizations. *(ME-195)*

GADE—Grupo de Apoyo al Desarrollo Étnico de Oaxaca, A.C.: 9/83–12/84; $37,436 To enable GADE—an organization dedicated to the cultural and economic development of the indigenous population of the state of Oaxaca—to provide technical assistance and financial support to ten small-scale production projects, including crop irrigation, improvement of traditional weaving techniques, and the construction and operation of a bakery, a ceramic workshop, and a carpentry workshop. GADE's goal was not simply to bring about economic gains, but also to introduce new technologies, all of which could be controlled by the indigenous communities and could expose the participants to creative, small-scale approaches to problem-solving. (See also ME-240.) *(ME-217)*

PPU—Promoción Popular Urbana: 9/85–9/86; $34,417 To implement a two-part community development program in a low-income neighborhood of Tijuana inhabited by Mixtec Indians. A consumer education component of the project involved informing Mixtecs of the services available through the public sector for housing and neighborhood improvement, food retailing, and primary health care. A human development component involved bilingual literacy classes, health education, and activities that emphasized cultural tradition and expression. (*ME-237*)

GADE—Grupo de Apoyo al Desarrollo Étnico: 9/85–4/87; $67,128 To offer technical assistance and training to ten isolated Indian communities managing production projects. These projects were designed to generate income and employ traditional technologies in such activities as silk production and carpentry. (See also ME-217.) (*ME-240*)

GER—Grupo de Estudios Regionales del Estado de Oaxaca: 7/86–1/89; $39,575 To conduct research with Indian women from four indigenous communities, investigating the role of traditional midwives in the provision of maternal-child health services. Immediate objectives were to systematize data on the theories and practices used by midwives, upgrade their skills, and disseminate these data to midwives, community women, and medical and academic institutions in Oaxaca. It is anticipated that a long-term outcome of this project will be improved integration of traditional and modern medicine at the community level. (*ME-249*)

Sna Jtz'Ibajom: 9/86-9/89; $52,730 To enable this Indian cultural organization to collect oral histories and native tales of the Tzotzil and Tzeltal Indians and share these materials with Indian communities and the public in general—through puppet theater, radio, and publications—in indigenous languages as well as Spanish. The purpose was to disseminate information and increase understanding about local history and culture. (*ME-262*)

Músicos—Comité de la Música de la Sierra Juárez: 9/87–9/88; $18,230 To design and implement a music course—covering music theory, composition, arranging, and writing—for musicians from thirty indigenous communities who play in municipal bands. Graduates of the course are expected to continue playing in their municipal bands, train other students, repair instruments, document traditional music, and organize musical exchanges among communities. (*ME-282*)

ADCCIO—Asociación para el Desarrollo Cultural de las Comunidades Indígenas de Oaxaca: 9/87–9/90; $61,740 To enable three Indian communities in the central valley of Oaxaca to establish community cultural centers. This entailed researching municipal archives, completing an inventory of local crafts and artifacts, documenting oral histories, preparing displays of traditional technologies, and offering workshops on such topics as textile design, natural dyes, construction, and farming techniques. (*ME-284*)

Centro de Capacitación Musical Mixe: 12/87–6/88; $3,948 To increase people's appreciation and understanding of traditional Mexican culture through a one-month visit to the United States by Mixe Indian students who met with community bands and choirs in four cities. The Mixe students are enrolled in a grassroots musical center in a town in the state of Oaxaca. (*ME-287*)

COMCAMP—Comunicación Campera, A.C.: 6/89–4/91; $89,840 To initiate an adult education program and provide economic assistance in establishing productive enterprises, benefiting Tzotzil and Tzeltal Indians from over sixty rural communities of Los Altos in Chiapas. The educational program trains Indian leaders to advise communities on legal problems, and it uses a group of Tzotzil and Tzeltal actors to dramatize legal problems on video tape and live, for group discussion and training in Indian communities. *(ME-314)*

Sna Jolobil, S.C.: 5/89–4/91; $82,800 To further capitalize this artisan organization of 700 Tzotzil and Tzeltal members, mostly women, by increasing its working capital fund, training new members in traditional weaving, repairing a dye workshop, and establishing an artisan center in San Cristóbal de las Casas. *(ME-318)*

Sna Jtz'Ibajom (Cultura de los Indios Mayas, A.C.): 9/90–3/91; $21,000 To enable this organization of Mayan Indian educators, writers, and performers to expand its literacy and cultural education program, providing new materials for its own instruction programs, for public schools, and for rural communities of the Chiapas highlands. Staff members travel frequently to rural villages to disseminate the new materials and present puppet and live theater works as part of the education program. *(ME-338)*

PANAMA

Fe y Alegría: 10/73–12/74; $4,800 To enable the communications arm of Fe y Alegría Comunicación Social y Teatro Popular—COSTEPO—to organize and provide technical assistance to twenty community theater groups in urban and rural areas, publish a manual on community theater, plan and carry out a national congress of theater groups, and research folklore, myths, and everyday life of individual communities. COSTEPO used theater as a means of communication and expression of the people, as well as a medium for raising consciousness about social problems. *(PN-013)*

CECOP—Centro de Comunicación Popular: 6/74–8/76; $81,115 To conduct a social analysis of Panama's mass communications media, including movies, television, radio, and newspapers; offer social communications workshops on techniques of moviemaking, journalism, and photography; and produce movies using fields and factories as the scenery, farmers and workers as the actors, and their life situations as the script. *(PN-020)*

AEK—Asociación de Empleados Kunas: 9/83–4/87; $498,552 To aid the Kuna in the establishment and demarcation of their reservation as a forest park and wildlife refuge, allowing the Kuna to control access to their traditional lands and protect the ecologically fragile watershed against deforestation. Funds were also awarded to assist the Kuna in constructing facilities for scientists and tourists at the park's central headquarters. Through these efforts, the Kuna are working to maintain their economic and cultural autonomy. (See also PN-093, PN-111.) *(PN-078)*

Asociación Panameña de Antropología: 5/83–5/84; $5,000 To collect and record oral histories, legends, and traditions surrounding two of the most important initiation ceremonies of the Guaymí Indians, the largest indigenous group in Panama. The information was translated into Spanish for use in bilingual education efforts. *(PN-079)*

AEK—Asociación de Empleados Kunas: 8/85–10/86; $21,150 To produce a documentary film portraying the problems created for the Kuna by the slash-and-burn agriculture that is practiced by peasant settlers throughout Panama's natural forest region and along the road connecting the Kuna reservation with the Pan-American Highway. The film documents the Kunas' agricultural practices, which are a unique mixture of traditional agroforestry techniques and modern ecological science, and will be used by the Kuna to educate their own people on the importance of integrating indigenous culture with natural resource management. (See also PN-078, PN-111.) *(PN-093)*

AEK—Asociación de Empleados Kunas: 2/87–12/90; $262,600 To enable the Kuna to implement the resource management, environmental education, and cultural preservation programs developed in its "Management Plan for the Kuna Reservation." Activities included completing the demarcation of the reservation's 200-kilometer border, finishing construction of its visitor center at Nusagandi, further training its personnel in resource management, and continuing to provide environmental education to Kuna youth, Kuna communities in general, and non-Kuna peasants living in the areas bordering the reservation. The long-term goal of this project is to increase the chances for the Kuna to survive as a people through establishing their reservation as a national forest park, relying heavily on existing cultural traditions in order to do so. (See also PN-078, PN-093.) *(PN-111)*

PARAGUAY

CEADUC—Centro de Estudios Antropológicos: 12/74–5/76; $134,379 To enable CEADUC—created in 1950 by private citizens concerned with the cultural preservation of the indigenous tribes of Paraguay—to carry out a series of dialogue sessions with seventeen indigenous groups, so as to stimulate a diagnosis of their present situation and future possibilities. CEADUC also provided the groups with information on their legal rights and their options for self-protection and self-development. In addition, CEADUC designed a media and conference campaign to educate the general population about the problems confronting indigenous people. (See also PY-026.) *(PY-011)*

Vicariato Apostólico del Pilcomayo: 1/75–6/75; $3,908 To publish 3,000 copies of a bilingual Nivacle-Spanish text for use by indigenous teachers in a literacy program for adults and children. (See also PY-026.) *(PY-015)*

Grupo Proyecto Aty-Ne'e: 7/75–9/76; $69,083 To strengthen the use of theater as a didactic vehicle for reflection, debate, and diagnosis in rural Paraguay. In implementing this goal, the proponents researched and compiled Paraguayan folklore, designed and staged plays, and planned and carried out theater workshops. (See also PY-025.) *(PY-016)*

API—Asociación de Parcialidades Indígenas: 3/77–10/80; $1,533,770 To enable API to unite Paraguayan Indian communities and strengthen itself as an independent Indian-managed organization capable of furnishing Indians with the means to improve their conditions and retain their cultural identity. IAF-supported activities included national meetings of the API membership and an economic plan to benefit seven indigenous communities, including the purchase of land, the establishment of a credit fund for production and marketing, and salaries for resident technical assistants in each community. *(PY-024)*

Grupo Proyecto Aty-Ne'e: 7/77–8/81; $115,150 To enable the Aty-Ne'e theater group to work in two rural areas to introduce agricultural assistance as requested by the communities, strengthen farmer organizations, and provide a recreational outlet that could be continued by the communities. Aty-Ne'e gathered extensive information about the myths and folklore of the region, prepared sketches based on local folklore that portray the dilemmas of rural life, presented improvisations incorporating elements of agricultural information, and taught improvisation and other theatrical techniques to local artists. (See also PY-016.) *(PY-025)*

Vicariato Apostólico del Pilcomayo: 8/77–8/80; $6,600 To compile and publish a Nivacle-Spanish dictionary that complements ongoing programs of bilingual education and literacy. The dictionary is now an indispensable tool in the area's bilingual education programs. (See also PY-015.) *(PY-026)*

Alter Vida—Centro de Estudios y Formación para el Ecodesarrollo: 8/87–8/88; $33,978 To enable Alter Vida to carry out a three-part project in four communities on the outskirts of the Greater Asunción metropolitan area. Alter Vida is a civil association dedicated to the promotion of community economic and cultural development within an ecological perspective. Project activities included the promotion of organic gardening with a women's organization, training of young adults in traditional and innovative techniques in the weaving of *karanda'y*, an indigenous palm fiber, and the revitalization of traditional forms of Paraguayan folk theater to be used as a means of self-expression and discussion of project and community issues. *(PY-118)*

Alter Vida—Centro de Estudios y Formación para el Ecodesarrollo: 11/88–8/91; $136,407 To carry out a project entailing traditional palm fiber weaving with the *karanda'y* palm, Guaraní folk theater, organic gardening, self-help housing, and community development in five low-income communities in suburban Asunción. *(PY-131)*

PERU

CEPTEL—Centro Latinoamericano de Producciones Tele-Educativas: 9/73–12/74; $10,660 To produce fifty scripts for a *telenovela* designed to introduce critical thinking and awareness of social change issues into Latin American television programming. (See also EC-023.) *(PU-033)*

ACP—Acción Comunitaria del Perú: 12/78–6/81; $154,960 To offer technical and business training to 400 artisans of Ayacucho, and to assist a nascent artisan association, COOSATEX. ACP provided COOSATEX with working capital to purchase raw materials from wholesalers and buy finished handicrafts from artisan members. ACP also helped COOSATEX to identify natural dyes and expand their use in the group's textiles, incorporate indigenous pre-Inca designs into their weavings, and initiate a reforestation program with 23,000 walnut seedlings. *(PU-083)*

Comité de Turismo de Taquile: 1/79–1/86; $67,219 To assist one of Lake Titicaca's traditional ethnic groups in responding to the upsurge and external control of local tourism, which served to improve local economic conditions while preserving their unique culture. Residents of the island of Taquile equipped locally made boats with outboard motors for the purpose of more swiftly transporting tourists from the mainland to the island, where they stay overnight in local Indian homes. This enabled the Taquileños to break the monopoly on tourist boat transport from the mainland that concentrated economic benefits in a small group of nonresident entrepreneurs. Taquileños also constructed a community-controlled museum to display some of the finest and oldest textiles made by the island's residents. *(PU-093)*

Yanapai Group: 4/79–2/82; $7,000 To publish, promote, and distribute an Andean children's book, *El Mundo de Santiago*, and its sequel, to be used as supplementary readers for first- and second-grade schoolchildren. The stories are told through texts and color illustrations that convey the wonder, adventures, and indigenous culture of a young boy in the mountains of Peru and are written in Spanish, Quechua, and Aymara for the target population of the central Andes and urban slums. *(PU-094)*

SEPAS—Servicio Evangélico Peruano de Acción Social: 5/80–8/84; $249,402 To provide technical assistance and training services to the Kamaq Maki Artisans' Association. On the organizational side, the project established Kamaq Maki as an independent, self-managed, financially self-sufficient grassroots organization, with a service program that went far beyond the original narrow handicraft marketing objectives. Economically, the increased income from craft sales helped many communities make it through an exceedingly difficult period for the Peruvian economy. Culturally, the project served to reinforce its beneficiaries' appreciation of the validity and worth of their handicrafts and cultural heritage. (*PU-117*)

Richard Chase Smith Study: 11/81–6/84; $49,020 To support an anthropologist in his research on development activities and issues that affect Indian groups in the Peruvian Amazon, and that have implications for the cultural and physical survival and well-being of indigenous peoples. (*PU-170*)

Centro de Estudios Andinos Rurales "Bartolomé de las Casas": 8/83–6/86; $139,250 To establish a campesino center in the city of Cuzco, offering lodging to peasants who must travel to the city from remote rural areas to market produce or tend to community affairs. The center serves as an informal training institution and a source of technical assistance in marketing and production, health care, and legal matters. It also houses the offices and recording studio of a radio station preparing programs in Quechua that are geared toward strengthening the cultural identity and awareness of the peasants, as well as communicating practical information. (*PU-199*)

CEICA—Centro de Investigación, Capacitación y Documentación: 5/83–4/86; $64,860 To raise the standard of living of the potters of Simbila, a group continuing a ceramics tradition that dates from pre-Columbian times. CEICA helped organize the potters and offered training in marketing, literacy, nutrition, and family vegetable gardening. (*PU-204*)

Asociación Civil Antisuyo: 6/83–10/86; $147,250 To support the work of Antisuyo, a service organization whose purpose is to establish a high quality commercial outlet offering fair prices for the products of jungle and highland artisan groups. Objectives of the project were to restore the quality of traditional handicrafts through technical assistance and training in design and production techniques, and to keep alive traditional Peruvian textile and pottery skills that reinforce the cultural values of artisan communities throughout Peru. (See also PU-256.) (*PU-205*)

CAAAP—Centro Amazónico de Antropología y Aplicación Práctica: 9/84–6/87; $97,880 To enable CAAAP—created in 1974 to develop a better understanding of the needs and the cultures of Indians in the Peruvian Amazon region—to conduct an agriculture and handicraft development program among five Aguaruna and twelve Chayahuita communities in the department of Loreto. This represents the first comprehensive development program established for these isolated beneficiary groups. (*PU-221*)

CEPCA—Centro de Estudios y Promoción de la Cultura Andina: 9/85–9/87; $110,900 To undertake and foster social and economic development programs and studies related to the Andean region, and later disseminate their results. CEPCA has been assisting migrant artisans who find it difficult to practice their crafts in Lima, distant from their homeland communities, their traditional looms, and sources of raw materials. Grant funds enabled CEPCA to assist migrants from the highlands by reconditioning a plot of land that was lent to it and establishing recreational facilities, handicraft workshops, vegetable gardens, and areas for small animal raising. *(PU-235)*

Asociación Civil Antisuyo: 9/86–3/91; $179,782 To enable Antisuyo to continue its work with remote jungle and highland Indian communities in the area of traditional handicrafts, including organizational training, raw material supply, quality control, and promotion of traditional artisan techniques. Antisuyo works to increase public awareness of the artisan traditions of Peruvian Indian cultures, through expositions, slide shows, and publications. In addition, it manages an artisan products store in Lima which sells the crafts of about sixty Indian communities from throughout Peru. (See also PU-205.) *(PU-256)*

Centro de Investigación Antropológica de la Amazonía Peruana: 8/87–7/88; $16,760 To design a culturally appropriate, bilingual education curriculum for eight Amazonian indigenous groups in the Department of Loreto, for implementation by the Peruvian Ministry of Education. *(PU-279)*

NCTL—Naturaleza, Ciencia, y Tecnología Local para el Servicio Social: 3/90–2/91; $49,926 To work to improve agricultural and land-use practices in several communities in Lima's Santa Eulalia river valley, by coordinating with these communities to conduct experiments, build demonstration plots, restore terraces, and provide classes in soil conservation, organic agriculture, small animal production, fish culture, reforestation, and irrigation. NCTL's work includes training local children in graphic and plastic arts and music. *(PU-310)*

ST. KITTS AND NEVIS

Nevis Crafts Studio Cooperative: 7/80–5/81; $10,655 To enlarge the studio's workshop, train new artisans in local crafts, and provide stipends to trainers and trainees. In addition to providing jobs and stable income to producers, the project aimed at preserving the handicraft traditions of Nevis by training young persons to carry on the techniques of elderly artisans, the only ones still engaged in screw-pine basketry, rugmaking, banjo-making, leather processing, and gourd decoration. *(NV-001)*

National Handicraft and Cottage Industries Development Board: 9/82–9/88; $280,320 To begin a traditional handicraft revival and development program by: equipping and operating four training and production centers; training 100 apprentice artisans to make everyday household articles from copper, wood, coconut shells, and fabrics; marketing crafts through local sales outlets and opening new foreign markets; and establishing credit funds for the purchase of raw materials and the marketing of finished products. (*SK-007*)

ST. LUCIA

FRC—Folk Research Centre: 8/89–7/91; $51,500 To purchase equipment to produce video and audio materials on St. Lucian folk culture to be used by the Ministries of Health, Education, and Tourism for nonformal educational activities in schools and self-help development activities. FRC's sale of videos on the local and tourist markets generates income for the support of the center's program and disseminates knowledge about traditional culture. (*SL-006*)

UNITED STATES

IED—International Educational Development, Inc.: 3/75–10/75; $45,760 To prepare and conduct a program of information interchange among Latin American and U.S. Spanish-speaking community organizations that use popular theater for social development purposes. The main activity of the program was a conference attended by representatives from these organizations. (*US-067/D*)

Wayne Ewing Films: 8/75–8/76; $23,030 To film the activities of the Jamaica National Dance Company, the Kingston Legal Aid Clinic, the Sugar Workers' Cooperative Council (Jamaica), and the Castle Bruce Cooperative (Dominica) for the Bill Moyers special entitled "The Other Caribbean." (*US-079/D*)

Institute for the Development of Indian Law, Inc.: 8/77; $22,500 To provide translation services and travel expenses for ten Latin American Indian delegates to attend a preconference planning meeting in the United States, and a Geneva conference entitled "Discrimination Against Indigenous Populations of the Americas," cosponsored by the Institute and the Indian Treaty Council. (*US-105*)

Centro de Arte: 8/80–11/80; $3,132 To enable the Centro de Arte to cover travel costs for the Second Andean Festival of Folk Music, held at George Washington University and featuring a well-known Bolivian musical group—Grupo Aymara—and a Washington, D.C.-based Bolivian group—Rumisonko. The objectives of the project were to educate non-Andean peoples (largely North Americans) regarding the cultural richness of the Andean region, to support and further the maintenance of Andean folklore, and to enrich and strengthen the Latin American cultural legacy within the United States. (*US-115*)

UNITED STATES AND MEXICO

Atlanta Association for International Education and the Centro de Investigaciones Superiores del Instituto de Antropología e Historia: 1/75–12/78; $111,738 To produce a film entitled "Double Feature" documenting the authentic face-to-face interaction between representative groups from a First World nation (affluent U.S. tourists) and representative groups from Third World nations (Mexican servants and vendors), and to initiate an educational program using the film as a catalyst in an active learning process. This film vividly and artistically conveys the preconceived images, attitudes, feelings, and myths that have traditionally determined how each group perceives its relationship with the other group. (*US-056/D*)

VENEZUELA

ADI—Asociación de Desarrollo: 9/85–7/91; $182,630 To carry out a three-year training and technical assistance program for women's organizations, cooperatives, and small businesses in Catia, a sprawling low-income neighborhood outside Caracas; to foster a network among these organizations to represent the interests of the community; and to coordinate the efforts of numerous local cultural groups to keep alive the tradition of indigenous music, dance, and theater by performing throughout Catia. (*VZ-044*)

Promoción Socio-Cultural Churuata: 11/85–7/90; $298,100 To enable Churuata to provide economic and technical support for three regional centers that coordinate the activities of more than 250 cultural groups throughout Venezuela. These *centros culturales* are perhaps the most dynamic form of grassroots organization in Venezuela and provide the impetus for local development activities. Through the centers, Churuata works with youth, artisans, and cultural expression groups. The grant included funds for materials and equipment for the establishment of workshops for ceramics, leathercraft, weaving and woodworking, and a crafts outlet in Caracas. Churuata was established to coordinate cultural and community development groups in Venezuela and to provide technical assistance for the creation of small artisan enterprises. It also helps support cultural exchanges between indigenous and nonindigenous youth, ages 6–12. (*VZ-047*)

PROANDES—Asociación Civil Promoción Social Los Andes: 9/86–8/90; $152,415 To enable PROANDES to strengthen and expand the

Centro Campesino Mucuchies, a campesino-run organization in the Rangel District, which is expanding its programs in marketing, agricultural training and technical assistance, handicrafts and cultural expression, nutrition, health, and organizational development. (*VZ-049*)

Grupo Cultural El Carmen: 7/88–8/90; $15,000 To expand its program to research, preserve, and perform folk traditions in the areas of music, dance, and drama, as well as to train its members in the production and marketing of handicrafts, and to improve its library for adult literacy programs and remedial education for children. (*VZ-064*)

Fundación Televisora Cultural Boconesa: 6/88–4/90; $86,000 To continue hands-on training in broadcast television for approximately 400 disadvantaged barrio youth, six to eighteen years of age, who operate a television station; expand educational and cultural programming, including the use of music and drama; and institute a program of outreach to community self-help organizations in the state of Trujillo. (*VZ-065*)

FECECENE—Federación de Centros Culturales del Estado de Nueva Esparta: 9/88–8/90; $29,400 To enable thirty-one member organizations to collect and preserve materials depicting the rich cultural heritage and history of the Island of Margarita. This would involve constructing a modest community and visitors' center to display materials, conducting educational programs, and selling traditional crafts, directly involving approximately 6,000 Margariteños, particularly youth. (*VZ-068*)

FLASA—Fundación La Salle de Ciencias Naturales: 9/90–7/91; $17,300 To prepare a manual explaining the medical practices of the Warao Indians and their use of herbal medicines, for use in teaching government, university, and private sector medical personnel about Warao customs. The manual was to be translated into the Warao language and distributed as reading material to schools and missions in the Orinoco Delta—currently, Warao language publications are almost all translations of Spanish stories that have little to do with Warao life and culture. (*VZ-077*)

Promoción Socio-Cultural Churuata: 8/90–9/93; $157,000 To continue Churuata's support for its network of some 350 cultural organizations in Venezuela, including the provision of training and technical, marketing, and management assistance to artisan promoters and local leaders, with special emphasis on youth. (*VZ-080*)

Select Bibliography

•

CARYL RICCA & CHARLES DAVID KLEYMEYER

This bibliography was designed to provide a tool to practitioners, students, and teachers of a culture-based approach to grassroots development among the poor and marginated peoples of Latin America and the Caribbean.

Although it primarily emphasizes English and Spanish language references on Latin America and the Caribbean, a number of relevant sources from Asia, Africa, and North America have been included to enable the reader to explore development experiences in other regions of the world.

The selection of entries, arranged by category (Culture and Development; Ethnic Identity and Cultural Preservation in Latin America and the Caribbean; Culture and Politics/Democracy; Cultural Policy and Cultural Rights; Music and Dance; Arts and Handicrafts; Tourism; Culture and Environment; Culture and Education; Mass Media; Sociodrama, Theater, and Puppets; Folk Tradition and Folk Media; Methodology; and General/Contextual Sources), does not represent an exhaustive review of the literature in any one category, only the best of the available resources. Nor are the categories intended to be mutually exclusive. The reader will find, for instance, that many references under the more general headings such as "Folk Tradition/Folk Media: Examples and Development Applications" are relevant to some of the more specific categories such as "Music and Dance" or "Sociodrama, Theater, Puppets."

More than three-fourths of the sources listed here are in the Library of Congress in Washington, D.C. A number of the entries are available from the sponsoring institutions listed at the end of the bibliography.

CULTURE AND DEVELOPMENT

African Cultural Institute (ACI). *La Dimension Culturelle du Développement* (proceedings of the international seminar, Dakar, April 20–25, 1983). Dakar: Regional Centre for Research and Documentation on Cultural Development (CREDEC), 1983.

Anacleti, Odhiambo. "Cultural Emancipation as a Means of Economic Development in East and Central Africa." *Cultures* 33 (1983): 26–46.

Ariyaratna, A. T. *In Search of Development: Sarvodaya Effort to Harmonize Tradition with Change*. Moratuwa, Sri Lanka: Sarvodaya Press, 1981.

————. "Learning in Sarvodaya." In A. Thomas and E. W. Ploman, eds. *Learning and Development. A Global Perspective*. Toronto: Ontario Institute for Studies in Education, 1985, pp. 108–124.

————. *A Struggle to Awaken*. Moratuwa, Sri Lanka: Sarvodaya Shramadana Movement, 1978.

Arizpe, Lourdes. "Culture in International Development." Paper delivered at the 19th World Conference of the Society for International Development, New Delhi, India, March 1988; published in *Development* (Journal of the Society for International Development) 1 (1988): 17–19.

Bryant, Coralie. "Culture, Management, and Institutional Assessment." Paper delivered at the International Conference on Culture and Development in Africa, World Bank, Washington, D.C., April 2–3, 1992.

Cadaval, Olivia. *Encuentro de Auto-Evaluación de los Proyectos de Mantenimiento Cultural*. 6–9 Diciembre 1984, Centro de Capacitación Bilingüe, Gatazo Hospital, Cantón Colta, Provincia de Chimborazo, Ecuador. Ecuador: Fundación Interamericana, 1985.

Camacho, Daniel. *La Dominación Cultural en el Subdesarrollo*. San José, Costa Rica: Editorial Costa Rica, 1972.

Cao-Tri, Huynh. "Identidad Cultural y Desarrollo: Alcance y Significación." *Cuadernos Americanos* 258.1 (1985): 105–119.

Casimir, Jean. "Culture, Discourse (Self-Expression), and Social Development in the Caribbean." *CEPAL Review* 25 (1985): 149–162.

Colchester, Marcus, ed. "An End to Laughter? Tribal Peoples and Economic Development." *Survival International Annual Review* 44 (1985): entire issue.

Colletta, N. J. "Folk Culture and Development: Cultural Genocide or Cultural Revitalization?" *Convergence* 10.2 (1977): 12–19.

————. "Folk Culture and Development: Cultural Genocide or Reconstruction Mentality?" *International Journal of Adult Education* 10.2 (1977): 12.

————. "The Use of Indigenous Culture as a Medium for Development: The Indonesian Case." *Indonesian Journal of Social and Economic Affairs* 1.2 (1975): 60–73.

————, ed. "Folk Culture and Development." *Convergence* 10.2 (1977): entire issue.

Colletta, N. J., R. T. Ewing, and T. A. Todd. *Cultural Revitalization, Non-Formal Education and Village Development in Sri Lanka: The Sarvodaya Shramadana Movement*. Chicago: Comparative Education Review, 1982.

Cultural Survival. "Grassroots Economic Development" *Cultural Survival Quarterly* 11.1 (1987): special issue.

Davis, Shelton H. *Victims of the Miracle: Development and the Indians of Brazil*. New York, NY: Cambridge University Press, 1977.

Dorfman, Ariel. "Bread and Burnt Rice: Culture and Economic Survival in Latin America." *Grassroots Development* 8.2 (1984): 3–25.

————. "Wandering on the Boundaries of Development." In Sheldon Annis and Peter Hakim eds. *Direct to the Poor: Grassroots Development in Latin America*. Boulder and London: Lynne Rienner Publishers, 1988, 166–184.

Dorfman, Ariel, y Armand Mattelart. *Para Leer al Pato Donald*. Buenos Aires, Argentina: Siglo XXI, 1972.

Durston, John W. "Los Grupos Indígenas en el Desarrollo Social Rural." *América Indígena* 40.3 (1980): 429–470.

Goodland, Robert. *Tribal Peoples and Economic Development: Human Ecologic Considerations*. Washington, DC: World Bank, 1982.

Guayasamín, Oswaldo. "Cultural Identity: The Key to Development in Latin America." *Cultures* 3.4 (1976): 69–75.

Gutiérrez, Paulina y Soledad Bianchi, "El Desarrollo del Campo Artístico Cultural." In *Una Puerta Que se Abre: Los Organismos no Gubernamentales en la Cooperación al Desarrollo*, Taller de Cooperación al Desarrollo. Santiago, Chile: Servicio Editorial, 1989, 411–453.

Haggerty, Patricia, Robert Mashek, Marion Ritchey, and Steve Vetter. "The Arts and Social Change." *Journal of the Inter-American Foundation* 3 (1979): 1–11.

Herrera, Xochitl, and Miguel Lobo-Guerrero. "From Failure to Success: Tapping the Creative Energy of Sikuani Culture in Colombia." *Grassroots Development* 12.3 (1988): 28–37.

Ideas and Action. "Culture and Rural Development." Special issue of *Ideas and Action (FAO)* 152.3–4 (1983): entire issue.

Institute for Development and International Relations (IRMO). "Network of Networks for Research and Cooperation in Cultural Development." *Culturelink* 8 (1992): 1–165.

Inter-American Foundation Learning Committee on Cultural Awareness. "Cultural Expression and Social Change." *Development Digest* 16.4 (1978): 47–61.

International Fund for the Promotion of Culture. *Culture Plus*—a journal published since 1989 by this subsidiary of the United Nations Educational, Scientific, and Cultural Organization (UNESCO).

————. *Reflections 1991*. Paris: UNESCO, 1991.

Jensen, Lois. "Old Cultures, New Beginnings: Cultural Development Takes on a New Life in Latin America." *World Development* (Journal of the United Nations Development Programme) 2.4 (1989): 4–9.

Katoke, Israel K., and Stephen A. Lucas. *Cultural Development as a Factor in Social Change*. Dar es Salaam: UNESCO, 1975.

Kazen, Felisa. *Culture and Development: An Inquiry into Policy and Practices in Selected International Agencies and Private Foundations*. Unpublished report commissioned by the Inter-American Foundation, 1982, 81 pages.

Kellerman, Luce. *The Cultural Dimension of Development: A Selective and Annotated Bibliography*. Paris: UNESCO, 1986; updated in 1991 in French: *La Dimension Culturelle du Développement: Bibliographie Sélective et Annotée, 1985–1990*.

Kirpal, Prem. "Culture and Development: The Incipient Crisis." *Cultures* 3.4 (1976): 83–89.

Kleymeyer, Charles David. "Cultural Energy and Grassroots Development." *Grassroots Development* 16.1 (1992): 22–31.

————. "What Is Grassroots Development?" *Grassroots Development* 15.1 (1991): 38–39.

————, comp. *La Expresión Cultural y el Desarrollo de Base*. Quito, Ecuador: Abya-Yala, 1993.

Langlois, Juan Carlos. "The Cultural Dimension in Development Projects." *Cultures* 7.3 (1980): 171–176.

McCarthy, Kathleen D. "From Cold War to Cultural Development: The International Cultural Activities of the Ford Foundation, 1950–1980." *Daedalus* 116 (1987): 93–117.

Macy, Joanna. *Dharma and Development: Religion as Resource in the Sarvodaya Self-Help Movement.* West Hartford, CT: Kumarian Press, 1985.

Maybury-Lewis, D.H.P. *The Social Impact of Development on Ethnic Minorities.* Washington, DC: U.S. Agency for International Development, 1980.

M'Bow, Amadou-Mahtar. "Latin America and the Caribbean: Cultural Dimension of the Development." *Cultures* 5.3 (1978): 11–17.

Moulinier, Pierre. *Programa de la Unesco para el Desarrollo Cultural: Presentación de las Actividades Realizadas desde 1960.* Paris: UNESCO, 1990.

Mowlana, Hamid, and Laurie J. Wilson. *Communication and Development: A Global Assessment.* Paris: UNESCO, 1985.

Mowlana, Hamid, and Laurie J. Wilson. *The Passing of Modernity.* New York: Longman, 1990.

Nettleford, Rex M. "Definition and Development: The Need for Caribbean Creativity." *Caribbean Review* 14.3 (1985): 6–10.

Nyang, Sulayman S. "The Cultural Consequences of Development in Africa." Paper delivered at the International Conference on Culture and Development in Africa, World Bank, Washington, D.C., April 2–3, 1992.

Pascallon, P. *The Cultural Dimension of Development.* Paris: UNESCO, 1982.

Paz, Octavio. *Children of the Mire.* Cambridge, MA: Harvard University Press, 1974.

Peel, J.D.Y. "The Significance of Culture for Development Studies." *IDS Bulletin* 8.2 (1976): 8–11.

Qureshi, Mahmud Shah. *Culture and Development.* Dhaka, Bangladesh: National Book Centre, 1983.

Ricca, Caryl. "Problems Encountered in Cultural Projects." Unpublished report under contract to the Inter-American Foundation, 1988, 23 pages.

Rivera, Anny. *Notas sobre Movimiento Social y Arte en el Régimen Autoritario.* Santiago, Chile: CENECA, 1983.

Rogers, E. M., N. J. Colletta, and J. Mbindyo. *Social and Cultural Influences on Human Development Policies and Programs.* Washington, DC: World Bank Staff Working Paper No. 403, 1980.

Rojas, Luís. "Ayni-Ruway: Indigenous Institutions and Native Development in Bolivia." *Ideas and Actions (FAO)* 152.3–4 (1983): 22–28.

Serageldin, Ismail, and June Taboroff, eds. *Culture and Development in Africa: Proceedings of the International Conference Held at the World Bank, Washington, D.C., April 2 and 3, 1992,* two volumes. Washington, D.C.: World Bank, 1992.

Serkkola, A., and C. Mann, eds. *The Cultural Dimension of Development.* Helsinki: Finnish National Commission for UNESCO, 1986.

Soares Pinto, Rogerio F. "Modern Development and Cultural Expression: Two Cultural Models." *Cultures* 33 (1983): 123–136.

Society for International Development. "Cultural Identity and Global Change." A special edition of *Development: Journal of the Society for International Development* (Lourdes Arizpe, guest editor) 4 (1992).

Tagger, Jutta. *Directory of Institutions Engaged in Research on the Cultural Dimension of Development.* Paris: UNESCO, Section for Cultural Policies and Studies on Cultural Development, 1989.

UNESCO (United Nations Educational, Scientific, and Cultural Organization). *The Cultural Dimension of Development. Proceedings of the International Symposium.* The Hague: Netherlands National Commission for UNESCO, 1985, 141–146.

———. "Culture: The Neglected Dimension of Development." *UNESCO Sources* 25 (April 1991): 6–16.

————. *List of Documents and Publications in the Field of Culture, 1984–1986.* Paris: UNESCO, 1988.

————. *List of Documents and Publications in the Field of Culture, 1987–1988.* Paris: UNESCO, 1989.

————. *List of Documents and Publications in the Field of Culture, 1989–1991.* Paris: UNESCO, 1992.

————. *Plan of Action for the Decade for Cultural Development.* Paris: UNESCO, 1990.

————. *A Practical Guide to the World Decade for Cultural Development, 1988–1997.* Paris: UNESCO, 1987.

————. *Strategy for the Implementation of the Plan of Action for the Decade for Cultural Development.* Paris: UNESCO, 1990.

————. "World Commission on Culture and Development." *Culture Plus* 10 (1993): 2–3.

van Nieuwenhuijze, C.A.O. *Culture and Development: The Prospects of an Afterthought.* The Hague: Institute of Social Studies, 1983.

Verhelst, Thierry. *Des Racines pour Vivre Sud-Nord: Identités Culturelles et Développement.* Bruxelles: Duculot Perspectives, 1987. Also in English: *No Life Without Roots: Culture and Development.* London: Zed Books, Ltd., 1990 (translated by Bob Cumming).

Wali, Alaka. "Living *with* the Land: Ethnicity and Development in Chile." *Grassroots Development* 14.2 (1990): 12–20.

Ziolkowski, Janusz. "Cultural Dimension of Development." *Cultures* 6.1 (1979): 17–29.

ETHNIC IDENTITY AND CULTURAL PRESERVATION IN LATIN AMERICA AND THE CARIBBEAN

Barth, Fredrik. *Ethnic Groups and Boundaries.* Boston: Little, Brown and Co., 1969.

Bonfil Batalla, Guillermo and Nemesio Rodríguez. *Las Identidades Prohibidas: Situación y Proyectos de los Pueblos Indios de América Latina.* Tokyo: Universidad de Naciones, 1981.

Bonfil Batalla, Guillermo, et al. *América Latina: Etnodesarrollo y Etnocidio.* San José, Costa Rica: Ediciones Flacso, 1982.

Breslin, Patrick. "The Mapuche Find Their Voice." *Grassroots Development* 13.2 (1989): 36–43.

————. "A Sense of Identity." *Grassroots Development* 10.2 (1986): 12–21.

————. "The Technology of Self-Respect: Cultural Projects Among Aymara and Quechua Indians." *Grassroots Development* 6.1 (1982): 33–37.

Bryan, Patrick. "African Affinities: The Blacks of Latin America." *Caribbean Quarterly* 17.3–4 (1971): 45–52.

Cámara Barbachano, Fernando. "Los Conceptos de Identidad y Etnicidad." *América Indígena* 46.4 (1986): 597–618.

Cotter, James T. "The Basic Need for Status." *Journal of the Inter-American Foundation* (Third Quarter 1979): 16–20.

Dorfman, Ariel. *The Empire's Old Clothes: What the Lone Ranger, Babar, and Other Innocent Heroes Do to Our Minds.* New York: Pantheon Books, 1983.

Goffman, Erving. *Stigma: Notes on the Management of Spoiled Identity.* Englewood Cliffs, NJ: Prentice-Hall, 1963.

Healy, Kevin. "Old Traditions and New Practices: Ayni-Ruway of Bolivia." *Journal of the Inter-American Foundation* 5.1 (1981): 2–5.

Isar, Yudhishthir Raj. *Why Preserve the Past? The Challenge to Our Cultural Heritage.* Washington, D.C.: Smithsonian Institution Press; and Paris: UNESCO, 1986.

Leon, Lydia. "Tengboche Culture Center in Nepal." *Cultural Survival Quarterly* 8.3 (1984): 69–70.

León-Portilla, Miguel. "Etnias Indígenas y Cultura Nacional Mestiza." *América Indígena* 39.3 (1979): 601–621.

Moreno Fraginals, Manuel, relator. *Africa en América Latina.* Mexico: Siglo Veintiuno Editores, 1977.

Nelch, Roger. "The Chinchero Center for Traditional Culture." *Cultural Survival Quarterly* 6.4 (1982): 26–35.

Nettleford, Rex M. *Caribbean Cultural Identity: The Case of Jamaica.* Los Angeles: UCLA, 1979.

Organización de los Estados Americanos. *Informe Final de la II Reunión Interamericana Sobre Administración de Casas de Cultura Popular.* Washington, DC: Secretaría General, Organización de los Estados Americanos, CIECC, 1984.

Pereira, João Baptista Borges. "Negro e Cultura Negra no Brasil Atual." *Revista de Antropología* 26 (1983): 93–105.

Pescatello, Ann M., ed. *Old Roots in New Lands: Historical and Anthropological Perspectives on Black Experiences in the Americas.* Westport, CT: Greenwood Press, 1977.

Rout, Leslie B. *The African Experience in Spanish America, 1502 to the Present Day.* New York, NY: Cambridge University Press, 1976.

Santa Cruz, Nicomedes. "Identidad Cultural y Descolonización." *Plural* 11.130 (1982): 68–71.

Shkilnyk, Anastasia M. *A Poison Stronger Than Love: The Destruction of an Ojibwa Community.* New Haven: Yale University Press, 1985.

Smith, Richard Chase. "The Amuesha Cultural Center." *Cultural Survival Newsletter* 4.2 (1980): 5–6.

Society for International Development. "Culture and Ethnicity." *Development: Seeds of Change* 1 (1987): entire issue.

Stavenhagen, Rodolfo. "Ethnocide or Ethnodevelopment: The New Challenge." *Development: Seeds of Change; Village Through Global Order* 1 (1987): 74–78.

UNESCO. *Conventions and Recommendations of UNESCO Concerning the Protection of the Cultural Heritage.* Paris: UNESCO, 1983.

———. "Focus: Raiders of the Cultural Ark." *UNESCO Sources* 28 (July/August, 1991): 6–16.

Varese, Stefano. "Cultural Development in Ethnic Groups: Anthropological Explorations in Education." *International Social Science Journal* 38 (1985): 201–216.

Whitten, Norman E., Jr., ed. *Cultural Transformations and Ethnicity in Modern Ecuador.* Urbana: University of Illinois Press, 1981.

CULTURE AND POLITICS/DEMOCRACY

African National Congress of South Africa. "The Role of Culture in the Process of Liberation." *Education with Production* (Botswana) 1.1 (1981): 34–46.

Ardiles, Osvaldo, et al. *Cultura Popular y Filosofía de la Liberación: Una Perspectiva Latinoamericana.* Buenos Aires: F. G. Cambeiro, 1975.

Aronoff, Myron J. *Culture and Political Change.* Political Anthropology, Volume 2. New Brunswick: Transaction Books, 1983.

Bonfil Batalla, Guillermo. "Lo Propio y lo Ajeno: Una Aproximación al Problema del Control Cultural." *Revista Mexicana de Ciencias Políticas y Sociales* 27.103 (1981): 183–191.

Cabral, Amilcar. *National Liberation and Culture*. Syracuse, NY: Syracuse University, 1970.

Deng, Francis M. *Cultural Dimensions of Conflict Resolution and Development: Some Lessons from the Sudan*. Paper delivered at the International Conference on Culture and Development in Africa, World Bank, Washington, D.C., April 2–3, 1992.

Dorfman, Ariel. "Chile: La Resistencia Cultural al Imperialismo." *Casa de las Américas* 17.98 (1976): 3–11.

————. "Niveles de la Dominación Cultural en América Latina: Algunos Problemas, Criterios y Perspectivas." *Ideologies and Literature* 2.6 (1978): 54–89.

Horowitz, Donald L. "Cultural Movements and Ethnic Change." *Development Digest* 16.4 (October, 1978): 62–70 Extracted from *The Annals* (The American Academy of Political and Social Sciences, Philadelphia, PA) 433 (September, 1977): 7–18.

Kouassigan, Guy Adjété. *Revolution ou Diversité des Possibles*. Paris: Coll. Points de Vue, 1985.

Maybury-Lewis, David. "Living in the Leviathan: Ethnic Groups and the State." In David Maybury-Lewis, ed. *The Prospects for Plural Societies*, 1982 Proceedings of the American Ethnological Society, Washington, 1984.

Moeckli, J. M. "Cultural Democracy." In *The Development of Cultural Policies in Europe*. Helsinki Conference, 1982 (Helsinki: Ministry of Education, 1982), 91–111.

Putnam, Robert D., Robert Leonardi, and Raffaella Nanetti. "Governance and the Civic Community." Paper delivered at the International Conference on Culture and Development in Africa, World Bank, Washington, D.C., April 2–3, 1992.

Reilly, Charles. "Cultural Movements in Latin America: Sources of Political Change and Surrogates for Participation." In Myron J. Aronoff, ed. *Political Anthropology, Volume 2: Culture and Political Change*. New Brunswick: Transaction Books, 1983.

Scott, James C. "Protest and Profanation: Agrarian Revolt and the Little Tradition, Part I." *Theory and Society* 4.2 (1977): 211–246.

————. "Protest and Profanation: Agrarian Revolt and the Little Tradition, Part II." *Theory and Society* 4.4 (1977): 1–38.

Thiong'o, Ngugi wa. *Barrel of a Pen: Resistance to Repression in Neo-colonial Kenya*. Trenton, NJ: African World Press, 1983.

Thompson, Dennis L., and Dov Ronen. *Ethnicity, Politics, and Development*. Newbury Park, CA: Sage Publications, 1986.

Whisnant, David E. *All That is Native and Fine: The Politics of Culture in an American Region*. Chapel Hill: University of North Carolina Press, 1983.

Young, Crawford. *The Politics of Cultural Pluralism*. Madison, WI: University of Wisconsin Press, 1970.

CULTURAL POLICY AND CULTURAL RIGHTS
(Note: Most UNESCO publications in this section also exist in Spanish.)

General

American Association for the International Commission of Jurists. *Toward an Integrated Human Rights Policy: A Commentary on the Interrelationship of Economic, Social, Cultural, Civil, and Political Rights*. New York: American Association for the International Commission of Jurists, 1980.

Bonfil Batalla, Guillermo, et al. *Culturas Populares, Política Cultural*. Mexico: Museo de Culturas Populares, 1982.

Brunner, José Joaquín. *Un Espejo Trizado: Ensayos sobre Cultura y Políticas Culturales*. Chile: Facultad Latinoamericana de Ciencias Sociales (FLACSO), 1988.

―――. *Políticas Culturales para la Democracia*. Santiago, Chile: CENECA, 1985.

Cultural Survival. "Intellectual Property Rights: The Politics of Ownership." *Cultural Survival Quarterly* 15.3 (1991): special issue.

"A 'Culture Bank'—The International Fund for the Promotion of Culture." *Cultures* 3.4 (1976): 182–187.

Ganji, Manouchehr. *The Realization of Economic, Social, and Cultural Rights: Problems, Policies, Progress*. New York: United Nations, 1975.

Girard, Augustin, and G. Gentil. *Cultural Development: Experience and Policies*. Paris: UNESCO, 1972.

Goodland, Robert, and Maryla Webb. "The Management of Cultural Property in World Bank–Assisted Projects." Washington, D.C.: World Bank, Technical Paper No. 62, 1987.

Ifias, I. "Cultural Diversity and Development." *Cultures* 4.2 (1977): 183–188.

Instituto Histórico Centroamericano. "Zigzagueos de la Cultura: Proceso de Autoevaluación." *Envió* (Nicaragua) 7.87 (1988): 30–48.

International Work Group for Indigenous Affairs (IWGIA). *Declaration of Barbados*. Copenhagen: IWGIA (Document No. 1), 1972.

Konare, A. O. "La Coopération Culturelle entre les Pays en Développement." In *La Culture et le Nouvel Ordre Economique International*. Institute for Developing Countries (Zagreb) and African Cultural Institute (Dakar), 1984, 123–157.

Lewis, Sulwyn. *Principles of Cultural Co-Operation*. Paris: UNESCO, 1971.

Lomax, Alan. "Appeal for Cultural Equity." *Journal of Communications* 27.2 (Spring 1977): 25–38.

Moya, Ruth. "Derechos Culturales de los Pueblos Indígenas." En *Los Derechos Humanos: El Caso Ecuatoriano*, editado por CEDHU. Quito: Editorial El Conejo, 1985.

Organization of African Unity. *Cultural Charter for Africa, Port Louis, 1976*. Addis Ababa, Ethiopia: Information Division, OAU General Secretariat, 1976.

Subercaseaux, Bernardo. *El Debate Internacional sobre Políticas Culturales y Democracia*. Santiago, Chile: CENECA, 1986.

UNESCO. *Convention Concerning the Protection of the World Culture and Natural Heritage*. Paris: UNESCO, 1972.

―――. *Cultural Development: Some Regional Experiences*. Paris: UNESCO, 1980.

―――. *Cultural Rights as Human Rights*. Paris: UNESCO, 1970.

―――. *Planning for Cultural Development: Methods and Objectives*. Paris: UNESCO, 1976.

―――. *Problems and Prospects: Intergovernmental Conference on Cultural Policies in Africa, Accra, 27 October–6 November 1975*. Paris: UNESCO, 1975.

―――. *Recommendation Concerning the Preservation of Cultural Property Endangered by Public or Private Works*. Paris: UNESCO, 1968.

―――. *Select Annotated Bibliography on Cultural Policies*. Paris: UNESCO, Division of Cultural Development, 1982.

―――. *Towards a Centre for Study, Research and Documentation on Cultural Development. Revised and Enlarged Version on the Basis of New Experiences*. Paris: UNESCO, 1977.

―――. *Towards a Documentation Centre for Cultural Development: Experiments and Suggestions*. Paris: UNESCO, 1975.

————. *World Conference on Cultural Policies (Mexico City—July 26–August 6, 1982) Final Report*. Paris: UNESCO, 1982.
"La UNESCO y la Lucha Contra el Etnocidio: Decalaración de San José." *Anuario Indigenista* 42 (1982): 157–165.
Vitanyi, I. "Cultural Policies: Typology and Effects of Cultural Policies." *Cultures* 33 (1983): 97–107.
White, Robert A. *Políticas Nacionales de Comunicación y Cultura*. Santiago, Chile: CENECA, 1985.

Latin American and Caribbean Countries

Alonso de Quesada, Alba. *Towards a Cultural Policy in Honduras*. Paris: UNESCO, 1978.
Ansión, Juan. *Anhelos y Sinsabores: Dos Décadas de Políticas Culturales del Estado Peruano*. Lima: Grupo de Estudios para el Desarrollo, 1986.
Baptista Gumucio, Mariano. *Cultural Policy in Bolivia*. Paris: UNESCO, 1979.
Bonfil Batalla, Guillermo, et al. *Políticas Culturales en América Latina*. Mexico: Grijalbo, 1987.
Brockmann Machado, Mario, et al. *Estado e Cultura no Brasil*. São Paulo: Difel, 1984.
Cardenal, Ernesto. "Democratization of Culture in Nicaragua." In Douglas Kahn and Diane Neumaier, eds. *Cultures in Contention*. Seattle: Real Comet Press, 1985.
Castells Montero, Carlos A. *La Revalida en Latinoamerica: Trabajo*. Montevideo, Uruguay: Ministerio de Relaciones Exteriores, Dirección de Asuntos Culturales y de Información, Departamento de Relaciones Culturales, 1980.
Catalán, Carlos, y Giselle Munizaga. *Políticas Culturales Estatales Bajo el Autoritarismo en Chile*. Santiago: Centro de Indagación y Expresión Cultural y Artística (CENECA), 1986.
Chaui, Marilena de Souza. *Política Cultural*. Porto Alegre, Brazil: Fundação Wilson Pinheiro, 1984.
Conselho Federal de Cultura (Brazil). *Aspectos da Política Cultural Brasileira*. Rio de Janeiro: O Conselho, 1976.
Dassin, Joan. "Cultural Policy and Practice in the Nova República." *Latin American Research Review* 24.1 (1989): 115–123.
El Salvador. Ministerio de Cultura. *Legislación Escolar, 1956–1959*. San Salvador: Ministerio de Cultura, Departamento Editorial, 1959.
FUNARTE. *Levantamento das Fontes de Apoio Financeiro a Area Cultural: Nível Federal*. Rio de Janeiro: FUNARTE, Núcleo de Estudos e Pesquisas, 1983.
García-Canclini, N. "Políticas Culturais na America Latina." *Novos Etudos* (CE-BRAP, Sao Paulo) 2 (1983): 39–51.
Guedez, Pedro Manuel. *Temas de Legislación Cultural Venezolana*. Caracas: Monte Avila Editores, 1986.
Harvey, E. R. *Cultural Policy in Argentina*. Paris: UNESCO, 1979.
Herrera, F. "Cultural Policies in Latin America and the Caribbean." In *Cultural Development*. Paris: UNESCO, 1980, 71–191.
Institute of Jamaica. *Cultural Policy in Jamaica: A Study*. Paris: UNESCO, 1977.
————. *A Guide to Cultural Policy Development in the Caribbean*. Washington, DC: General Secretariat, Organization of American States, 1984.
Martínez, E. *Cultural Policy in Mexico*. Paris: UNESCO, 1977.
Massiani, F. *Cultural Policy in Venezuela*. Paris: UNESCO, 1977.
Moreira, Darío. *Cultural Policy in Ecuador*. Paris: UNESCO, 1979.
Nicaragua. Ministerio de Cultura. *Hacía una Política Cultural de la Revolución Popular Sandinista*. Managua: Ministerio de Cultura, 1982.

Núñez de Rodas, Edna. *Cultural Policy in Guatemala*. Paris: UNESCO, 1981.
Panama. National Institute of Culture. *Cultural Policy in the Republic of Panama*. Paris: UNESCO, 1978.
Peru. National Institute of Culture. *Cultural Policy in Peru*. Paris: UNESCO, 1977.
Rovinski, Samuel. *Cultural Policy in Costa Rica*. Paris: UNESCO, 1977.
Ruíz, Jorge Eliecer. *Cultural Policy in Colombia*. Paris: UNESCO, 1977.
Saruski, J., and G. Mosquera. *Cultural Policy in Cuba*. Paris: UNESCO, 1977.
Seymour, A. J. *Cultural Policy in Guyana*. Paris: UNESCO, 1977.
Sobre Política Cultural na América Latina: 1º. Seminário Interamericano de Mudanças e Políticas Culturais, Aspen, Colorado, agosto 1978: 3º. Curso Interamericano de Administração Cultural—Política e Gerência, CNRC, Brasília, outubro a dezembro 1978. Ouro Preto, n.p., 1979.
Sosnowski, Saul, comp. *Represión, Exilio y Democracia: La Cultura Uruguaya*. Montevideo: Ediciones de la Banda Oriental, 1987.
Stansifer, Charles L. *Cultural Policy in the Old and the New Nicaragua*. Hanover, NH: American Universities Field Staff, 1981.
UNESCO (United Nations Educational, Scientific, and Cultural Organization). *Intergovernmental Conference on Cultural Policies in Latin America and the Caribbean. Bogota, January 10–20, 1978. Problems and Prospects*. Paris: UNESCO, 1978.
———. *Intergovernmental Conference on Cultural Policies in Latin America and the Caribbean. Bogota, January 10–20, 1978. Situation and Trends*. Paris: UNESCO, 1978.
———. *Intergovernmental Conference on Cultural Policies in Latin America and the Caribbean. Bogota, January 10–20, 1978. Final Report*. Paris: UNESCO, 1978.
———. *Situations and Trends in Cultural Policy in Member States of Latin America and the Caribbean. World Conference on Cultural Policies, Mexico City, 26 July–6 August, 1982*. Paris: UNESCO, 1982.

U.S. Government Policies and Programs

Banks, Ann, ed. *First-Person America*. New York: Knopf, 1980.
Bloxom, Marguerite D. *Pickaxe and Pencil: References for the Study of the WPA*. Washington, D.C.: Library of Congress, 1982.
Coe, Linda. *Folklife and the Federal Government*. Washington, D.C.: American Folklife Center, Library of Congress, 1977.
McKinzie, Richard D. *The New Deal for Artists*. Princeton: Princeton University Press, 1973.
National Endowment for the Arts. Office of Research. *Federal Funds and Services for the Arts*. Judith G. Gault, comp. Washington, D.C.: Office of Education, U.S. Government Printing Office, 1967.
National Endowment for the Arts. National Council on the Arts. *Our Programs*. Washington, D.C.: National Endowment for the Arts, 1972.
O'Connor, Francis V. *Federal Support for the Visual Arts: The New Deal and Now; A Report on the New Deal Art Projects in New York City and State with Recommendations for Present-Day Federal Support for the Visual Arts to the National Endowment for the Arts*. Greenwich, CT: New York Graphic Society, 1971.
United States. Library of Congress. American Folklife Center. *Cultural Conservation: The Protection of Cultural Heritage in the United States: A Study*. Carried out in cooperation with the National Park Service, Department of the Interior; coordinated by Ormond H. Loomis. Washington, D.C.: Library of Congress, 1983.

————. *A Report on the Chicago Ethnic Arts Project*. Washington, D.C.: Library of Congress, 1978.
United States. Library of Congress. Education and Public Welfare Division. *Millions for the Arts*. Washington, D.C.: Washington International Arts Letter, 1972.
Weisberger, Bernard A. *The WPA Guide to America: The Best of 1930s America as seen by the Federal Writers' Project*. New York: Pantheon Books, 1985.

MUSIC AND DANCE

Carawan, Guy and Candie, comps. and eds. *Sing for Freedom: The Story of the Civil Rights Movement Told Through Its Songs*. Santa Cruz, CA: New Society Publishers, 1990.
Carrasco, Eduardo. *La Nueva Canción en América Latina*. Santiago, Chile: CENECA, 1982.
Chase, Gilbert. *A Guide to the Music of Latin America*. 2d ed., revised and enlarged. A joint publication of the Pan American Union and the Library of Congress. Washington, D.C.: Pan American Union, 1962.
Constant, D. *Aux Sources du Reggae: Musique, Société et Politique en Jamaïque*. Roquevaire: Editions Parentéses, 1982.
González, Juan Pablo. *El Estudio de la Música Popular Latinoamericana*. Santiago, Chile: CENECA, 1987.
Latif, A. "The Use of Folk Songs in Family Planning Communication (Bangladesh)." Supplement to *IEC Newsletter* (East-West Centre), No. 20, 1975.
Mella, Luís, et al. *Seminario: La Canción Popular Chilena*. Santiago, Chile: CENECA, 1983.
Moore, Sylvia. *Music for Life's Sake: The Media of Roles and the Rules of the Media; Education Through Music in Industrially Developing Countries: Priorities and Policies*. The Hague: Centre for the Study of Education in Developing Countries, 1983.
Nettleford, Rex. *Dance Jamaica: Cultural Definition and Artistic Discovery*. New York: Grove Press, 1985.
New York Times. "Cambodia Is Putting Propaganda to Music." November 13, 1977.
Ochsenius, Carlos. *Cuerpo y Cultura Autoritaria*. Santiago, Chile: CENECA, 1984.
Reagon, Bernice Johnson. *Voices of the Civil Rights Movement: Black American Freedom Songs, 1955–1965* (three-volume record set, with booklet). Washington, D.C.: Smithsonian Institution, Program in Black American Culture, 1980.

ARTS AND HANDICRAFTS

Agosín, Marjorie. *Scraps of Life, Chilean Arpilleras: Chilean Women and the Pinochet Dictatorship*. Trenton, NJ: Red Sea Press, 1987.
"Artesanato e Identidade Cultural." *Cultura* (Brazil) 12.42 (1984): 18–31.
Baca, Judith Francisca. "Our People Are the Internal Exiles." From an interview with the Chicana muralist by Diane Neumaier, with a brief history of the Social and Public Art Resource Center by Nancy Angelo. In Douglas Kahn and Diane Neumaier, ed. *Cultures in Contention*. Seattle: Real Comet Press, 1985.

Berg Salvo, Lorenzo. *Artesanía Tradicional de Chile*. Santiago: Departamento de Extensión Cultural del Ministerio de Educación, 1978.

Boynton, Linda L. "The Effect of Tourism on Amish Quilting Design." *Annals of Tourism Research* 13.3 (1986): 451–465.

Comunidec. *Primer Encuentro de Artesanos Populares*. Conocoto, Ecuador: Comunidec, 1988.

Cook, Scott. "Craft Production in Oaxaca, Mexico." *Cultural Survival Quarterly* 6.4 (1982): 18–20.

Cultural Survival. "Ethnic Art: Works in Progress?" Special year-end issue of *Cultural Survival Quarterly* 6.4 (1982): entire issue.

———. "Inuit Craft Industry." *Cultural Survival Newsletter* 2.2 (1978): 4.

Deitch, Lewis I. "The Impact of Tourism upon the Arts and Crafts of the Indians of the Southwestern United States." In Valene L. Smith, ed. *Hosts and Guests: The Anthropology of Tourism*. Philadelphia: University of Pennsylvania Press, 1977.

Fernández, Adelfa. "The Ixchel Museum of Indian Clothing: Guatemalans Labor to Save Endangered Traditional Textiles." *Américas* 35.4 (1983): 8–11.

García Canclini, Nestor. *Arte Popular y Sociedad en América Latina*. Mexico: Editorial Grijalbo, 1977.

———. "Conflictos de Identidad en la Cultura Popular: Bases para una Política Artesanal en América Latina." *Revista Mexicana de Sociología* 43.2 (1981): 713–26.

Goff, Brent. "Mastering the Craft of Scaling-Up in Colombia." *Grassroots Development* 14.1 (1990): 13–22.

Graburn, Nelson H.H. "The Evolution of Tourist Arts." *Annals of Tourism Research* 11.3 (1984): 393–419.

———. ed. *Ethnic and Tourist Arts: Cultural Expressions from the Fourth World*. Berkeley: University of California Press, 1976.

Israel, Pamela. "The Amazon in Plexiglass." *Cultural Survival Quarterly* 6.4 (1982): 15–17.

Leon, Lydia. "Art, Ecology, and the Huichol's Future." *Cultural Survival Newsletter* 5.2 (1981): 10–11.

———. "Artisan Development Projects." *Cultural Survival Quarterly* 11.1 (1987): 49–52.

Maguire, Robert. "Crafts and Creole in the Eastern Caribbean." *Grassroots Development* 8.1 (1984): 54–55.

Nason, James D. "Tourism, Handicrafts, and Ethnic Identity in Micronesia." *Annals of Tourism Research* 11.3 (1984): 421–449.

New, Lloyd H. *Institute of American Indian Arts; Cultural Difference as the Basis for Creative Education*. Washington, D.C.: U.S. Indian Arts and Crafts Board, 1968.

Pita S., Edgar, and Peter C. Meier. *Artesanía y Modernización en el Ecuador*. Quito: CONADE, 1985.

Rivera, Anny. *Arte y Autoritarismo*. Santiago, Chile: CENECA, 1982.

———. *Transformaciones Culturales y Movimiento Artístico en el Orden Autoritario. Chile: 1973–1982*. Santiago, Chile: CENECA, 1983.

Salles, Vicente. *Bibliografia Analítica do Artesanato Brasileiro*. Rio de Janeiro: FUNARTE, Instituto Nacional do Folclore, 1984.

Schneebaum, Tobias. "The Asmat Museum of Culture and Progress." *Cultural Survival Quarterly* 6.4 (1982): 36–37.

Stephen, Lynn. "Culture as a Resource: Four Cases of Self-Managed Indigenous Craft Production in Latin America." *Economic Development and Cultural Change*, forthcoming, 1990.

————. "Zapotec Weavers of Oaxaca: Development and Community Control." *Cultural Survival Quarterly* 11.1 (1987): 46–48.

Stevens, Jonathan. "Museums and Indigenous Peoples: Through the Display Glass." *Cultural Survival Quarterly* 6.4 (1982): 38–39.

Susnik, Branislava. *Artesanía Indígena: Ensayo Analítico*. Asunción, Paraguay: Asociación Indigenista del Paraguay, 1986.

Whitten, Dorothea. "Amazonian Ceramics from Ecuador: Continuity and Change." *Cultural Survival Quarterly* 6.4 (1982): 24–25.

TOURISM

Bugnicourt, Jacques. "La Otra Cara del Turismo: Sus Efectos Culturales." *Comercio Exterior* 28.5 (1978): 593–595.

CEDHU (Comisión Ecuménica de Derechos Humanos). "Fiesta del Yamor: Resistencia del Pueblo Quichua." En *Los Derechos Humanos: El Caso Ecuatoriano*, editado por CEDHU. Quito: Editorial El Conejo, 1985.

Cultural Survival. "Breaking out of the Tourist Trap, Part One." *Cultural Survival Quarterly* 14.1 (1990): special issue.

Cultural Survival. "Breaking out of the Tourist Trap, Part Two." *Cultural Survival Quarterly* 14.2 (1990): special issue.

de Kadt, E., ed. *Tourism—Passport to Development? Perspectives on the Social and Cultural Effects of Tourism Development in Developing Countries*. New York: Oxford University Press, 1979.

Esman, Marjorie R. "Tourism as Ethnic Preservation: The Cajuns of Louisiana." *Annals of Tourism Research* 11.3 (1984): 451–467.

Healy, Kevin, and Elayne Zorn. "Lake Titicaca's Campesino-Controlled Tourism." *Grassroots Development* 6.2 (1982): 3–10.

————. "Taquile's Homespun Tourism." *Natural History* 92.11 (1983): 80–93.

Lange, Frederick W. "The Impact of Tourism on Cultural Patrimony: A Costa Rican Example." *Annals of Tourism Research* 7.1 (1980): 56–68.

Noronha, R. *Social and Cultural Dimensions of Tourism*. Washington, D.C.: World Bank Staff Working Paper No. 326, 1980.

Smith, Valene L. *Hosts and Guests: The Anthropology of Tourism*. Philadelphia: University of Pennsylvania Press, 1977.

Swain, M. B. "Cuna Women and Ethnic Tourism: A Way to Persist and an Avenue to Change." In V. L. Smith, ed. *Hosts and Guests: The Anthropology of Tourism*. Philadelphia: University of Pennsylvania Press, 1977.

CULTURE AND ENVIRONMENT

Carroll, Thomas F., and Helga Baitenmann. "Organizing Through Technology: A Case from Costa Rica." *Grassroots Development* 11.2 (1987): 12–20.

Chapin, Mac. *In Search of Ecodevelopment*. West Hartford, CT: Kumarian Press, Inc., forthcoming, 1992.

————. "The Seduction of Models: Chinampa Agriculture in Mexico." *Grassroots Development* 12.1 (1988): 8–i7.

Chapin, Mac, and Patrick Breslin. "Conservation Kuna Style." *Grassroots Development* 8.2 (1984): 26–35.

Gill, Sam D. *Mother Earth: An American Story*. Chicago: The University of Chicago Press, 1987.

Herman, Marina Lachecki, Joseph F. Passineau, Ann L. Schimpf, and Paul Treuer. *Teaching Kids to Love the Earth.* Duluth, MN: Pfeifer-Hamilton, 1991.

Hufford, Mary. *One Space, Many Places: Folklife and Land Use in New Jersey's Pinelands National Reserve.* Washington, D.C.: American Folklife Center, Library of Congress, 1986.

Lyman, Francesca. "If I Can't Sing, I Don't Want to be Part of Your Revolution." *Environmental Action* (March 1982): 26–29.

Palmer, Paula, Juanita Sánchez, and Gloria Mayorga. *Taking Care of Sibö's Gifts: An Environmental Treatise from Costa Rica's Kéköldi Indigenous Reserve.* San José, Costa Rica: Asociación de Desarrollo Integral de la Reserva Indígena Cocles/Kéköldi, 1991.

Reichel-Dolmatoff, G. "Cosmology as Ecological Analysis: A View from the Rain Forest." *Man* 11.3 (1976): 307–318.

Richards, P. W. *Alternative Strategies for the African Environment; Folk Ecologies as a Basis for Community-Oriented Agricultural Development.* London: International African Institute, African Environmental Special Report No. 1: Problems and Perspectives, 1975.

Stahl, Ann B. "Valuing the Past, Envisioning the Future: Local Perspectives on Environmental and Cultural Heritage in Ghana." In Serageldin, Ismail, and June Taboroff, eds. *Culture and Development in Africa: Proceedings of the International Conference Held at the World Bank, Washington, D.C., April 2–3, 1992,* two volumes. Washington, D.C.: The World Bank, 1992, 415–427.

Taboroff, June. "Bringing Cultural Heritage into the Development Agenda: Summary Findings of Report of Cultural Heritage in Environmental Assessments in Sub-Saharan Africa." In Serageldin, Ismail, and June Taboroff, eds. *Culture and Development in Africa: Proceedings of the International Conference Held at the World Bank, Washington, D.C., April 2–3, 1992,* two volumes. Washington, D.C.: The World Bank, 1992, 332–339.

CULTURE AND EDUCATION

Formal and Nonformal Education

Aceredo, Juan. "La Historieta Popular: Un Movimiento de los 70." En Luís Peirano, ed. *Educación y Comunicación Popular en el Perú.* Lima: Centro de Estudios y Promoción del Desarrollo, Centro de Estudios sobre Cultura Transnacional, 1985.

Amadio, Massimo, Stefano Varese, y César Picon Espinosa, comps. *Educación y Pueblos Indígenas en Centroamérica: Un Balance Crítico.* Santiago, Chile: UNESCO, OREALC, 1987.

Amodio, Emanuele, comp. *Educación, Escuelas y Culturas Indígenas de América Latina.* Quito, Ecuador: Ediciones Abya Yala, 1986.

Cordero C., Carlos H. y Humberto Malean L. *Teatro, Música y Educación en Bolivia.* La Paz, Bolivia: Centro de Estudios Sociales (CENDES), 1989.

Cultural Survival. "Identity and Education." *Cultural Survival Quarterly* 9.2 (1985): special issue.

Deleon, Ofelia. *Folklore Aplicado a la Educación Guatemalteca.* 1st. ed. Guatemala: Centro de Estudios Folklóricos, Universidad de San Carlos de Guatemala, 1977.

"Ecuador: La Educación No-formal: Un Método de Participación." Quito: Dirección Nacional Técnica, Ministerio de Educación Pública y Deportes, 1976.

Epskamp, Kees, José Matos Mar, and Giorgio Alberti. *Education and the Development of Cultural Identity: Groping in the Dark.* The Hague: CESO, 1984.

Feijoó, Mary. "Gente y Cuentos: La Literatura en la Educación Popular." *El Porteño* 11.18 (1983): 44–47.

Folklore y Curriculum: Un Estudio de las Culturas de Tradición Oral en Venezuela Aplicado a la Educación Básica. Dos volúmenes. Caracas: Consejo Nacional de la Cultura, Instituto Interamericano de Etnomusicología y Folklore, 1983.

Freire, Paulo. *Education for Critical Consciousness*. New York: Seabury Press, 1973.

————. *Pedagogy of the Oppressed*. Translated by Myra Bergman Ramos. New York: Continuum, 1986.

————. *The Politics of Education: Culture, Power, and Liberation*. Hadley, MA: Bergin and Garvey, 1985.

Healy, Kevin. "Animating Grassroots Development: Women's Popular Education in Bolivia." *Grassroots Development* 15.1 (1991): 26–34.

Hilton, David, ed. "Health Teaching for West Africa: Stories, Drama, Song." New Brunswick, GA: MAP International, 1985, 30-page manual.

————. "Storytelling for Health Teaching." *Contact* 100 (December 1987): 1–11.

Inter-American Center for Caribbean Cultural Development (CARICULT), Jamaican Cultural Training Centre, Institute of Jamaica. *The Potential of the Arts in Caribbean Education: Alternatives in Education IV*. Final Report from the Workshop on Cultural Relevance in Curriculum Development, Kingston, Jamaica, 19–23 May 1986. Kingston: CARICULT, 1986.

Kidd, Ross. *The Performing Arts, Non-Formal Education and Social Change in the Third World: A Bibliography and Review Essay*. The Hague: Centre for the Study of Education in Developing Countries (CESO), 1981.

Kidd, Ross, and N. J. Colletta, eds. *Tradition for Development: Indigenous Structures and Folk Media in Non-Formal Education*. Bonn: German Foundation for International Development, 1981.

La Belle, Thomas J. *Nonformal Education in Latin America and the Caribbean: Stability, Reform, or Revolution?* New York: Praeger, 1986.

Nahmad Sittón, Salomón. "Indoamérica y Educación: Etnocidio o Etnodesarrollo?" Reunión de Expertos sobre Etnodesarrollo y Etnocidio en América Latina. San José, Costa Rica: UNESCO-FLACSO, 1982.

Non-formal Education in Ecuador, 1971–75. Amherst, MA: Centre for International Education, School of Education, University of Massachusetts, 1975.

Nurcombe, Barry. *Children of the Dispossessed: A Consideration of the Nature of Intelligence, Cultural Disadvantage, Educational Programs for Culturally Different People, and of the Development and Expression of a Profile of Competencies*. A Culture Learning Institute monograph, East-West Center. Honolulu: University Press of Hawaii, 1976.

Organización de los Estados Americanos. *Alternativas de Educación para Grupos Culturalmente Diferenciados: Estudio de Casos*. Washington, D.C.: OEA, 1983.

————. *Alternativas de Educación para Grupos Culturalmente Diferenciados. Tomo III: Museos y Educación*. Washington, D.C.: OEA, 1985.

Paco, Delfina. *Bibliografía de Cultura Popular y Educación en América Latina*. La Paz, Bolivia: Centro Boliviano de Investigación y Acción Educativas, 1986.

Peirano, Luís, ed. *Educación y Comunicación Popular en el Perú*. Series: Experiencias de Desarrollo Popular No. 1. Lima: Centro de Estudios y Promoción del Desarrollo, Centro de Estudios Sobre Cultural Transnacional, 1985.

Roman de Silgado, Manuel, Alejandro Ortíz, and Juan Ossio. *Educación y Cultura Popular: Ensayo Sobre las Posibilidades Educativas del Folklore Andino*. 1° ed. Lima, Perú: Universidad del Pacífico, Centro de Investigación, 1980.

Russell, Robert. "Cultural Groups as an Educational Vehicle." In D. C. Kinsey and J. W. Bing, ed. *Non-Formal Education in Ghana: A Project Report.* Amherst, MA: Centre for International Education, University of Massachusetts, 1978.

Tetzner, Bruno, Jürgen-Dieter Waidelich, Andreas Wiesand, and Diethard Wucher, eds. *Concept for Cultural Education: Positions and Recommendations.* Bonn: German Cultural Council, 1988.

Varese, Stefano. "Etnias Indígenas y Educación en América Latina." En *Educación, Etnias y Descolonización.* Santiago: UNESCO, 1983, 15.

Varese, Stéfano y Nemesio Rodríguez. "Etnias Indígenas y Educación en América Latina." En *Diagnóstico y Perspectivas en Educación.* Mexico: UNESCO-III, 1983, 7.

Werner, David. *Helping Health Workers Learn.* Palo Alto, CA: Hesperian Foundation, 1982 (NB: Chapter 13 on storytelling).

Zuñiga Castillo, Madeleine, Juan Ansión, and Luís Cueva, eds. *Educación en Poblaciones Indígenas: Políticas y Estratégias en América Latina.* Santiago, Chile: UNESCO, OREALC, 1987.

Bilingual/Bicultural Education and Language Issues

Alford, Margaret R. "Developing Facilitative Reading Programmes in Third World Countries. A Culturally Relevant Programme for Teaching Reading in the Mother Tongue: The Karanja Indians of Brazil." *Journal of Multilingual and Multicultural Development* 8.6 (1987): 493–511.

Atucha Zamalloa, Karmele, et al. *Bilingüismo y Biculturalismo.* Barcelona: CEAC, 1978.

Bennet, Louise, ed. *Jamaica Maddah Goose.* Kingston: Jamaica School of Art, 1981.

Blake, Robert. "El Planeamiento Lingüístico en el Perú: Antecedentes de la Oficialización del Quechua del 1975." *Ideologies and Literature* 1.3 (1985): 51–73.

Briggs, Lucy Therina. "On Bilingual Education." *Latin American Indian Literatures* 8.2 (1984): 104–110.

Corbera, Angel, comp. *Educación y Lingüística en la Amazonía Peruana.* Lima, Perú: Centro Amazónico de Antropología y Aplicación Práctica, 1983.

Corvalán, Grazziella E. de. *Lengua y Educación: Un Desafío Nacional.* Asunción, Paraguay: Centro Paraguayo de Estudios Sociológicos, 1985.

Escobar, Alberto. *Lenguaje y Discriminación Social en América Latina.* Lima: Editorial Carlos Milla Batres, 1972.

———, ed. *El Reto de Multilingüismo en el Perú.* Lima: IEP Ediciones (Instituto de Estudios Peruanos), 1972.

Fortune, David, and Gretchen Fortune. "Karanja Literary Acquisition and Sociocultural Effects on a Rapidly Changing Culture." *Journal of Multilingual and Multicultural Development* 8.6 (1987): 469–491.

Giménez, Aleida. "Educación Intercultural Bilingüe." *América Indígena* 42.2 (1982): 235–252.

Glock, Naomi. "Extending the Use of Saramaccan in Suriname." *Journal of Multilingual and Multicultural Development* 4.5 (1983): 349–360.

Hernández, Franco Gabriel. "De la Educación Indígena Tradicional a la Educación Indígena Bilingüe-Bicultural." *Revista Mexicana de Ciencias Políticas y Sociales* 25.97 (1979): 27–39.

Hernández Hernández, Severo. "Planteamientos Básicos para una Educación Indígena Bilingüe y Bicultural en México." *América Indígena* 42.2 (1982): 281–288.

Jamaica School of Art. "Maddah Goose." *Journal of the Inter-American Foundation* 2 (1981): 8–9.

Larson, Mildred L., Patricia M. Davis, and Marlene Ballena Dávila, eds. *Educación Bilingüe: Una Experiencia en la Amazonía Peruana.* Lima: I. Prado Pastor, 1979.

Lindahl, Carl. "Latin American Indian Literatures and Languages: A Checklist of Periodicals and Monographic Series." *Latin American Indian Literatures* 3.1 (1979): 34–49.

Macdonald, Theodore, Jr. "Shuar Children: Bilingual-Bicultural Education." *Cultural Survival Quarterly* 10.4 (1986): 18–20.

Mauviel, M. "Le Multiculturalisme (Pluralisme Culturel): Aspects Historiques et Conceptuels." *Revue Francaise de Pédagogie* 61 (1982): 61–71.

Mayer, Enrique. "Los Alcances de una Política de Educación Bicultural y Bilingüe." *América Indígena* 42.2 (1982): 269–280.

Methelier, Georges. *Pédagogie et Bilinguisme en Haiti.* Port-au-Prince: Université d'Etat d'Haiti, 1976.

Minaya-Rowe, Liliana. "Sociocultural Comparison of Bilingual Education Policies and Programmes in Three Andean Countries and the U.S." *Journal of Multilingual and Multicultural Development* 7.6 (1986): 465–477.

Mosonyi, Estéban Emilio. "La Educación Intercultural Bilingüe." En *Educación, Etnias y Descolonización.* México: UNESCO-III, 1983, 219.

———. "Responsabilidad del Lingüísta Frente a los Pueblos Indígenas Americanos." *América Indígena* 42.2 (1982): 289–300.

Pierola, Virginia. *Aportes sobre Educación Bilingüe, 1952–1982.* La Paz: Centro Boliviano de Investigación y Acción Educativas, 1983.

Plaza, Pedro, y Juan de Dios Yapita. "La Discriminación Lingüística y Social." (Policopiado; proyecto de investigación.) La Paz: INEL 1974.

"Revitalización de las Lenguas Indígenas." *América Indígena* 47.4 (1987): entire issue.

Riester, Júrgen y Graciela Zolezzi. *Identidad Cultural y Lengua: La Experiencia Guaraní en Bolivia.* Quito: Ediciones ABYA-YALA/Ayuda para el Campesino-Indígena del Oriente Boliviano, 1989.

Rodríguez, Nemesio J., Elio Masferrer K., y Raúl Vargas Vega, eds. *Educación, Etnias y Descolonización en América Latina: Una Guía para la Educación Bilingüe Intercultural.* Mexico: UNESCO, III, 1983.

Sanders, Thomas Griffin. *Education, Language, and Culture Among the Contemporary Maya.* Hanover, NH: American Universities Field Staff, 1979.

Varese, Stefano. "Notas Para una Discusión Sobre la Educación Bilingüe y Bicultural en Latinoamérica." *América Indígena* 42.2 (1982): 301–314.

Vásquez Fuller, Beatríz. "La Lengua Vernácula en la Educación: Actitud del Indígena Frente a los Programas de Desarrollo." *Guatemala Indígena* 6.4 (1971): 141–168.

Velasco Toro, José. "Educación y Etnicidad: Hacia la Creación de una Pedagogía Bilingüe-Bicultural?" *La Palabra y el Hombre,* no. 56 (1985): 29–32.

Yáñez Cossio, Consuelo. *Estado del Arte de la Educación Indígena en el Area Andina de América Latina.* Ottawa, Canada: Centro Internacional de Investigaciones para el Desarrollo, 1987.

MASS MEDIA: RADIO, TELEVISION, FILM

Albo, Xavier. *Idiomas, Escuelas y Radios en Bolivia.* Sucre, Bolivia: ACLO-UNITAS, 1981.

Annenberg School of Communication, University of Pennsylvania. "When Cultures Clash." Special section of *Journal of Communication* 27.2 (1977).

Beltran, S., and E. Fox de Cardona. "Mass Media and Cultural Domination." *Prospects* 10.1 (1980): 76–89.

Brown, Jim (Dir.). *We Shall Overcome: The Song That Moved a Nation*. New York: Ginger Group Productions, 1989 (58-minute documentary film).

Chander, R. *TV Treatment of Folk Forms in Family Planning Communication*. Presented at the UNESCO Inter-regional Seminar-cum-Workshop on the Integrated Use of Folk Media and Mass Media in Family Planning Communication Programmes, New Delhi, 7–16 October 1974.

Clay, Jason. "Radios in the Rain Forest." *Technology Review*. 92.7 (October 1989): 52–57.

Clearinghouse on Development Communication, Washington, D.C.. "Folk Culture for Radio." *Instructional Technology Report*, No. 15, 1976.

———. "Health Education by Open Broadcast." *Instructional Technology Report* 15. Washington, D.C.: Clearinghouse on Development Communication, 1976.

Corella, M. Antonieta Rebeil. "What Mexican Youth Learn from Commercial Television." *Studies in Latin American Popular Culture* 4 (1985): 188–199.

"Culture in the Age of Mass Media." *Latin American Perspectives* 5.1 (1978): entire issue.

Dublin, S. "Broadcast of Folk Messages Carries the Development Message in Malaysia." *Instructional Technology Report* 13. Washington, D.C.: Clearinghouse on Development Communication, 1976.

East-West Communication Institute. *Using Folk Media and Mass Media to Expand Communication: Report on a Workshop in New Delhi, India, October, 1974*. Honolulu: Communication Institute, 1975.

Encinas Valverde, Orlando. "La Radio al Servicio de la Liberación Indígena: Radio Mezquital." *Nueva Sociedad* 25 (1976): 85–94.

Gargurevich, Juan. "La Radio Popular en el Perú." En Luís Peirano, ed. *Educación y Comunicación Popular en el Perú*. Lima: Centro de Estudios y Promoción del Desarrollo, Centro de Estudios sobre Cultura Transnacional, 1985.

Haket, Lenneke. *Theatre for Development: Annotated Catalogue of Documents Available at CESO Library and Documentation Centre*. The Hague: Centre for the Study of Education in Developing Countries (CESO), 1991.

Hein, Kurt. "Popular Participation in Rural Radio: Radio Baha'i, Otavalo, Ecuador." *Studies in Latin American Popular Culture* 3 (1984): 97–104.

Hosein, Everold N. "The Problem of Imported Television Content in the Commonwealth Caribbean." *Caribbean Quarterly* 22.4 (1976): 7–25.

Hoxeng, James. "Programming by the People: An Ecuadorian Radio Experiment." *Educational Broadcasting International* 10.1 (1977).

IPPF (International Planned Parenthood Federation). *Folk Media and Mass Media: Their Integrated Use in Communication Programmes for Social Development and Family Planning*. London: IPPF, 1974.

Leon, Lydia. "Shuar Bicultural Radio Education." *Cultural Survival Quarterly* 9.2 (1985): 4–5.

McAnany, Emile G. "Cultural Policy and Television: Chile as a Case." *Studies in Latin American Popular Culture* 6 (1987): 55–67.

MEDIACULT—International Institute for Audio-Visual Communication and Development. *Selected and Annotated Bibliography on Cultural Industries in Third World Countries*. Paris: UNESCO, Division of Cultural Development, 1988.

The Program on Social Change and Development. *The Media as a Forum for Community Building: Cases from Africa, Asia, Latin America, Eastern Europe and the United States*. Washington, D.C.: The Program on Social Change and

Development of the Nitze School of Advanced International Studies (SAIS) at the Johns Hopkins University, 1992.

Romero, Rocío. "Culture Andine, Culture de Résistance: La Radio au Pérou." *Amérique Latine* 9 (1982): 58–61.

Skinner, Ewart C., and Richard Houang. "Use of United States Produced Media in Caribbean Society: Exposure and Impact." *Studies in Latin American Popular Culture* 6 (1987): 183–195.

UNESCO. *Folk Media and Mass Media in Population Communication.* Paris: UNESCO, 1982.

UNESCO/IPPF (International Planned Parenthood Federation). *Folk Media and Mass Media: Their Integrated Use in Communication Programmes for Social Development and Family Planning.* Working document prepared for expert group meeting, London, November 1972. London: UNESCO/IPPF, 1972.

White, Robert A. "Limitaciones y Posibilidades de una Radioemisora Educativa y Cultural en el Proceso de Desarrollo Rural: Radio Santa María." *Estudios Sociales* (República Dominicana) 9.8 (1976): 204–229.

Williams, Glen. *A Simple Solution: How Oral Rehydration Is Averting Child Death from Diarrhoeal Dehydration.* A UNICEF Special Report. New York: UNICEF, 1987.

SOCIODRAMA, THEATER, AND PUPPETS

General

Adult Education and Development. "Popular Theatre: Cross Cultural Reflections." Special issue of *Adult Education and Development* 23 (1984): entire issue.

Baird, B. *Puppets and Population.* New York: World Education, 1971.

Bappa, Salihu. "Popular Theatre for Adult Education, Community Action and Social Change." *Convergence* 14.2 (1981): 24–35.

Bappa, Salihu, and M. Etherton. "Popular Theatre—Voice of the Oppressed." *Commonwealth Arts Association* 25.4 (1983): 126–130.

Beltrán, L. R. *Puppets Go to the Country.* Visual Aids in Agricultural Extension Series. Scientific Communication Service, Inter-American Institute of Agricultural Sciences. Washington, D.C.: Organization of American States, n.d.

Boal, Augusto. *Teatro del Oprimido y Obras Poéticas Políticas.* Buenos Aires: Ediciones de la Flor, 1974.

———. *Theatre of the Oppressed.* New York: Urizen Books, 1979.

Bruyn, Louise. "Theatre for the Living Revolution." In S. T. Bruyn and P. M. Rayman, ed. *Non-Violent Action and Social Change.* New York: Irvington Publishers, 1980.

Edwards, Nancy. "The Role of Drama in Primary Health Care." *Educational Broadcasting International* 14.2 (1981): 85–89.

Epskamp, Kees. "Going 'Popular' with Culture: Theatre as a Small-Scale Medium in Developing Countries." *Development and Change* 15.1 (1984): 43–64.

———. *Theatre in Search of Social Change: The Relative Significance of Different Theatrical Approaches.* The Hague: Centre for the Study of Education in Developing Countries (CESO), 1989.

Espinosa Domínguez, Carlos. "Raquel Rojas: 'El Teatro Popular Debe Ser Desbordamiento Imaginativo y Desafío a la Fantasía.'" *Conjunto* 54 (1982): 104–119.

Etherton, M., and Ross Kidd, eds. *Third World Popular Theatre.* London: Hutchinson, 1985.

Horn, Andrew. "Theatre in Community Development." *WUS News* (August-September 1983): 7–11.

Kidd, Ross. "Didactic Theatre." *Media in Education and Development* (British Council) 16.1 (1983): 33–42.

————. "Folk Theater: One-Way or Two-Way Communication?" *Development Communication Report* 28 (1979): 5–7.

————. "People's Theatre, Conscientization and Struggle." *Media Development* 27.3 (1980): 10–14.

————. *The Performing Arts, Non-Formal Education and Social Change in the Third World: A Bibliography and Review Essay.* The Hague: Centre for the Study of Education in Developing Countries (CESO), 1981.

————. *The Popular Performing Arts, Non-Formal Education, and Social Change in the Third World.* The Hague: Centre for the Study of Education in Developing Countries, 1982.

————. "Popular Theatre, Conscientization and Popular Organization." In A. Fuglesang, *Methods and Media in Community Participation.* Uppsala, Sweden: Dag Hammarskjold Foundation, 1984.

————. "Popular Theatre, Conscientization and Struggle." *IFDA Dossier* 30 (1982): 14–25.

————. *Popular Theatre for Education and Development.* New York: Longmans, 1985.

————. "Popular Theatre and Nonformal Education in the Third World: Five Strands of Experience." *International Review of Education* 30.3 (1984): 265–287.

Kidd, Ross, et al. *The Koitta Papers: International Dialogue on Popular Theatre.* Toronto: International Popular Theatre Alliance, 1984.

Lambert, Pru. "Popular Theatre: One Road to Self-Determined Development Action." *Community Development Journal* 17.3 (1982): 242–249.

Motos Teruel, Tomás. "El Sociodrama como Procedimiento para Solucionar Creativamente Problemas Sociales." *Innovación Creadora* 8 (1978): 3–25.

Naaraayan, B. "Puppetry as a Medium of Communication for Family Planning." Supplement to *IEC Newsletter* (East-West Centre), No. 20, 1975.

Ochsenius, Carlos. *Expresión Teatral Poblacional, 1973–82.* Santiago, Chile: CENECA, 1983.

————, ed. *Encuentro de Teatro Poblacional.* Santiago, Chile: CENECA, 1982.

Ochsenius, Carlos, y José Luis Olivari. *Métodos y Técnicas de Teatro Popular.* Santiago, Chile: CENECA, 1984.

Ráez, Ernesto. "El Teatro en la Educación Popular." En Luís Peirano, ed. *Educación y Comunicación Popular en el Perú.* Lima: Centro de Estudios y Promoción del Desarrollo, Centro de Estudios sobre Cultura Transnacional, 1985.

Shank, Theodore. "Political Theater, Actors, and Audiences: Some Principles and Techniques." *Theater* (Yale) 10.2 (1979): 94–103.

SONOLUX Information. "People's Theatre for Development." A special issue of *SONOLUX Information* 6 (1982): entire issue.

Suárez Radillo, Carlos Miguel. "El Negro y su Encuentro de si Mismo a través del Teatro." *Cuadernos Hispanoamericanos* 271 (1973): 34–49.

UNESCO (United Nations Educational, Scientific, and Cultural Organization). "Puppets for Nutrition Education." *Rural Development* 1.4, 1972.

Latin America

Aramayo, Vicky, y Gastón Aramayo. "El Teatro de Títeres: Dos Experiencias." En Luís Peirano, ed. *Educación y Comunicación Popular en el Perú.* Lima:

Centro de Estudios y Promoción del Desarrollo, Centro de Estudios sobre Cultura Transnacional, 1985.

Breslin, Patrick. "Puppets in the Pampas." *A Propos.* (American Centre for the Union Internationale de la Marionnette) (Fall 1985): 8–10, 34.

Bustos, Nidia. "MECATE, the Nicaraguan Farm Workers' Theatre Movement." Based on an interview with Ross Kidd. *Adult Education and Development* 23 (September 1984): 129–139.

———. *Teatro ICTUS.* Santiago, Chile: CENECA, 1980.

———. *Transformaciones del Teatro Chileno en la Década del 70.* Santiago, Chile: CENECA, 1983.

Escuela Primavera, Osorno. *Documentos sobre una Experiencia de Teatro con Campesinos Huilliches.* Santiago, Chile: CENECA, 1985.

Espinosa Domínguez, Carlos. "El Teatro Quechua: Una Tradición que se Reafirma." *Conjunto* 28 (1976): 4–15.

Frischmann, Donald H. "Active Ethnicity: Nativism, Otherness, and Indian Theatre in Mexico." *Gestos* 11 (April 1991): 113–126.

———. *El Nuevo Teatro Popular en México.* Mexico City: INBA/CITRU, 1990.

———. "New Mayan Theatre in Chiapas: Anthropology, Literacy, and Social Drama." A paper prepared for the meetings of the Latin American Studies Association, Los Angeles, September 1992, 28 pages.

Grupo Cultural Yuyachkani. *Allpa Rayku: Una Experiencia de Teatro Popular.* Lima, Peru: Grupo Cultural Yuyachkani, 1983.

Gutiérrez, Sonia, ed. *Teatro Popular y Cambio Social en América Latina.* Ciudad Universitaria Rodrígo Facio, Costa Rica: Editorial Universitaria Centro Americana, 1979.

Harrop, J., and J. Herta. "The Agitprop Pilgrimage of Luís Valdéz and El Teatro Campesino." *Theater Quarterly* 5, 1975.

Hostetler, S. "Non-formal Education at Work in the United States: El Teatro Campesino, Farm Workers' Theater." *Instructional Technology Report* 12. Washington, D.C.: Clearinghouse on Development Communication, 1975.

Hurtado, María de la Luz, y Carlos Ochsenius. *El Taller de Investigación Teatral.* Santiago, Chile: CENECA, 1980.

———. *Teatro ICTUS.* Santiago, Chile: CENECA, 1980.

Jaraba-Pardo, Enisberto. "Curtain Up!" *Americas* 30.9 (1979): 18–25.

Kuhner, María Helena. *Teatro Popular.* Río de Janeiro: Livraria F. Alves Editora, 1975.

Leis, Raúl. "The Popular Theatre and Development in Latin America." *Educational Broadcasting International* 12.1 (1979): 10–13.

Luzuriága, Gerardo, ed. *Popular Theater for Social Change in Latin America: Essays in Spanish and English.* Los Angeles: UCLA Latin American Center Publications, 1978.

Muñoz, Diego, Carlos Ochsenius, José Luis Olivari, y Hernán Vidal. *Teatro Poblacional Chileno: 1978–1985 (Antología Crítica).* Minneapolis, MN: The Prisma Institute—CENECA, 1987.

Murillo Selva, Rafael. "El Bolívar Descalzo: Original Experiencia Teatral Colombiana." *Repertorio Latinoamericano* 2.14 (1976): 10.

Nacimiento del Teatro Popular Chileno: Desde Chile, Trabajos de los Talleres Culturales Populares. Madrid: Ediciones Conosur, 1980.

Núñez, C., and G. Núñez. "Popular Theatre and Urban Community Organizing in Mexico." In Ross Kidd and N. J. Colletta, ed. *Tradition for Development: Indigenous Structures and Folk Media in Non-Formal Education.* Bonn: German Foundation for International Development, 1982.

Ochsenius, Carlos. *Expresión Teatral Poblacional 1973–1982.* Santiago, Chile: CENECA, 1983.

————. *Teatro y Animación de Base en Chile (1973–1986)*. Santiago, Chile: CENECA, 1987.

————. comp. *Práctica Teatral y Expresión Popular en América Latina*. Buenos Aires, Argentina: Ediciones Paulinas, 1988.

Royaards, Rense. *De Quién Vienen Ustedes: De Dios o del Diablo; Experimentos de Teatro en América Latina*. La Haya, Holanda: Centro para el Estudio de la Educación en Paises en Via de Desarollo (CESO), 1989.

Weaver, A. J. "An Experience of Educational Theatre in Community Development in Nicaragua." *Journal of Communication* 27.2, 1977.

Caribbean

Association for Christian Communication. "Folk Media for the Caribbean." *Action* 28.7, 1978.

Corsbie, Ken. *Theatre in the Caribbean*. London: Hodder and Stoughton, 1984.

Ford-Smith, Honor. "Sistren: Jamaican Women's Theater." In Douglas Kahn and Diane Neumaier, ed. *Cultures in Contention*. Seattle: Real Comet Press, 1985.

————. "The Sistren Women's Theatre Collective: Process and Perspective." In M. Etherton and Ross Kidd, ed. *Third World Popular Theatre*. London: Hutchinson, 1985.

————. "Women's Theatre, Conscientization and Popular Struggle in Jamaica." In Ross Kidd and N. J. Colletta, ed. *Tradition for Development: Indigenous Struggles and Folk Media in Non-Formal Education*. Bonn: German Foundation for International Development, 1982.

Gillette, A. "'Rough Theatre' Serves Literacy in Jamaica." *UNESCO Features* 667, 1974.

Hill, Erroll. *The Study and Practice of Drama and Theatre in Adult Education in the West Indies*. Kingston, Jamaica: Department of Extra-Mural Studies, University of the West Indies, 1956.

————. *The Trinidad Carnival: Mandate for a National Theatre*. Austin: University of Texas Press, 1972.

Maguire, Robert. "Theater and the Caribbean: An Interview with Ken Corsbie." *Journal of the Inter-American Foundation* 4.2 (1980): 4–11.

The Sistren Theatre Collective. "Women's Theater in Jamaica." *Grassroots Development* 7.2 (1983): 44–52.

Wasserstrom, Robert. "Sistren: Women's Theater in Jamaica." In Robert Wasserstrom. *Grassroots Development in Latin America and the Caribbean: Oral Histories of Social Change*. New York: Praeger, 1985.

Asia

Abrams, Tevia. "Folk Theatre in Maharashtrian Social Development Programmes." *Educational Theatre Journal* 27.3 (1975): 395–407.

Ampo. "Theatre as Struggle: Asian People's Drama." Special Issue of *Ampo* (Pacific-Asia Resource Centre, Japan) 11.2–3 (1979): entire issue.

Asian Action. "Asian Rural Drama." Special issue of *Asian Action* (Asian Cultural Forum on Development, Bangkok) 7 (1977): entire issue.

Crawford, R. H., and R. Adhikarya. *The Use of Traditional Media in Family Planning Programs in Rural Java, No. 2*. Ithaca, NY: Department of Communication Arts, Graduate Teaching and Research Center, Cornell University, 1972.

Fernández, A. "Jargan: Theatre of the People." *Seva Vani* 6.1, 1976.

Foley, Kathy. "Drama for Development: Sundanese Wayang Golek Purwa, an Indonesian Case Study." *East-West Culture Learning Institute* 6.1 (1979): 1–6.

Gunawardana, T. "Folk Theatre in Family Planning Communication (Sri Lanka)." Supplement to *IEC Newsletter* (East-West Center), No. 20, 1975.

How. "People's Theatre." Special issue of *How* (New Delhi) 6.1–2 (1983): entire issue.

Kamm, Henry. "Burmese Theater: Outlet for Dissent." *New York Times*, October 7, 1977, p. A8.

Kidd, Ross. "Domestication Theatre and Conscientization Drama in India." In Ross Kidd and N. J. Colletta, ed. *Tradition for Development, Indigenous Structures and Folk Media in Non-Formal Education.* Bonn: German Foundation for International Development, 1982.

Kidd, Ross, and Mamunur Rashid. "Aranyak: Performing for the People in Bangladesh." *Adult Education and Development* 22 (March 1984): 101–116.

———. "Theatre by the People, for the People, and of the People: People's Theatre and Landless Organizing in Bangladesh." *Bulletin of Concerned Asian Scholars* 16.1 (1984): 30–45.

Krishnan, Prabha. "Catalyst Theatre." *Indian Journal of Youth Affairs* 2.1 (1980): 27–36.

Labad, Gardy. *Towards a Curriculum for a People's Theatre.* PETA Theatre Studies No. 3. Manila: Philippines Educational Theatre Association, 1979.

University of the Philippines. "Report on the Social Role of Asian Theatre." *UP Newsletter* 5.11, 1977.

van Erven, Eugene. *Stages of People Power: The Philippines Educational Theater Association.* The Hague: Centre for the Study of Education in Developing Countries (CESO), 1989.

Africa

Bame, K. N. "Comic Plays in Ghana: An Indigenous Art Form for Rural Social Change." *Rural Africana* 27 (Spring 1975): 25–41.

Blecher, Hilary. "Goal Oriented Theatre in the Winterveld." *Critical Arts* (South Africa) 1.3 (1980): 23–39.

Byram, Martin, and Ross Kidd. "Popular Theatre as a Tool for Community Education in Botswana." *Assignment Children* (UNICEF) 44 (1978): 35–65.

Byram, Martin, et al. *Report of the Workshop on Theatre for Integrated Development (Swaziland).* Swaziland: Department of Extra-Mural Services, University College of Swaziland, 1981.

Crow, B., and M. Etherton. "Popular Drama and Popular Analysis in Africa." In Ross Kidd and N. J. Colletta, eds. *Tradition for Development: Indigenous Structures and Folk Media in Non-Formal Education.* Bonn: German Foundation for International Development, 1982.

Etherton, M. *The Development of African Drama.* New York: African Publishing Co., 1982.

Kerr, David. "Didactic Theatre in Africa." *Harvard Education Review* 51.1 (1981): 145–155.

Kgatleng District Extension Team. *Botswana-Bosele Tshwaraganang: A Popular Theatre Campaign by Kgatleng District Extension Team, 1977.* Mochudi, Botswana: University College of Botswana, Institute of Adult Education, 1977.

Kidd, Ross. "A Botswana Case Study: Popular Theatre and Development." *Convergence* (1977) 10.2: 20–30.

———. "Liberation or Domestication: Popular Theatre and Non-Formal Education in Africa." *Educational Broadcasting International* 12.1 (1979): 3–9.

———. *From People's Theatre for Revolution to Popular Theatre for Reconstruction: Diary of a Zimbabwean Workshop.* The Hague: Centre for the Study of Education in Developing Countries (CESO), 1984.

————. "Popular Theatre and Popular Struggle in Kenya: The Story of the Kamiri-ithu Community Educational and Cultural Centre." *Race and Class* 24.3 (1983): 287–304. Also in Douglas Kahn and Diane Neumaier, eds. *Cultures in Contention.* Seattle: Real Comet Press, 1985.

Kidd, Ross, and M. Byram. "A Fresh Look at Popular Theatre in Botswana: Demystifying Pseudo-Freirian Non-Formal Education." *Rural Development Participation Review* 3.1 (1981): 19–24.

————. *Laedza Batanani: Folk Media and Development—A Botswana Case Study.* Botswana: Botswana Extension College, 1976.

Mlama, Penina. "Theatre for Social Development: The Malya Project in Tanzania." In Ross Kidd, et al., eds. *The Koitta Papers: International Dialogue on Popular Theatre.* Toronto: International Popular Theatre Alliance, 1984.

Nwansa, Dickson. "Popular Theatre as a Means of Education: Suggestions from Zambia." *Adult Education and Development* 16 (1981): 98–104.

————. "Theatre as a Tool for Communication." *IFDA Dossier* 42 (1984): 23–32.

Pickering, A. K. "Village Drama in Ghana. *Fundamental and Adult Education* (UNESCO) 9.4 (1957): 178–182.

Theatre Research International. "Popular Theatre in Africa." Special issue of *Theatre Research International* 7.3 (1982): entire issue.

Thiong'o, Ngugi wa. "The Language of African Theatre." In Ngugi wa Thiong'o. *Decolonising the Mind: The Politics of Language in African Literature.* London: James Currey, 1984.

————. "Women in Cultural Work: The Fate of Kamiriithu People's Theater in Kenya." In Ngugi wa, Thiong'o. *Barrel of a Pen: Resistance to Repression in Neo-colonial Kenya.* Trenton, NJ: African World Press, 1983.

FOLK TRADITION AND FOLK MEDIA:
EXAMPLES AND DEVELOPMENT APPLICATIONS

Caribbean Folk Arts for Communication and Education (FACE). *Report of the Caribbean FACE Production Workshop in Trinidad, June 1975, initiated and coordinated by the Folk Institute of the Antilles.* Port of Spain, Trinidad, 1976.

Carvalho-Neto, Paulo de. "Historia del Folklore de las Luchas Sociales en América Latina." *Cuadernos Americanos* 189.4 (1973): 133–156.

Catalán, Carlos, Rodrígo Torres, y Jaime Chamorro. *Cultura y Recolección Folklórica en Chile.* Santiago, Chile: CENECA, 1983.

Chonati, Irma, et al. *Tradición Oral Peruana: I. Hemerografía (1896–1976).* Lima: Instituto Nacional de Cultura, 1978.

Chumpí Kayap, María Magdalena. *Los "Anent": Expresión Religiosa y Familiar de los Shuar.* Quito: Instituto Normal Bilingüe Intercultural Shuar (Bomboiza) y Ediciones Abya-Yala, 1985.

CINEP (Centro de Investigación y Educación Popular). *Experiencias en Comunicación Popular: Contando Historias, Tejiendo Identidades.* Bogotá: Departamento de Comunicación Popular, CINEP, 1987.

Clearinghouse on Development Communication, Washington, D.C.. "Folk Media in Development." *Instructional Technology Report* 12 (1975): entire issue.

————. "Village Festivals and Folk Media." *Instructional Technology Report* 15. Washington, D.C.: Clearinghouse on Development Communication, 1976.

Colletta, Nat. "The Use of Indigenous Culture as a Medium for Development: The Indonesia Case." *Instructional Technology Report* 12. Washington, D.C.: Clearinghouse on Development Communication, 1975.

Compton, J. L. "Indigenous Folk Media in Rural Development in South and South-East Asia." In D. W. Brokensha, et al., eds. *Indigenous Knowledge Systems and Development*. Lanham, MD: University Press of America, 1980.

Díaz Bordenave, Juan E. *Communication and Rural Development*. Paris: UNESCO, 1977.

————. "The Role of Folk Media: A Point of View." *Instructional Technology Report* 12. Washington, D.C.: Clearinghouse on Development Communication, 1975.

Dissanayake, W. "New Wine in Old Bottles: Can Folk Media Convey Modern Messages?" *Journal of Communications* 27.2 (1977): 122–124.

Ewert, D. Merrill. "Proverbs, Parables and Metaphors: Applying Freire's Concept of Codification to Africa." *Convergence* 16.1 (1981): 32–42.

Fiofori, Ferdinand O. "Traditional Media, Modern Messages: A Nigerian Study." *Rural Africana* 27 (1975): 43–52.

Folklore y Curriculum: Un Estudio de las Culturas de Tradición Oral en Venezuela Aplicado a la Educación Básica. Caracas, Venezuela: Consejo Nacional de la Cultura, Instituto Interamericano de Etnomusicología y Folklore, 1983.

Gadis, Diego. "A Maya Community's Path to Life." *Reflections 1991*. Paris: International Fund for the Promotion of Culture, UNESCO, 1991, 1–4.

García Salazar, Juan. *La Poesía Negrista en el Ecuador*. Esmeraldas: Banco Central del Ecuador, 1982.

Gutiérrez, Paulina. *Agrupaciones Culturales: Una Reflexión*. Santiago, Chile: CENECA, 1983.

Hilton, David. "Tell Us a Story: Health Teaching in Nigeria." In D. Morley, et al., eds. *Practising Health for All*. Oxford: Oxford University Press, 1983.

Huerta, Jorge A., ed. *A Bibliography of Chicano and Mexican Dance, Drama, and Music*. Oxnard, CA: Colegio Quetzalcoatl, 1972.

IPPF (International Planned Parenthood Federation). *Folk Media in Family Planning Communication: Resource List, IPPF*. London: Information and Education Department, IPPF, 1973.

Jekyll, Walter, ed. *Jamaican Song and Story: Anancy Stories, Digging Sings, Ring Tunes, and Dancing Tunes*. New York: Dover Publications, 1966.

Kleymeyer, Carlos David. *¡Imashi! ¡Imashi! Adivinanzas Poéticas de los Campesinos Indígenas de Mundo Audino: Ecuador Peru y Bolivia*. Quito: Mundo Andino/Abya Yala, 1993.

Kleymeyer, Charles David, and Carlos Moreno. "La Feria Educativa: A Wellspring of Ideas and Cultural Pride." *Grassroots Development* 12.2 (1988): 32–40.

Lent, John. "Grassroots Renaissance: Folk Media in the Third World Nations." *Folklore* 91.1 (1980): 78–91.

Long, R. "The Folk Media, Their Potentiality and Role in Social Development: A Background Paper." Paper prepared for the UNESCO/IPPF Expert Group Meeting on the Integrated Use of Folk Media and Mass Media in Family Planning Communication Programmes, held in London, November 20–24, 1972. Universiti Sains Malaysia, Minden, Penang, Malaysia.

Malya, Simoni. "Traditional Oral Literature for Post-Literacy Reading Materials." *Prospects* 6.1, 1976.

Moss, William W., and Peter C. Mazikana. *Archives, Oral History, and Oral Tradition*. Paris: General Information Programme and UNISIST, UNESCO, 1986.

Nketia, J.H.K. "The Influence of Traditional Media on Social and Individual Behaviour." Ghana: Institute of African Studies, University of Ghana, n.d.

Ochsenius, Carlos. *Agrupaciones Culturales Populares 1973–1982*. Santiago, Chile: CENECA, 1983.

O'Sullivan-Ryan, J., and M. Kaplun. *Communication Methods to Promote Grass-Roots Participation.* Paris: UNESCO, 1979.

Palmer, Paula R. "Self-History and Self-Identity in Talamanca, Costa Rica." *Grassroots Development* 6.2 (1983): 27–34.

———. *"Wa'apin Man": La Historia de la Costa Talamanqueña de Costa Rica, Según sus Protagonistas.* Traducción por Quince Duncan y Paula Palmer. San José: Instituto del Libro, 1986.

———. *"What Happen": A Folk-History of Costa Rica's Talamanca Coast.* San José, Costa Rica: Ecodesarrollos, 1977.

Parlato, Ronald, Margaret Burns Parlato, and Bonnie J. Cain. *Fotonovelas and Comic Books: The Use of Popular Graphic Media in Development.* Washington, D.C.: Office of Education and Human Resources, Development Support Bureau, Agency for International Development, 1980.

Parmar, Shyam. *Traditional Folk Media in India.* New Delhi: Gekha Books, 1975.

Patanjali, S. V. "Rural Entertainment Forms." *Kurukshetra* 25.21, 1977.

Proceedings of the Third Asian-Pacific Conference on the Preservation of Cultural Properties and Traditions—Folklore: November–December, 1980, Taipei. Seoul: Cultural and Social Centre for the Asian and Pacific Region, 1981.

Rangananth, H. K. *Using Folk Entertainments to Promote National Development.* Paris: UNESCO, 1981.

Roeder, Hans, ed. *De Superman a Superbarrios: Comunicación Masiva y Cultura Popular en los Procesos Sociales de América Latina.* Santiago, Chile: Consejo de Educaciión de Adultos de América Latina (CEAAL), 1990.

Roy, Rati Ranjan. "Folk Poetry in Bangladesh: Updating Traditional Forms to Carry Timely Messages." *Development Communications Report* 34 (June 1981): 2.

Ruíz, Wilson. "Communication and Tradition." *The IRDC Reports* 4.2 (1985): 19–20.

Tamu, Ahmed Tejan. *Folk Media, Theatre for Development, and Non-formal Education: A Case Study of CARE's Project "Learn" in the Pujehun District.* Freetown: Institute of Adult Education and Extra-Mural Studies, Fourah Bay College, University of Sierra Leone, 1986.

Tanna, Laura. *Jamaican Folk Tales and Oral Histories*, No. 1, Jamaica 21 Anthology Series. Kingston, Jamaica: Institute of Jamaica Publications, Ltd., 1984.

Toelken, Barre. *The Dynamics of Folklore.* Boston: Houghton Mifflin, 1979.

Wasserstrom, Robert. *Grassroots Development in Latin America and the Caribbean: Oral Histories of Social Change.* New York: Praeger, 1985.

Wigginton, Eliot, and Margie Bennett, eds. *The Foxfire Book: Hog Dressing; Log Cabin Building; Mountain Crafts and Foods; Planting by the Signs; Snake Lore, Hunting Tales, Faith Healing; Moonshining: and Other Affairs of Plain Living.* The first book in a series on North American Folklife. Garden City, NY: Doubleday, 1972.

METHODOLOGY: CULTURAL ACTION, PROMOTION, RESCUE, PRESERVATION, AND MAINTENANCE

Allen, Barbara, and William Lynwood Montell. *From Memory to History: Using Oral Sources in Local Historical Research.* Nashville, TN: American Association for State and Local History, 1981.

Catalán, Carlos, Rodrigo Torres, y Jaime Chamorro. *Cultura y Recolección Folklórica en Chile.* Santiago, Chile: CENECA, 1983.

Colombres, A. *Manual del Promotor Cultural: Bases Teóricas de la Acción.* Toluca, Mexico: Centro Cultural Mazahua, 1980.

Cornejo Polar, J. "A Promoter of Culture for Latin America." *Cultures* 33 (1983): 159–174.

Dunway, David K., and Willa K. Baum, eds. *Oral History: An Interdisciplinary Anthology.* Nashville, TN: American Association for State and Local History in Cooperation with the Oral History Association, 1984.

The Free Form Arts Trust. *Cultural Action for Community Development. A Report on the Goldsmith's Square Estate (London FS).* Paris: UNESCO, 1985.

Freire, Paulo. *Cultural Action for Freedom.* Harmondsworth: Penguin Books, 1972.

——. *Sobre la Acción Cultural: Ensayos Escogidos.* Santiago, Chile: Instituto de Capacitación e Investigación en Reforma Agraria, 1969.

Gebhard, Krysztof M. *Community as Classroom: A Teacher's Practical Guide to Oral History.* Regina: Saskatchewan Archives Board, 1985.

Heider, Karl G. *Ethnographic Film.* Austin, TX: University of Texas Press, 1976.

Hermosilla, Maria Elena. "Ceneca in Chile" Cultural Action in Stormy Waters." *Reflections 1991.* Paris: International Fund for the Promotion of Culture, UN-ESCO, 1991, 18–23.

Higgs, John Walter Yeoman. *Folk Life Collection and Classification.* London: Museums Association, 1963.

Ives, Edward D. *The Tape-Recorded Interview: A Manual For Field Workers in Folklore and Oral History.* Knoxville: University of Tennessee Press, 1980.

Jackson, Bruce. *Fieldwork.* Urbana and Chicago: University of Illinois, 1987.

Jones, Suzi. *A Brief Guide to Folklore Collecting.* For the Archives of Northwest Folklore, University of Oregon. Eugene, OR: S. Jones, 1974.

Kyvig, David E., and Myron A. Marty. *Nearby History: Exploring the Past Around You.* Nashville, TN: American Association for State and Local History, 1982.

Lindahl, Carl, Sanford Rikoon, and Elaine J. Lawless. *A Basic Guide to Fieldwork for Beginning Folklore Students: Techniques of Selection, Collection, Analysis, and Preservation.* Bloomington, IN: Folklore Publications Group, 1979.

Marc, Alexandre O. "Community Participation in the Conservation of Cultural Heritage." Paper delivered at the International Conference on Culture and Development in Africa, World Bank, Washington, D.C., April 2–3, 1992.

Martinic, Sergio, y Horacio Walker, eds. *El Umbral de lo Legitimo: Evaluación de la acción cultural.* Santiago, Chile: Centro de Investigación y Desarrollo de la Educación (CIDE) y Centro de Investigación y Capacitación del Campesinado (CIPCA), 1988.

Moeckli, J. M. "The Social Role of the Animateur." In Council of Europe, *Explorations in Cultural Policy and Research.* Strasbourg: Council of Europe, 1978, 50–58.

Poujol, G. *Action Culturelle, Action Socio-Culturelle, Recherches.* Marly-le-Roi: Institut National d'Education Populaire, 1983.

Renuka. "The RCDA Experience: Organizing the Poor Through Cultural Action." *How* 1.5 (1978): 17–23.

Trask, David F., and Robert W. Pomeroy, eds. *The Craft of Public History: An Annotated Select Bibliography.* Westport, CT: Greenwood Press, 1983.

UNESCO. *Educational Action, Communication, Cultural Action; International Seminar, Sornetan, Switzerland, 17–21 October, 1983.* Porrentruy, Switzerland: Université Populaire Jurassienne, 1984.

——. "Towards Developing Tools for Integrating the Cultural Dimension into Development Plans and Projects." Information Document presented at the International Conference on Culture and Development in Africa, World Bank, Washington, D.C., April 2–3, 1992.

————. *The Training of Cultural 'Animators.'* Paris: UNESCO, 1981.
Wigginton, Eliot. *Sometimes a Shining Moment: The Foxfire Experience.* Garden City, New York: Anchor Press/Doubleday, 1985.

GENERAL/CONTEXTUAL SOURCES

Annis, Sheldon, and Peter Hakim, eds. *Direct to the Poor: Grassroots Development in Latin America.* Boulder: Lynne Rienner Publishers, 1988.
Barth, Frederick, ed. *Ethnic Groups and Boundaries: The Social Organization of Culture Differences.* Boston: Little, Brown, and Company, 1969.
Berger, Peter. *Pyramids of Sacrifice.* New York: Anchor Press, 1967.
Breslin, Patrick. *Development and Dignity: Grassroots Development and the Inter-American Foundation.* Rosslyn, VA: Inter-American Foundation, 1987.
Dyal, William. "Report from the President." *Annual Report 1979.* Rosslyn, VA: Inter-American Foundation, 1980, 5–6.
González Casanova, Pablo. "El Colonialismo Interno." En *Sociología de la Explotación*, 2d ed., por Pablo González Casanova. Mexico City: Siglo Veintiuno Editores, 1969. Translated into English and published as "Internal Colonialism and National Development." In Irving Louis Horowitz, José de Castro, and John Gerassi, eds. *Radicalism in Latin America: A Documentary Report on Left and Nationalist Movements.* New York: Random House, 1969.
Goulet, Denis. *The Cruel Choice: A New Concept in the Theory of Development.* New York: Atheneum, 1971.
Herrera, Felipe. *El Escenario Latinoamericano y el Desafío Cultural.* Santiago, Chile: Galdoc, 1981.
Hinds, Harold E., Jr., and Charles M. Tatum, eds. *Handbook of Latin American Popular Culture.* Westport, CT: Greenwood Press, 1985.
Hirschman, Albert O. "The Principle of Conservation and Mutation of Social Energy." *Grassroots Development*, 7:2 (1983), 6–8.
Hirschman, Albert O. *Getting Ahead Collectively: Grasssroots Experiences in Latin America.* New York: Pergamon Press, 1984. Also available in Spanish: *El Avance en Colectividad: Experimentos Populares en la América Latina.* Mexico: Fondo de Cultura Económica, 1986.
Kahn, Douglas, and Diane Neumaier, eds. *Cultures in Contention.* Seattle: Real Comet Press, 1985.
Kleymeyer, Charles David. *Poder y Dependencia Entre Quechuas y Criollos: Dominación y Defensa en la Sierra Sur del Perú.* Lima: Centro de Investigaciones Socioeconómicas del Departamento de Ciencias Humanas de la Universidad Nacional Agraria, 1982.
Lerner, Daniel. *The Passing of Traditional Society.* New York: Free Press, 1955.
Minc, Rose S., ed. *Literature and Popular Culture in the Hispanic World.* Gaithersburg, MD: Hispamerica, 1981.
Ochsenius, Carlos. *Agrupaciones Culturales Populares.* Santiago, Chile: CENECA, 1983.
Reichel Dolmatoff, Gerardo, and Alicia Reichel Dolmatoff. *The People of Aritama: The Cultural Personality of a Colombian Mestizo Village.* London: Routledge and Kegan Paul, 1961.
Subercaseaux, Bernardo. *Sobre Cultura Popular.* Santiago, Chile: CENECA, 1985.
UNESCO (United Nations Educational, Scientific, and Cultural Organization). *Cultural Industries: A Challenge for the Future of Culture.* Paris: UNESCO, 1982.

————. *Cultura y Sociedad en América Latina y el Caribe.* Paris: UNESCO, 1981.
Wasserstrom, Robert. *Grassroots Development in Latin America and the Caribbean: Oral Histories of Social Change.* New York: Praeger, 1985.
Wolf, Eric R. "Culture: Panacea or Problem?" *American Antiquity,* 49:2 (April 1984): 393–400.

ADDRESSES FOR OBTAINING PUBLICATIONS

Centre for the Study of Education in Developing
   Countries (CESO)
P.O. Box 90734
2509 LS, The Hague, The Netherlands

Centro de Indagación y Expresión
Cultural y Artística (CENECA)
Casilla 1348—Correo Central
Santiago, Chile

Cultural Survival
215 First St.
Cambridge, Massachusetts 02142, USA

Inter-American Foundation (IAF)
901 N. Stuart Street, 10th floor
Arlington, Virginia 22203, USA

United Nations Educational, Scientific,
   and Cultural Organization (UNESCO)
7 Place de Fontenoy
75700 Paris, France

OTHER RELEVANT ADDRESSES

American Folklife Center
Library of Congress
10 First St., SE, Room G-08
Washington, D.C. 20540, USA

Association pour la Diffusion de la Recherche sur
   L'Action Culturelle (ADRAC)
3 rue Paul Dupuy
75016 Paris, France

Association pour la Recherche Interculturelle (ARIC)
41 rue Gay-Lussac
75005 Paris, France

Center for Folklife Programs and Cultural Studies
955 L'Enfant Plaza, SW, Room 2600
Washington, D.C. 20560, USA

CULTURELINK: Network of Networks for Research and
    Cooperation in Cultural Development
Institute for Development and International Relations (IRMO)
Ul. Lj. Farkasa Vukotinovica 2
P.O. Box 303
41000 Zagreb, Croatia

Fondation Europeenne de la Culture
Jan Van Goyenkade, 5
NL-1075 HN Amsterdam, The Netherlands

Gesellschaft für Bedrohte Völker
Gronnerstrasse 40
3400 Göttingen, Germany

International Fund for the Promotion of Culture
    UNESCO
7 Place de Fontenoy
75700 Paris, France

International Work Group for Indigenous Affairs (IWGIA)
Fiolstraede 10
1171 Copenhagen K, Denmark

South-North Network—Cultures and Development Office
    for International Coordination
174 rue Joseph II
B-1040 Brussels, Belgium

Survival International
310 Edgware Road
London W21DY, England

Traditions pour Demain; Tradiciones para el
Mañana; Traditions for Tomorrow
B.P. 477–07
75327 Paris Cédex 07, France

Working Group on Indigenous People
Human Rights Subcommission
Center for Human Rights
United Nations
1211 Geneva 10, Switzerland

World Commission on Culture and Development
    UNESCO
7 Place de Fontenoy
75700 Paris, France

World Decade for Cultural Development
UNESCO
1 rue Miollis
75732 Paris, France

Index

Traditions for Tomorrow, 10, 283

Ujajs (chant for warriors), 154
UNICEF, 134
Unidad de Educación in Ecuador, 59,
    60, 63, 64, 65, 66, 67
United Nations, 10, 28
United Nations Educational, Scientific,
    and Cultural Organization
    (UNESCO), 11, 134, 202, 208, 281
United States, 7; cultural expression
    projects and, 249–250; social
    movements in, 33
Universal Declaration of Human
    Rights, 28
Urban-centered nations, 22
Uyari (solidarity act), 165–166

Valdez, Leonidas, 55–56
Vallenatos (protest songs), 30
Venezuela and cultural expression
    projects, 250–251

Wali, Alaka, 195–196
Weaving: Aymara (Chile) women and,
    174–175; Taquile Islanders (Peru)
    and, 137, 141–142, 143
Westernization, vii-viii, 91–95, 198;
    technology and, 28, 83–84, 95–100,
    198
What Happen: A Folk History of Costa
    Rica's Talamanca Coast (Palmer),
    45, 116

Wildlife reserve in Panama, 55, 83–84,
    95–100, 198
Winning of the West, The (Roosevelt),
    ix
Women: breast-feeding and Sikuani
    Indians, 189; influence of
    Ecuadorian, 64, 66; Jamaican theater
    and, 71–82; protest culture in Chile
    and, 30; spiritual work chants and,
    150, 154–157; Taquile island (Peru),
    143; textile projects and Aymara
    (Chile), 174–175; water problems
    and Sikuani Indians, 185–186
Work and tradition: collective work
    forms of Quichua Indians (Ecuador)
    and, 151–152, 199; cultural forms
    and, 165–166; oral traditions of
    Shuar Indians (Ecuador) and,
    149–151; potato dig of Llinllín
    campesinos (Ecuador) and, 162–165;
    spiritual chants of Shuar Indians
    (Ecuador) and, 152–160
World Bank, 134, 202
World War II, vii
World Wildlife Fund (WWF), 83
Wretched of the Earth, The (Fanon),
    viii

Yumbos Chahuamangos, Los
    (Ecuadorian musical group), 19, 23

Zapotec people (Mexico), 20

About the Book

Arguing that a people's own cultural heritage is the foundation on which equitable and sustainable development can best be built, this book presents an innovative, culture-based approach to grassroots development in Latin America and the Carribbean.

The approach seeks to retain a population's special cultural strengths and contributions while enabling them to achieve necessary changes in their social and economic conditions. Their "cultural energy"—a concept introduced in the book—is thus tapped into, and in turn drives further development efforts.

The authors provide illustrations from 215 cases in 30 countries, ranging from handicraft production, adult literacy centers, and community bread ovens to collections of folktales and harvest chants, and reforestation and conservation efforts.